The Thoughtful Guide to God

To Eric
with all good wishes

Howard Jones

The Thoughtful Guide to God

DR HOWARD A JONES

BOOKS

Winchester, U.K.
New York, U.S.A.

First published by O Books, 2006
An imprint of John Hunt Publishing Ltd., The Bothy, Deershot Lodge,
Park Lane, Ropley, Hants, SO24 0BE, UK
office@johnhunt-publishing.com
www.o-books.net

USA and Canada	Singapore
NBN	STP
custserv@nbnbooks.com	davidbuckland@tlp.com.sg
Tel: 1 800 462 6420	Tel: 65 6276
Fax: 1 800 338 4550	Fax: 65 6276 7119
Australia	South Africa
Brumby Books	Alternative Books
sales@brumbybooks.com	altbook@global.co.za
Tel: 61 3 9761 5535	Tel: 27 011 792 7730
Fax: 61 3 9761 7095	Fax: 27 011 972 7787

New Zealand
Peaceful Living
books@peaceful-living.co.nz
Tel: 64 09 921 6222
Fax: 64 09 921 6220

Design: Jim Weaver Design
Cover design: Book Design, London
ISBN 1 905047 70 3

A CIP catalogue record for this book is available from the British
Library.

Printed by Maple-Vail, USA

Contents

Preface

This book has been written to try to reconcile world-views derived rationally from science and philosophy with those originating from mystical insight to develop a coherent approach to the concept of the divine. This has been a challenging issue for theologians, particularly, for two thousand years. Why should this presentation have anything new to say? Because the majority of apologists for religion, not surprisingly, have been theologians. Where scientists have entered the argument, it has been mainly to explain Creation without invoking the notion of God. This treatment presents empirical evidence and rational argument in an attempt to validate the concept of a divine spiritual field.

Although we live in a materialistic age, there are many for whom concern with spiritual values is still a cornerstone of their lives. Surveys suggest that some 80% of people in Britain, for example, believe in a reality beyond the sensory level. But what kind of reality is this? Does God exist? If so, what form does God take and what meaning can we give to the idea? What evidence do we have of God's interaction with the human world? Despite the decrease in numbers of people professing to practice a formal religion, these are still questions of vital importance to a majority of people on the planet and for which many are seeking answers.

There are those who feel they can answer these questions to their own satisfaction, logically or intuitively through their faith. But there are also many who are troubled by the apparent incompatibility between the now predominant rational scientific or philosophical view of the world and the picture of reality that emerges from revelation. Those who do believe in what others may describe as superstitious nonsense often feel self-conscious or vulnerable to social criticism. Certainly, scientists enter this field of research at their professional peril.

Ideas as to the nature of God or the gods have evolved with humankind into a diverse spectrum of beliefs, some of which are outlined in the first chapter of this book. As pointed out there, it is pertinent to remind ourselves that all the predominant Western religions, with their frequently bloody conflicts, have their origin in the same one scriptural source, the Bible, and differ basically only in the matter of interpretation. Of course, this is simplistic, and there is mystical input from other divinely inspired persons in each religion that has produced additional scriptures. Also, nationalistic and territorial issues are often interwoven with religious differences in provoking regional conflicts – they cannot be blamed entirely on religious fanaticism. Nevertheless, it behoves us to re-examine just how far apart these various interpretations of the one source of what is claimed as the Word of God have moved.

We should also remember that religions are man-made social institutions and that it is a few charismatic individuals claiming divine revelation who have shaped the fundamental tenets of most of the major world religions. The scriptures on which these religions are based, while purporting to be transmitting direct divine revelation, have passed through many human hands and minds of scribes, interpreters and translators in the course of their long evolution. As there are many fundamental contradictions between one set of religious beliefs and another, it is logically untenable that any one of these accounts should be regarded as expressing unequivocal and unilateral divine truth, as this condemns the remaining religious beliefs to falsehood. The various bodies of scriptures should therefore be regarded as presenting accounts of different paths to the divine, created for different peoples at different times and different places in different social situations. Chapter 1 highlights this diverse origin of some of the world's scriptures and the religions that have evolved from them and it also gives some indication of the extent of the input by human agency. The chapter ends with more recent ideas as to the nature of God's message that were developed in the 19th and 20th Centuries by others claiming divine inspiration or presenting deep philosophical insight.

The Bible has been subjected to many revisions and translations since its original creation, as we shall see: it is pertinent therefore to question how much of the original text is likely to remain and even how much was truly original and veridical in the first place. Although there may be many people, places and events in the Bible that are historically valid, this does not imply that all the stories told of them are true, since many similar tales are to be found in other cultures, and accounts were usually written down many years after the lives of the people and events they describe. This, however, does not exclude the possibility of divine inspiration of the founding prophets and even of those scribes who recount their lives to help them in portraying a moral message to help sustain a people in their times of need. Furthermore, it does not preclude religion and its scripture from serving as a path to spiritual enlightenment for those individuals who wish to take it; and religion has certainly provided social cohesion of nations since its inception. Some of the developments that have occurred in arriving at the Bible as we know it today are outlined in this first chapter to illustrate its somewhat tortuous evolutionary path.

The philosophers of ancient Greece were the first in Western civilisation to systematically question and debate many of the key issues concerning the nature of the world and the purpose of human existence. The answers the philosophers produced have inspired, either consciously or unconsciously, much of Western thought, particularly in philosophy and science, but also in theology since that time and this is discussed in Chapter 2. When thoughts and ideas are created, or new facts are discovered about the world, it is part of human nature to want to correctly attribute their source, and we can follow a line of development from the ancient Greek philosophers to philosophers, scientists, and theologians in the post-Renaissance period with regard to many of the concepts discussed in this book. Furthermore, as we shall see in the last chapter, post-Renaissance thinkers may not always have come by their knowledge by direct reading of ancient texts: it is possible that their knowledge has a more spiritual source. This is not to undervalue the achievements of the more modern thinkers: on the contrary, knowledge created or recreated in this way illustrates a more highly developed spiritual awareness and an ability to communicate beyond the material plane, as discussed in Chapter 6 on. The discussion of Greek philosophy is restricted to those issues relevant to this argument.

As well as the churchmen themselves, the academic philosophers have also made great contributions to theology. Some views of the principal medieval theological philosophers of Judaism, Christianity and Islam that are relevant to this discussion are therefore outlined briefly in Chapter 3. Probably the main issue that provoked the burgeoning theological tracts in these times was the attempt to interpret the rational presentations of Greek philosophy, newly available in Latin translations, in a way that was compatible with the texts of scripture.

Chapter 4 describes the rise of science during the Renaissance, sometimes from these earlier Greek ideas presented in Chapter 2. The development of science in the following centuries against the background of resistance from the predominant Western Christian belief system is described in this chapter. Again, the discussion is confined to those ideas we shall need to use later, though some brief biographical details are given for general interest and to put the personalities involved into their cultural context. It was in these centuries that the medieval antinomies between rationalism and revelation were replaced by the conflict between religious tenets and scientific empiricism. However, as we shall see, scientific discovery in turn often influenced religious thought or attitude. With the continual expansion of knowledge, these early scientific ideas subsequently evolved into the 20th Century science that provides us with an interpretation of the universal divine spirit that permeates the tenets of many world religions. Thus there is a time-line in the thought processes of theology, philosophy and science as discussed in these first four chapters that have shaped our 21st Century world and led to the developing ideal of the fusion of science and mysticism in the modern world.

One specific major problem that science and philosophy have wrestled with for centuries is that of the nature of mind or consciousness; but, as we are thinking creatures, no-one at least disputes that some human function that we can distinguish as mind does exist. In the corresponding theological realm however, another challenge has been to interpret the meaning of the equally non-material soul: there are many conservative scientists and philosophers, and even a few theologians who dismiss the notion as a socially useful but in no sense a real entity. So what meaning can be given to the concept of soul in this rational approach, and how is soul related to mind? This subject is explored in Chapter 5.

Assuming, at least for the purpose of this discussion, that soul may be regarded in some sense as a real entity, this concept is expanded on in Chapter 6 with examples of phenomena that believers could ascribe to participatory events involving *individual* soul. The published literature abounds with reliably documented but anecdotal examples of such events and only a small representative sample can be given of these various facets of soul; but the unprejudiced reader will find that the empirical evidence for their existence is overwhelming even if their interpretation is equivocal. Some aspects of what may be regarded as spiritual or psychic events have been studied under scientifically rigorous conditions, and several of these experiments are described here by way of validation of the anecdotal accounts.

The evidence in the first chapter makes it clear to what extent human agency has determined the prescriptivism of the various religions: the Bible and other scriptures are not meticulously transcribed verbatim accounts of God's dealings with humankind, for all that the fundamentalists would wish it so. Expanding global communication has made us more aware of the great diversity of religious belief. For those who are thereby disenchanted with the contradictions between the various orthodox religions, and between religion and reason, and are disillusioned with regard to the authenticity of scripture, where lies the path to communion with the divine? The answer may lie for some internally in the contemplations of the soul, and externally in experience of the joy of the natural world around us and the aesthetic beauty of the many facets of human creativity. There are many expressions of human soul that represent communion with the divine spirit other than the practice of the ritual and dogma of organised religion: such are the examples given in Chapter 6.

Having considered a definition of soul in relation to mind, and examined some instances of the *individual* soul in action, in Chapter 7 we return again primarily to the philosophers and see how the idea of a *universal* soul or spirit has been suggested in various forms and contexts over two millennia, from the time of the ancient Greeks to the present-day. Such a concept is found also among the writings of some theologians and poets. Sometimes the idea is that of an over-arching unified but remote World Soul; in other contexts it is described as a ubiquitous individual soul that may be regarded, in wider view, as a community of souls or Communal Soul. If scripture and the religions based on it are, in some sense, artificial and created by Man, we may establish direct communion with this divine universal soul or spirit through the experiences of our individual souls in meditation, through human loving, in the enjoyment of natural beauty, in the appreciation of music and the other arts, and through psychic experiences, as described in the previous chapter.

Chapter 8 then takes these rather disparate ideas from science, philosophy and theology and tries to provide a unifying scientific interpretation or rationale. This is not merely an esoteric academic argument. It is imperative that people are persuaded that how they conduct their lives is of importance, not only to themselves individually, but is of vital significance for the wellbeing of humankind as a whole and of our planet, both now and in perpetuity. What better way is there of doing this than to present each of our actions as participation in a divine plan embracing all of humanity and our environment.

The last chapter of the book is a personal reflection on how my own thoughts on the spiritual dimension of the world have progressed from outright disbelief and atheism, through healthy scepticism, to total belief and commitment to the concept of a universal divine spirit.

In the past four centuries science has provided so many answers to questions about the way the world works. In many respects, science has enhanced the quality of life for millions of people. But in so doing it has also undermined some of the tenets of religion by showing them to be factually or logically untenable: the notion of God has lost its relevance to the everyday lives of many people because of its seeming irrationality. Not only are science and religion seen as incompatible in many respects, so are the world- views of the different religions themselves. In the face of contradictory claims by science and by the various religions, some choices must be made: it is a logical impossibility that the spiritual views of everyone could completely, unequivocally and unilaterally be representing truth. Such religious views of the world, while they are beyond explanation by science, should not, at least, conflict with reason. For reason and language for its expression are the distinguishing faculties of humankind, and if we regard ourselves as potentially the greatest of God's creations, to ignore reason in our religious beliefs is to deny the wisdom of God in granting us this faculty. Even if a rational interpretation for the nature of the divine spirit can be found that is not incompatible with science, the sense of wonder and awe and mystery of the divine and the human creativity it inspires, and the relationship of the divine spirit with the created world remain ineffable. There is no suggestion that science has found all the answers to humankind's greatest mysteries.

The overzealous and at times indiscriminate application of science and technology have produced problems undreamed of four centuries ago, problems that threaten our very survival as a species on Earth. There is a desperate need to find some common thread behind the different paths to the divine essence, whether it is called God, Elohim, Yahweh, Allah, Holy Spirit, Brahman, Universal Mind or World Soul. With increasing materialism and innovation all around us, the world is crying out for the peace and stability of a more spiritual world-view that emphasises our interconnectedness to one another and to our environment, the Earth. Service to the divine spirit is so much more than following the rituals and tenets of a particular religion: it involves maintaining our own bodily health insofar as we are able to do so, and refraining from practices that we know are physically harmful, while striving to enhance the lives of others towards ever greater fulfillment; and honouring our guardianship of the environment for future generations. This is as much the practical expression of love and devotion to the divine as the practices of a formal religion.

My hope is that the contents of this book may encourage and enable others to embrace a more spiritual outlook on life as well as suggesting a spiritual theme that could provide a unifying link between science and religion, between rationalism and revelation, and even, with a will, between the disparate notions of the divine that have arisen in the various religions of the world. Religious fundamentalism is the fanatics' way to power when they lack the moral courage to face truth. They are content to live in a *demi-monde* of fantasy and delusion. Because they deceive themselves, they must retreat into an elitist conclave to the exclusion of all others: this is *not* the way forward to global harmony.

Developments in physics in the 20th Century provide prospects that there may be a scientific interpretation for the human concepts of the divine and of the soul that accord with a spiritual and yet rational world-view. This book is an attempt to present logically a search for the divine, a view, a hope – in every sense, a prospect of God.

Finally, I must acknowledge those who have helped me in the preparation of this manuscript: my wife, Jennifer, who has kept me on the spiritual path when I tended to stray too far into my scientific rationalism; Verena Tschudin of the Alister Hardy Society, who has been a constant source of encouragement during the writing of this book; my friends in the Baha'i faith with whom I have shared many stimulating Fireside discussions – it was the preparation of a talk to one of their Easter meetings more than a decade ago that first set me thinking along these lines; and my Christian, Jewish and Spiritualist friends who have given me religious insights I probably would not otherwise have had. My thanks to you all. I hope this book may help others as you have helped me towards a more spiritual world view.

1 The nature of God: What the scriptures tell us

The gulf between science and religion seems to be as wide now as it ever was. Because science requires so much jargon, it is not easily accessible to those who study any of the humanities, whether it be theology or one of the arts. Scientists similarly are reluctant to delve too deeply in any academic way into the arts or theology [438]. In our scientifically and technologically driven world, we have all tended to become sceptical of ideas that do not seem to be based in logic, such as those of the scriptures allegedly given to us by divine revelation. Some are quite comfortable with rejecting notions of God or soul as irrational concepts, but are still in need of human love, of continual spiritual refreshment through participation in the arts, or of periods of relaxation in natural surroundings – activities that could be interpreted by believers as involving the human soul or communion with the divine. There are few who can remain productive, healthy and contented without this periodic or even continual spiritual uplift, though they may not regard it as such, because the pressure and materialism of our contemporary everyday world leaves us with little time or energy for us to even think about spiritual issues. Then there are others who have a great need to believe, but find that their rational self rejects any notions of the supernatural, or who fear that they will engender some lack of respect from their peers for demonstrating belief in paranormal experiences of any kind. Thankfully, we are now several centuries away from burning witches at the stake to 'cleanse their souls', but still psychics or spiritual healers are viewed by many as 'strange' individuals with eccentric personalities, not conforming to the norms of society as they see them. And finally there are those whose spiritual faith is firm, without any need for rationalisation, but who are then viewed by some rationalists as fantasists, in need of an emotional prop. So some kind of rationalisation of religious beliefs would go some way to resolving the differences in these points of view of the numinous and, hopefully, lead to greater tolerance of those who are different from ourselves.

For many of us, an awareness of a higher being gives purpose, direction and a sense of ethical values to govern our interaction with other people – what we describe as our faith, with our notion of divinity at its head. To constantly renew that faith, some participate with fellow believers in the rituals and traditions and constructs of a formal religion. But there are a large number of people who, though they do not 'belong' to any formal religious organisation, still have a faith and a belief in some kind of supernatural force or being. Conversely, it must be said, there are also those who profess to belong to a religious group who show little sign of a constructive faith.

What is it about the human psyche that continually quests after God? Primitive people, faced with the awesome might of Nature, attributed its vagaries to 'the gods' – gods having dominion over almost every facet of the natural world in which they lived and to which they attributed human characteristics. This anthropomorphism was the means of establishing a relationship with the gods. As these gods had such power, the people wanted at least to appease them so that they did them no harm and, if possible, to get them working for their benefit. Much as many believers in the West pour scorn on those who made offerings to the gods, is this not what many do today in supplication to the God of Western theology in their prayers and rituals? As Israel Regardie wrote in his book *The Tree of Life*: the gods 'were not mere idle inventions by the ignorant ... men who having nothing else better to do, occupied themselves in storytelling and in weaving pleasant and unpleasant fictions about the figments of their minds' and perceptively 'Primitive man did not 'create' the Gods ... What he really did, perhaps unconsciously, was to apply names (and even these names were significant) and quasi-human faculties to these 'powers' or great forces of Nature which he so accurately observed, and which he believed rightly enough to be manifestations or symbols of the divine' [397].

The pagans and less sophisticated peoples than those in Western civilisation today attach great importance to the influence of ancestors and of the environment, which is regarded as alive with the spirit of their forefathers. Environmental features, such as rocks or trees, and burial grounds of ancestors are venerated as holy places to which the people go for comfort and inspiration, just as we may visit a cemetery today to commune with the spirit of a loved one. Those who lose their sense of awe at the wonders of the natural world lose their connection with spirituality. These primitive people have an intimate and reciprocal relationship with their natural environment – they care for it and, in return, it protects and nourishes them, physically and spiritually. The anthropologist Lucien Levy-Bruhl (1857–1939) said of such people that they live at one with their environment in a state of 'mystical participation'. In our ever-expanding urbanisation and materialism, we are tending to lose sight of this respect for our heritage and for our environment, in the broadest sense, and with it a respect for the wisdom of our elders, both living and those who are no longer physically among us. There is a great store of knowledge and power in those who have departed to the afterlife after many years on Earth – both from their years of earthly experience and from the access to supernatural knowledge that they now possess.

A belief in some spiritual reality that we call our God or gods inhabiting a realm beyond our normal sensory experience is commonplace amongst such peoples that we in the West regard as 'primitive' or 'pagans'. Indigenous peoples everywhere, since the beginning of human history, as far as we are aware, have relied on tribal members called *shamans* who have particular expertise in communing with these spiritual forces. Individuals with the highest spiritual aura may even be regarded as *avatars* or messengers of the gods or even divine Manifestations.

The very word 'God' seems to be derived from the Sanskrit word *ghut*, an invocation to extracorporeal spirits [Oxford English Dictionary]. According to the Greek theologian Eusebius (*ca.*265–*ca.*339 CE), Bishop of Caesarea, belief in a divine spirit is derived 'from those natural notions which are implanted in men's minds', and many other theologians have subsequently regarded our belief in a divine being as innate in human nature. The English word 'God' originated sometime in the late 16th Century (*ca.* 1565–1586) and it appears frequently in the works of Shakespeare (d.1616) and other contemporary writers, so it had already become an accepted concept in the language.

The 19th Century Austrian psychoanalyst, Sigmund Freud (1856–1939), maintained that humankind invoked the notion of God as a father figure, to provide comfort in times of stress: 'God is nearest when the need is greatest'. It is likely also that people, always seeking understanding and control of their environment, had to resign themselves to forces bringing hardship and tragedy into their lives, and over which they had no control – the notion of an all-powerful God was, at least, some kind of explanation for this distress and suffering, and provided someone to blame in moods of anger. Freud thought that religion was 'ancient, baneful, and eradicable' and that it should be replaced by science; he felt that "mankind collectively had most to fear from the phenomenon of 'illusion'; that is to say, from 'beliefs moulded by wishes'" [524].

The Swiss psychiatrist Carl Gustav Jung (1875–1961) on the other hand believed that religion was one of the highest priorities for humankind. It helped people to resolve their emotional conflicts to achieve wholeness in developing their personality – a process that Jung called 'individuation'. It also gave people a social focus, again, an important facet of being human. Jung believed that our lives are governed by two psychological phases. The first phase, up to 'middle age', is the *acquisitive phase*, in which we are primarily concerned with developing our social standing, selecting a partner, establishing a career and building a home and family. The second period, in the latter half of life, was the *inquisitive phase* in which we no longer needed to strive for wealth and position but had more time for reflection, to think about the meaning and purpose of life. This was the time when religious issues became of even greater importance to us. Though Jung was a psychiatrist, he read widely and was well aware that many of the myths associated with Judaism and Christianity recorded in the Bible were in fact reworkings of stories from earlier times and that similar tales were to be found in many other cultures. This was one example of what Jung called 'archetypes', which will be discussed further in Chapter 7.

The Judeo-Christian religions have shaped western society for two millennia, as Islam has influenced the people of the Middle East, and Hinduism, Buddhism and Confucianism have shaped the Eastern philosophy of life. The pagan religions of the Inuit of North America, the Australian aborigines, the Celts, and the present Wicca and Neopagans have generated a fascinating rich cultural heritage which we are perhaps only now beginning to appreciate fully. Everywhere, religion is an essential indispensable facet of society, whether to support individual faith or to provide social cohesion of a society.

For more than 3000 years, from at least 1500 BCE to the Renaissance, since worship of God was formalised into the great Western religions, these religions were regarded as possessing the key to all natural phenomena, to the rules of human behaviour, and to the fate of the human soul. At the heart of Western religion is the worship of God, but the vision of the nature of any such God or gods has evolved through human history. Some of the principal ideas are outlined below for some early civilisations (Egyptian, Greek and Roman) and for those Western religions with the greatest number of adherents – Judaism, Christianity and Islam.

1.1. Egypt

The 1st dynasty of the archaic Egyptian civilisation of the Bronze Age has been dated at 4000 BCE, but there was habitation along the banks of the Nile for some 2000 years before that. Egyptian civilisation was organised as a single state – one of the first in the world – under one god-like ruler, the pharaoh. But in ancient Egypt, there was a multiplicity of gods in addition to their deified kings and pharaohs. Horus, son of Osiris, was the falcon god and was often regarded as god of the sun; there are tales about his incarnation by a virgin birth and that he was 'a fisher of men with twelve followers' [233]. Animals were often held as symbols or even incarnations of the gods: the cobra represented the goddess Wadjyt; the ibis was an incarnation of the god Thoth, the god of wisdom, who could also appear as a baboon; the frog was associated with the goddess Heket; Anubis incarnated as a dog; and though cats were domesticated, they were regarded as symbols of the gods Bastet and Ra. The crocodile and the scarab beetle were also venerated, the latter as a symbol of resurrection and rebirth; and there were many others. Significantly, some of the carvings of scarabs on Egyptian tombs have crosses carved on their backs. Some gods were half animal, half human: the Sphinx has the head of a pharaoh but the body of a lion. Then there were anthropomorphic mythological deities like Osiris and his wife and sister Isis.

Many of the tales that appear in the Old and New Testaments have earlier versions in Egyptian mythology: for example, before Jesus raised Lazarus from the dead (John, Chap. 11) an Egyptian shaman brought El-Azar back to life. The name 'Jesus' itself as a saviour of the world appears in Greek literature as Iesous and in Egyptian as Iusa.

The Egyptians believed that as long as their gods were appeased their life of relative comfort and prosperity would be preserved, and continuity and maintenance of the daily order was paramount. As well as the cross, symbol of the crucifixion to Christians, Egyptian tombs also carry symbols of the ankh, a modified cross with a loop at the head, and the swastika, now forever tarnished by its association with the Nazis. But the swastika is also part of the symbol of the theosophists and the word comes from the Sanskrit *svastika* meaning 'cross of good fortune'. The symbol is found at Hindu sites, as would be expected, but also in Central America, so these are universal cultural symbols. Amongst pagans generally, the horizontal of the cross is intended to indicate the natural world of which man is a part, and the vertical indicates the spiritual component of creation, along which an individual can move spiritually either upward or downward.

With this polytheism came a corresponding diversity in belief, often and inevitably, mutually incompatible. It was left to the ancient Greek philosophers to try to mould consistent views of the nature of the world and our role in it. But amongst this societal polytheism, there was one Pharaoh, Akhenaten (also known as Ikhnaton, or Amenhotep IV, *fl.* 1375 BCE), who was regarded as a heretic – he was a monotheist who worshipped only the sun-god, Re, who was now designated as Aton. The sun was deified for the light and heat it provided to sustain life. During the reign of Akhenaten, the Egyptian empire grew mightily and with it the status of their pharaoh. He tried to convert those who did not share his beliefs and banish the worship of the old god Osiris. In times of prosperity, he met with some success; but as the empire crumbled, so did his following, and worship of Osiris continued on in the Roman Empire for many centuries. The boy-king Tutankhamun was Akhenaten's son-in-law.

The overriding principle that shaped the life of the ancient Egyptians was that the universe was essentially static. Of course, there were obvious changes in their day-to-day immediate surroundings, like day and night, floods and droughts, the passing of the seasons of the year, but these were relatively superficial; overall, to the ancient Egyptian, the world was changeless – there was equilibrium between opposites. As Henri Frankfort, formerly Professor of Oriental Archaeology at the University of Chicago, commented in the Preface to his book on *Ancient Egyptian Religion* [188]: '[this world view] informed not only his theology but also his moral and political philosophy ... it determined the forms he gave to his state and his society, to his literature and his art.' Any season would wane, to be replaced by another; but the same seasons came around again each year. In the animal kingdom, an individual animal would die, but it was replaced by another of the same species. They knew nothing of extinction of species: as far as they were concerned, the species as a whole survived with new individuals.

So human death had to be fitted into this cyclic but essentially unchanging world view: death was an interruption in the life cycle, but not its annihilation. There was, in some sense, a life after death: the body's vital force, *ka*, was not extinguished. The ancient Egyptians therefore firmly believed in the existence of the afterlife. There was regular communication with the spirits of the dead, even by writing letters to them [203]. The appearance of dead relatives in dreams and visions kept the spirit world alive in the hearts and minds of the living: the concept formed part of everyday social life. Bodies were embalmed because the body was regarded as the seat of the soul and had to be preserved for afterlife in the Field of Reeds. Coffins contained ornaments and jewellery, pots and tools. Small human effigies called *shabtis* made of faience were buried with the bodies of noble Egyptians to act as servants in the afterlife, so that they could continue to live a life of leisure, though we have little indication of the nature of existence in the afterlife as the Egyptians saw it. Wealthy noblemen and women of rank were often buried in *mastabas* – underground tombs with another chamber above ground for offerings. The pharaohs and their queens were buried in tombs with huge monuments above – the pyramids, of which about eighty are known today from the time of the ancient Egyptians, built around 3000–2000 BCE. The largest pyramid known, the Great Pyramid at Giza, was built for the pharaoh Khufu.

The sages of each generation, after active lives and successful careers, wrote of their experiences to pass on as 'teachings' to future generations, so that they too might live good, happy and useful afterlives. The name of God appears frequently in translations of these texts. Encouraging a placid demeanour Amenemope counsels: 'Put thyself in the hands of God and thy tranquillity shall overthrow them (the enemies)' [189]; or again, in encouraging truth and honesty: 'Speak not to any in falsehood, the abomination of God;' [190]. In these contexts, the word 'God' may refer to the predominant deity at that time and place, or to 'gods' in general, or to some unspecified but felt spiritual entity, as was common in pagan belief.

The language of these ancient Egyptians lives on with the Coptic Christians, Copt being the transliterated form of the Arabic word *gypt* or *qubt* (which gives us 'Egyptian'). This sect represents about one-sixth of the 60 million inhabitants of predominantly Islamic Egypt, and there are more than a million others scattered worldwide. The Church was formally instituted by St. Mark, who some believe to have been martyred by the Romans under Emperor Nero in 68 CE. Other authorities believe that it was Mark who wrote the second-placed but earliest of the gospels and this has been dated at around 70 CE. The remains of his body are now reputedly buried in St. Mark's Coptic Cathedral in Cairo. The Coptic language evolved from Greek after the invasion of Egypt by the Greek general, Alexander the Great in 313 BCE. The Egyptians were taught the Greek language that comprised only 24 pronounceable characters. This replaced the Egyptian script which, at that time, was made up of over 400 hieroglyphs, but which nevertheless was adequate to facilitate communication and commerce. The Coptic language evolved from this in the next few centuries. The Copts or Coptics are important because it was they who established the Christian monastic tradition through which Greek learning has been transmitted to us over the intervening two millennia. They also set up a school in Alexandria, the Didascalia, to promote the contention that reason and revelation, philosophy and theology, were compatible, complementary, and each essential for the understanding of the other. The most famous scholars from the Didascalia were Pantaenus and Origen (185–254 CE), whose spiritual and allegorical interpretation of the Bible was ignored by the Church in the Middle Ages. Instead, the Bible came to be regarded as a historical account of events, but this was not the view of the early Christians in the first century.

When Alexander the Great invaded Egypt he set up his base at Neapolis on the outskirts of the ancient town of Rhacotis, renaming it Alexandria. From that time on, aided by the establishment of its Museum and Library, Alexandria became a second centre of learning in the Hellenic Empire. The conquest of Egypt by Alexander changed a way of life there that seems to have flourished essentially unchanged for the previous three millennia.

1.2.   Greece and Rome

In the societies of ancient Greece and Rome, again there were many gods to worship, generally anthropomorphic, with Zeus (in Greece) or Jupiter (in Rome) at the head, with their respective wives Hera or Juno. Their daughter Athena (Greek) or Minerva (Roman) was goddess of war, of wisdom and of the arts and crafts, especially handicrafts, and protectress of cities. Most of the gods were associated with aspects of everyday life: for example, Ares (Greece) or Mars (Rome) was the god of war and was held next to Zeus/Jupiter in importance. Helen, daughter of Zeus, and the most beautiful woman in Greece according to legend, was the patron saint of sailors; but she was also associated with trees, when she took the name Dendritis. Demeter (Greece) or Ceres (Rome) was the goddess of corn; Poseidon or Neptune was god of the sea; Hermes (Greece) or Mercury (Rome) was the messenger of the gods, and was associated with movement or circulation of goods or people. Mithras, a sun-god, was the principal deity of a Roman cult that flourished two or three centuries after the time of Jesus. He had been a prominent god in Indo-Iranian culture of the Hindus and Zoroastrians, though in the *Rig Veda* he is referred to as Mitras. To the Zoroastrians he was the son of their god, the Creator, Ahura Mazda, and saviour of humankind. In the words of Ahura Mazda in Zoroastrian scripture, Mithras was 'as worthy of prayer as myself'. The gods of the Egyptians lived on too, for the Romans were still building monuments to Isis and Osiris some 3000 years after their appearance as deities in Egypt. The animal gods of Egypt had disappeared, but the Greeks learned from the Egyptian stonemasons how to build huge effigies of their gods.

In the ancient world, there were many people associated with the administration of religion and preparation of temples and sacred sites for religious festivals or *synodoi* (the later Christian synods), and these festivals were primarily agriculturally based – rather like the Christian Harvest Festival. There was nothing resembling a clergy or priesthood: the officials were elected officials who held office for six to twelve months, often along with other secular duties. Sacrifices of food and drink, including parts of animals, were an integral part of the act of worship so that humans could participate in the ritual of the feast with the gods. This also symbolised an implied reciprocity – humans would take care of the gods if they responded with their protection. The Christian Eucharist, while commemorating the Last Supper, is also a token of this pagan sharing of a meal with the gods. Singing of pagan hymns and dancing also accompanied the ceremonies. While dancing is not usually part of Christian church practice, the singing of hymns is, in most denominations. In Greece, particularly, in the ancient world there were competitions in sports and in music and drama to accompany religious celebrations. The Olympic Games are reputed to have started in this way in 776 BCE and thereafter were held every four years. For the Greeks, their religion was an intimate part of their everyday life to provide explanations for human experience, to give meaning to the past, and to provide hope for the future.

The Greco-Roman culture attached great importance to prophecy. The Greeks had their Delphic Oracle located at the base of Mount Parnassus, established around the 9th Century BCE; but Greek communities were small and scattered at the time so the site probably had only local significance then. As Greece became established as a nation in the succeeding centuries, the significance of the Oracle grew so that by the 6th Century BCE and for more than a thousand years until the coming of Christianity it had a huge effect on Greek social, political and religious life. At Delphi, the site of the temple of Apollo, the prophetess or Pythia burnt laurel leaves and barley meal on the altar or *hestia* to induce a trance-like state to make her pronouncements by divine inspiration. But there was no creed of a formal religion, no book of revelation, no scriptures of any kind until the late Sibylline oracles. Sibyl was a prophetess first mentioned by Heraclitus in the 6th Century BCE, and was probably a specific person, but later Sibyl was taken as the name of other prophetesses in general. The temples were simply shrines for the gods – they were not buildings for communal worship.

The first Roman king Lucius Tarquinius Priscus (616–578 BCE), whose wife was the prophetess Tanaquil, is said to have bought three books of prophecy from the Cumaean Sibyl for consultation by the senate in times of crisis. These were housed in a temple atop one of the hills of Rome, the Capitolium, but this was destroyed by fire in 83 BCE. These books were replaced by a more diverse collection of prophesies which the emperor Augustus Caesar housed in the temple to Apollo built on the Palatine hill. Divination in Rome was a matter for the state and was employed frequently before military expeditions. Julius Caesar, so Shakespeare tells us, was warned by his own personal soothsayer to beware the ides of March, but independent prophets and prophetesses were not common in Rome.

Early Jewish and Christian writers assembled (or wrote) their own collection of fourteen *Sibylline Oracles* to try to gain converts to their respective religions from paganism, but these probably originate from the 2nd to 4th Centuries CE.

The Greeks practiced both burial and cremation on death of the body. The epic poems by Homer (*fl.* 8th Century BCE), the *Iliad* and *Odyssey*, refer often to the fact that the soul leaves the body at death to begin its journey to Hades, the dominion of the dead, and that cremation is more effective at releasing the soul than inhumation. The fact that offerings were left at the tombs of the dead indicates that the living felt their ancestors still had influence in the everyday world. Deceased heroes and heroines in the community functioned as intermediaries in supplications to the gods, and their practical help was often requested, and expected. The gods were also believed to mete out rewards or punishment amongst the souls of the dead for good or evil deeds enacted on Earth, so by the end of the 5th Century BCE, images corresponding to the Christian notions of Heaven and Hell were already commonplace. Ideas of reincarnation and metempsychosis (reincarnation in another kind of being, like an animal or insect) may have been derived from the Eastern religions or, as Herodotus (*ca.*484–*ca.*420 BCE) suggested, from the Egyptians. As was mentioned earlier, the Egyptians had many nature-gods, some of whom were associated with animals. It was important that each body, friend or foe, should receive proper burial rites; failure to see to this brought divine retribution on those responsible from the Erinyes, the spirits charged with maintaining the natural order of things, as is related often again by Homer and his slightly earlier predecessor, Hesiod (*fl. ca.* 800 BCE).

These poets did much to establish the new wholly phonetic Greek alphabet from which arose the works of the philosophers and also Greek drama for the entertainment of the *theatai* (spectators), and which gave us our 'theatres'. The origins of their dramatic plays are obscure but they are thought to have arisen from the singing, chanting and dancing associated with the religious festivals; theatres had become an established feature of Athenian life by the 5th Century BCE [179].

In his book, *The Nature of the Gods*, the Roman orator and statesman Cicero (106–43 BCE) [120] presented somewhat similar arguments for the existence of the Roman gods as those found later in the writings of the Christian theologians as rational evidence for the existence of their God. He credits the Greek philosopher Epicurus with the contention that 'gods must exist because nature herself has imprinted an idea of them in the minds of all mankind' [121]. So the idea of the existence of 'the gods' Cicero regards as innate – and anthropomorphic: 'all of us of every race can conceive the gods only in human form' [122]. In Book II, he attributes the existence of seers who can foretell the future as another reason for supposing gods exist; and there is the abundance of blessings bestowed on humankind; we see awe-inspiring events in Nature, like floods and earthquakes; and the existence of the rhythms and cycles of Nature – all these are taken as signs from the gods. However, at one point, Cicero comes close to a monotheistic, though pantheistic, vision of the divine: 'God and the world of Nature must be one, and all the life of the world must be contained within the being of God.' – note the capitals! [124].

The First Cause Argument for the existence of God that was developed later by St. Thomas Aquinas (see section on Christian philosophers in Chapter 3) is pre-empted in Cicero (at least, for gods, plural) by 'all things are ordered by a sentient natural power, impelling them towards their own perfection', while Aquinas' Cosmological Argument appears in 'all the wonders of the earth and sky' that Cicero attributes to the gods [126]. Cicero's gods are also immanent in the world: 'if you admit their existence, you must also admit that they are active in the highest sense. What could be better than that their activity should be the government of the world?' Even the famous 'clock' argument of the English theologian William Paley (1743–1805), is here: 'When you see a sundial or a water-clock, you see that it tells the time by design and not by chance. How then can you imagine that the universe as a whole is devoid of purpose and intelligence, when it embraces everything, including these artifacts themselves and their artificers?' [127]. And again we read 'When we see some example of a mechanism, such as a globe or clock or some such device, do we doubt that it is the creation of some conscious intelligence? So when we see the movement of the heavenly bodies, the speed of their revolution, and the way in which they regularly run their annual course, so that all that depends upon them is preserved and prospers, how can we doubt that these too are not only the works of reason but of a reason which is perfect and divine?' [128]. This became known as the Teleological Argument or the Argument from Design that inferred the existence of God from the coordinated structure of the universe. French philosopher Denis Diderot (1713–1784), principal editor of the Enlightenment *Encyclopédie*, saw an Argument from Design based on the Guiding Hand he believed responsible for the organisation of the minutia of the natural world: he maintained that wonders like the germination of the seed or the emergence of the butterfly were too complex as processes to happen by chance. So belief in a god or gods, and attempts at rationalisation of that belief, has a long history.

1.3.   Paganism

The Egyptians, Greeks and Romans, as well as the indigenous natives of western Britain, the Celts, were all pagans. Paganism is more a philosophy for living, like some of the Eastern religious philosophies, rather than a formal religion, at least in its modern form. The word 'pagan' is derived from the Latin *pagus*, meaning a village or country district, and particularly referring originally to a region outside Rome where Christianity had not yet taken hold. It tends to be used by adherents of Western religion disparagingly as synonymous with 'heathen', 'barbarian', 'illiterate savage', or 'practitioner of the occult'; this is implied even by such an eminent authority as the Oxford English Dictionary. But pagans are not atheists in the broadest sense and they are certainly not Satanists or devil worshippers; nor were their cultures 'primitive'. The building of such architectural structures as those of the ancient world that we in more recent times described as the Seven Wonders is testimony to their knowledge of engineering and the physics of materials, and the design of their pottery and jewellery indicated a strong sense of aesthetic beauty.

Centuries ago, those who practiced pagan rituals, especially if they demonstrated any degree of psychic power or healing ability, other than through herbal treatments, and often even then, were branded as witches. There were famous witch trials and executions in America at Salem still in 1692, but the last execution of witches in The Netherlands had occurred in 1610, and in England in 1684. However, it was into the next century before France and Germany abandoned the practice, in 1745 and 1775, respectively. Today, spiritual healers and clairvoyants are increasingly to be found in Western society.

While there may be many variations in beliefs and rituals between different groups of pagans, one principle that is common to all is the belief in a divine and sacred universal spiritual force. Some identify this divine spirit with Nature itself (*pantheism*); some believe in a God that is transcendent as well as within Nature (*panentheism*). Some may believe in a multiplicity of gods, but they still have an awareness that there is a unifying divine spirit all around them constantly: there are those who identify this with a form of living soul (a divine spiritual energy) in the objects of the natural world (*animism*; Latin: *anima* – soul).

The idea of the divine spark incarnate in all individuals, and manifest to highest degree in tribal shamans, with the hope for a Saviour or Messiah or *Christos* in the Greek term, a god incarnate, to lead the group to physical betterment and spiritual salvation was not unknown even in Babylon and Egypt, as we saw earlier [233, 238]. Harpur implies that, in his view, the pagan religion is the original and authentic faith: 'It's almost as though long ago, there was one virtually cosmic religion that eventually and gradually deteriorated over eons' [234]. It is the later religions that many feel have created obstructions in communion between humankind and the divine, rather than facilitated spiritual peace of mind. In their preoccupation with their man-made tenets and rituals, they ignore the immense amount of suffering some of those edicts create, and they perpetuate the subconscious and often overt belief that suffering is in some way good for the soul. Where Christians focus on the afterlife for individual salvation, on human suffering and on the agony of Jesus on the cross as the central image, pagans celebrate the joy of this life on Earth to be shared with all. This does not imply that pagans do not believe in an afterlife – only that one must extract the maximum fulfilment for oneself and others from this life first, with constant awareness of our earthly interconnectedness. In his book, *The Way of Wyrd* [46], Brian Bates puts these words into the mouth of his pagan mystic in an effort to explain his world to a Christian scribe: 'You are labelling pieces of the world with words, then confusing your word-hoard for the totality of life. You see life as if you were viewing a room by the light of a single moving candle; then you make the error of assuming that the small areas you are seeing one at a time are separate and cannot be seen as one. Since the small areas of your life are thus seen as separate, you have to invent ways of connecting them. This is the fallacy of the ordinary person's view of life, for everything is already connected.'

This account might be regarded as a modern version of Plato's allegory of the cave [367]. Here, there is a story of prisoners in a cave, which is only dimly lit by firelight. The men have been there since childhood. Other men, hidden from the prisoners by a low wall, carry statues of people and animals such that they cast shadows on the wall. All the prisoners know of the world is what they see in those shadows. It is only when they emerge into the light from the shadow world in the cave that they achieve understanding of the true nature of their cave world. Some prisoners opt to return to their world of illusion, if they lack the courage to face reality. A world of religion based on fallacy and irrational propositions is like that of the prisoners in the cave – theirs is a world of illusion in the half-light imposed on them by others, until they emerge free into the natural world. If we believe that a God has created us then surely reason and language are humankind's greatest faculties, and these serve little purpose if we allow our lives to be ruled by the fantasies created by those questing for power.

The holding sacred of the natural environment and the interconnectedness of all life are the overriding principles of paganism: they value and try to preserve the abundance and diversity of Nature. They also place great store by personal responsibility and freedom of thought and action, gender equality and community spirit: 'if it harms no-one, do what you will'.

We are told by commentators on these things that the Christian churches are being forsaken in contemporary Europe, and even in America, the home of evangelism and Christian fundamentalism, for a return to a kind of Nature religion, a Neopaganism. There are now many people (some 13% of the world's population we are told [www.MissionFrontiers.org]) who do not follow any organised religion but many of whom still believe in a divine reality. Only 2½% of the world's population claim to be atheists. Some see in paganism the purest religion of communion between humankind and the divine, without all the human excrescences (and bitter controversies!) of the organised religions that developed subsequently, so often in a quest for power.

In Britain, one group of pagans whose direct descendants are with us still, perpetuating their cultural heritage, were the Celts. The Celts were a well-defined group of Western-European pagans living some two millennia ago. They were the Iron Age inhabitants (*ca.* 600 BCE to 100 CE) of Alba (Scotland), Breizh (Brittany, France), Cymru (Wales), Eire (Ireland), Kernow (Cornwall) and Mannin (Isle of Man). Most of what little we know of the Celts comes from the writings of their Roman conquerors, so almost inevitably we shall get a biased or prejudiced view. Regrettably, we have to get our information second-hand because the early Christians did their best to expunge all trace of pagan learning – which was considerable. There was a centre of ancient Gaelic learning at Arles from some 2000 years BCE, but this was sacked by a Christian mob in 270 CE. The same fate befell the irreplaceable collection of scrolls and books in a college at Bibracte in 389 CE [300]. These acts of desecration, and the even greater outrage of the destruction of the library at Alexandria, give a clear indication of 'the overwhelming hatred of learning and education' held by the converts to the new Christian religion and the continual fear of knowledge they displayed up to and beyond the Inquisition [235]. Harpur tells us that the last school of pagan philosophy in Athens was closed by decree of the Church in 529 CE [236].

The learned men and women of the Celtic tribes, who functioned as sages, seers, poets, astronomers, astrologers and healers, were called Druids. They formed the cornerstone of Celtic cultural life and guided the interaction of their people with their environment. Their wisdom was compared by the Roman writer Diogenes to that of the Chaldeans, the priest-kings that ruled over the Babylonians in the 7th Century BCE. Pliny the Elder maintained that the oak tree, and more especially any mistletoe found to be growing on it, were held sacred by the Druids [372], and their name is sometimes interpreted as being derived from *dru-wid* or 'wise oak'.

The stone circles at Stonehenge and Avebury in England that were originally attributed to the Druids date from a much earlier period, probably the second millennium BCE, though they were probably used by the Druids later, just as they are used by Neopagans now. Archaeologists believe that they were built as sacred sites to honour the sun and moon. Some archaeologists believe that, as these civilisations developed from Stone Age to Iron Age, they moved from hunter-gatherer communities that hunted in groups and often by moonlight, when animals were asleep, to agricultural communities working the land for crops as food, with individuals owning land that they had to tend during the day by the light of the sun. It may be that their god-worship moved at that time from allegiance to the moon-god to the god of the sun. While the Egyptians built their pointed pyramids as tombs for their god-kings, the pagan civilisations of Central and South America, the Aztecs and Mayans, built their pyramids with flat tops as temples to their sun and moon gods; the pagans of Europe likewise built flat-topped monuments and stone circles to honour their gods. The best surviving examples of stone tombs amongst these early pagans, long before the time of the Celts, are to be found in the Eastern part of Ireland, with the Newgrange megalithic tomb the outstanding example. These structures probably date back to before even the pyramids of Egypt, more than 3000 years BCE. They were probably used both for burial of the elders of the tribes and as temples to the sun and moon.

The Celts were much less sophisticated as societal groups than their Mediterranean counterparts and predecessors. Each society or clan was made up of a number of extended families, all of whom participated in child-rearing, rather like a contemporary Israeli kibbutz, and the clans banded together loosely in tribes. Women however were rather more emancipated in their communities than in many parts of the world today; they were not merely chattels but had a fair measure of independence, as indicated by the fact that some became Druids or priestesses. The families lived in timber houses with thatched roofs and made their living from farming. It was probably the Celts who brought the iron plough to Britain as they migrated to the western regions of the British islands from all over Western Europe, tied together by a similar if not common language and life style. What trade they had was largely dependent on iron working and agriculture. Mining, quarrying and farming have long been major industries in Wales, Cornwall and the Isle of Man. As a relic of their pagan past, the Welsh hold a regular festival of music and poetry, the National Eisteddfod (*Eisteddfod Genedlaethol Cymru*), which involves the ceremony of crowning of the bard, the most illustrious poet in the land. The Eisteddfod was started in 1176 when the first one was held in Aberteifi (Cardigan). The sites of the Eisteddfodau are still commemorated by the erection in the town or village of a circle of standing stones, the Gorsedd stones, similar to those at the ancient sites in England.

Celts, like other pagans, had many gods, most of whom were associated with Nature. There was a widespread belief in *animism* – that there was a spiritual force permeating all of the objects of Nature, organic and inorganic. There is a closely allied concept known as *panpsychism*, the idea that all of Nature is sentient, capable of responding in some way to the universal spiritual energy. Yet another related term is *hylozoism* (Greek: *hyle* – matter; *zoion* – animal), coined by the Cambridge philosopher Ralph Cudworth (1617–1688) in his book *The True Intellectual System of the Universe* [132]. Although he created the term 'hylozoism', Cudworth argued against this idea and in the same work coined the term *theism* to describe belief in a God that interacted with humans, but not inanimate matter. He described a dualistic theory of inorganic matter and life, though admitted that all life forms might respond consciously or unconsciously (instinctively) to the divine spirit. Today, these terms to describe a divine spirit throughout the natural world are often used synonymously. The Catholic Encyclopaedia describes the whole concept as a 'childish, inexperienced way of looking on nature' and dismisses the 'personification of nature in primitive races'. In fact, as we shall see in the final chapters of this book, it is a concept that, in modified form, has been accepted by several Nobel Prizewinners in science over the last century.

Some of the Nature spirits took human form, others animal, and some a combination of the two, as in Egypt; some spirits were benign while others were malevolent. Those that were benevolent were called Elementals: they were regarded as being the agents of the life-force, and were ruled over by archangels. The archangels Gabriel, the messenger, and Michael, the warrior and overseer, are mentioned in the Old Testament in the Book of Daniel, a prophet who lived in the 6th Century BCE. The archangels now have become venerated figures in Western religion: it was Gabriel who brought the news to Zacharias that his wife Elizabeth was to bear him a son in her old age [Luke 1:13] and also told Mary of the impending birth of Jesus [Luke 1:31]; and it was Gabriel also who appeared to Muhammad to reveal the scriptures that became the *Qu'ran* in Islam. The idea of archangels as spiritually advanced beings is thus found in Judaism and Christianity as well as in Neopaganism.

In contemporary paganism, there is no priesthood to act as intermediaries between each individual and the universal spiritual force: no-one is required to participate in specific rituals or to believe in something they cannot see or feel. Modern Druids simply guide novices towards a better understanding of how they can live in harmony with Nature. Pagans hold great respect for the wisdom of their ancestors, with whose spirits they commune in rituals and even in everyday life. Talking, silently or audibly, to the spirit of a loved one who has passed into the spiritual world is not a psychosis: what else is prayer but supplication to an unseen spirit? Pagans are not sexual deviants; they may perform rituals by moonlight, and often in woodland, near water, sometimes naked as free spirits, but they are not deranged – eccentric, perhaps, but as sane as anyone else. Their rituals never involve slaughter or mutilation of any living thing. Some of the neopagans live in simple, humble dwellings in the countryside; but others may be ordinary members of the community in any modern metropolis, escaping to the sanctuary of the wilderness at every opportunity. Many neopagans are well educated, middle-class citizens who are spiritually troubled by the materialistic, growth-obsessed lifestyles to be found in all major cities of the developed West, and especially in North America where there is such a strong accent on 'success' as judged by material possessions.

This whole western philosophy of a quest after growth and progress by continual material acquisition is anathema to the

Neopagans, who believe life should be lived in harmony with the cycles of Nature, not by its desecration and exploitation. The need to secure our energy from renewable sources instead of from nuclear fission or fossil fuels has, at long last, become a matter of concern for some governments. For humankind to live in harmony with the rest of the natural world is part of the ethos of service to the divine spirit. Paganism has enjoyed a resurgence especially since the 1960s, which saw a revival of the need for spiritual values and concern for the natural environment.

*   *   *

The Western religions are all based primarily on the Bible as scriptural text, though other scriptures are also important in the various faiths. The Bible is a work of historical fiction, a series of tales and myths, based on historical fact, but elaborated into parables and allegories in such a way as to convey a spiritual message. Many of the individuals described in the Bible undoubtedly existed, and some of the events may have actually occurred, but not necessarily at the times and places as recorded. That this is so has been confirmed from other literary sources or is borne out by archaeological investigations. Many writers have criticised unthinking adherence to the edicts of Christianity, in particular, and have pointed out that Christian beliefs are man-made principles based on tradition and a will-to-power of early Church fathers rather than some divine instruction [see, for example, refs. 197, 233, 238, 398, 505]. The historical details of the Old and New Testaments are all presented in the form of tales created by storytellers from the sayings of prophets and divine manifestations or from events in their lives to present guidance as to how, initially, the Jewish people of the time should live noble and moral lives – lives that would enhance their spiritual and physical wellbeing, and that would allow them to live together in social harmony as one nation. The storytellers were not concerned with historical accuracy but with conveying a spiritual message. It is only since the evolution of the rational approach to knowledge ushered in by the Renaissance that we demand that all information should be factually correct.

That these were re-workings of tales from earlier civilisations was well-known to theological writers at the time, like Origen. Similar stories are found also in other civilisations of both East and West. Just as Satan tempted Jesus with material wealth [Matthew 4, 1–11], so Siddhartha Gautama was tempted by Devaputra Mara with visions of beautiful women as he underwent his enlightenment. God gave the Ten Commandments to Moses on Mt. Sinai [Exodus, Chap. 20]; Jesus went up into Mt. Hermon for his transfiguration [Matthew 17, 1–8]; Muhammad went up into the hills above Mecca to receive the words of archangel Gabriel [*Qu'ran, surah* 2, *Al-Baqarah*]. The Egyptian god Horus, the Persian god Zoroaster, and the Hindu god Krishna were all reputed in various tales to have been incarnated by a virgin birth. The incarnation of the divine in human form was a widely held belief in many civilisations. For all their differences, there are very many parallels in the myths that make up the scripture of the major world religions. Some religious authorities have insisted on the historical validity of their scripture as a means of exerting control over their people; but fundamentalists who so vehemently affirm the unequivocal and unilateral truth of their particular faith by scriptural quotations are building on quicksand. Though one may regard scripture with great reverence for the moral messages it proclaims, and the beauty of its literary expression, and admire the spirituality of its founders, one cannot rationally regard it as *theopneustos*, 'God breathed'. It conveys a spiritual message in various forms for humankind, transmitted and interpreted over many generations by other human hands and minds, with all their fallibilities.

It is perhaps worthwhile therefore to review some of the main principles of those Western religions with the most adherents, and some of the newer religions from 19th Century America, all claiming to transmit the Word of God as found in the Bible to see how it has been interpreted by humankind at different times to give different views of the nature of God, and most certainly quite different views of the divine message as to how we should live our lives. It is a sobering thought how much carnage has been wreaked over the past two millennia by groups of people who believed that their human constructs of the Bible's message was the only one rendering truth, and who felt that any who failed to agree should be slaughtered.

1.4. Judaism

The Babylonian and Assyrian cultures from, respectively, the southern and northern regions of Mesopotamia (corresponding roughly to what is now Iraq) flourished around 3000 BCE. Mesopotamia was given its name by the Greeks from its situation between two great rivers, the Tigris and Euphrates (Greek: *meso* - between; *potamos* - river). Here, society was arranged as a number of small and independent city-states, as was the Hellenic system that followed. The southern part of Mesopotamia was called Sumer, its language and people Sumerian. The people believed that certain objects of the natural world were pervaded by a life-force or *mana*, and that amongst these natural objects dwelt the deities or *elohim*. Their world was created out of some chaotic primordial matter that had existed for eternity – they did not believe that the world was created from nothing. The natural world, including humankind, and the gods themselves were all fashioned out of the same material from this same original source. This pagan world-view was what we now describe as *monistic* or *holistic* – all that was, was one. These pagans did not consider themselves demeaned as unworthy creatures in comparison to their gods but rather that the gods were paragons of excellence to which they should and could aspire. A deity that was totally devoid of human characteristics was not one that could inspire any kind of meaningful relationship and certainly not spiritual commitment. Two of the principal gods of the Sumerians were the sun-god Marduk and the moon-god Sin, from which Sinai derives its name. The probable shift of allegiance from moon-god to sun-god with a change in life-style from hunter-gatherers to land cultivators was described in the previous section on paganism.

The Sumerians used the waters of their rivers to irrigate the dried-out alluvial mud of the flood plain and turn it into fertile crop-land. Little wonder that the people thought of this region of lush vegetation amidst the desert as Paradise, and they called it Edeen, later to become the biblical Eden. They planted gardens even on the upper levels of their stepped temples, or ziggurats, to give a spectacular display of foliage that, in one instance, was to become known as one of the seven wonders of the ancient world – the Hanging Gardens of Babylon.

Annually in this pagan culture there was a great festival at the start of the New Year, when the natural world would begin its cycle of regeneration. This was held in the month of April or Nisan, which later became the Easter festival of Christendom; it also marks the beginning of the new financial year in most present-day Western commercial organisations. The New Year Festival was a time to re-establish communion with the *mana* of the natural world and with the divine, which amounted to much the same thing.

One of the early kings of Mesopotamia about whom we have a fairly detailed record was Gilgamesh who ruled the city of Uruk (or, in the Bible, Erech) during the first half of the 3rd millennium BCE. His exploits are written down in one of the west's earliest epic poems, written mainly in one of the principal languages of the region, Akkadian. One of the tales told of him (in Tablets ix to xi) was how he and his animals took refuge when the whole region was devastated by a flood – an obvious model for the biblical story of Noah and the Ark [Genesis, Chaps 6–9].

The capital of Sumeria was at Ur, a city situated in what is now south-eastern Iraq, about 150 miles south-east of Baghdad. It became a focus for growth and prosperity in the region, as is the role of big cities in our own western cultures. The materialistic Sumerians were visited from time to time by famines, droughts and plagues that may well have been interpreted at the time as retribution from the gods for overindulgence in material pleasures; however, such occurrences are also quite familiar to us at the present time as a result of regional over-exploitation of resources. Again, there are obvious parallels here with the biblical tales of the plagues of Egypt [Exodus, Chaps 8–11] brought about for defying God's will. In fact, as indicated previously, there are numerous clear secular and historical antecedents for several of the stories of the Old Testament, and mythological parallels in earlier cultures dating back to the Egyptians and Babylonians.

It seems to have been overdevelopment and the substantial growth in population which followed that finally outstretched the natural resources of the region leading to the eventual downfall of the Sumerian civilisation around 1500 BCE. At the time when the culture was weakened from within, it was attacked by marauders from the north. The devastation of Ur by the Elamites, a tribe from a region around south-western Persia, is believed to have occurred shortly after 2000 BCE.

The first books of the Bible represent the first attempts in Western civilisation to present a world-view, a prescription for individual moral behaviour and recommendations for practices that would produce social cohesion of what was to become the Jewish nation. The writings tell us that amongst the Sumerian people was a family headed by Terah (or Terach) who lived in Haran, near Ur. Terah's eldest son was called Abram, and he was charged by God to take his family away from the war-ravaged area to resettle in the comparative safety of Canaan [Genesis, Chap. 12, vs 1–5], the land that subsequently became Palestine. Abram's entourage included his sister Sarah and Lot, his nephew. Terah remained at Haran and died there many years later. The biblical account then describes how Abram experienced the first of several visions of God at this time. As a result of his encounters, Abram is said to have become imbued with the concept of a single omnipotent God who was Creator of Heaven and Earth. This event represents the first recorded break with Babylonian polytheistic tradition. Abraham, as he was now to be called [Gen 17.5], thence entered into a covenant with God [Gen. 17. 2–4], converting his people to his vision of monotheism, and he has thus become acknowledged as the founder of Judaism. When he and his family migrated, Abraham took with him the myths, fables and historical dramas of the Sumerians, stories that became incorporated into the books of the Old Testament.

Archaeologists of the 19th and early 20th Centuries tended to interpret their finds on the basis of the assumed historical truth of these accounts in the Bible. Such archaeologists thus deduced that Abraham lived in the Holy Land between 2000 and 1500 years BCE. This date was arrived at by interpretation of the historical evidence from excavation of local sites and seemed to be of the same order as that calculated from biblical sources. The biblical account records that there were 42 generations between Abraham and Jesus [Matthew 1.17]. Allowing 30 years per generation we get a total of 1260 years, which is not too far adrift from the earlier archaeological dating. However, modern studies have failed to find any concrete evidence that the biblical Abraham was an actual historical figure. The modern interpretation is that there may have been a charismatic leader called Abraham living *at some time* in the early history of the Israelites, such that epic tales were told of his life. These stories, recounted orally over many generations, were then subsequently elaborated so that he became an inspirational symbol of the birth of the Jewish nation. As for his having converted the Israelites to monotheism, there is much incontrovertible archaeological evidence that polytheism was still practiced for many centuries after the time of this biblical Abraham.

Another key figure in the founding of Judaism is Moses, but the same situation exists historically for Moses as for Abraham: Moses was a common enough name in the Levant then as now, and probably another charismatic leader arose a few centuries after Abraham who also shaped the destiny of his people and he became the biblical figure of Moses. The time of the life of Moses has been dated by biblical scholars at around 1400 BCE. It is said that the Canaanites, who later became the Israelites, were driven from their homeland into Egypt to work as slaves. It was Moses who led the Israelites out of Egypt back to their homeland in Canaan [stories told in Exodus and Numbers], though again there is no archaeological or independent literary evidence of this. It was on the way back to Canaan that Moses had an encounter with God on Mount Sinai [Exodus, Chap. 20] and was given the tablets containing the Ten Commandments or Decalogue.

Moses had encountered God earlier on Mount Horeb (Sinai) when an angel of the Lord set fire to a bush without destroying it (Exodus 3, vv. 2–3). A monastery dedicated to St. Catherine is now built on the supposed location of Moses's encounters with God on Mount Sinai to perpetuate this idealised account.

The problem with the historicity here is that the Israelites were too large a group of people (perhaps as many as two million) to have possibly left Egypt for Canaan *en masse* – it would have represented a huge migration in those times, especially if it occurred within a short period of time. Also, Canaan was itself an Egyptian territory at the time, in the late Bronze Age, when the exodus was supposed to have occurred, and it contained an important garrison town, so the Canaanites would not have escaped Egyptian rule by moving to Canaan. On the contrary, they would have been more likely to be subject to its dictates than in their original home. Moses and his people were said to have spent 40 years in the desert [Exodus 16, v.35], so it could only have been by miracles, as recounted in the Bible, that they would ever have found enough food or water in that wilderness for a large number of people. Although such a mass migration was therefore unlikely, there are actual records of *some few groups of people* who lived as nomads at this time, and there was known to be constant migration back and forth between Egypt and Canaan.

Moses died on the last stage of this migration [Deuteronomy, Chap. 34], so Joshua took over leadership of the Israelites [Joshua, Chap.1]. They waged war against the Canaanites during which the city of Jericho was taken, and the walls were said to have fallen with the blast of the trumpets by the priests. However, archaeological evidence again indicates that the city of Jericho was no longer occupied or even standing at this time (13th Century BCE) having been destroyed – probably by an earthquake – at least a century or two previously. Many of the cities described in the book of Joshua as having been conquered were not occupied in the late Bronze Age, and Hazor is the only one for which historical evidence suggests collapse around the 13th Century BCE, consistent with the biblical account. So again, historical facts were probably elaborated on so as to glorify the achievements of Joshua as leader of the people.

Archeological excavations carried out in the correct location and for the right time periods as described in the Bible (*ca.* 1000 BCE) have also found no evidence of the wealth and power of such prominent biblical personalities as David and his son Solomon [1 Samuel, 1 Kings, 1 Chronicles], supposedly kings of Israel. Rulers of such wealth must have left some indications of their prosperous existence. Archaeology indicates that Israel itself at this time was apparently a region of small scattered villages to the north of Judah and lacking a major city and therefore unlikely to be ruled by powerful kings. That such a region should possess great wealth and power also seems unlikely. However, there is evidence of the existence of a King David a few centuries later, but the remains of cities like Gezer and Megiddo, that might have been built by Solomon, have been dated by radiocarbon methods, and indicate dates of 9th-8th Centuries BCE, again some centuries after the dates derived from the biblical accounts.

The establishment of the new Judaic religion, and of later Christianity, occurred gradually and never completely extinguished the old beliefs, but King Hezekiah, king of Judah around 700 BCE, also did much to reaffirm the monotheistic faith and prohibit idol worship. Judah was a territory just to the south of Israel, with its capital at Jerusalem. When the Assyrians under Sennacherib attacked Jerusalem, the biblical version describes how Hezekiah handed over vast wealth to try to placate the opposing armies but that the help of the angel of the Lord was needed to overcome more than 5000 of the enemy who died mysteriously in the night [2 Kings, Chap. 18–20; Isaiah, Chap 36–39]. Assyrian wall carvings from a somewhat later period however record this battle as a great victory for them. Again, both sides claimed victory for propaganda reasons to maintain the morale of their people. We do not know therefore whether or not the biblical account is historically accurate.

Hezekiah's great-grandson Josiah, king of Judah *ca.* 640–609 BCE, tried to carry on this monotheistic religion but he was killed at the battle of Armageddon (Hebrew: *har megidda* – hill of Megiddo), a strategic battle location from Hebrew times to the present day (even in World War II). Armageddon is used in the book of Revelations [Chap. 16] as a symbol for the battleground of good against evil. Many Jewish people believe that, as God's chosen people, they are continually made to suffer in order to atone for the sins of the world, in much the same way as Christians regard the suffering of Jesus on the cross. After the death of Josiah the people looked to the prophet Isaiah, whose accounts are the best preserved of those in the Dead Sea Scrolls. After this crushing defeat of a good king, it was from this time on that the expectation of a Saviour or Messiah to restore their fortunes became a focal point of Judaic belief, as it had been with their Egyptian and Babylonian predecessors in difficult times. This was also the aspect of Isaiah's pronouncements that had greatest appeal to the Christians in their deification of Jesus. It was at this point, around the 5th Century BCE, that the Judahites became the nation of the Jews.

The Isaiah text in the Dead Sea Scrolls, as well as predicting catastrophes for the world, also talks about techniques of prayer: 'The paths of the Infinite Garden must be traversed by the body, the heart and the mind as one' [*The Essene Gospel of Peace* from ref. 89]. In other words, prayer should be all-consuming; it is most effective when it is directed not so much to supplication but to meditation on a constructive theme as if it were already accomplished and accepting that one is a participant in the divine plan. This meditative technique has been used extensively by some complementary therapists in recent decades to produce remission from some highly debilitating diseases. For the Jews, in the time of Isaiah, belief in a Saviour thus became a cornerstone of their faith.

The Bible is one of the key Scriptures of western religion, and its precepts form the foundation of the code of law and civil behaviour of western society. The five Books of Moses or Pentateuch elaborate the 613 ritual observances or *mitzvoth* that Jews are required to practice. It was thought originally that these were texts actually written by Moses, but more recent scholarship has established the existence of at least four separate authors, or groups of authors, described enigmatically as J (who called God 'Jahweh'), P ('the priest', who was concerned largely with ritual observances), E (who designated their God as 'Elohim', taking the name of the pagan nature spirits to represent the one God of many attributes), and D (the emphatic monotheists of Deuteronomy). As the Pentateuch also includes an account of the death of Moses, at least some of this text must have been written later. The importance of the Pentateuch, and particularly the books of Leviticus and Deuteronomy, is that these books lay down for the first time the rights and duties of the individual, and the need to worship one God for the social cohesion of the emerging nation.

The different groups of writers had somewhat different views of the nature of God. The Jahwehists have God interacting directly with humankind (as in Exodus 3 and 4, where Moses talks with God to receive instructions, or when the angel lights the burning bush to get Moses's attention to speak to God). The Elohimists prefer to have God interacting with humankind through dreams and angels. The basic Pentateuch is believed to have been essentially complete by about the 7th Century BCE with writings from all the different sources. The text, in Hebrew, seems to have changed little to this day, as evidenced by the discovery in 1947 of the Dead Sea Scrolls that originated from the Essenes, and it forms the *Torah* (Hebrew: teaching), the cornerstone of Jewish scripture. The *Torah* was now sealed and unchangeable, for all its apparent contradictions, because it was regarded as sacred. All that remained now was commentary and interpretation. A copy of the *Torah* is housed in every synagogue at its focal point in a structure called the Ark of the Covenant, corresponding to the altar in Christian churches.

Scholars now believe that it was the priest and scribe Ezra who, around the middle of the 5th Century BCE (458 BCE is a date sometimes given), brought together versions of the scripture from the north and south of the region, from Israel and Judah, to form one authoritative version of the *Torah*, and possibly some of the other books of the Old Testament as well. The Old Testament as a whole was probably compiled over a period of some 1000 years and may well have involved as many as 100 to 150 scribes over this period, so we can hardly expect uniformity and total historical accuracy in the stories told. More texts were gradually added to form the Old Testament as we know it today, and one of the earliest and most important Greek translations of the complete work was the *Septuagint*, compiled in the 3rd Century BCE.

The battle in the writing of the *Torah* was to win the hearts and minds of the pagan people of the Mesopotamian region, to make them abandon their worship of idols and to pay homage to the same one God, in an effort to bind them into one nation. In Exodus, Chapter 7, we are told of the battle between Moses and Aaron with their divine powers and the sorcerers of the Egyptian Pharaoh. In the biblical version, the serpents conjured up by Moses and Aaron from their staffs devour those of the Pharaoh's men; but in the Egyptian version of the same tale, it is the magic of the old sorcerers that wins. Again, the tale is told from the perspective of those who need to use it for social and political propaganda.

Archeology can tell us little or nothing about myths, and it is now generally held that religiously inspired archeologists might have been too enthusiastic in interpreting the results of their finds in such a way that they corroborated biblical stories. More recent excavations with more careful interpretations, over a much broader range of times and places in the Middle East, suggest that many biblical accounts are historically inaccurate and are probably often completely incorrect. But the important thing is that the Old Testament describes an epic story of the founding of the Jewish nation, and the principles of personal and social conduct and their presentation as literature are still sound and inspiring, even if the factual details of people and places are not always correct.

The central core of Judaism is belief in one personal God, Yahweh (YHWH) or Elohim, who enacted a covenant with the people of Israel, first through Abraham and then with Moses. God is denoted by YHWH because the ancient Hebrew script had no vowels – these were added *ca.* 60 CE by the Masoretes. The biblical story is that the monotheistic vision of Abraham was perpetuated by his son

Isaac, his grandson Jacob, and by the twelve sons of Jacob, founders of the Twelve Tribes of Israel. But there was a constant battle to establish the new faith and there were periodic relapses when times were good into a predominant polytheism (worshipping Baal, Anat and Asherah) and the worship of idols (for example, the golden calf described in Exodus, Chap. 32). The prophets of Israel were very intolerant of this behaviour, as when Elijah called for the execution of those who persisted in idol worship (1 Kings 18, verse 40).

This one God of the Jews was imbued with the qualities that pervaded the whole of Judeo-Christian religion. He was seen as *Creator of the universe*: 'For all the gods of the peoples are idols; but the Lord made the heavens' [Psalm 96, v.5]. He was *infinite and eternal*: 'from everlasting to everlasting thou art God' (Psalm 90, v.2) and 'The Lord will reign for ever and ever' [Exodus 15, v.18 and Psalms 146, v.10]; *omnipotent* [Psalm 104]; and *immanent and omnipresent* (the *Shechinah* or Indwelling One): Whither shall I go from thy spirit? Or whither shall I flee from thy presence?' [Psalms 139, v.7]. He is also *incorporeal*: as David J. Goldberg and John D. Rayner put it in their book on *The Jewish People* [213], even though the Bible refers to God in human terms 'He is pure spirit, without a body.' The all-pervading divine spirit described as the *Shechinah* is regarded in some contexts as implying the feminine aspect of the divine. Another of the holy Hebrew scriptures is the *Talmud*, comprising the *Mishnah* of Rabbi Judah (135–217 CE) and the commentary thereon, the *Gemara*. This work describes the necessary participation of humankind to fulfil God's purpose on Earth: 'The conception of divine purpose fulfilling itself through human history and human life determines all the teachings of Judaism about God.' [174]. This is a very uplifting idea, since it makes every act of every individual, however seemingly trivial, important to God. Individuals should never humiliate other people, even non-Jews, because this is considered a sacrilegious denial of God's image [*Baba Metziah* 58b]. Similarly, it is offensive to spread malicious gossip about other people [*Arakin* 15b]. Charity and loving kindness are the most important of the *mitzvoth* (commandments or religious duties). This view of a God that evolves with humankind is found again in the idea of process theology, discussed later at the end of this chapter.

Judaism today has some 20 million adherents throughout the world. Their relatively small numbers are out of all proportion to the immense contribution that people of Jewish extraction have made throughout human history to the disciplines of theology, philosophy and science, and to the creative arts.

The medieval Jewish philosophers are discussed in Chapter 3 while Jewish theologians of the Enlightenment, Solomon Formstecher and Samuel Hirsch, are discussed in Chapter 7.

1.5. Christianity

The view of God inherited from Judaism was passed on to Christianity for, of course, Jesus and his disciples were Jews. The philosophy of Jesus laid emphasis on forgiveness of our enemies to receive the grace of a loving God. Simon Peter was regarded as the first pope because he was the first of the apostles to be called by Jesus (Matthew, Chap. 4, vv.18, 19), he was the first to claim that Jesus was the Messiah (Matthew, Chap. 16, v.16), and the first of the apostles to see what he believed to be the risen Christ (1 Corinthians, Chap. 15, v.5). His given name was Simon but he was called Peter or Cephas, which mean 'rock' in Greek and Hebrew, respectively.

In the first centuries after the time of Jesus, most of Western Europe was under the rule of the pagan Roman Empire, of which Britain formed part. In 306 CE, Flavius Valerius Constantinus was with his father, Constantius Caesar Augustus, at Eboracum (York) when the latter died. The local troops immediately proclaimed his son as Emperor Augustus, the emperor later to be known as Constantine the Great, because Constantine Jr. was, like his father, a highly successful general.

In the time of Jesus and for at least two centuries after, Christians were regarded as troublemakers, railing against excesses of the Roman military, and were therefore ruthlessly persecuted. Constantine decided to try to get them on his side rather than against him and the Edict of Milan (313 CE) stipulated toleration of Christians and pagans. For him, the promotion of Christianity was a matter of political expediency, providing a code of social conduct and a group of administrative officials that the people would listen to in order to help bind together his decaying empire and control the masses. The early Church fathers were astute enough to adopt and adapt many of the pagan beliefs into the Christian system. The emperor wore purple robes at his public audiences – so did the Church hierarchy. At these congregations, incense was burnt so that the emperor would not be offended by odours from the unwashed attendees – another practice adopted by the Church. The Easter festival is the pagan celebration of the new natural year. The pagan festival of the winter solstice became the time chosen to celebrate the birth of Jesus: 25th December has no significance whatever in terms of the actual birth date of Jesus. Indeed, his very existence as a real person is still a matter of debate amongst scholars. December 25th was originally chosen by emperor Aurelian in 274 CE as the birth date of the unconquered sun-god (*natalis solis invicti*). The decoration of the pine-tree at the winter solstice was an Anglo-Saxon pagan custom introduced into England from Europe in the 19th Century by Queen Victoria's consort, Albert. Its Christian symbolism was justified by the passage in Isaiah Chap. 60, v.13 about using the pine and box trees as religious decoration.

The Christians were also useful in improving social cohesion because they offered messages of hope and ultimate salvation to a poor and enslaved people, who had little real comfort in their lives. By the third century CE, the Christians had already established some kind of rudimentary social health care system often provided by widows of soldiers who had been killed defending the Empire – the beginnings of the establishment of the orders of nuns who now minister to the sick. In these centres, the women would offer free food to the poor and dispossessed.

Constantine thus became a patron of Christianity and helped the early church to persecute not only non-Christians but even other Christians, like the Gnostics and the Arians, to reinforce the imposition of just one Establishment set of doctrines. Twenty-four volumes by the Gnostic philosopher Basilides (*fl. ca.* 2nd Century CE), *The Exegetica: Interpretations Upon The Gospels*, along with thirty-six volumes by Porphyry (233–304 CE), all apparently critical of the emerging religion, were wantonly destroyed because they did not conform to Establishment Church doctrine. Even before the tenets of Christian belief were formally established (see below), Porphyry made a long and bitter attack on Christian principles and their assertion of the historical truth of the scriptures. Origen (*ca.*185–254 CE), Jewish philosopher Celsus (*fl. ca.* 178 CE), and founders of Neoplatonism like Plotinus were all aware that the precepts of the new Christian religion were simply reworkings of long-established myths and that the Bible was essentially allegorical. Christian propaganda was made to work more effectively in the Church's favour by the fortuitous historical development of parchment instead of papyrus for written texts. The spiritual and allegorical interpretation of the Old Testament by such eminent theologians as Clement of Alexandria (*ca.*150–215 CE) and Origen was repudiated and substituted by assertion of literal truth and historical accuracy. This brutal conformity all worked in Constantine's interest in expanding and securing his empire, but he still retained his pagan beliefs and only embraced Christianity so far as it suited him. He was only baptised on his deathbed in 337 CE. From its very beginnings, in its bid for power, Christianity felt it had an obligation to convert the whole of humankind, unlike Judaism, which was essentially a local religion of the Hebrew people.

It was Constantine who built the Church of the Nativity in Bethlehem and another church on the site of Jesus' tomb in Jerusalem that was to become the Church of the Holy Sepulchre to consolidate his new-found religion. Thus Constantine was responsible for sanctifying the supposed sites of Jesus' birth and death some 300 years after the Crucifixion. As part of the official establishment of Christianity, Constantine declared Sunday a public holiday, the *dies solis* when the Roman pagans celebrated their invincible sun-god Mithras. He formalised the system set up by his predecessor,

Emperor Diocletian, whereby imperial vicars governed the thirteen regions of the Empire, called diocese. The system was later expanded and taken over by the monasteries in the Middle Ages, when vicars were administrative officials of both the lords of the manor and of the Church; later, they became appointees of the Church alone, but the origin of the system was entirely secular. It was also not difficult for the Romans, who had for centuries revered their Emperor as a God, to transfer these god-like qualities to another man, the founder of the Christian faith. In the first century after the time of Jesus, Christianity was a very spiritual faith and still retained such pagan beliefs as that of reincarnation and universal salvation. After the Councils of Nicaea and Chalcedon (see below), it moved along the path of transformation into the religion we know now, nominally abjuring anything to do with paganism but still absorbing pagan practices as if they had some specific Christian significance.

Because Rome was still a largely pagan city, in 324–6 CE Constantine set up his base in the Eastern part of the Empire at Byzantium, which he renamed Constantinople (now, officially since 1930, Istanbul). The Eastern Roman Empire flourished there as a centre of learning and culture for a thousand years until its overthrow by the Muslim Ottomans in the fourteenth century. Art and architecture from the Byzantine period have had a great influence on culture in Eastern Europe. The domed roofs of the cathedrals, like those of neighbouring mosques are in marked contrast to the spires and vaulted ceilings of European Gothic cathedrals. The music of the Byzantine period was derived, not from early Greek music but from the Hebrew chants in the Jewish synagogues.

Constantine is therefore venerated by the Catholic Church as the Emperor who converted Rome, and subsequently a large part of Western Europe, to Christianity through enactments of the Edict of Milan (313 CE) and the Council of Nicaea (325 CE), at which Constantine presided. Here, the form of the Bible as we know it today was established, with many writings eliminated and with many others, as we now know from comparison with original sources like the Dead Sea Scrolls, altered to suit control required by the Church Fathers. Two verses at the end of the Book of Revelation that concludes the Bible warn against any tampering of the officially approved text, by addition or deletion, on pain of death [Revelation Chap. 22, verses 18, 19].

Some parts of the Bible, like the Pentateuch, the Prophets and the Psalms, must have existed for some time, perhaps several centuries, before the birth of Jesus; this must have been the Bible as he knew it. The original texts were written in Hebrew and Aramaic: but already there were translations of what became the Old Testament available even then, the most important of which was the Greek translation known as the *Septuagint*, compiled in the 3rd Century BCE. Some time after the death of Emperor Constantine (337 CE), Pope Damasus I (366–384) authorised his secretary, Jerome (*ca.*345–420 CE), to translate the Bible from the predominantly Greek texts into Latin. The authorised Greek versions of the New Testament were the *Codex Sinaiticus* and the *Codex Vaticanus*, which also date from about this time and are thought to have been prepared by copyists in Alexandria. Jerome worked from pre-existing Latin or Greek texts for the Gospels, the Old Testament was translated from Hebrew and the Psalms from the Greek *Septuagint*.

Most of the New Testament was written by Paul, probably in the decade 50–60 CE, in the form of letters to various groups of Christians scattered throughout the Roman Empire giving advice on theological issues; there were probably some 14 letters in all. Two or three years later he was put to death in Rome. The spread of Christianity was a gradual process, as missionary converts travelled through the Empire after the death of Jesus. The gospels, of which Mark is now believed to have been the first, were written within a decade or two after Paul's death: so none of these accounts is an observer's description of Jesus's life and ministry as it happened, as they were all written many years after the events. The Acts of the Apostles was probably written by Luke. The Bible was to go through many more revisions after Nicaea before reaching the version we know today.

The classical scholars Gerald Massey and Alvin Boyd Kuhn

claim that all the essentials of the life of Jesus, as presented in the Gospels, were already written in Babylonian and Egyptian times. The temple at Luxor, built by pharaoh Amenhotep III, has a mural that is interpreted as displaying scenes of angels telling shepherds of the coming of God on Earth, with an archangel telling a virgin that she was to be the mother of the incarnation, and three sages paying homage to the newborn infant [336, cited in ref. 237]. The name, Jesus, is by no means unique to the person Christians call their Messiah. In Egyptian folklore there was a Messiah called Iusa, which became the Hebrew Ieshua, the Greek Iesous and finally the Latin Iesus (there was no letter 'J' in these languages, or in any English language until the 14th Century, and its use did not become widespread in English until the 17th Century). The symbol of the cross and the *chi-rho (XP)* monogram (from Χριστος Ρήγας, *Christos Reegas*, Christ the King) used by Christians had their origin in Egyptian or even Babylonian times, as they have been found as inscriptions on Egyptian tombs, as related above.

The preparation of the new Latin version of the Bible by Jerome was primarily an attempt to convert the pagans who still made up the majority of the population of Rome. Jerome did not regard himself as divinely inspired. He maintained that it was the prophets who were inspired and he regarded himself only as translator and interpreter. This translation became known as the *Vulgate Bible* and it was the standard version used in the Catholic Church for over 1000 years. It was also the version used by Christian religious scholars throughout the Middle Ages, as Latin was the language of communication within the Church. Spanish Muslims even translated the Bible into Arabic for Christians in the Iberian Peninsula.

The first of the translations into English was the notable version, produced around 1384, of John Wycliffe (or Wyclif) (*ca.*1320–1384) and his followers, carried out under pain of death, for any translation not authorised by the Church was forbidden. Wycliffe, a student and later master at Oxford University, worked from the deeply flawed Latin Vulgate Bible of Jerome. He regarded the Bible as presenting 'the infallible rule of truth'. After his death, Wycliffe's bones were dug up and burned by the Church as retribution for his actions. His followers, the Lollards, were persecuted well into the next century: the Church thus suppressed original thought at Oxford on theological issues for many years. William Tyndale (*ca.* 1492–1536) produced a more authentic English Bible working from a Hebrew version of the Old Testament and a Greek version of the New Testament, probably the 4th Century *Codex Sinaiticus*. As a result, he was hounded out of England to continental Europe, but still the Church authorities hunted him down and executed him by strangulation and burning at the stake. You went against the Church on any matter at all at your peril, and you certainly did not interfere with matters theological without authorisation! It is difficult for us now to appreciate that in the Middle Ages, the Church was as ruthless a dictatorship as any we have seen in Germany or Russia in the 20th Century. Tyndale died as Henry VIII's dissolution of the monasteries (1536–39) was just beginning, though Matthew Parker, the first Archbishop of Canterbury in the new Church of England, was not appointed for another twenty years (1559).

Then, as part of the Protestant movement, with the English Church now free of the dictates of the Church of Rome, an English version of the Bible was authorised by King James in 1604–1611, the text of which follows closely that of its predecessor by William Tyndale. The Westminster Confession of 1647 confirmed the authority of this Bible, saying it presented 'infallible truth'. With so many successive translations into different languages by successions of scribes it is not rationally plausible that one could believe in the literal and historical accuracy of every word or passage. Every translator must essentially produce their own interpretation of text. So even if historical events are described, they almost certainly would have become embellished with passage through many hands and minds. However, this is not to deny the validity of the moral message, or the divine inspiration of the key figures of the scriptures.

In shaping the early Christian tenets, one of the key declarations of the Church Fathers at the 1st Ecumenical Council, the Council of Nicaea (325 CE), at which Constantine presided, was that Jesus was at one with God ('of the same substance' – *homoousion*), though of two natures, human and divine in one being – the so-called hypostatic union. This edict was reaffirmed at the 2nd Ecumenical Council, the Council of Constantinople (381 CE), and again at the 4th Ecumenical Council, the Council of Chalcedon (451 CE), together with the divinity of Father, Son and Holy Ghost., and this was to give rise to immense difficulties for Christianity in later centuries. It was one of the prime factors in the rise of Islam – to counter this dilution of the 'one-God' system of belief. The deification of Jesus was introduced primarily to counter the rising influence of the cult of Arianism that regarded Jesus as of human rather than of divine essence – *homoiousion* – just one iota of difference! The nature of Jesus as the *logos*, the Word made flesh, was the primary concern of the 3rd Ecumenical Council at Ephesus (431 CE). At Nicaea, Athanasius (*ca.*296–373 CE), Bishop of Alexandria, was one of the most outspoken critics of Arianism, following the theme of his most important work, *On the Incarnation*, written some years earlier. The Arians, so-called after the Alexandrian theologian Arius (*ca.*250–*ca.*336 CE), rejected the idea that the being of God could be transferred to any other. Although the Arian rejection of the Trinity and of the divinity of Jesus was quashed at Nicaea, this belief still persisted amongst some Christians, so the Cappadocian Fathers (Basil of Caesarea, his brother Gregory of Nyssa and Gregory of Nazianzus) found it necessary to press for this principle again as part of Christian belief in the later Ecumenical Councils. In 1098, in the early years after the first schism (see below), Pope Urban II still found it necessary to ask St. Anselm of Canterbury to prepare a defence of the Western Church's position on the origin of the Holy Spirit for the Council of Bari, in an effort to heal the rift. Anselm spoke at the Council and in 1102 produced a work on this theme, *On the Procession of the Holy Spirit*.

It was also at these Councils that the idea arose that Jesus' crucifixion should be regarded as an atonement for the 'sin' of Adam in tasting the fruits of the tree of knowledge: knowledge has always tended to be regarded by the Christian Church as dangerous! Jews and the later Muslims regarded the suggestion that Jesus *was* God incarnate as idolatry, undermining the concept of their *one* God, Yahweh or Allah, and they regarded Jesus simply as a prophet.

As a result of these rather arbitrary dictates by the early Church Fathers, the first major schism within the Christian Church occurred in the 11th Century (*ca*.1054), when the friction that had existed for centuries between the Church in Rome and the Byzantine Church centred in the east at Constantinople finally erupted in a formal break between the two. There had long been a political struggle, dating back to Roman times, between the Latinate centre at Rome and the Greek clergy at Constantinople. This animosity was exacerbated by the founding of the Holy Roman Empire when Pope Leo III crowned Charlemagne (768–814 CE) as Emperor in 800 CE. The Holy Roman Empire was to continue for a thousand years until its dissolution in 1806. The papacy saw the Empire as a secular administrative institution established by and therefore responsible to Rome, exerting only such authority as was directly delegated to it. The emperor however saw himself as possessing a fair degree of autonomy by virtue of his own military conquests and, in respect of his appointment, answerable to no-one but God. Whatever role the Empire was to fulfil, it was an authoritative and powerful body, largely independent of Rome, and even taking upon itself the power to appoint bishops. Having been set up deliberately by Rome, the Empire could not fail to undermine the power and security of the Eastern Church.

At the time when the formal break occurred between east and west Leo IX was Pope and Emperor Constantine Monomachus was head of the Eastern Church. Worried by the spread of the Norman Empire with the successes of William the Conqueror (later William I of England) the Pope sent his legates to Constantinople to heal existing divisions. Instead, because of the personalities involved and the fact that Leo IX died in the midst of these negotiations, the discord erupted into a final break: the Pope's envoy, Cardinal Humbert, laid a letter of excommunication on Patriarch Michael Cerularius and his associates in the Eastern Church. But the schism was far from being only the result of an exaggerated personal dispute; there were also significant doctrinal and procedural differences. The Byzantines disagreed with the enforced celibacy of clergy; the concept of Purgatory was held by Rome but denied by Constantinople; the shaving off of beards and the use of musical instruments during services of worship the Eastern Church regarded as contrary to Apostolic practice; and, in its administration, the Papacy was a dictatorship under the Pope while the Greek Church was a federation of Churches run by an oligarchy of bishops, one at the head of each Church.

Another serious dispute was over the so-called *filioque clause* added in 589 CE by Rome to the Creed. This stipulated that the Holy Spirit emanated from God the Father *and* the Son, in order to protect the integrity of the Holy Trinity; according to the Eastern view, however, the Holy Spirit emanated only from the Father (John, Chap. 15, v.26).

Political rivalry between the Greek and Latin theological empires in the years after 1054 ensured that the break between the Churches was maintained. Constantinople was also an important centre in the Muslim world and this gave the Popes a pretext, during the Crusades, for continual attacks on the Eastern Empire under the guise of removing the 'infidel' from the Holy Lands. Constantinople itself was sacked in 1204 during the fourth crusade. In the wake of the schism, Pope Boniface VIII (papacy, 1294–1303) issued a bull (*Unam Sanctam*, 1302) that stated that neither salvation nor forgiveness was to be secured outside of the Church of Rome, specifically excluding followers of the Eastern Church – as well as the majority of humankind!

Scarcely had the Church adjusted to this major division amongst its followers than it was beset by another, generated in the wake of the humanism of the European Renaissance. This was the Reformation of the 16th century and it created the branch of Christendom that became known as Protestantism. The main proponents of the movement in its early days were German religious reformer Martin Luther (1483–1546), together with the Swiss theologians, Huldreich (or Ulrich) Zwingli (1484–1531) and John Calvin (1509–64).

There were several issues that caught Luther's attention. The ethical and moral behaviour of the papacy had been questionable for some time, reaching their most recent nadir in the conduct of the Borgias – Cardinal Rodrigo Borgia who became Pope Alexander VI (from 1492 to 1503), his son archbishop Cesare Borgia (1475–1507) and daughter Lucrezia Borgia (1480–1519). It was not so much the sexual immorality of the popes and clerics that was of concern, for this was commonplace; it was more the papal interference in affairs of state that aroused indignation, particularly when they conducted alliances with Muslim Turks or were implicated in acts of murder for political ends.

Another criticism was that the Church was engaged in simony, the selling of holy office for money. The Holy Roman Emperor had long made no secret of the reason for his enthusiasm for appointing bishops – to raise funds for his military campaigns to extend the area of influence of the Empire. There were suspicions too about the spiritual propriety of the sale of Indulgences, defined by the Roman Catholic Church as 'the remission before God of the temporal punishment due to sin after the guilt has been forgiven'. The forgiveness was drawn from a 'fund' of benefice created by the acts of Jesus and the saints – but it had to be paid for in hard cash as well as spiritually. Monasteries had long accepted payment in cash for prayers offered on behalf of their parishioners, and many religions from the early Jews to present-day churches have a system of tithing by which followers pay a small fraction of their income to the church. Indulgences were used in profusion by Pope Leo X, for example, to raise funds to rebuild St. Peter's basilica in Rome. That priests should administer such an act of forgiveness, particularly for profit, was felt by the Protestants to externalise an act of penance that should be a matter of individual conscience, even if this was justly administered – which itself was debatable.

The disquiet erupted on the eve of All Saints Day, October 31, in 1517, when Martin Luther nailed his 95 theses concerning Indulgences and other issues to the door of Wittenberg church.

Luther was a Professor of Theology at Wittenberg University and his act was provoked by theological principle. It did, however, reflect a growing disenchantment amongst ordinary people with the abuse of authority by the Church of Rome, and the growing affluence of the monasteries that were set up supposedly for quiet reflection and prayer in humble and austere surroundings, uncorrupted by worldly goods. It is said that Luther was spurred to action by Erasmus' interpretation of the words marking the beginning of Jesus' ministry in Matthew 4:17 – Repent: for the kingdom of heaven is at hand. This was taken to mean not just a call to reform one's own behaviour but to try to persuade others to do the same. For the next four years, Luther was engaged in dialogue with the Church, but the dispute was ultimately unresolved and it resulted in his excommunication in 1521.

The Protestant Reformation was followed by a Catholic Counter-Reformation that tried to address some of the Church's shortcomings elaborated by Luther. The theologians tried to use some of the rationalism of emerging scientific discovery to good effect in justifying religious principles and beliefs, just as the earlier medieval monks had done with Greek philosophy (see Chapter 3). The priesthood renounced material acquisitions. The Spanish nobleman, St. Ignatius of Loyola (Inigo Lopez de Loyola), founded a mendicant order, the Society of Jesus or the Jesuits, that was approved as a religious order by Pope Paul III in 1540. Ignatius began the movement by gathering around him six fellow students from the University of Paris. Their aim was to live a simple life by an exacting code of conduct while studying not only theology but also philosophy and science, as advocated by their medieval predecessors (Chapter 3). It is this academic approach to religion, as well as strict observance of the usual vows of poverty, chastity, and obedience that characterises Jesuit practice, maintained to the present day. The Counter-Reformation also inspired the promulgation of mystical expression through such pious individuals as the Spanish St. Theresa of Avila (1515–1582) and St. John of the Cross (San Juan de la Cruz; 1542–1591) and the German mystic Jakob Böhme (1575–1624).

In keeping with the spirit of the Renaissance, and with the rise of a more sophisticated merchant middle-class, Christianity also became a more individually oriented religion during the Counter Reformation. The ministers were now university-trained intellectuals rather than humble members of the community with little more learning than the rest, but given to a power of oratory. But the simple country folk did not abandon their old ways easily. In medieval Britain, pagan practices and belief in the power of magic and the presence of guardian spirits were still widespread. Most of the executions of witches in England, by burning at the stake to purify their souls, took place between about 1560 and 1680 (see the Paganism section, above). In the latter half of the 20th Century there has been an increasing interest in alternative or complementary therapies for the treatment of ailments; many of these involve traditional herbal folk remedies and practices that have evolved from centuries of pagan practice. Many spiritual healers are Christian, but many others are overtly pagan. All believe in guardian spirits guiding their work and establishing communion with the universal divine. Use of alternative medicine is still widespread in Germany and France in the 21st Century, and Italy still has its band of 'white witches', *la veccia religione*, despite the strength of the Catholic Church in that country. An article in *Encyclopaedia Britannica* on witchcraft describes its followers as 'the more ignorant members of the community'. On the contrary, there are many today who would view such people as the more enlightened and far closer to Nature and the Universal Spirit than those who practice the later formal religions.

Returning to the developments of the Counter-Reformation: Protestantism focused on the actions required to try to merit receiving the grace of God that was needed for individual salvation. For Protestants, emphasis was on the Bible, the Ten Commandments and the sacrifice of Jesus on the cross, a symbol of the common Christian belief that suffering is in some way good for the soul. The Roman Catholic Church focused on the Creed, the Trinity, the role of the Blessed Virgin Mary as the mother of Jesus and the importance of the confessional. As Protestant churches and chapels became more austere, with the sermon as the focus of the service, the emergence of the ornate figuration of the Baroque period in music and architecture moved in the opposite direction to produce magnificent, highly ornamented churches and cathedrals for Catholics. The pure polyphonic style of Palestrina was the only one acceptable for performance in church services at this time. Although the Fourth Lateran Council of 1215 required attendance at confession only once a year, it became regular practice to expect attendance every week; and the use of the confessional box made the acts of contrition totally individual.

Living a century after Luther, the English philosopher Thomas Hobbes (1588–1679) was equally wary of the power wielded by the Church, of any denomination. Hobbes was born of an impoverished clerical family in Malmesbury, Wiltshire. He was highly sceptical about allegiances to any large organisations, whether of church or state. His most famous work, *Leviathan*, was published in 1651. The title (from Job 41) refers to a sea monster devouring all in its path and is a metaphor for the evil wrought by the unbridled power of the church or the state. In his day, he was considered to be a symbol of atheism and heresy. His whole outlook was negative, sceptical or even nihilistic, and he held 'the life of man nasty, solitary, brutish and short' [260]. In his reservations about the abuse of power, Hobbes was criticising the state and Church of his time, but we would do well to heed it as an apposite warning about industrial mega-organisations in our own day, who too often put material concerns and satisfying the greed of directors and shareholders before the wellbeing of employees or of the public they are meant to serve. This aspect of industrial development has certainly become a symptom, and perhaps a significant cause, of the lack of spirituality in society in the most developed nations in the western world, as well as contributing to the desecration of our environment.

The various Protestant groups within Christianity have subsequently developed their own diverse views of the role of God and of Jesus, of the importance and literal truth of the Bible, and of the relationship of humankind to God. But the overall aim of Protestantism was not only what they regarded as theological purification but also the achievement of individual spiritual sustenance in everyday life and social wellbeing through communion with God, directly, effectively and responsibly, without the interpolation of an authoritarian Church. The Danish philosopher Søren Kierkegaard (1813–1855) thought that there was too much emphasis on the rituals and doctrines of the Church, which had become something of an end in themselves, and that the Christian religion had gone too far away from the message of Jesus. The need, he wrote, was to *live* the teaching of Jesus.

In the 19th Century, German philosopher Ludwig Andreas Feuerbach (1804–1872), a pupil of Hegel (see Chapter 7), also criticised the Christian Church in his book *The Essence of Christianity* (1841) because it set humankind the impossible goal of attaining the perfection of Jesus and thereby made them feel perpetual failures. But it is surely for just this reason that Christianity posits the human and divine nature of Jesus, for it is he who represents the human face of an otherwise unattainable God. To Feuerbach, God is the outward projection of the spirit of humankind; through Jesus, he is the paragon of goodness, of love and understanding, and of moral behaviour.

The role and significance of the Old and New Testaments of the Bible has been an issue in Christian religions since the Reformation. The 20th Century Swiss Christian theologian Karl Barth (1886–1968) saw the Bible as the only true source of knowledge about God. He rejected the rationalism of natural theology, but he also rejected the necessary validity of mystical experience because he felt that the human mind is unreliable. Christianity he felt had nothing to learn from the other world religions. The significance of religion, the Church, and the whole of theology, is diminished in his eyes as human creations: 'the church ... cannot try to prove the truth of God's Word either directly or indirectly ... the truth will prove itself' [45]. He even regarded religion as 'alien to life', but he felt that human life only makes sense if there exists a transcendent reality [from ref. 173].

Since the Councils of Nicea and Chalcedon, which set out the precepts of the Christian Church, the doctrinal view of Jesus, and other aspects of the dogma of Catholicism have been continually subjected to revision through the years. For example, the concept of *transubstantiation* by which, through the words of the Eucharist, the bread and wine of the ceremony become, in some sense, the body and blood of Jesus Christ was declared as Church dogma as early as 1215 by the Fourth Lateran Council, and verified by the Council of Trent (1545–1563). The idea that the soul of the Virgin Mary was free from original sin from the moment of her conception and, with this, that Jesus was conceived by the Holy Spirit became Church dogma only in 1854 by the declaration of the Constitution of the Church made by Pope Pius IX, though philosopher Duns Scotus had earlier proposed the Immaculate Conception as dogma consistent with the regard in which Jesus and Mary were held. Papal infallibility was an even later addition, being declared as dogma, again by Pius IX, only in 1870 at the First Vatican Council. The Catholic Encyclopaedia (2004) states that the term 'infallibility' implies that 'the Church is infallible in her objective, definitive teaching regarding faith and morals, not that believers are infallible in their subjective interpretation of her teaching.'

There are now some 2000 million people in the world who profess to be Christians and this is the most numerous of all the world religions (approximately one-third of the world population); it is also one of the most fragmentary in the number of different interpretations of what is supposed to be the message of Jesus Christ as presented in the New Testament.

1.6. Islam

The overriding principle of Islam is a thoroughgoing monotheism (*tahwid*): there is but one true God, *Allah*, and any form of worshipping of idols, statuettes or photographs, as is commonplace in Catholicism and Hinduism, is strictly forbidden. True belief demands *ikhlās*, a total devotion to God alone.

The founder of Islam, Muhammad (or Mohammed or Mahomet) was born in Mecca around 570 CE. As he was an orphan by the age of six, he was raised by an uncle, Abu Talib, and spent his childhood in poverty amongst the local Bedouin shepherds, despite the fact that he was descended from one of the prominent families of Mecca. Arabia was at the focus of the traffic between Europe and Asia and the land had several busy trading centres, of which was Mecca was one. On reaching maturity Muhammad himself became a merchant there.

When he was 25, Muhammad married a local widow for whom he acted as agent and who was somewhat older than himself. They lived happily together for 20 years and she bore him several children. It was just before her death, when he was in his early 40s, that Muhammad began preaching.

It was around the year 610 CE, on one of the occasions when Muhammad went alone into the hills around Mecca to pray, that he had a vision of the Archangel Gabriel calling him to preach the Word of God. For the next two or three years he was tormented by self-doubt but he had further revelatory experiences of hearing voices and seeing visions calling him to his destiny.

By the year 613 CE he had resolved his inner conflicts and began proclaiming Allah as the One God. He did not claim that his was a new message but simply a revival of the passionately monotheistic declarations of the former Judaic prophets. Muhammad was particularly disturbed by the worldliness of his fellow Meccan traders, by the social injustice perpetrated in the quest for wealth and power, by the poverty he saw all around him and which he had experienced first-hand as a child, and by what he saw as the pseudo-polytheism created by the hypostases of the Christian Trinity with their deification of Jesus. Jesus was seen as another in the line of divine messengers sent to the Jewish people.

With his criticisms of the established social order in the largely affluent Meccan community, Muhammad made many enemies. As a result, he was persecuted and forced to flee the city. He took refuge in the oasis at Yathrib, just over 200 miles due north of Mecca. A strong Jewish community there was less hostile to his monotheistic doctrines than the Christians and pagans in Mecca. Gradually he gathered a following around him there before returning to his native city on the death of his wife and uncle in 619 CE.

The Meccans now grew fearful of Muhammad's influence and resolved to have him killed. As a result, in 622 CE, he and his followers fled once more in what has become known in Islam as the migration (*hegira* or *hijra*) to settle in Yathrib. In honour of the refuge which this city gave to Muhammad it became known as 'Madinat an-Nabi', the city of the prophet, or more commonly, Medina. Henceforth, Islam was to become a formal religion and a social institution in the region, gaining converts from Judaism, Christianity and paganism. Muhammad however always stressed the essential unity of the western monotheistic religions, despite his criticism of the status accorded to Jesus by the Church. Muhammad never claimed any special divine powers, though the myths that grew up about him after his death tended to embellish his exploits with extraordinary and supernatural powers. Muhammad himself asserted that he was an ordinary mortal man, charged with a mission from God, through his encounters with the Archangel Gabriel, to establish monotheism amongst his people. He claimed to be the last in the line of Hebrew prophets from Abraham, through Moses, David and Jesus.

The Word of God, as revealed to Muhammad by Gabriel, is described in the *Qur'an* (or *Koran*), the holiest of the Muslim Scriptures. The revelations are set out in 114 chapters or *suras* (or *surahs*). The word '*Qur'an*' means 'recitation' (of the Word of God through Muhammad). The book is set out in a series of exhortations from God, in the manner used by the *kahins* or Arabian soothsayers. Scholars debate how much, if any, of the *Qur'an* was actually written down by Muhammad himself. Opinion generally favours the view that most of the work was compiled by scribes from the sayings of Muhammad, or by his successor as head of Islam, Abu Bakr, and by subsequent *caliphs*, as the heads of the faith after Muhammad were designated. But these sayings, although emanating from

Muhammad, were believed to have originated from God, written on a tablet in Heaven, and all but one begin with a phrase known as the *Bismillah* that may be translated as 'God has said ...', or 'In the name of God, the Compassionate, the Merciful ... '. As the Arabic language was itself developing in the centuries after Muhammad – a process to which the existence of the *Qur'an* made a significant contribution – there are some variations in text in different editions that are acknowledged as authoritative by different sects. Also, the *Qur'an* was originally written in the Cufic (or Kufic) script of ancient Babylon, which like ancient Hebrew contained no vowels, and the meanings of words could have been altered by the addition of diacritics, which were originally omitted. It is not known when these were added or by whom. So there was much scope for variations in text and interpretation, but one authoritative version of the *Qur'an* is now used almost universally.

There are no arguments presented in the *Qur'an* for the existence of God: this is assumed as axiomatic. From then on, the central messages are: '*lā ilāha illa'llāh* – there is no God but Allah' and, separately, '*muhammadun rasūlu'llāh*' – Muhammed is the Apostle of God [208], which constitutes the creed for Muslims. One can attain the grace of God only by devotion, through prayer, alms-giving and good works in the service of others. The most important attributes of God that are emphasised by the *Qur'an* are unity, power and goodness. The demand for regular prayer, morning and evening, has subsequently been ritualised into prayers at five specific times of day, with ritual washing beforehand. The *Qur'an* also calls for fasting during the hours of daylight during *Ramadan*, the ninth month of the lunar year. This celebrates the month in which the Word was revealed to Muhammad. As it follows the lunar calendar, the feast moves progressively through the year, each year it occurs. These practices – prayer, alms-giving, and fasting, together with pilgrimage to the Holy Land and recitation of the creed – are known as the Five Pillars of Islam. There is little discussion of the attributes of God, since to ascribe qualities to God undermines His unity. Certainly, all forms of anthropomorphism of the deity were strenuously rejected. The *Qur'an* contains passages that suggest a predestination determined before birth: 'Every misfortune that befalls the earth, or your own persons, is ordained before We bring it into being' [*sura* 57]; but there are other passages that can be interpreted as giving to humankind free-will to determine their own life path: 'God will recompense each soul according to its deeds' [*sura* 14].

The Old and New Testaments are sacred books in Islam recounting the lives of the prophets before Muhammad. Just as Orientals have their moment of enlightenment (*wu* – Chinese; *satori* – Japanese; *anātman* – Indian), so Muslims have their *ihsan* ('realisation' – of the truth of the *Qur'an*) that for a true Muslim must rapidly lead on to *taqwa* ('God-consciousness'). Muslims must be aware in every moment of their lives that everything they do, they do in the sight of *Allah*, in obedience to His will.

Like Christianity, Islam has had its major schisms. The most significant was the division that occurred in the 7th and early 8th centuries, not long after the death of the prophet. The first three caliphs were former companions of Muhammad and held closely to the tradition of the community. The fourth caliph was Muhammad's son-in-law, Ali, whom many felt should have held the title previously. When Ali and his two sons were killed, followers were divided between those who felt succession should stay with the traditionalists (the Sunni) and those who felt the caliphate should be occupied by members of Muhammad's family (the Shi'ites). The Shi'ites also felt that their appointed spiritual leaders, the imams, could receive divine revelation to supplement the teachings of the *Qur'an* and *Hadith*. This the Sunni regarded as heresy. Thereafter, Islam was split into two major divisions and, as with other religions, fragmentation into other sects followed. There are now over 1000 million Muslims distributed throughout the world, with the greatest number in the Middle East, Pakistan and Indonesia, where some three-quarters of the population are Muslim.

One of the Shi'ite sects was the Shaikiya, and Ali Muhammad was one of its followers. The Shaikiya saw the Imams as 'gates' through which the faithful entered into their communion with

God. At the age of 25, Ali Muhammad proclaimed himself to be the latest in such a line of divine prophets. He began pressing for social reform, as Muhammad had himself done in his lifetime. High on his list of priorities was the raising of the status of women who, to this day, occupy a subordinate place in Muslim society. Ali Muhammad subsequently became designated as the 'Bab' (or 'Gate') and those who followed him were known as Babis. Because of his religious views, which the orthodox regarded as heretical, Ali Muhammad was executed in 1850. The followers of the Bab formed themselves into a separate religion called the Baha'is. It is one of several new religions to arise in the 19th century and one of the most important to have its origins, not in the United States, where most of the newer religions have arisen, but in the Middle East, fount of Judaism, Christianity and Islam.

1.6.1. Baha'i. At the end of the previous section we saw how Ali Muhammed (1819–50) broke away from orthodox Shi'ism and in 1844 proclaimed himself to be the Bab or Gate to the kingdom of God, assuming the title Imam or spiritual leader in the process. The last of the 12 Imams of the Shi'ites (Imam Mahdi) disappeared in the 9th century but they believe that he will reappear on the Day of Judgement. Ali Muhammed subsequently claimed that he was the expected *Mahdi*, returned to proclaim that one would come after him who would be the next in a succession of earthly Manifestations of God. It was these claims that distinguished Babism from orthodox Shi'ism.

After the Bab's execution in 1850, the Babis were increasingly persecuted and in some disarray. In 1856, there arose amongst them one Mirza Husain Ali Nuri (1817–92) who claimed to be the Manifestation foretold by the Bab, thereby coordinating the movement and giving it fresh impetus. He assumed the name *Baha'u'llah* ('the Glory of God'), from which the followers of the movement were subsequently designated as Baha'is. Although his father was a prominent landowner and government official, Baha'u'llah's political activity was humbly directed at the social and spiritual welfare of the people.

At the end of his life, Baha'u'llah was finally allowed to live in peace in the country, but only after he had spent many years in prison, most notably in Akka (or Acre) in Turkish (Ottoman)-controlled Syria. On the death of Baha'u'llah (1892), leadership of the movement passed to his eldest son, Abbas Effendi (1844–1921), known within the faith as *Abdu'l Baha* ('the servant of Baha'). He furnished interpretive commentary on his father's writings and during his period of leadership (from 1892–1921) the first Baha'i communities were established in the United States (1894).

After *Abdu'l Baha*, the succession of leadership passed to his eldest grandson, Shoghi Effendi Rabbani (1897–1957), who died without leaving children. Since 1963, the Baha'i faith has been administered by the Universal House of Justice in Haifa, Israel, the world centre of the faith. Although the Baha'i faith had its origins in Shi'ite Islam, it has now moved so far away in its beliefs and practices that it must be regarded as a separate religion. It is no more a sect of Islam than Christianity is of Judaism, or Buddhism a sect of Hinduism.

The Baha'is have carried with them the Islamic belief in the utter unknowability of God the Creator other than through the Manifestations and the revelations they convey. Baha'is believe that divine Manifestations have appeared throughout the history of humankind and in this they differ fundamentally from followers of Islam, for whom Muhammad has a unique status as prophet. The best known of the Baha'i Manifestations are Abraham, Moses, Zoroaster, Buddha, Krishna, Jesus, Muhammad and, most recently, the Bab and *Baha'u'llah*.

The purposes of God are seen to be progressively unfolded to humankind through such intermediaries. The primary purpose of life is spiritual fulfilment. The physical needs of humankind are acknowledged but these are considered subordinate to the higher spiritual goal. Thus there is no advocacy of celibacy, but human sexuality should be expressed in the context of a loving relationship.

There is a prohibition on the drinking of alcohol – another legacy of the Islamic origins – but not on the eating of any kind of meat.

Many Baha'is do seem however to be inclined to vegetarianism as an ecologically sound philosophy if not for other religious reasons, and Abdu'l Baha predicted that the time would come when humankind gave up the eating of meat in favour of grain. We know now that it takes much more energy to rear meat for human consumption than to grow appropriate crops for nutrition. Concern for the environment has long featured prominently amongst the Baha'i philosophy.

Periodic fasting is seen to be spiritually uplifting and physically cleansing. The most important fast is that of the Baha'i month of Ala (March 2–20) when followers are enjoined to abstain from food or drink during the hours from sunrise to sunset, as Muslims do at Ramadan. As is usual in such prescriptions, the very young or old, the sick, pregnant women or nursing mothers are excused adherence.

Another major concern is the achievement of the spiritual unity of humankind. The Baha'is do not see themselves as an elite with a unique path to eternal salvation; however, they do see their beliefs and practices as offering the most expedient solutions to the problems of society and they believe that Baha'u'llah has revealed insight into these solutions.

There is great feeling too for the emancipation of women that they may fulfil their true potential, both as individuals and as contributing members of society. As the wellbeing of society begins with the children who will form that society in the next generation, the right education of children is a prime concern, as in Confucianism. If children are not given adequate opportunities to learn, if they are denied moral direction, subjected to inadequate instruction and exposed to unwholesome example, it is small wonder that we have major problems with discipline in adolescents.

There is no formal priesthood amongst the Baha'i: all are equal, though some are obviously better acquainted with the doctrines and more observant of religious practices than others. There are Local and National Spiritual Assemblies that organise the administration of the faith, and believers and others interested in Baha'i ideas are welcomed at periodic meetings called Firesides held in the homes of members of the faith.

As with Jews, Baha'is attach great importance to the role of the family, as the stabilising kernal of society, and to the education of children. Homes may well have a picture of *Abdu'l Baha* prominent but it is considered disrespectful to make images of *Baha'u'llah*.

Where some religions tend to focus on ritual or on the worship of their particular divine Manifestation, Baha'is see their faith and Baha'u'llah as media for the physical and spiritual wellbeing of humankind. That is not to imply that Baha'u'llah is not a venerated figure in the faith, but he is seen as a route to God, as with Muhammad in Islam, rather than as a figure for worship as is Jesus in Christianity.

Attention of the Baha'i is focused on the progression of human spirituality and on the practical steps to be taken to achieve equality of status for women, to reduce the disparity of wealth within and between nations, to see that children are properly educated, both academically and morally, and to encourage people who are at present unconcerned to have consideration for the environment of Earth, all precepts laid down by Baha'u'llah over a century ago.

The teachings of Baha'u'llah are recorded in his books, of which the best known are the *Hidden Words*, *Gleanings*, *Tablets*, *Certitude*, and *Prayers and Meditations*. The precepts of the faith were subsequently amplified by Abdu'l Baha in his own original writings and commentaries on those of his father.

Baha'i is perhaps the least self-indulgent of all of the newer religions and the one that most accords with a rational approach to the physical and spiritual fulfillment of humankind, both as individuals and as communities, and one that cares deeply about the wellbeing of the environment. With its emphasis on global harmony between different faiths, the emancipation of women so that they are treated as equals in the still-predominately paternalistic Western culture, concern for the family, social cohesion and for the environment, Baha'i is a faith well attuned to the needs of the 21st Century. So many of the pronouncements of Baha'u'llah over a century ago have either been fulfilled or have been adopted as working principles by those who subscribe to the New Age Philosophy, as it has become known – those who see these ideas as providing the only logical route to the spiritual expansion and fulfillment of humankind and, indeed, perhaps its very survival. [For further reading, see ref. 437]

1.7.   The newer religions

A reaction against the materialism of society in the wake of the Industrial Revolution, together with the self-expressionism encouraged by the Romantic Movement, combined in the 19th century to produce a number of individuals claiming divine insight and whose followers instituted a new religion. Most of these arose in America which, at the time, was just being developed. Lawlessness and violence were prevalent in the frontier towns of the west and the use and abuse of slaves in the more developed cities of the east and in most territories of the south was becoming a significant moral and political issue, one that finally erupted in the American Civil War of 1861–5.

The instability caused by rapid growth within the country as a whole and the insecurity of individuals who were surrounded by violence and innovation in a prevailing atmosphere of material expansion combined together to predispose people towards an eagerness to welcome those who claimed to have new insight of moral purpose and spiritual values. The situation could be given a religious interpretation by saying that the moral fabric of society was degenerating to such an extent that God saw the need to instil a new sense of ethical values in humankind and sent prophets for that purpose. This is hardly a convincing argument, however, for there have been concentrations of far greater evil at various times and places in human history when no prophet appeared, as far as we are aware. And in 19th century America there were so many! The undiminished popularity of evangelism in contemporary America testifies to the religious devotion, or desperate sense of need, or naive gullibility of the American people, depending on the degree of cynicism with which you view the historical situation.

It is difficult therefore to see this burgeoning of religions in 19th century America as a direct intervention by God. What is more likely is that these religions arose in New England in the last century primarily as a result of social factors and the charisma of the individuals concerned, though we have no reason to doubt the sincerity of what they believed were divine revelations.

In the wake of the scientific revelations in the 19th century, especially those of Darwin and Lyell, counter movements reasserting the validity of the Bible were very likely to develop. And where more likely than America, which was being colonised by people of adventurous spirit, eager for innovation, and who were actively seeking to develop a country away from the conservatism of Europe. The ethos of the age was right for spiritual adventure. The result was the creation of several new religions or sects, many of which have subsequently become established world-wide.

1.7.1. Church of Jesus Christ of Latter-Day Saints. Founded by Joseph Smith of Vermont and established in 1830 at Fayette, N.Y., this faith is based on acceptance of the validity of the revelations that were claimed by him in adolescence. The faith regards itself as re-establishing the Logos or message of God as revealed through Jesus and passed on by the prophets to Joseph Smith (1805–44). These revelations, together with the Bible, constitute the Scriptures of the faith.

The Book of Mormon is a sacred record of God's dealings with the ancient peoples of the Americas. These civilisations originally came to America, it is claimed, from the Holy Lands when the area was invaded by the Babylonians (586 BCE) or previously when God confounded the tongues after the building of the Tower of Babel (Gen. 11. 1–9). Jesus is alleged to have appeared to one of these tribes, the Nephites, soon after his resurrection. The resettled peoples divided into two groups – the faithful and the pagans. The faithful group died out in 421 CE while the savages live on as the North American Indians.

The prophet Mormon passed on an account of these events,

written on gold plates, to his son, Moroni, who in turn appeared as an angel before Joseph Smith, for the first time in 1823. He appeared again in 1827 to tell Smith that the plates were hidden in a cave at Mt. Cumorah, in New York State. In 1820, young Joseph as a boy of 15 had seen a vision in which it was revealed to him that the existing religions did not proclaim the true Gospel. When he found the plates, they were accompanied by two jewels that served as 'lenses' with supernatural powers to decode the writing on the tablets. Smith interpreted these jewels as the Urim and Thummim that had adorned the breastplate of Aaron [Exodus 28.30].

The present-day *Book of Mormon* comprises 15 Books of revelations to prophets of the ancient peoples, including Mormon and Moroni. It is this text that gives the Latter-Day Saints their popular name of Mormons. The other Scriptures, apart from the Bible, are the *Doctrine and Covenants*, a selection of revelations to and inspired declarations of Joseph Smith, and *The Pearl of Great Price*, a series of revelations to Moses and Abraham not found in the Old Testament but revealed anew to Smith. The Bible is thus a work of Mormon scripture that is interpreted as confirming the later revelations to Joseph Smith.

The Mormons were persecuted in a number of locations in which they tried to settle, partly because of the exclusivity of their sect and partly because of their practice of polygamy, a practice recorded also in the Old Testament. In 1843 Joseph Smith was arrested and jailed at Carthage, Illinois, where he was killed by a group of vigilantes. Brigham Young (1801–77) took over leadership of the group and in 1847 moved the centre of the faith to a new site which the followers established beside the Great Salt Lake in Utah, from which it operates to this day.

The doctrine of the Church today includes belief in continual revelation direct from God or from His angels or from the Holy Spirit; that Man is punished for his own sins but not those of Adam; and that Zion will be re-established in America, together with restoration of the lost Ten Tribes of Israel, when Jesus reappears to reign on Earth. The Church administers a system of tithing in which a portion of each follower's salary is given to the Church. Every adult male undertakes missionary work abroad, if there is no physical impediment to his doing so. The practice of polygamy was abandoned in 1896 as a condition of entry of Utah into the Union to become the 45th State of America.

There is a Law of Health amongst the Latter-Day Saints which regards the body as the sanctuary of the soul and therefore to be treated with respect. Excesses of food or sex are discouraged and there is a prohibition on the use of tea, coffee or any other stimulating hot beverages, on alcohol and on tobacco, and on all 'recreational' drugs. In the light of these restrictions it is not surprising to find that the health of the residents of the State of Utah, which is largely under Mormon control, is considerably better than that of the rest of America, and premature deaths from drug overdose, from degenerative diseases like cancer and arteriosclerosis, or from viral infections like AIDS, are significantly lower than in the rest of America.

The Latter-Day Saints lay great emphasis on the education of children into the principles of the faith and their religion brings God very much into the everyday practice of their lives.

1.7.2. Adventism. This movement began with the teaching of William Miller (1782–1849) from Pittsfield, Massachussetts. He began preaching in 1831 that the end of the world was imminent, specifically in 1843/44 when Jesus was due to reappear on Earth (an interpretation of Daniel, 8.13, 14). That the expected apocalypse failed to occur then, or on a revised date a year later, was no deterrent to believers in Miller's message. They believed this was because of a failure to keep the Sabbath holy and they simply decreed that it would occur at some unspecified time in the near future: more than a century later they are still waiting for the Second Advent. This will mark the start of the Millenium, the 1000–year rule of God as Jesus on Earth [Rev. 20.1,2].

Today there are several Adventist groups of which the most numerous are the Seventh Day Adventists. They adopted their name in 1860 with strict observance of a Sunday Sabbath according to their interpretation of the Bible: the Book of Revelation is particularly important to Adventists. They also believe in the unity of a personal God, appearing as Father, Son and Holy Spirit; that on the Day of Judgement the righteous shall receive immortality while the damned shall burn in hellfire [Rev. 20.13, 14]; that the body is the temple of the soul, bestowed by God, and as such should be cared for and not subjected to abuse by drugs, stimulants, tobacco or alcohol [1 Corinth. 6. 19–20]; and that time for repentance of sins is short because Advent is near [Rev. 22.10].

1.7.3. Christian Science. This religion was pioneered by Mary Baker Eddy (1821–1910), inspired by her own experience of self-induced faith healing. Mary Baker, born near Concord, New Hampshire, suffered from a spinal complaint from the earliest years of her life. She also bore a child from her first marriage, and this probably aggravated her condition. She was treated unsuccessfully by homeopathy but then had a temporary remission from her condition after treatment by mesmerism. The illness recurred however, so she sought help from a faith healer, Phineas Parkhurst Quimby. Again there was temporary relief but the ailment returned after she had a bad fall in 1866. With her aversion to orthodox treatment for her malady, she read the New Testament while she was bedridden and became permanently cured by meditating on the life and works of Jesus.

As a result of her experience she believed that she had discovered the healing method of Jesus, namely, through faith alone. She began to teach others to act as healers and wrote of her experiences and philosophy in the book *Science and Health*, published in 1875. Two years later she married for the third time, her new husband, Asa G. Eddy, being one of her followers. Mary Eddy's book, now called *Science and Health with Key to the Scriptures*, sets out the basic doctrines of the faith which was formally instituted in Boston, Massachussetts in 1879 and originally called The Church of Christ, Scientist.

The cornerstone of Christian Science belief is healing by non-invasive techniques through faith. The faith teaches that 'God is incorporeal, divine, supreme, infinite Mind, Spirit, Soul, Principle, Life, Truth, Love' [*Science and Health*, p. 465]. Man, being made in His image, is also essentially spiritual. God, Mind, Soul or Spirit represents ultimate reality. Matter, evil, pain and sickness are only manifestations of Spirit discernible by the human condition when lacking faith. It is because orthodox medicine treats the body as matter and virtually ignores the spiritual dimension that Christian Scientists will have nothing to do with conventional treatment for illness. The whole training programme of medical students today tends to be focused on organs or, at most, systems and not on the organism as a whole, and little attention is paid to spiritual or mental issues. As there is now a whole branch of medicine, iatrogenic medicine, devoted to illnesses caused by the prescription of unsuitable pharmaceutical drugs or by incorrect or incompetent surgery, there is much to be said for the Christian Science approach. Perhaps the best path is the Middle Way – not to eschew the use of drugs completely but to use them only when absolutely necessary, and then, to make these as natural as possible. The beneficial effects of positive thought of both the patient and others who know and love them is well documented, as we shall see in Chapter 6.

1.8.   Process theology

This is a view of the nature of God as a being that changes with the evolution of the universe, as opposed to the omnipotent and unchanging God of Western theology. The notion of God embraces the created universe, but God is not identical to material creation. God has a dual nature: there is a transcendent part of God, constant and perfect, but the God immanent in the world changes and evolves with humankind and creation. Reality does not comprise objects that endure through time but rather is a series of events in a constantly changing milieu. Everything, including humankind, is characterised by free-will or self-determination. God provides the possibilities, the potentialities, the spiritual goal, but the actualities come about through human and other agents exercising free will. Every event again is dipolar representing a physical as well as a spiritual interaction between material objects, living or inorganic.

Several names are associated with process theology, but the original seminal ideas are generally attributed to the mathematician and philosopher Alfred North Whitehead (1861–1947) in the 1920s, particularly with his books *Concept of Nature* [511] and *Process and Reality* [514]. In the former, Whitehead argued against attempts 'to bifurcate nature into two divisions, namely into the nature apprehended in awareness and the nature which is the cause of awareness ... The meeting point of these two natures is the mind' [512]. As he saw it, it is the business of science simply to explain connections between natural events, not to speculate about their origination or ultimate nature. Ideas of space and time are also mental constructs, he said, not properties of reality: 'space and time are merely ways of expressing certain truths about the relations between events' [513].

The ultimate real things of which the world is made up are the 'actual occasion' (event) and 'actual entity' (object) [515], each one of which is only momentary, partly self-determined and partly influenced by other actual entities. 'In a sense, every entity pervades the whole world' [516], and 'every actual entity is present in every other actual entity' [519], a concept to be expanded on in detail by David Bohm (see Section 8.3). Actual entities differ from one another in the way they turn potentiality into actuality. Humans represent complexes of actual entities, the supreme example of which is God. 'God's immanence in the world in respect to his primordial nature is an urge towards the future' [517] or what Whitehead calls 'a principle of unrest' (*cf.* the Buddhist *dukkha*, described later). 'The things which are temporal arise by their participation in the things which are eternal. The two sets are mediated by a thing which combines the actuality of what is temporal with the timelessness of what is potential. The final entity is the divine element in the world' [518]. 'Thus the continuum is present in each actual entity, and each actual entity pervades the continuum' [520]. The 'continuum' is what would now be identified in New Age spirituality with the akashic field or in science with the zero point field (see Chapter 8).

Another key theologian who developed the ideas of process theology was Charles Hartshorne (1897–2000). He emphasised the concept of *panpsychism* – the idea that all matter, both organic and inorganic, possessed in some sense a sentient quality. For if God is immanent in the world then clearly everything must have an awareness of the divine energy: 'the God who creates and the inclusive creation are one God' [246]. Hartshorne also emphasised the interactive nature of the universe: 'the social structure is the ultimate structure of all existence' [240]. This social principle applies at all levels of being – at the lowest, to the components of atoms and molecules and, at the highest, to God: 'deity is the supreme case of the social principle' [241]. The idea of the dual aspects of God appears again – the absolute or abstract aspect and the relative or consequent aspect of the God immanent in the world and interacting socially with it. As long as the amount of goodness in the world exceeds the amount of evil, 'there will always be a *net increment* of value accruing to God at each moment' [242]; and 'the actual state of the deity will be determined partly by the creatures' [245]. Just as each of us is grateful to others for providing uplifting experiences, 'so God is indebted to *all* persons for the much fuller enjoyment of the same privilege' [243]. Hartshorne disagrees with those who argue for a God as an impassive, omnipotent, unchanging and unreachable deity: 'Such guardians of the divine majesty in my opinion know not what they do' [244]. As Carl Jung was to say a little later in interpreting the reason for human consciousness: 'That is the meaning of divine service, or the service that man can render to God, that light may emerge from the darkness, that the Creator may become conscious of His creation, and man conscious of himself [286]. So lives devoted to service to others, to improve their welfare, and to preserve the world in which we live and, as a prerequisite of these, to keep ourselves in optimum health and fitness is a life of service to the divine – a life of involvement with one another and with the divine.

Other religious philosophers who are associated with process theology are the American philosopher Daniel Day Williams (b.1910) and the British Jewish philosopher Samuel Alexander (1859–1938). Alexander, born in Sydney, Australia but teaching most of his career in the University of Manchester, believed that higher levels of existence emerge when lower orders become sufficiently complex. Thus the divine emerged but was still evolving through mind. His book *Space, Time and Deity* [1] presents a working out of his ideas.

The Eastern religions are discussed briefly in Section 5.1 with regard to their differing views of soul.

Summary

Several highly significant conclusions can be drawn from the above material. It is claimed that scripture reports the lives, the words and the deeds of divinely inspired individuals. In many cases, and certainly for the Bible, which forms the core text of the three major Western religions, and of many others, those records were compiled, as in the case of the Old Testament, from an oral tradition perpetuated over many generations. It was written down by scribes some time after the events they describe – scriptures are rarely current records of events. With subsequent amendments and translations by other human hands and minds, with the extensive interpretations that these processes inevitably involve, scripture cannot rationally be regarded as the literal word of God. It represents divine revelation to the extent that the central characters in each body of scripture, and to some extent those who wrote of their lives, were in harmony with the divine and universal spiritual energy and were therefore in a position to present meaningful guidance as to how we should live our lives.

The language in which the texts were written was sometimes itself developing extensively, such as by the addition of vowels or diacritics, which must give rise to uncertainty about the meaning of original writings. Scripture is not therefore, as the theologians say, *theopneustos* – the breath of God.

Much evidence has been presented in this chapter to indicate the predominately allegorical rather than historical nature of the Bible. Many of the events described in the Bible, in both the Old and New Testaments, are obvious re-workings of traditional myths that have been found in the records of earlier civilisations in that region, or that can be found within other disparate social groups from around the world, some of which are still extant today. The value of scripture lies in providing stories concerning spiritually enlightened heroes as models to which individuals should aspire in their own lives. There is no other literary or archaeological evidence for many of the key people or events described in the Bible, for example, and in some cases evidence has been found that directly contradicts biblical accounts.

Rationally then, scripture should be regarded as the presentation of myths, parables and allegories woven around one or more charismatic individuals; it was intended, by its content and style of presentation, to provide spiritual uplift for the individual and social cohesion of a specific group of people at some particular time and place, and therefore relevant to those particular people. At the time of its creation, scripture was never intended to be a universal prescription for all humankind.

The whole purpose of scripture is to provide myths that use the issues of everyday life to build a series of stories into gripping allegorical narratives with moral purpose. When these stories have some historical or factual basis, this adds weight to the moral message, but this is not an essential component.

The various scriptures represent different but spiritually equivalent paths to communion with the divine. They cannot rationally be regarded as historically accurate documents or as conveying direct and verbatim records of some unique divine message. The scriptures provide a variety of emotionally uplifting messages that, *if not taken literally and held unilaterally*, can give humankind, individually and communally, a number of alternative paths to spiritual uplift and enlightenment.

Religions are wholly human constructs based on the various

bodies of scripture. They are intended to establish and continually renew a code of moral conduct – a faith – in individuals through a body of traditional beliefs and rituals. Religions constantly evolve and new beliefs and practices are added, while others become obsolete. As we have seen, many religions in the West are based to a greater or lesser extent on this one literary source, the Bible, and it is different interpretations of this one text that have given rise to a number of religions with different beliefs and rituals that are often mutually incompatible but which provide alternative paths to the divine. Despite the huge amount of human input into religion and the scripture on which it is based, it provides a fund or reservoir of development-inducing spiritual metaphors.

Which religion an individual follows usually depends, in the first instance, on their place of birth, and then often subsequently on that religion whose beliefs and practices resonate most harmoniously with the spiritual ethos of the individual. No religion can therefore be regarded as presenting unequivocal and unilateral 'truth', because by implication those that differ radically must be presenting falsehoods. All the religions that have been discussed in this chapter originated within a specific social and temporal setting, so there is no logical reason why any one religion should be preferred over another and thus be universally applicable. The vehement declarations of fundamentalists that their beliefs represent unequivocal truth to which all should assent are simply not rationally tenable and are potentially divisive and dangerous to humankind. For fundamentalism all too easily becomes fanaticism, and that in turn leads to hatred and enmity, which is no basis at all on which to build a collaborative loving brotherhood of humankind.

Such extensive input from human agency into both scripture and religion that we have reviewed briefly in this chapter must logically challenge the assertion of divine authority and infallibility. In this sense therefore, religions and the scriptures on which they are based are largely artificial (human rather than divine or 'natural') constructs, however divinely inspired their original message or messenger may have been. They represent interpretations by the prophets or manifestations of a perceived message from a divine universal spiritual energy as to the best route to communion with the divine.

For those who are thus bewildered by the multiplicity of orthodox religions, disenchanted with the irrationality of much that is taken as scripture, disillusioned by its contradictions and inconsistencies, both internally and from one religion to another, the foundation of their spiritual life may be undermined. We need to find something to put into the vacuum that might be created, because faith or spiritual belief is the foundation of all moral behaviour and, with it, social cohesion and stability. Many do find inspiration still in orthodox religion and, for them, religion is a necessary path to communion with the divine. Religion is the externalised expression of those spiritual values that we share with other people by participation in supplication and thanksgiving, and in the performance of rites and rituals. For those who need and enjoy this communalistic expression of belief represented by structured religion, this option remains, as long as others for whom this has no appeal are not pressured into adherence. To find at least some potential common thread to unite religious differences is also a high priority for our survival and prosperity. Ultimately, it is in our own material interests that humankind should work in harmony as one global community without constant religious-based conflict.

But, in a world where rational thought predominates, many are rejecting organised religion. For those who are disturbed by the artificiality of religion, a return to the basic empathy of the individual with the natural environment and appreciation of the aesthetic that is found in primitive civilisations, without the excrescences added to religion by human agencies, may present an acceptable path to communion with the divine spirit. It is not necessary to 'belong to' a particular formal religion in order to live a spiritually fulfilling life dedicated to the welfare of others. The essential criterion is to have faith – the internalised system of moral values that we use to guide our actions in life; and faith is the expression of the human soul. This simple, unadorned philosophy represents a return to the most basic and earliest of all faiths – that of (neo)paganism, without all the obfuscation of human additions to the worship of the divine. As we saw above, there are no rules or dogma, no prescribed rituals, no authoritarian priesthood in paganism, just direct communion with the all-embracing divine through the human soul: this can be expressed in many ways, as illustrated by the examples given in Chapter 6. Belief in a spiritual realm beyond the world of appearances and embracing a community of souls has a long and eminent pedigree from theologians and philosophers, and this is explored in Chapter 7. For those who seek some rationalisation of this concept of a divine spiritual energy, Chapter 8 explores the contemporary science that makes this a reasonable world-view.

First, we should seek the origins of some of the ideas we shall be discussing in later chapters. For this we need to explore some of the various ways in which ancient Greek philosophy has influenced post-Renaissance science, philosophy and theology, directly or indirectly, and this we shall do in Chapter 2. We should also consider how the medieval theologians of the West tried to relate these rational views from Greek philosophy with their own world-views derived from revelation, and this is the subject of Chapter 3. The foundations of science that have led to the developments in the subject over the past century form the basis of Chapter 4. After a consideration of mind and soul (Chapters 5 to 7) we shall see how these writings, in turn, have given rise to the ideas in Chapter 8 that lay the groundwork for a rational view of God and soul that is not incompatible with 21st Century scientific thought.

2 Some ideas of the ancient Greek philosophers and their influence on post-Renaissance thought

The Greek philosophers, living some 600–300 years before the time of Jesus, focused their attention on a number of topics concerning the world and our place in it. First, they wrote about the fundamental nature of the constituents of the created world (metaphysics). Later, they debated what constitutes the 'good life' for Man that would produce individual happiness and fulfilment, and allow harmonious social development, living to best advantage to ourselves and to others (ethics); what is the nature of the gods that seem to rule our lives (theology) and they examined how we obtain our knowledge of the world (a study we now distinguish as epistemology). Some of the conclusions they reached have found parallels in, or even formed the basis of, ideas in post-Renaissance philosophy and science, providing a spiritual link between kindred minds separated by two thousand years of human history. In some cases, the later philosophers and scientists read of the ideas of their ancient Greek predecessors. In other cases, the modern thinkers created original ideas that had parallels in, or were a development of, the topics debated in ancient Greece. When they wrote of their ideas, they typically used the style of a dialogue or debate between a number of advocates of various points of view. This was simply a more permanent record of the style they used in teaching – to have students and tutor gathered together in a more or less informal way to discuss various subjects. It was because one of their number, Socrates, used this technique to encourage the youth of Athens to challenge any received opinion that he was put to death by the authorities for 'corrupting' their young people.

Greek philosophers often present holistic, monotheistic one-world views that resonated both with the existing religious philosophies of East and West and with some of the religious, philosophical, social and scientific thoughts of today, ideals that many see as the best hope for securing a peaceful, uplifting development of humankind without ongoing religious disputes. In particular, some Greek and Roman philosophers saw in the order of the universe the rationale for belief in the power within one spiritual God.

Greek philosophers have thus had an immense influence on the development of western theology since that time – Judaic, Christian and Islamic – and especially with the works of Plato (through Plotinus and Augustine) and Aristotle (through Averroes and Aquinas). Some thoughts from the theologians are considered in the next chapter. Where earlier world-views were derived from divine revelation (in the Pentateuch in the West, and in the *Shruti* texts of the four *Vedas* in the East), the next major input to human knowledge came from these rational world-views of the Greek philosophers. They have influenced the development of science and the systems of law and government in the western world ever since. So the views of the ancient Greek philosophers are still of great relevance today, and especially so in any debate about the relative merits of knowledge obtained by reason, by observation or through revelation, quite apart from providing us with a more or less continuous time-line in the development of human knowledge from the ancient world to the modern.

One of the earliest groups or schools of philosophers of whom we have knowledge today flourished in the 6th Century BCE at Miletus in Asia Minor, a region that corresponded in its greatest part to present-day Turkey. The earliest of the philosophers were Thales (*ca.*625–*ca.*545 BCE), Anaximander (*ca.*610–*ca.*540 BCE) and Anaximenes (*ca.*585–*ca.*528 BCE). These Miletian philosophers are known as pre-Socratics because they lived before Socrates, one of the most renowned of the ancient Greeks. They were also known as the 'naturalists' because they enquired about the constitution of the natural world, as opposed to the mythological and poetic school of Homer and Hesiod (both *fl. ca.* 750 BCE) and their followers. The 'four elements' of the Miletians – earth, water, air and fire – that they believed comprised the essential stuff of which the world was made correspond, in essence, to the four states of matter defined by scientists today – solid, liquid, gas and plasma (the material we get when we knock bits off the outer surfaces of atoms in a gas to produce collections of charged particles). These same four elements are found as the basic atoms of matter in *Vaiseshika* philosophy in Hinduism, which flourished around 200 CE, but had its origins many centuries earlier at the time of the *Vedas* (see Chapter 5). Clearly there must surely have been some cross-fertilisation of ideas between the Greek and North Indian cultures. It was said that the four elements were represented by the points at the ends of the arms of the symbol of the cross. The cross was also seen as a symbol of humankind, the horizontal arm representing the universal brotherhood of Man, and the vertical arm communion between heaven and earth.

The Miletians wanted to know what the world was made of, the nature of ultimate reality. One favoured air as the basic stuff of matter, another water, another fire, but it was left to the much later Greek philosopher Empedocles (*ca.* 490–430 BCE) to suggest that all four components were necessary to produce the diverse material forms found in Nature. He also added two other essential components – 'love' and 'strife' –to describe what we would now call forces of attraction and repulsion. The cosmologists or philosophers of the *Vaiseshika* Hindus added five more immaterial components to the four kinds of atoms that made up the fundamental stuff of the material world: space, time, ether, mind and soul. The cosmologists among the Miletians also thought that there was life of some kind in all matter such that it needed the elements of air and water – a notion described as *hylozoism*. Scientists in the 19th Century revived this idea with their concept of *vitalism*.

Another of the earlier Greek philosophers of whom we have some record is Xenophanes of Colophon (*ca.* 560–480 BCE). He left little in writing that has passed down to us, but he is regarded as the founder of what became known as the Eleatic School. His view of the writings of the Greek poets Homer and Hesiod was that they tended to glorify war and power, and that reverence for these values would undermine respect for law and virtue, essential components of a stable society [145, 253, 262]. In his theology, Xenophanes is interpreted as a monotheist and pantheist, at a time when polytheism was the norm. He believed that the whole of the created world is God. In this he was a forerunner of Parmenides (another of the Eleatics – see below) and, amongst the post-Renaissance philosophers, Spinoza (see Section 6.1), to mention but two of the many philosophers who shared the views that 'the all is one and the one is God'.

Anaxagoras (*ca*.500–428 BCE) was a friend of the great Greek statesman and soldier, Pericles. Anaxagoras noted the processes of change in things of the material world – substances could be burnt to ash; when we ate food like cereals, we were able to turn the raw materials into flesh and bone; animal and vegetable matter left in the air would putrify. From this he supposed that there were fundamental elements of all things in everything. Every object, say, the grains of wheat, contained an infinite number of extremely small components. These were then passed into the body to be rearranged or transformed in some way to become components of our flesh and blood. In his belief that there were, in this sense, portions of blood and bone within the wheat, Anaxagoras was quite correct – those portions we now distinguish as atoms and molecules, and some of the later Greek philosophers developed this idea. The Greek word *atomon* means atom, item or individual. The very same atoms that form the flesh of our bodies do also constitute the grains of wheat. Anaxagoras believed that all material objects were mixtures of these components and that such changes in the natural world (like what we would now call digestion, for instance) were processes of separation and rearrangement. This idea was elaborated more fully by the atomists (see below). There is also a sense in which the 'everything contains components of everything else' idea resonates with David Bohm's view of the structure of an object being implicate or encoded in each of its component parts (see Section 8.3).

This 'fundamental particle' notion of Anaxagoras was expanded on more precisely by other Greek philosophers. Leucippus of Miletus (*fl.* 5th Century BCE) and Democritus of Abdera (*ca.*460–*ca.*360 BCE), the latter certainly a contemporary of Socrates, are the names predominantly associated with the school of atomism. They suggested that matter was composed of tiny particles called atoms. The atoms of Democritus (Greek: *atomon* – atom, particle, item) were indivisible and indestructible and were always in motion; they had shape, size and weight, but no other discernible properties. The objects of the world that we observe were formed by combinations of atoms – into what we now call molecules – and it was these atomic combinations that gave rise to the perceptible properties of colour, taste and smell. Atoms of different shapes and sizes give rise to combinations that produce different properties. With the addition of the term 'molecules', this is so close to our view of the material world today. The most direct development of this idea in recent centuries was the Atomic Theory proposed by John Dalton in 1803: the properties he ascribed to atoms closely resemble those of the atoms of Democritus, whose work Dalton fully acknowledged. This concept of the atom was held by chemists for nearly two hundred years until observation of the phenomenon of radioactivity.

Lucretius (*ca.* 94–55 BCE) maintained that the fundamental state of atoms is perturbed in the universe to produce spinning vortices that give rise to the objects of the real world perceived by our senses. The 19th Century physicist, William Thompson, Lord Kelvin, discoverer of the Second Law of Thermodynamics also believed that atoms were vortices spinning in the vacuum of 'the ether'. This was a sufficiently convincing theory at the time to number even James Clerk Maxwell, creator of the mathematical theory of electromagnetism, and Joseph John (J.J.) Thomson, discover of the electron, amongst its adherents. French philosopher Rene Descartes (1596–1650) thought that great vortices of some unknown invisible substance (for there could be no such thing as a vacuum) moved the planets and the stars through the heavens. It is a theme that was taken up recently by science writer David Ash in his book *The New Science of the Spirit* [21] in using the vortex hypothesis 'to show how matter is formed out of energy and how energy can be stored, in potential form, in the particles and forces associated with matter'. We now know that outer space, the region between the stars and planets, is not a vacuum, as it was formerly understood. It is filled with a low level of background radiation, an energy field that is found here on Earth too within all matter, which corresponds to what was known formerly as 'the ether'.

Hippocrates of Cos (*ca.*484–*ca.*420 BCE) was a physician and an empiricist. He denied the common belief that illness was due to some kind of divine intervention or retribution, or that sickness arose from chance. Instead, he believed that rational origins of diseases should be sought in the natural laws of the material world. He attributed illness to an imbalance of the 'four humours' – blood, phlegm, yellow bile and black bile – that gave rise to the four temperaments, sanguine, phlegmatic, bilious and melancholy. Though these ideas are considered outmoded today, there is much truth in the notion that illness is strongly influenced by the disposition or temperament of the individual; and the concept of an organic rather than supernatural or random origin for disease has long since been adopted by the medical profession. The oath of conduct proposed by Hippocrates is used as the standard declaration of ethical behaviour for physicians today, although in modified form.

The next physician of eminence in the ancient world was Galen (*ca.*130–*ca.*200 CE). Though born in Pergamum in the Greek Empire he spent most of his adult life in Rome. He had an outstanding knowledge of anatomy, physiology and surgery for that time, but also had a keen interest in both religion and philosophy. He was a monotheist, seeing God as Creator and Designer, and he believed that God's purpose for the world could be deduced by a study of His works. In his medical practice he was a keen advocate of the use of plant extracts to treat ailments, and herbal medicine has subsequently become a recognised form of therapy in the armamentarium of the modern complementary therapist – indeed, it was almost the only medicinal method of treatment of ailments until the 20th Century.

The curative properties of compounds found in plants and animals are also explored intensively today by the pharmaceutical industry, which has become increasingly aware of the costs and problems involved in the creation of new synthetic chemicals for use as drugs.

The views of Hippocrates and Galen that each disease has a specific cause and should have a specific treatment were shared by the Renaissance physician Paracelsus (*ca.*1490–1541). Paracelsus disagreed with Galen however in the method of treatment for, usually, in his case the treatment he recommended involved the use of metal-based chemical compounds rather than the herbal tinctures favoured by Galen. In this respect it could be said that Paracelsus' ideas were the forerunner of the pharmaceutical treatment of disease that predominates today, involving synthetic drugs, and which has replaced herbal treatments of illnesses since the beginning of the 20th Century. Only now are herbal remedies making a comeback along with other alternative forms of medical practice.

The sophist philosopher Protagoras (*ca.* 485–415 BCE) claimed that 'Man is the measure of all things' – a view that became the rallying cry of the Renaissance for humankind to express its individuality in the face of religious dogmatism. Protagoras maintained that an assessment of truth is made according to our personal assumptions and social conventions, not from any objective reality. All truth (and that would include ethical truth or moral values) is relative: there is no absolute truth, only what is held to be true by an individual or by a society. This pragmatic view of truth was revived by the American philosopher Charles Sanders Peirce (1839–1914), son of a famous Harvard mathematician Benjamin Peirce, and founder of the philosophical movement known as *pragmatism*. In his most famous essay, *How To Make Our Ideas Clear* (1878), he says that 'the opinion which is fated to be agreed to by all who investigate it is what we mean by truth' [364]. The other principal exponent of pragmatism in more recent times was William James (1842–1910), Professor of Psychology and Philosophy at Harvard, and a friend of Peirce. The most notable of James' works are the *Principles of Psychology* (1890), *The Varieties of Religious Experience* (1902) and *Pragmatism* (1907).

His father Henry James was a Swedenborgian (see Chapter 4), which stimulated William James' interest in psychical research. His brother, also called Henry James, was a novelist. It was in *Pragmatism* that he stated 'Truth happens to be an idea. It becomes true, it is made true by events.' So a proposition cannot be judged as true independent of its consequences as judged by experience. Truth is usually defined as conformity to the facts relevant to the statement and is tested by observation with the five senses and reason.

In the field of ethics, the ancient Greek principle of 'The Golden Rule' – to treat others as you would wish to be treated yourself – and found also in Matthew (Chap. 7, verse 12) was framed in other words, but with the same message, by Thomas Hobbes (1588–1679): 'every man that hath attained to the use of reason is supposed to know he ought not to do to another what he would not have done to himself' [261]. German philosopher Immanuel Kant (1724–1804) stated it more formally as his Categorical Imperative: "I will be constrained by reason to act only on that maxim which I can at the same time will as a universal law" [423]. This was intended as a universal moral law by which humankind should live.

Thucydides (*ca.* 460–400 BCE) also sought natural laws that would explain human behaviour. He was particularly concerned with explaining the human outlook that precipitated wars, focusing on the Peloponnesian War of 431–404 BCE between Greece and Sparta. Although his interest was focused and local, he thought that such laws would be of more general interest to other times and places if they could be established – 'a possession for ever'. Thucydides observed that as we all compete for limited resources that we all want, we will each have desires that conflict with those of other people. So we quest after power and control over others to prevent them from usurping our needs [258]. His comments certainly resonate with those we see exhibited repeatedly in the modern world where individual and national competition for limited resources is engendering stress and conflict.

Thucydides's translator, Thomas Hobbes (1588–1679), taking up this same theme, expressed this idea more forcibly and pessimistically:

'So that in the first place, I put for a general inclination of all mankind a perpetual and restless desire of power after power, that ceaseth only in death. And the cause of this is not always that a man hopes for a more intensive delight, than he has already attained to; or that he cannot be content with moderate power; but because he cannot assure the power and means to live well, which he hath present, without the acquisition of more.' [259].

The idea of competition for limited resources suggested by Thucydides and Hobbes was also the main thesis of English economist Thomas Malthus (1766–1834) in his great work *An Essay on the Principle of Population*, the first edition of which was published in 1798. Malthus believed that populations have a tendency to increase more rapidly than the resources to support them. Put mathematically, populations increase exponentially or in geometric progression while resources increase in arithmetic progression. Malthus' work, in turn, had a great influence on Charles Darwin (1809–82) in his monumental work, *Origin of Species*, published in 1859. One of Darwin's earliest and most enthusiastic supporters was Herbert Spencer (1820–1903) who coined the phrase most often used as a summary of Darwin's work: 'It cannot but happen ... that those will survive whose functions happen to be most nearly in equilibrium with the modified aggregate of external forces ... This survival of the fittest implies multiplication of the fittest' [442]. These authors produced their works from their own observations and they were probably not even aware of Thucydides' suggestions, but it is an apposite description of the world we live in today, where 'fittest' equates with 'richest and most powerful'. It is precisely this ethos of ruthless and impersonal competition that has led to the expansion of industrial empires, over-exploitation of Earth's resources and deterioration of spirituality in society.

The Greek philosopher Parmenides (*fl. ca.* 5th Century BCE) wrote his philosophy in Homeric poetic style, but nonetheless followed a rigid and disciplined approach in his arguments. He owed his ideas he said to divine inspiration from the Goddess of Justice. He reflected the view of the ancient Egyptians that the world was uncreated and essentially imperishable overall, despite the obvious waxing and waning of the seasons, the coming of night and day, and other natural phenomena of cyclical change. Things changed their form, but nothing new could be created and nothing totally destroyed. The cyclic nature of things was a dominant belief in both ancient Greece and Egypt. A similar principle is to be found as part of the philosophy of the theosophists that when we die, both our material and our spiritual bodies simply assume other forms – they are not annihilated: existence is continuous.

In the field of modern science, the German philosopher and physicist Hermann Helmholtz (1821–1894) concluded that the energy of the universe was constant: it could not be created or destroyed, only converted from one form to another – an important law of Nature that later became known as the First Law of Thermodynamics. Albert Einstein was to extend this notion further in his Special Theory of Relativity by including mass as another form that could be interchanged with energy using the famous $E = mc^2$ relation. During the 1950s and 1960s there was a model of the universe called the steady-state theory, proposed by Hermann Bondi, Thomas Gold and Fred Hoyle [83] that made use of this same concept in maintaining that matter was continuously created out of energy as the universe expanded such that its space-time properties remained unchanged. This meant that the universe had always existed, thus dispensing with the need for a Creator. This was the accepted view of the ancient Greeks, and of the Egyptians before them. So scientists too see certain aspects of the universe as imperishable.

A contemporary of Parmenides, and one of the Pythagorean School, Heraclitus (or Heracleitus) of Ephesus (*fl. ca.* 500 BCE) took a rather different view of the world. He believed that the universe was in a state of constant flux, oscillating between poles of extremes. This idea of a dynamic equilibrium between opposites, or *enantiodromia* as Heraclitus called it, had a profound effect in shaping Carl Jung's theory of human psychology (see Chapter 7). Since the material world was forever changing, knowledge of ultimate reality was impossible, for what was known at any instant would change at the next: all is change – 'you cannot step into the same river twice'. Life should be lived in harmony with this balance between opposites – thoughts very much reflecting that of the pagans and of the Eastern religious philosophers. Ideas originating from twentieth century physics envisage a similar state of flux between the subatomic particles that make up the very stuff of matter, with a balance between 'opposites' – mass and energy, particles and waves. This will be expanded on in Chapter 8.

Parallels have been drawn by American physicist Fritjof Capra [104] of the harmony between these two thought systems – Eastern mysticism and 20th Century physics – as discussed in Section 8.3. The idea that all is change or process, including the divine, is also the fundamental tenet of process theology, discussed in Chapter 1.

Heraclitus' notion of change may well have been inherited from the Buddhist idea of a century or so earlier that life essentially involves impermanence (*anicca*) leading to unhappiness or unease (*dukkha*) (the First Noble Truth) in all things, which in its turn produces yearning or striving for security and esteem (the Second Noble Truth). Much as we enjoy change in surroundings, food and social contacts when we go on holiday, for example, we are usually glad to be back in the security of our own home, jobs and partners or families. Evolution itself demands change and as such it is unavoidable. But, in a world where processes of change seem to be accelerating all around us, a philosophy that embraces change for its own sake as necessarily an improvement in every system is misguided, as reflected upon by a famous Roman orator, Petronius Arbiter. He was a poet and reputed author of the first western European novel, who died in 66 CE: 'We trained hard, but it seemed that every time we were beginning to form up into teams, we would be reorganised. I was to learn later in life that we tend to meet any new situation by reorganising: and a wonderful method it can be for creating the illusion of progress while producing confusion, inefficiency and demoralisation'.

While innovation and change is exciting to some, especially to the younger generation, it brings unease and fear and weariness to others, especially if it is unceasing. In our western society, change and material growth have become equated with 'progress'. In many respects, our lives are of better quality now, especially materially, than those of people living even one century ago. But in many respects we have also lost – in leisure time spent with family and friends, in lack of spiritual contemplation, and in living in an environment that too often is desecrated or polluted. The change needed now is in human perspective and philosophy of living. In this, the question of spiritual faith is of prime importance if we are to heal some of the ills of society and ensure our, and the planet's, survival into the next millennium.

Xenocrates (*ca.*396–*ca.*314 BCE), one of the 'directors' of the Academy after Plato's death, had an interesting view of the three-fold nature of reality as comprising objects of sensory perception, objects of true knowledge and objects of opinion to mediate between them: these last owed their origins to the sphere of the heavens. We might say now that it is the soul-engendered emotions that mediate between the senses and reason. We shall see in Chapter 6 that the Romantics saw the primacy of our emotions in our assessment of the world in which we live, and our emotions are a reflection of our genes, on the one hand, but of our faith and soul on the other. The post-Renaissance philosophers debated whether it was sensory experience or reason or both that gave us our knowledge of the world and it was left to the Romantics in late 18th Century Germany to add the component of the emotions. In this three-fold vision of the acquisition of knowledge, it could be said that they were pre-empted by Xenocrates.

Some of the ideas about deity presented by the philosophers of ancient Greece seem to have been inherited from travellers from the East or the Egyptians with whom the Greeks came into contact through trade. Plato (*ca.* 428-347 BCE) was a pupil of one of the first great Greek philosophers, Socrates. Plato's philosophical output consists of some two dozen dialogues, each on one or a number of themes, and in which Socrates is usually presented as one of the debaters. The dialogue is usually named after one of his opponents.

We are thus never quite sure when the views expressed are those of Socrates or of Plato or those of one of the other protagonists. There are however certain ideas that appear consistently or which evolve gradually within the dialogues and which are therefore attributed to Plato or Socrates.

In the *Phaedrus* and *Republic* Plato introduces us to his Tripartite Theory of the Soul. The human soul, Plato suggests, is made up of three components: reason or intellect (*nous*), desire or appetite (*epithymia*) and spirit or energy (*thymos*). Plato's Socrates compares the soul (in *Phaedrus*) to a charioteer driving a team of two horses, one noble and the other of opposite character: the charioteer is reason, the good horse is spirit and the ignoble one is desire. As well as giving a very graphic metaphor for the human personality, this picture is in keeping with the view of Socrates and early Plato that knowledge or intellect represents virtue or the greatest good and that physical needs are to be subordinated to the spiritual or mental.

In the dialogues *Phaedo* and *Meno* Plato proposes his Theory of Forms (Greek: *eidos*) or Ideas (Greek: *idea*). The knowledge we acquire in earthly existence is not only recollected, sensory and transient, but is made up of a number of particular instances of a series of ideal, eternal and unchanging concepts, forever beyond the senses and representing reality. We derive our ideas in our first earthly existence from a series of ideal spiritual templates, eternal and unchanging concepts that are forever beyond the senses and which represent ultimate reality. Thus, such Ideas as Beauty, Goodness, Justice, Equality, Heat, Cold, Oddness and Evenness we can know only by reason through access to a spiritual domain in which these concepts have eternal existence. The Form of the Good is considered to be the highest of the Ideas and corresponds to the concept of God. We form our own ideas only by communion with this spiritual world. The Greek words for these concepts are usually translated as Forms or Ideas; but there is a sense too in which these are ultimate standards or templates (Greek: *paradeigma*) from which God (Plato's Craftsman or Demiurge, in Greek, *demiourgos*) created the world, or created with the world, and of which we experience imperfect earthly examples.

The Ideas are known to the soul only beyond earthly existence but they provide our source of knowledge, through mind or soul, of the material world. As mentioned previously, the terms 'soul' and 'mind' are used interchangeably in most writings in Greek philosophy but, to Plato, the human soul is eternal like the Ideas and existed before it was incarnated in an individual. By extension, therefore, there must be a realm of eternal individual souls, or community of souls. Though Buddhist teachings reject the concept of the soul, they do postulate an Infinite Mind that retains knowledge of the quality of each human life lived in order to implement their karma, a system of instigating the teaching of the soul necessary in each incarnation to achieve the state of no-soul or *nirvana*.

Plato maintains (in the *Timaeus*) that God's creation of the world was an act of establishing order out of the pre-existing undifferentiated chaos. Most Gnostic belief adopted this idea. In this sense therefore the existence of the world is infinite and eternal. The Christian belief in Creation *ex nihilo* is usually interpreted as a bringing into being of the universe 'from nothing', as a literal translation of the Latin indicates, which implies a universe that is finite in time; others give Creation *ex nihilo* the same meaning as Plato – the establishment of order out of chaos.

Following the ideas of immortality and reincarnation of the soul that originated in Eastern religious philosophy, to be revived in Greek philosophy with the Eleatics, Plato suggested (in *Meno*) that all knowledge is recollection of what we once knew in past lives. One logical problem with this is the source of first knowledge – that which we acquire in our first earthly existence – if all knowledge is recalled from past lives. Plato overcomes this by postulating an eternal immortal soul (which could correspond to our idea of mind) from which our knowledge is derived and which may be interpreted as God. Though there is no concept of 'soul' in Eastern philosophy, there is an idea of a consciousness that survives death to become part of an Infinite Mind so that it may be carried over to the next incarnation.

Plato's *Philebus* introduces the idea that the pursuit of happiness or pleasure is also an essential component of human fulfilment: wellbeing cannot be achieved by virtue or knowledge alone. This modifies the position taken by the younger Plato and introduces the famous Doctrine of the Mean: the ideal life of greatest fulfilment is achieved with moderation between indulgence and abstinence (as had been discovered by Gautama Siddharta in his enlightenment), and a balance between the physical and the spiritual.

In the *Philebus* and *Timaeus* Plato develops the concept of a World Soul or Cosmic Soul that designed and maintains the order of the Universe, and is invested in us as individual soul. In some sense, the Universe is viewed as having a self-awareness that transcends mortal existence. As Socrates is made to say: '. . . the Cause...exists within everything [and] provides us with a soul ... in general producing harmony and health and being regarded as universal wisdom.' Plato's 'allegory of the cave' was discussed in Chapter 1 in relation to the undesirability of our living in a world of irrationality and fantasy.

Sometime in his 40s(?) Plato founded a school in Athens called the Academy at which other young philosophers practiced their skills. Amongst his pupils was the teenage Aristotle who studied there for twenty years until Plato's death in 347 BCE. A decade or so later Aristotle founded a school of his own in Athens, the Lyceum. These were not institutions like universities, with formal lectures and examinations. They were meeting places for discussion and gymnasia – places to exercise minds and bodies – and they were free and open to all.

Aristotle (384-322 BCE) was born in the town of Stagira in Macedon in northern Greece. His father, Nichomachus, was court physician to the King of Macedon and this profession may well have kindled Aristotle's interest in the life sciences. It was also probably influential in generating Aristotle's insistence on experiment, observation and classification of the natural world as essential prerequisites to theorising about it. He was the first to stress the importance of empiricism. Where Plato had continued the interest of the early Greek philosophers in conceptual and social issues,

Aristotle was more interested in the study of material things. He established a code of practice that became the standard procedure of science – only, in his day, with virtually no equipment with which to make measurements. Science today is all about practical measurements underpinned with mathematical theory.

Aristotle's philosophical work, of which only about one-fifth seems to have passed down to us, consists mainly of treatises on a range of subjects as diverse as politics, ethics, metaphysics, logic, literature, and what we would now call science, a range of work far exceeding that covered by either Socrates or Plato.

Aristotle also endorsed Plato's Doctrine of the Mean, that the happy life is one of balance and moderation, involving the achievement of what he called *eudaimonia*, literally, having a good demon or benevolent (guardian) spirit. This implies much more than the usual translation of the word as 'happiness'; rather it is a deep-seated fulfilment derived from knowledge, wisdom and beneficence, of being 'in touch' with Plato's Cosmic Soul. It means living a virtuous life, which generally involves avoiding extremes or excesses. Plato believed that *akrasia* (weakness of will) arose only because a person did not know what was in their best interests. Aristotle maintained that *akrasia* arose when someone acted for short-term gain – like the Hedonists – without a vision of what was in their best interests in the long-term to generate *eudaimonia*. The Epicureans were much more selective in their pleasures.

Both Plato and Aristotle believed that there were three agencies responsible for producing the events of the world: Nature (*physis*) embraced those events that occurred regularly without any human intervention; Art (*techne*) included events that were brought about by humans; and Chance (*tyche*) was considered to be the agency that caused things to happen, without any human intervention, but which also did not follow any regular pattern or, as we would say nowadays, that did not happen according to natural laws. The last of these would include what Christians would designate as 'miracles' and those that others would describe as 'supernatural' or 'paranormal'.

One of Aristotle's books on logic, the *Prior Analytics*, introduces the idea of the proposition as a logical statement consisting of subject and predicate, something we can say about the subject. This is how we describe the world in which we live. The *Analytics* also define the *syllogism*, the tripartite structure of logical argument that is the standard form of mathematical deduction and, to a significant extent, of induction in science: given a fact or premise x, if the statement y is true, then the conclusion z follows.

Aristotle's writings on logic shaped this branch of philosophy for two thousand years up to the present century. Euclid (*fl.* 300 BCE) used the method of Aristotle's *Posterior Analytics* extensively in his exposition of geometry called *Elements*. Little is known of Euclid except that he founded a school at Alexandria in the reign of Ptolemy I, but his system of logical argument of the properties of planar figures formed the basis of high-school geometry up to the 20th Century, though his work had been forgotten until the late Middle Ages.

The classification of sciences into the separate disciplines of the present day also owes its origin to Aristotle. In the *Physics* (Greek: *physis* - nature) and in *De Anima* (*On The Soul*) Aristotle sees science as the study of those events or changes in what we may predicate about the objects of the natural world. The subject under study possesses a constant potential (Greek: *dunamis*, which gives us our word 'dynamic'), the nature of which emerges as we observe a succession of properties or actualities (Greek: *energeia*) that are produced in the subject through its purpose or intrinsic character or *entelechy* (Greek: *en* - in; *telos* - goal; *echein* - to have). The substance or matter of an object represent its potential(ity); its character, nature or form is its actuality. Entelechy turns potentiality into actuality. The essential characteristic of humans is activity or work (*ergon*): we all have this potential but we need entelechy to bring it into being. Science as it was practiced by Aristotle was necessarily descriptive or qualitative rather than the systematic quantitative measurement of properties with mathematical backing that distinguishes the subject today: the technical instruments enabling accurate measurement were simply not available. Nevertheless, Aristotle's work was largely observational practice rather than the purely mental and conjectural activity that characterised the work of the mathematicians and most other philosophers of his day and he is regarded by some as the first scientist, certainly in spirit.

The term and concept of entelechy arise again in 20th Century science with German biologist and philosopher Hans Driesch in regard to the development of sea-urchin embryos. Portions of embryos were found to develop normally into whole, undeformed adults, suggesting a potential for development in each cell – its entelechy (see Chapter 7). Today we would probably describe such processes in terms of cellular DNA. The germ of the whole being contained in each of its parts is David Bohm's view of he world as a whole (Chapter 8).

Entelechy lies in things organic and inorganic, but the entelechy of a living organism is its soul [15] and since all living matter possesses a soul, souls come in varying degrees of complexity. Soul must always be associated with a living body; but it is not seen as a spiritual component *within* the body, like energy. It is rather like a skill that someone possesses – an ability to act in a certain way [41]. Aristotle here seems to reject the hypothesis of the immortality and reincarnation of the soul found in Plato and many earlier writers [42] – a point of view reflected in those of many scientists today. But Aristotle is ambiguous on the point, and the opposite view that thought can exist apart from the body [43] appears in other places in *De Anima* and elsewhere. In *Generation of Animals* we are told: 'Hence it remains that thought alone comes in from outside, and that it alone is divine; for corporeal actuality has no connection at all with the actuality of thought' [43], for intellect may be active or passive, and some kinds of thought may be 'immortal and eternal' – again, a version of the Buddhist belief in the continuity of some form of consciousness of the individual after earthly life. D.J. Allen in *The Philosophy of Aristotle* [2] similarly interprets the role of *nous* (mind, reason) as a component in the *psyche* (life-force) as having 'no bodily counterpart and [that it] may well be capable of separate existence'.

Another crucial idea of Aristotle's that certainly does form the basis of science today is that of 'cause' and 'effect'. Science views all events as having rational causes that fit the established thought-scheme or *paradigm* that is current at the time. Any alleged incident that does not fit in with this scheme is held not to exist – as is the case in the minds of many scientists with the whole body of psychic or paranormal experiences. Aristotle said that change (Greek: *kinesis*) comes about as a result of Four Causes: (i) the Material Cause, the object being constituted as it is, the substance or composition of the object; (ii) the Formal Cause, the form or shape or nature of the object; (iii) the Efficient Cause, that which changes the matter of an object into its form; and (iv) the Final Cause, the reason for the change or purpose of the object. These ideas lie behind the cause-and-effect structure that has underpinned scientific investigation ever since its inception. In the latter half of the 20th Century, the American-born physicist David Bohm challenged the view that events could always be attributed to simple or single causes: no event he felt should be separated from its multiple contributing causes and myriad effects in the world as a whole. All 'causes' and 'effects' were interrelated. In the Middle Ages, Aristotle's final, formal and efficient causes of things were identified with God the Father, Son and the Holy Ghost. The material cause was the primordial stuff of the universe that God had created out of nothing.

There is a long-standing debate in philosophy as to the extent to which moral values are absolute or relative: does a statement like 'thou shalt not kill' represent truth at all times and under all circumstances? Aristotle regarded ethics or morality and politics as pursuing the same goal of promoting and maintaining human happiness and wellbeing that he called *eudaimonia*.

When Copernicus formulated his heliocentric theory of Earth moving around the sun, he acknowledged his indebtedness to Aristarchus of Samos (*fl. ca.* 270 BCE), who made a similar suggestion around 300 BCE, though even he was probably not the first; but more of this in Chapter 4. This was one of two theories concerning the motion of the heavens. The other theory – that Earth is the centre of the heavens – is generally attributed to the Greek astronomer Claudius Ptolemy (*fl. ca.* 127–148 CE). Like Aristotle, Ptolemy took the observation that the sun, moon and stars *appear* to revolve around the Earth to indicate that Earth was indeed the centre of the solar system, and this was adopted as official Church doctrine. Ptolemy's view of the solar system also influenced the medieval Islamic mystic Abu Nasr al-Farabi (died *ca.* 950 CE). He proposed that the One generated ten successive emanations, each of which produced one of the Ptolemaic spheres. The spheres were geometrical constructions that Ptolemy had produced, following Hipparchus (*fl.* 146–127 BCE), to allow him to calculate the orbits of stars and planets around Earth. Jewish mystics also hold that ten *sefiroth* emanated from *En Sof,* the Creator.

Thus many of the ideas of the ancient Greek philosophers have exerted a considerable influence on the development of theology, philosophy and science during the past five centuries, as the above examples show. To establish some kind of cognitive structuring of the development of knowledge is satisfying to the human psyche and thereby conducive to maintaining emotional and thence physical wellbeing. The later post-Renaissance concepts referred to here rather briefly will be developed in the following chapters. The earlier ideas may have been transmitted directly by modern thinkers reading about the works of the Greek philosophers, or from the original texts themselves; they may have been created out of the minds of the modern thinkers; or, to utilise a theme that is the focus of this presentation, it may be said that modern thinkers have unconsciously tuned in to the akashic field, the record of all human experience reposit in the spiritual domain: this last notion will be discussed in Chapter 8. This does not denigrate or devalue the achievements of post-Renaissance thinkers. On the contrary, it is the contention here that creative inspiration is an activity of soul that derives from resonance with the universal spiritual field. Just how science and philosophy developed during the Enlightenment from these early ideas in the context of the religious upheavals of the Renaissance period will be explored in Chapter 4 after we have examined how the medieval philosophers of religion struggled to interpret the works of the ancient Greek philosophers, that had been written on the basis of rational logic, in a way that was compatible with their religious tenets derived from revelatory scripture.

3 Some ideas of the medieval philosophers of religion

The predominant subject matter of the writings of philosophers of religion in the medieval period, which in philosophy encompasses everything from around the time of Jesus right up to the Enlightenment, is their attempt to reconcile the contribution to knowledge from divine revelation found in the Bible with that derived by reason in the works of the ancient Greek philosophers. This was especially important since some of the latter writings contain ideas similar to, and perhaps derived from, the Eastern mystical philosophies. The subject of medieval philosophy is a vast topic in its own right, so this short commentary focuses on those concepts relevant to the central thesis in this book, with some short biographical details to put the writers into their respective contexts.

3.1. Medieval Jewish philosophy

One of the first Jewish philosophers to attempt reconciliation between philosophical rationalism and the divine revelation of scripture in the *Torah* was the Alexandrian Jew Philo Judaeus (*ca.*20 BCE - 50 CE). He was a contemporary of Jesus and lived in one of the centres of scholarship in the Greek empire. He spent his whole life in Alexandria apart from a short trip to Rome. His work had little influence on Judaism but considerable effect on later Christian writing. His works were all written in Greek and he may not even have been able to read original manuscripts in Hebrew. His primary concern was with exegesis rather than creating any original philosophy.

In his writings on the Pentateuch, he interpreted the lives of the patriarchs Abraham, his son Isaac and grandson Jacob to be exemplars of the Jewish law as presented in the Books of Moses. In an important series of writings, called *Allegorical Interpretation*, he presents both literal and philosophical interpretations of this core of the Old Testament. He follows Plato in distinguishing between the material world and a higher spiritual realm representing ultimate truth. The human soul quests to achieve this understanding, reaching out to God, but the spirit of God also inhabits the human soul. But God itself is utterly transcendent and is immanent in the world only through intermediaries as angels or incorporeal souls. Any direct relationship between God and the material world would demean his perfection and purity. This infinite variety of divine agencies are the *logoi* that bring the Word of God to humankind, and amongst them is a highest *Logos*. It was this concept that had such appeal to the Christians, who saw Jesus as just such a Supreme *Logos*. Though Philo mainly follows Plato in his philosophy, this idea of angels as intermediaries corresponds to Aristotle's 'intelligences' that allow communion between the Prime Mover and the material world.

Abraham ibn Daud (1110–1180) was born in Cordoba in Southern Spain and remained in Spain all of his life. He was a physician, astronomer, and religious philosopher and historian. His most important work is the *Emunah Ramah* (*Exalted Faith*) written around 1160. In this he attempted to show how revealed scripture is compatible with Aristotelian philosophy. Where there is conflict or contradiction between the two, scripture must be interpreted according to reason. For ibn Daud, the divine essence is essentially incorporeal and he regarded as heresy any attempts to interpret the Bible literally and attribute anthropomorphic characteristics to God. Such qualities were ascribed to God only because lay people would tend to believe that what is not material could not exist: hence they would be inclined to reject a purely spiritual image of God. It therefore required a more advanced degree of understanding to comprehend the message of the sages and prophets.

The Jewish philosopher, physician and astronomer Moses ben Maimon or Maimonides (1135–1204) was also born in Cordoba at the time of Moorish rule. He was the son of a *dayyan*, a rabbinical judge. His family left Cordoba when it was overrun in 1148 by the Berber group known as the Almohads. After many years of wandering around various places in North Africa, Maimonides ended up in Cairo as physician to the sultan of Egypt. It was there that he wrote his *Guide for the Perplexed* (ca.1190, written in Arabic) which, after translation into Hebrew, formed the basis of Jewish philosophy and rational faith. It was intended as a guide to the more erudite Jews on how to live their lives according to Jewish law but also to have regard for what their intellect told them, in other words, to seek out the harmony between faith and reason to resolve their perplexity at seeming incompatibilities between the *Torah* and Greek philosophy, primarily that of Aristotle. The work draws on earlier Muslim interpretations of Aristotle by ibn Sina and al-Farabi.

An equally important writing was his *Mishneh Torah* (the Second Teaching or Repetition of the Law), a commentary on Jewish law that acquired a status in Judaism comparable to that of the *Sentences* of Peter Lombard (ca. 1100–1160) commenting on Christian theology. Maimonides also influenced Christian theology through Thomas Aquinas after the *Guide* was translated into Latin. He maintained that nothing could be said about the qualities of God – the so-called *via negativa* – for such description undermined the absolute unity of God: 'All attributes ascribed to God are attributes of his acts, and do not imply that God has any qualities.' [*Mishneh Torah*, quoted in ref. 87]. In the words of Aquinas: 'the diversity implied is to be attributed not to God himself but to our way of conceiving him' [11]. He felt that to predicate any qualities of God was to endanger His absolute unity: whatever qualities God possessed, they were unknowable. In describing God as, for example, 'incorporeal' we are saying that he has no material body, and by such negative statements we approach a truer understanding of the meaning of God. The negation of attributes denies what would otherwise be some imperfection in

God. This was a view that came in for some criticism from other Jewish scholars in the following centuries.

He also had some original ideas on the source of inspiration of the prophets. The traditional religious view was that people became prophets or healers because they were chosen by God. Philosophers on the other hand believed that people possessed the gift of prophecy by chance (or by genetic programming, as we would say now) and that study and application were necessary to cultivate this gift. Maimonides rejected both these absolute points of view, but produced a theory that embraced elements of both. He believed that, while the original inspiration came from God, it also required activation by the Universal Mind of God, or the Active Intellect in Maimonides' terminology, together with the receptive intellect and imagination of the person concerned to perfect this skill – a view that accords perfectly with the philosophy of this book. On the basis of his ideas, Maimonides classified human beings into three types: those with developed intellect but poor imagination (philosophers); those with highly developed imagination but poor intellect (statesmen and politicians); and the third group, the prophets, with both intellect and imagination both finely tuned to the Active Intellect, or Universal Spirit, or the Mind of God. Maimonides shared the view of the Christian philosopher St. Augustine that evil was the privation of good and arose only through the human heart expressing misdirected free will.

Moses ben Nahman or Nahmanides (1194–1270) was born in Catalonia in the north-eastern corner of Spain. He came from a prominent rabbinic family. He was a physician by profession but also the head of a *yeshivah* (a Jewish Academy) in his home town of Gerona. His standing was such that King James I of Spain called upon him to represent the Jewish viewpoint in a disputation on the position of Jesus in scripture against a Jewish apostate called Pablo Christiani. Nahmanides was so successful in his arguments that the Dominicans, who had instigated the disputation, sought the backing of Pope Clement IV to prosecute him for heresy against the Christian faith. As a result, he was forced to leave Spain and he fled to the Holy Land, first to Acre and then on to Jerusalem where he founded another *yeshivah*. He returned to Acre shortly before his death.

In his lifetime he wrote many tracts on the *halakhah* (Jewish law). With regard to the divinity of Jesus Nahmanides wrote: 'The doctrine in which you believe and which is the foundation of your faith cannot be accepted by reason, and nature affords no grounds for it, nor have the prophets ever expressed it. Nor could even the miraculous stretch so far as this' [quoted in ref. 129]. The Arian position on the irrationality of this belief has been attested to repeatedly by non-Christians ever since Nicaea.

Levi ben Gershom or Gersonides (1288–1344) was not only a religious philosopher but also a mathematician and astronomer of some note for the time. He made observations of several eclipses of the sun and of the moon and many other astronomical events using a device known as Jacob's Rod (*baculus Jacob*) that he either invented or at least improved to measure angular distances between stars or planets. From these, he called into question Ptolemy's geocentric theory of Earth as the centre of the universe – the official Church tenet. He wrote one of the earliest European treatises on trigonometry – *De Sinibus, chordis et arcubus*. His most famous writing is the work *Wars of the Lord* (1317–29). In this, he used the Argument from Design – the presence of order in the cosmos – to verify the existence of God; and the Cosmological Argument to deduce that the world must have had a beginning in time as an 'effect' that resulted from a divine 'cause'. Interestingly, he took issue with Aristotle's arguments for the eternal existence of the universe on the grounds that the physical laws of Nature that operated now need not be the same as those that operated at the moments of Creation. This is in accord with the views of 21st Century cosmologists. He also did not agree with Maimonides that the act of Creation of the universe from pre-existing primordial matter would infringe the absolute unity of God.

He also criticised Maimonides' negative attitude to ascribing attributes to God: the attributes of humankind are but reflections of the attributes of God. Although God has knowledge of our ultimate fate, this does not negate the possibility of our free-will. By exercising this quality we can break free from the constraints of determinism. This does not undermine the essential attributes of God, because knowledge of our actions day-to-day is not part of these. He did believe however that the extent of divine guidance in our lives increases with our degree of spiritual enlightenment. In modern terminology we might say that our actions are guided by the extent of our resonance with the universal spiritual field.

Salient points in the life and work of Israel ben Eliezer (Baal Shem Tov), whose theology was both a product of the Enlightenment and a reaction against it, are discussed in Chapter 4. The philosophies of the 19th Century Jewish theologians Solomon Formstecher and Samuel Hirsch are described in Chapter 7 in relation to the concept of a Universal Soul.

3.2.   Medieval Christian philosophy

The medieval Christian theologians were mostly members of a mendicant monastic Order. The beginning of monasticism is generally attributed to St. Anthony in Egypt in the 3rd Century or to St. Mark, whose monastery gave rise to the Coptic tradition there. The works of Plato and, more particularly, Aristotle formed the subjects of much theological debate in the Middle Ages. Christian theologians were trying to interpret their revelational scriptures, and the role of Jesus, in a way that was compatible with the rational logic of the Greeks. There was a constant dichotomy between the spiritual and revelational approach to theology and that compatible with rational thought and empirical observation. It was these congregations of monastic Orders that were to become the forerunners of the universities. The universities represented a formalisation of the teaching systems of the ancient Greeks, but with theology as the central topic of instruction rather than metaphysics or epistemology.

Benedict of Nursia (*ca.* 480–550 CE), who was the inspirational source of the Benedictine Order founded at Subiaco and Monte Cassino in Italy, advocated a life of moderation, without extreme asceticism. Pope Gregory (*ca.* 540–604 CE) also encouraged a balance between active service to God, whatever that entailed by way of self-denial, and spending time in mystical contemplation as advocated in Eastern philosophy. These ideas recall the 'Middle Way' advocated by the Greek philosophers.

While Greek philosophy entered into Islam to a significant extent only after the 9th Century, Christian theologians like the Benedictines adopted ideas from their Greek pagan predecessors within the first few hundred years after the time of Jesus. Christian and Islamic scholars translated the principal works of Plato and Aristotle into Arabic and then Latin. Greek philosophy therefore influenced Christian theology directly from its earliest days, most significantly in what is described by philosophers as the 'medieval period' with the theologians Philo Judaeus, who adopted ideas from both Plato and Aristotle; Augustine, a NeoPlatonist; and Aquinas, an Aristotelian.

St. Dominic (1170–1221) founded his mendicant Order of monks in 1215 with a philosophy of service to others and serious study of theological issues: the Dominicans have always been regarded as one of the most academic of religious Orders.

In 1209, St. Francis of Assisi (*ca.*1181–1226) heeded a call from God to live a life devoted to poverty and instruction to others in the ways of God. To do that, it was necessary that he and his small band of followers became sufficiently well versed in theological matters themselves. So he established a mendicant brotherhood around him and in 1209 it was approved by Pope Innocent III by the issue of a Rule. This was confirmed by a papal Bull in 1223 by Pope Honorius III. Thus the Franciscan Order was established. St. Francis' call for renunciation of worldly wealth struck a discordant note in the medieval Church, not noted for its frugality. The Church felt itself bound to reject this call officially and thus St. Francis inadvertently provided ammunition for critics of the Church in the Reformation.

The Carmelite nuns, or White Friars, driven from their seclusion at Mount Carmel in Palestine by the failure of the Crusades in the 13th Century, resettled in several sites in Europe. They lived an austere life of individual seclusion, silence and abstinence. Their Order later included the mystical St. Teresa of Avila (1515–1582), noted for her writings on the practice of prayer. Her work *Interior Castle* describes the highly effective metaphorical concept of a sanctum that, during prayer, one can enter, walk about and leave at will. The mystic St. John of the Cross (1542–1591), noted for his work *Dark Night of the Soul* that describes the purification of the soul after death before union with the divine, was amongst the monks who helped Teresa to re-establish greater spirituality in the Order.

The establishment of these Orders represented the first time that Christian preaching had been formalised since Augustine had set up his small devotional group in Thagaste (see below). Another Order, the Augustinians, a collection of hermits inspired by Augustine's life and work, came together in 1256. The 12th and 13th Centuries saw a fervent expansion in universities and monasteries to allow the members of the mendicant Orders to pursue Christian theology in relation to Greek philosophy with the same passion as that with which Muslims had studied Islam in their mosques and Jewish theological philosophers the *Torah* in their *yeshivot* for several centuries, striving for compatibility with Greek rationalism.

The Dominicans and Franciscans were pre-eminent in establishing centres of instruction. The very first universities, the *studia provincialia*, were like lecture tours by prominent theologians. The tutors moved around from place to place gathering students around them in each location. *Studia generalia* or permanent universities were established by the Dominicans and Franciscans in Bologna, Vicenza, Padua and Naples in Italy, and elsewhere at Toulouse, Paris, Lisbon, Oxford and Cambridge during the 13th century. Many others sprang up throughout Europe in the next hundred years or so, including that at St. Andrews in Scotland in 1410. It was not until the next century (1591) that Ireland had its first University in Trinity College, Dublin, and the University of Wales was not established at Aberystwyth until 1872. They were staffed by academic theologians, clerics and monks who were devoted to a study of theology, law, medicine and mathematics and the instruction of theological students who were themselves preparing to take holy orders. Both students and tutors travelled freely between them communicating in Latin as the international language. In the early years of universities the students decided for themselves with whom they wished to study and the topics they wanted to investigate, but in the late 13th Century formal syllabuses were established with a curriculum to follow with prescribed teachers. But theology and a knowledge of Latin were always primary requirements and it was not until 1875 that theological tests before the awarding of academic degrees were abandoned by Oxford and Cambridge Universities. Initial and higher degrees began to be awarded, the latter for work at a more advanced level but not necessarily including any original research.

Medieval Christian theologians were preoccupied with the idea that the existence and qualities of God could be inferred by reason – what we now call natural theology. One of the most influential of the early philosophical theologians was Augustine. St. Augustine (354–430 CE) lived most of his nearly eighty years in Roman-occupied North Africa, the last thirty-four as bishop of the town of Hippo (now called Annaba) in Algeria. In 388, Augustine returned to his home town of Thagaste, intending to spend the rest of his life in quiet contemplation with a few friends. Their community, which existed for two and a half years, broke up when Augustine was called to serve first as presbyter and then as Bishop in Hippo.

Augustine saw God as beyond our human notions of space and time – of necessity if God is Creator of all that is: God is Being itself. Because of the limitations of language, we can only describe the qualities of God by the way that God is related to the universe and, in particular, to humankind. He believed that God was the 'immutable and supreme Good' [26] and that everything created by God was good, including our freedom not to sin. This was a defence against the dualistic view of Manichaeism, of which Augustine was a follower for nine years, that the world comprised opposing forces of Light (that is, God, Goodness, Spirit) and the Darkness of the created material world. There is a very long tradition of associating the divine with light or with the sun. To Augustine, everything that God created was good but human nature had an intrinsically evil side – 'evil' in the sense of lacking the goodness of perfection, of being egotistical and selfish not necessarily evil in the sense of creating malicious acts. Evil arose through the exercise of free will by humankind, choosing to err, and did not originate from God. We therefore needed God's grace to achieve happiness: 'there is no other good which can make any rational or intellectual creature happy except God' [26]. We needed the illumination of the Holy Spirit from God, the sun of souls. Augustine was well aware that many of the stories that formed the basis of Christian scripture and the principles on which their religion was founded had a long history dating back to antiquity: 'The very thing which is now called the Christian religion existed among the ancients also, nor was it wanting from the inception of the human race until the coming of Christ in the flesh, at which point the true religion, which was already in existence, began to be called Christian' [29]. The Bible should not be regarded as the only medium of divine revelation [30]: it used myths to represent symbolically the divine message for humankind. This message was lost if the Bible was treated as a historical document.

The Manichaeans were extreme ascetics. The degree of asceticism that is required for devotion to the divine has always been a contentious matter within the Christian Church (following Matthew 19, v.12; 1 Corinthians, Chap.7). Jews and Muslims, while abstaining from certain practices, like the drinking of alcohol or the eating of pork, have never advocated abstinence from the joys of living. Augustine renounced physical pleasures only later in his life.

Anselm of Canterbury (1033–1109) was born at Aosta in Lombardy, Italy. As his father died while he was still young, Anselm travelled north in search of an education. He joined a school associated with a new abbey at Bec in Normandy which had been set up by a fellow Italian from Pavia called Lanfranc. While there,

Anselm decided he wanted to take holy orders. In a treatise called *Cur Deus Homo* Anselm tries to justify the divine incarnation in Jesus as God's attempt to redeem his own honour tarnished by the supposed Fall of Man in the Garden of Eden, who paid for the sin with his life. As the Adam and Eve story is itself only allegorical, it seems to build a justification for Jesus as the Christ on very shaky ground. As we saw in Chapter 1, after the schism, Anselm was also involved in trying to defend the Western Church's view on the emanation of the Holy Spirit from Jesus as well as from God in his publication *On the Procession of the Holy Spirit*. In his *Proslogion* Anselm declared God's existence to be self-evident inasmuch as the human mind is capable of envisaging degrees of greatness; if we envisage a Being, of which none greater can be conceived, that Being is God. This is known as the Ontological Argument for the existence of God. It lays itself open to the criticism that because such a being can be conceived this does not imply its existence: we can conceive of such creatures as unicorns and hobbits, but this does not mean they exist. If we add to the Argument the contention that existence makes the Being greater than non-existence, this is challenged on the ground that existence is not a quality, for an object must exist before anything can be said of it at all. In 1093 Anselm succeeded Lanfranc as Archbishop of Canterbury.

The Catholic theologian St. Thomas Aquinas (*ca.*1225–1274 CE) was born in Italy and went to school with the Benedictines at Monte Cassino. He joined the newly formed Dominican Order in the 1240s while he was a student at the also newly inaugurated University of Naples, then he went on to Paris to study with Albert the Great (*ca.*1200–1280). He produced two major influential works: the *Summa contra Gentiles* is a book of theological argument against the views of unbelievers; *Summa Theologiae* was written for theology students beginning their studies.

In the *Summa Theolgiae* Aquinas outlined *Five Ways* he thought that the existence of God could be deduced logically [11]. The first way observes that changes take place in the world around us and, with Aristotle's Four Causes in mind, he noted that every change requires a cause, as deduced from the axiom of cause and effect, and someone to initiate or bring about that cause: 'We arrive then at some first cause of change not itself being changed by anything, and this is what everybody understands by *God.*' Here, God is Prime Mover. 'The second way is based on the very notion of cause ... one is forced to suppose some first cause, to which everyone gives the name *God.*' – this is God as Uncaused Cause or First Cause. The third way is based on the observation that there is something rather than nothing: everything could exist or not exist; 'One is forced to suppose something which must be, and owes this to nothing outside itself; indeed it itself is the cause that other things must be.' Before anyone had posited a 'Big Bang' to initiate Creation, the very fact that there was a universe at all surely implied the existence of a Creator. These three arguments are variations of what is generally known as the *Cosmological Argument* for God's existence.

The argument that is offered to counter the Cosmological Argument as evidence of the handiwork of God as Creator is that, when scientists reach a conclusion by induction, it is based on several examples that have been observed of the same phenomenon. As there has been only one Creation, the argument goes, we cannot make any generalisations on the basis of that. Indeed, there are some philosophers who deny the very existence of the cause-and-effect reasoning itself. William of Ockham (*ca.* 1285–1349), a Franciscan friar who was born in Surrey and who studied at Oxford, and the Scottish philosopher David Hume (1711–96) maintained that all we see are events occurring together in succession – in 'constant conjunction': we never see any factor that specifically and uniquely unites the two events [266]. But the cause-and-effect argument appears to be consistent with human experience and so is generally accepted – and, indeed, forms the basis of the inductive method of scientific reasoning and the way we make sense of the world.

The fourth way posited by Aquinas as proof of the existence of God defines God as paragon of excellence. We observe gradations of goodness or excellence in all things: 'Something therefore is the truest and best and most excellent of things ... And this is what we call

God.' The fifth way is what is now called the Argument from Design or *Teleological Argument* for God's existence. As Aquinas says: 'The fifth way is based on the guidedness of nature' – the fact that there seems to be a purpose to the complexity of Nature that makes it all work in harmony, regarded as a self-evident truth even before the laws of Nature had begun to be investigated: 'Everything in nature, therefore, is directed to its goal by someone with understanding, and this we call *God.'* [11]. A comparable argument was advanced by the English religious philosopher William Paley (1743–1805), who used the analogy of encountering the complexities of a watch lying in the sand on the seashore, which he said would imply the existence of a skilled craftsman as watchmaker. The vastly greater complexity of Nature in our world surely suggested a Grand Designer to plan such a scheme. It is interesting to note that this same argument is also to be found in the work of the pagan Roman orator Cicero (106–43 BCE) in his book *The Nature of the Gods*, except that the pocket-watch of Paley is replaced by sundials and water-clocks [123].

Aquinas was critical of Anselm's Ontological Argument as proof of the existence of God for the reasons given above, which are presented early in Chapter 1 of *Summa Theologiae* on God. Aquinas argued that simply because we could conceive of such a Being does not guarantee its existence, and that existence is not an attribute. Amplifying the argument, Aquinas quotes Boethius saying: 'though an existent may have other properties as well, existence is simply existence' [12].

Aquinas was not suggesting that rationality alone was sufficient to prove the existence of God, only that it was necessary. He quotes St. John of Damascus (656–747 CE) in saying 'the awareness that God exists is implanted by nature in everybody' [9] – the instinctive feeling even amongst pagan societies that the grandeur of the world must have a Creator. But Aquinas qualifies this by saying that our awareness of God is neither clear nor specific. He also quotes St. Paul in saying that we deduce the qualities of God by His works: 'we know the hidden things of God by looking at the things that he has made' [St. Paul's Letter to the Romans, 1: 20]. Both Aquinas and his Franciscan contemporary, St. Bonaventura (1221–74), asserted the primacy of personal experience of God through faith, though they valued philosophical argument that substantiated the existence of God.

Like his contemporary Roger Bacon, Aquinas deplored the proliferation of tracts discussing the so-called 'disputed questions' in theology that arose partly from incompatibilities between Aristotelian and Christian thought, and partly from comparison of Jerome's Vulgate Bible in Latin with original Greek or Hebrew texts. Aquinas did however try to classify these discussions systematically.

In his rational exploration of causes, in the manner of Aristotle, Albert the Great (*ca.* 1200–1280), teacher of Thomas Aquinas, explored the possibilities of 'action at a distance', as exhibited in the influence of God on humankind. This theme of 'action at a distance' was to become of great importance to post-Renaissance scientists in studying electricity and magnetism, radiation and, in the 20th Century, the interactions between subatomic particles. Just as Aquinas later defined the individuality of an object by its position in time and space, Albert debated whether locations could be characterised in the same way when objects were moved in or out of them. Does each location have a specific identity irrespective of what it may contain?

One of the key reformers of the early university curriculum was Roger Bacon (*ca.*1220–1292), who was the first to try to make measurements of phenomena in the natural world. He was a student at Oxford and was probably influenced there by Robert Grosseteste (*ca.*1170–1253). In 1257, he became a friar in the new Franciscan order.

In his writing Roger Bacon listed the ways that believers could be led into error in their faith, just as his later namesake, Francis Bacon, listed the errors that humankind could make in their perceptions in his 'doctrine of idols'. Bacon deplored the succession of tracts that were appearing discussing controversial theological issues, which often arose from interpretation of Greek philosophy: he believed that theologians would have been better to spend their time studying the scriptures in their original languages. Bacon petitioned the Pope to try to reform the university curriculum maintaining that knowledge of Greek and Hebrew was essential to understand the Bible.

In his writings, the *Opus maius* of 1267, and the later *Opus Tertium,* Bacon also recommended that mathematics and careful practical observation and measurement were essential to understand the natural world that God had created. Like St. Bede (*ca.* 673–735 CE), in his own work *De rerum natura,* in the *Opus maius* Bacon tried to interpret natural phenomena in theological terms, like his explanation of the rainbow by the passage of light through raindrops. This marked an abandonment of the Platonic notion of perfect Forms or Ideas from which we developed imperfect earthly copies to be used in rationalisation. In the *Opus Tertium* Bacon maintained that all arguments should be supported by experimental verification – a very Aristotelian approach – even though this meant working with imperfect material copies of the Ideas. This approach to the investigation of Nature in order to understand God's handiwork also motivated the post-Renaissance scientists themselves. They were not setting out to destroy the foundations of the Christian religion but rather to support it, or at least to establish the need for a God as Creator and Designer of the world. The word 'science', with the meaning it has today, comes from the Latin *scire* meaning 'to know' and came into use around 1725. Up to that time, those we now call scientists, like Newton, were known as natural philosophers.

Siger of Brabant (*ca.*1240–*ca.*1284) was an academic working in Paris who did not belong to one of the established mendicant Orders. He was considered a danger to the Church because his rational arguments, inspired by those of Aristotle and presented in his work *Quaestiones in Physicam,* asserted that the universe must have existed for eternity (and was therefore not created by God), that morality was defined by humankind (and therefore was not absolutely decreed by God) and that there was a Universal Mind (as found in some Eastern religious philosophies and Averroes' interpretation of Aristotle also). Because of the heretical nature of his philosophy, his influence soon waned.

The Dominican friar Eckhart von Hochheim, known as Meister

Eckhart (*ca.*1260–*ca.*1328) was influenced in his theology by the Neoplatonist Plotinus and by Jewish philosopher Maimonides. He continued a spirit of mysticism in the Catholic Church in the Rhineland that had been started by Hildegard of Bingen (1098–1179), though he claimed no divine insight. For a decade from 1314, Eckhart lectured and preached in Strasbourg, in Cologne and in the University of Paris but his mystical philosophy did not win the approval of the Church, despite his popularity. In 1326 he was summoned to appear before the Archbishop of Cologne on a charge of heresy. Despite a direct appeal to Pope John XXII, he was forced to recant his beliefs and died a short time later. The pope issued a Bull in 1328 condemning 28 propositions of his philosophy as heretical.

Eckhart maintained that the most important thing we could say about God was that He exists; beyond that we could say nothing of him (compare the philosophy of Maimonides, above). The created world *has* being, but God *is* being: it is He who created being. The human soul is that part of the divine within us: the Father engenders the Son in the soul, the *Seelenfünklein* or 'spark of the soul' that unites with the divine (*cf.* Anthony Freeman's 'God in us', in Chapter 7). Eckhart also posited an unknowable Godhead beyond the God immanent in the world with whom we commune in prayer and supplication; but even God is unknowable in the sense we use the term of the world: 'The proof of a knowable thing is made either to the senses or the intellect, but as regards the knowledge of God there can be neither a demonstration from sensory perception, since He is incorporeal, nor from the intellect, since He lacks any form known to us' [quoted in ref.18]. We know the divine only through mystical experience using our sixth sense.

We saw above that Aquinas believed that objects were characterised by their location in space and time. The medieval Franciscan theologian John Duns Scotus (*ca.*1266–1308) defined a concept of intrinsic individuation with respect to material objects that he called *haecceitas* (literally, 'thisness'). The concept goes deeper than that of the individuality of a thing given by Aquinas. To Scotus, there is a distinctive quality that is intrinsic in each object, and the *haecceitas* of the human organism is our soul. According to the *Catholic Dictionary of Theology*, Scotus was the first to champion the view of the Immaculate Conception of Mary as fundamental to Christian belief, though the doctrine did not become an article of faith in the Catholic Church until 1854. Scotus is said to have had a vision of Mary with the infant Jesus on Christmas night in 1299. He advanced a complex criticism of Aquinas' Five Ways to proof of God's existence because they were based on observed facts about the universe and were therefore contingent, that is, not necessarily true like the deductions of logic. Born in the village of Duns in Berwickshire, Scotland, he studied and lectured at Oxford and Cambridge, and in Paris. His birthplace and the almost incomprehensible complexity of his arguments have given rise to the now pejorative word 'dunce' in the English language.

William Ockham (or Occam; *ca.*1285–1347), so-called after his probable birthplace, Ockham in Surrey, was a Franciscan who studied at Oxford sometime in the early 14th Century. He suggested that any statement should not be regarded as true unless it is self-evident, or it can be verified by sensory experience, or by reasoning, or is known by divine insight; or it can be derived by reasoning from observation or revelational experience. This conforms to the accepted sources of knowledge: empiricism, rationalism or revelation. It has been suggested that this is the true meaning of 'Occam's Razor' [67] rather than the Principle of Parsimony with which his name is usually associated: the simplest explanation is most probably the correct one, or, to give the version that is a more literal translation of his Latin, 'beings ought not to be multiplied except out of necessity'. William also advocated the authority of scripture over that of the pope, as did many theologians after the Reformation. He even suggested that the pope himself was guilty of heresy in the stand he took over the question of poverty within the Church hierarchy. This called into question the authority of the pope to govern the Church if he was not infallible. It is not surprising therefore that he was accused of heresy and summoned to Avignon, home of the exiled pope, to explain himself.

Thomas Bradwardine (*ca.*1295–1349) was born in Chichester, Sussex. As Proctor at Oxford in 1325/6, he was instrumental in securing independence for the university from Episcopal authority. He became Archbishop of Canterbury in 1348, but died of the plague the following year. He explained the existence of human free will compatible with the prescience of God by saying that although people are inspired by God in their actions, already known to God, they are not aware of his having done so and are hence free agents. This is totally compatible with the view presented in this book that mind events, especially those involving spiritual, mystical or inspirational experience, are derived from resonance between the individual and the universal spiritual field. Apart from his theological work, Bradwardine also wrote treatises on mathematics – in geometry (*Geometria speculativa*) and in mechanics (*Tractaus de proportionibus*). In his derivation of a formula for uniform acceleration in terms of initial and final speeds, Bradwardine was perhaps the first to express physical concepts in terms of mathematics, several centuries before Newton.

Some medieval theologians saw human spiritual history as recorded in the Bible in terms of three Ages: the Old Testament represented the Age of the Father; the New Testament recorded the Age of the Son (or one might say the age of the prophets for non-Christians); evolving into a Third Age, the Age of the Holy Spirit. Rupert of Deutz (*ca.*1075–*ca.*1130), Anselm of Havelberg (*ca.*1100–1158) and Joachim of Fiore (*ca.*1125–1202) were the main protagonists of this view. This is interesting because of its resonances with the modern situation of an increasing awareness of the spiritual dimension of the world, which is discussed in Chapters 6 and 7.

3.3.   Medieval Islamic philosophers

The Persian philosopher and physician, Abu Ali ibn Sina or Avicenna (980–1037 CE), wrote of logic, medicine and the natural sciences, but unfortunately most of what he wrote has been lost. However, his most famous medical work was used extensively in Arabic and Latin translation in Islam and Christendom for several centuries. Avicenna never doubted that it was possible to establish the existence of God by human reason.

Another of the early medieval theological philosophers of significance was Abū Hāmid al Ghazzāli (1059–1111 CE), a professor of religion in Baghdad, who sought in his writings to place the mystical faith of the Sūfis at the heart of Islamic belief. In his work *The Incoherence of the Philosophers* he made a passionate attack on both the reverence for the philosophical arguments of Plato and Aristotle and on Christian belief. He never believed it was possible to establish the existence of a Supreme Being by reason alone. Amongst the twenty chapters of his attack were that he deplored 'the vanity of their assertion that the world had no beginning and that it will have no end'; 'their denial of the Divine attributes'; 'their inability to prove that the world has a maker and a cause'; 'their assertion that the souls of the heavens know all particulars', undermining some of the key tenets of Christian belief.

However, al-Ghazzāli's views were not universally accepted. Averroes, Abu al-Walid ibn Ahmad ibn Rushd (1126–1198 CE), like Maimonides, who was one of his pupils, and ibn Daud was born in Cordoba. He eventually became a judge there, after serving in the same capacity in Seville, but died in exile at Marrakesh, Morocco.

Averroes used Aristotelian and Neoplatonic logic to take issue with each of the points made by al-Ghazzāli in his book *Incoherence of the Incoherence*. This work was of such significance that it was translated into Latin and into Hebrew in the 14th Century. He also wrote on astronomy, with some criticism of the ideas of Ptolemy on his geocentric theory. In his theological philosophy Averroes affirmed the later Greek philosophical contention that the world was infinite and eternal; otherwise, God would have had to make a decision in time to create the world, which would have involved a change in God, which was unthinkable in Islam. However, as Thomas Aquinas puts it: 'From eternity God willed that the world should be, but he did not will that it should be from eternity.' [quoted in ref. 219], returning to the earlier Greek philosophy of a finite universe. If the universe was infinite and eternal, this would remove the need for the role of God as Creator in Christian theology. These three philosophers represent the pinnacle of medieval Islamic academic theology, but there were others too of lesser standing.

*   *   *

We have seen, in this chapter, how medieval philosophers from the three principal religions of the West – Judaism, Christianity and Islam – expended much effort in reconciling Greek rationalism with the divine revelations of their respective faiths. One Christian scholar from the early Middle Ages who was active in this regard was Johannes Scotus Erigena (*ca*.810-877). He believed passionately that faith and reason were not mutually exclusive and that philosophy could be used as a means of establishing the existence of God. Before we move on to look at the science that emerged in the Renaissance we should just briefly explore the historical development of the cultural systems in Europe between the time of the Greeks and the Renaissance.

During the years that philosophy and drama flourished in ancient Greece, the country, specifically Athens, was constantly at war, especially with Persia and even with Sparta, the most powerful state of the Peloponnese in the southernmost region of Greece. Architecture and sculpture flourished too – the temples of the Acropolis, including the Parthenon, were built in the 5th Century BCE, as was the temple of Poseidon in Attica at the time when Democritus, Protagoras and Hippocrates were creating ideas that shaped Western civilisation and Sophocles, Euripides and Aristophanes were entertaining the *theatai* (audience). The conquests of Alexander the Great (356-323 BCE), a pupil of Aristotle's, represented the acme of the Hellenic empire. With his death the Empire fragmented into self-administered states once more.

The foundation of what was to become the Roman Empire was being laid in the 7th Century BCE, long before the supremacy of Athens in the Mediterranean region. At this time, several independent communities in the region around Rome gathered together to form a single city state as a monarchy that lasted just over a century. The first king was Lucius Tarquinius Priscus (king from 616 to 578) and the last, Tarquinius Superbus, who ruled from 534 to 509 BCE. With his assassination, Rome became a republic in 509 BCE. Over the next two centuries, the influence of Rome spread ever wider until the Empire occupied the whole of Western Europe and much of the Middle East, surviving for nearly a thousand years.

Ironically, it was the Roman Emperor Constantine (ruling from 316 to 361 CE) who, having done so much to establish Christianity in Europe to consolidate the Empire, then contributed significantly to its downfall by establishing his administrative centre in Byzantium at the city that was named Constantinople. In many respects, he was a feeble ruler, but this was not the only factor that led to the crumbling of the dominance of Rome. Subsequent internal power struggles and material decay together with pressure from the barbarian hordes to the north brought about the final collapse. According to Gibbon [209], Rome was sacked by the Frankish Visigoths under Alaric in 476 CE.

The Goths, Visigoths and Vandals overran Europe for the next three centuries. By the beginning of the 5th Century, the Vandals, originating from Scandinavia, had occupied much of the lands around the Mediterranean, including Spain and Italy. Many Visigoths remained, some converting to the local religions. As Arians, the Vandals might well have thought that theirs was an act of piety in displacing the barbarians, but they were just as ruthless in conquest.

We saw in Chapter 1 that the Islamic faith began with Mohammed (*ca.*570-632) in Medina after the Prophet was forced to flee from his home in Mecca. After his death, the faith was administered by the four Rightly Guided Caliphs (Arabic: *khalifa* – successor): Abu Bakr (632-634); Umar (634-644); Uthman (644-656); and Ali (656-661). Ali was cousin and son-in-law to the Prophet and was his choice as successor. It was Ali's second son, Hussain, and his supporters who formed the Shi'ite faction of Islam, believing that the faith should be ruled by descendants of the Prophet. When Ali was assassinated, a new dynasty began to rule Islam, the Umayyads, the first of whom was Mu'awiyah. He was the Governor of Syria and based in Damascus, so this became the centre of Islam. The Umayyads survived for less than a century before the ruling royal family was massacred in 750 – except for one, whom we shall meet shortly. The new Caliphate was assumed by followers of a descendant of Abbas, one of the Prophet's uncles, and they took his name – Abbasids. With the new dynasty, the centre of operations moved to Baghdad in Iraq. Umayyads and Abbasids expanded the influence of Islam throughout Europe and the Middle East, but both dynasties were as interested in cultural development as they were in military conquest. They established libraries of ancient texts to an extent not seen in the region since before the dawn of the Christian era. The followers of these dynasties believe that the faith should be ruled by the most authoritative of the elders, following the *Qu'ran* and the commentary on it, the *Sunnah*, which also perpetuates the oral traditions of the faith. These are the Sunni Muslims, who represent the majority 80-90% of the adherents of Islam, the Shi'ites representing the remainder.

While this power struggle progressed in the Middle East, another group of Muslims in North Africa, the Berbers, invaded Spain in 711 and subsequently Sicily and Italy from 827. They named Spain, the Land of the Vandals, al-Andalus. It was in 755 that the only survivor of the Umayyad royal family, Abd al-Rahman, turned up in Spain to settle in Cordoba. From there, under his leadership, another arm of the Muslim Empire developed, again with emphasis on culture but with religious harmony. It was in this environment that Jewish, Christian and Islamic scholars worked together, side-by-side, free of persecution, to bring the scholarship of the ancient world to Christendom. This state of collaboration was known locally as *convivencia*. Here, art, architecture, philosophy, theology and science flourished, nourished by work that continued in Damascus and Baghdad. For example, the book on mathematics by al-Khwarizmi of Baghdad in the 8th Century, *Al-jabr wa'l muqabalah*, became so popular throughout Europe that the name of one of the most important branches of mathematics, algebra, is derived from it. In later centuries the centre of learning in Spain moved from Cordoba to Toledo and on to Granada and Seville, the last bastion of Islamic scholarship before the territory was seized by the Christians in 1492. The crusades against Islam were initiated in 1095 by Pope Urban II (*ca.*1042-99; pope from 1088) and the Christians gradually took control of Spain over the next four centuries as the Islamic rule was weakened by in-fighting.

Without the cultural attitude of the Islamic Empire in Europe for some six centuries, scholarship in Christendom would probably never have recovered the treasures of the ancient world that the early Church did its best to eradicate. Thus Greek philosophy had an enormous influence over the medieval theology of the Jews, Muslims and Christians, and over many of the ideas of the scientists who began to emerge in the period we call the Enlightenment, and whose work we shall consider next.

4 The beginnings of science and its influence on post-Renaissance thought

'Man is the measure of all things': so began Protagoras in his book on *Truth* in the 5th Century BCE and he was expressing a view that permeated the society of ancient Greece. But with the decline of the Roman Empire that followed that of the Greeks, some four centuries after the time of Jesus, for the next thousand years, this attitude of mind was largely forgotten while philosophers concentrated their thoughts on the existence and nature of God and His role in the world. The religious scholars of the West, from whom society took its lead, had a traditional disdain for worldly affairs. Imbued as they were with the Christian ideas of the innate sinfulness of Man through Adam, they shut themselves away in their monasteries to debate these academic issues while the peasantry of Europe got on with the routines of everyday existence, which revolved around the monastery. As we saw in Chapter 3, there was an expansion in the mendicant orders: the Dominicans and Franciscans were established at this time. Availability of the writings of the Greek philosophers in Latin for the first time opened up a whole new world of rationalism for the Christian theological scholars – but also conflicts with revealed scripture that needed to be resolved.

In the 11th and 12th centuries, the population of Europe grew rapidly and the people had to be fed and clothed. The situation demanded the attention of the clerics. Forests were cleared and marsh lands reclaimed for agriculture, as a result of which, new towns became established, many of them built around magnificent new cathedrals and castles, or existing monasteries. The Normans, who colonised Britain at this time, were particularly vigorous developers. As a result of the Crusades, European trade expanded eastwards, with Christian merchants now following the routes of their Muslim predecessors. As population grew, and a new middle or merchant class emerged in Continental Europe, people found the dimensions of their daily lives expanding. They began increasingly to focus their attention on the needs of this life as well as preparing themselves for the life to come. This new attitude of mind generated a surge of mental, spiritual and practical creative activity.

This was the setting for the development of science and the humanities in western civilisation that comprises the cultural revolution that we call the Renaissance, where once again Protagoras's world view became dominant. The Renaissance movement began in Italy, and most notably in Florence, in the 13th to 14th Century. Italy was located geographically at the junction of important trading routes, a centre of commerce and banking; it was the home of some of the first universities, and within that country lay the seat of the Holy Catholic Church. All these factors probably played their part in the cultural revolution.

Many aspects of life began to change: there was a rediscovered sense of the joy of living through sensuousness, naturalism and realism to replace the idealism and asceticism of the medieval period; experimentation, observation and rational interpretation became a basis for the acquisition of knowledge where before there had been authoritarian obscurantism; the knowledge acquired itself opened up still further avenues for exploration. However, the changes were gradual and occurred over many centuries, subsequently embracing many different revolutions.

With the emergence of the Renaissance, the re-birth of knowledge and Man's freedom of expression, the field of scientific discovery burgeoned from around 1500 CE. After some 3000 years when religion was taken as providing answers to the great questions of life, with a mere 500 years or so of Greek rationalism in the years before Jesus, gradually it was science – empirical knowledge underpinned with mathematical theory – that came to be regarded as giving us solutions to the mysteries of human existence. Many of the discoveries of the scientists made literal acceptance of the events described in the Bible impossible. It is difficult for us today to imagine the disquiet this information must have caused even to the scientists, let alone the lay public. Some theologians, even early writers that had greatly influenced the Christian Church, like Philo, Origen, and Augustine, and the medieval Jewish Kabbalists, urged that the Bible should be treated as myth and allegory. However, the Christian Church in this Renaissance period, both Catholic and Protestant, insisted that the events described in the Bible were literally true, thereby further undermining the credibility of the Christian religion.

The existence of God may only be unequivocally ascertained by transcendental or mystical experience, but it can be supported, even if not proven in the mathematical or logical sense, by rational argument. The Flemish Jesuit priest, Leonard Lessius (1554–1623) was a Catholic scholar noted for his views on predestination and justice, and his work on providence and immortality of the soul, *De Providentia Numinis* of 1613, was translated into several other European languages and even into Chinese. But he too was caught up in the excitement of the new scientific age and in *The Divine Providence* seemed to regard God as another facet of the natural world, the existence of which was to be explained as with any other aspect of Nature. Lessius considered the existence of God as Creator and Sustainer logically self-evident from the existence and order of the world (the Cosmological and Design Arguments again!), even before any of the complexities of the laws of physics had begun to be unravelled.

Richard Hooker (1554–1600), a close contemporary of Lessius and a well respected English theologian, maintained that God's purposes for Man are accessible by human reason without divine revelation. However, reason is limited to investigation of the natural world and Hooker disagreed with Lessius in asserting that reason is not competent to investigate God or soul: these were concepts that were accessible only by faith or revelation (fideism). His masterpiece, *The*

Laws of Ecclesiastical Polity, published in 1593, upheld the validity of the new Church of England: the first Archbishop of Canterbury in the new Church, Matthew Parker, had been appointed only in 1559 after Henry VIII's dissolution of the monasteries. He also tried to chart a middle way in religious politics between the attitude of the Church of Rome in asserting the equal primacy of scripture and tradition and that of the Calvinist Puritans who regarded the Bible as sole authority.

Legend has it that the Italian mathematician, astronomer and physicist Galileo Galilei (1564–1642) noticed the regular oscillations of a lamp in Pisa cathedral, and this awakened his interest in studying mathematics and the laws of the physical world. Largely self-taught, he rose to become Professor of Mathematics at Padua University. Using the telescope he had invented, Galileo made observations on the motion of sunspots across the face of the sun that confirmed what the Polish astronomer Nicolaus Copernicus (1473–1543) had said: that the sun was the centre of the orbits of Earth and the other planets, not Earth. The so-called geocentric theory putting Earth at the centre of our solar system seems to have been suggested first by Eudoxus of Cnidus (409–356 BCE); it was taken up by Heraclides (*fl.* 4th Century BCE) and then expounded in much greater detail with mathematical justification by Claudius Ptolemy (85–165 CE), a Greek astronomer of Alexandria. The geocentric theory, with planets moving around Earth in perfect circles, was preferred by the Church fathers, like Isidore of Seville (*ca.*560–636 CE), in the early centuries because it put Earth and humankind, the greatest of God's creations, at the centre of the universe, and the circle was a perfectly symmetrical shape. This thereby became the official view of the Church for over a thousand years; so Copernicus' theory brought him into direct conflict with established Church doctrine. Fortunately, Copernicus was rather reticent about publishing his heliocentric theory, probably because he knew it would meet with a hostile reception from the Church. In fact, Copernicus' work *De revolutionibus orbium coelestium* was not published until 1543, the year of his death, and then only as a result of the efforts of one of his students. So Galileo, like Copernicus, was equally cautious about making his astronomical observations public.

King Ferdinand V of Aragon and Queen Isabella of Castille, who married in 1469, instigated the Spanish Inquisition in 1492, following the expulsion of the Arabian conquerors from Granada. But many other purges of non-believers (that is, non-adherents of the Church of Rome) were set up by various popes both before and after this date: like those of Pope Innocent IV in 1252, and that of Pope Paul III in 1542. Their purpose was to monitor that anything that was written was acceptable to the orthodoxy of the Church of Rome. The tribunal had the power not only of censorship but also of excommunication and even execution of those who refused to recant their beliefs. The Italian theological philosopher Giordano Bruno (1548–1600) was burnt at the stake for heresy because of his publications. Many Jews and Muslims rapidly 'converted' to Christianity – or, like Spinoza's ancestors (see Section 6.1), moved away from Spain and Italy to countries like Holland that were more tolerant of 'heretical' views! Bruno had spent his life moving around Europe to avoid persecution. By this time, Catholicism was already on the defensive against the rise of Protestantism, which is generally regarded as beginning with Martin Luther's nailing of his 95 theses of protest to the door of Wittenberg Castle church in 1517. So the Church was very sensitive to any critical publications.

Nevertheless, Galileo did publish his *Letters on the Sunspots* in 1613 and, as a result, in 1616 he had to appear before the Inquisition. He survived this encounter and in 1632 was even allowed, under licence from the Pope himself, to publish a comparison of the two prevailing theories of the Earth's motion – *Dialogue Concerning the Two Chief Systems of the World* – though coming down clearly on the side of Copernicus. The Jesuits thought the publication would do more to undermine Catholic dogma than the accusations of Luther and Calvin put together. For this publication, Galileo was denounced to the Inquisition again for 'blasphemous utterances'; he subsequently stood trial in 1633, was forced to recant his observations, and was sentenced to house arrest on his small estate near Florence for the rest of his life. That same year, 1633, French philosopher René Descartes wisely abandoned his plan to publish his own book, *The World*, because it too supported Copernicus. It was 1992 before the Vatican apologised for its treatment of Galileo. However, as a result of his persecution, Galileo had time to work on some of his earlier observations in mechanics, like the oscillating lamp in Pisa cathedral. He subsequently used these observations to make a pendulum to regulate clockwork, and the Dutch physicist and astronomer Christiaan Huyghens (1629–1695) was able to put this into practice in 1656 with the first mechanical clock. Galileo is also usually credited with being the first to construct a thermometer, though the mercury-in-glass instrument of 1714 invented by the German Gabriel Fahrenheit (1686–1736) was the first of real practical importance.

Meanwhile in England, a contemporary of Galileo's, Francis Bacon (1561–1626), Viscount Verulamium, Lord Chancellor of England, was advocating greater investigation of the workings of Nature so that it could be exploited for the benefit of humankind. This may be seen as an inspiration to the philosophy of the Industrial Revolution. He was not interested in knowledge for its own sake, nor did he believe that a study of Nature would in some way lead us to knowledge of the divine: 'We do not presume by the contemplation of nature to attain to the mysteries of God ... Divers great learned men have been heretical, whilst they have sought to fly up to the secrets of the Deity by the waxen wings of the senses' [quoted in ref. 391]. He had little time for mathematics, however, because this could not be put to obvious and immediate practical use. Astronomy was similarly disregarded as being of little or no utility. He did however stress the importance of public dissemination of investigations of Nature, as opposed to the secrecy surrounding occult practices, and emphasised the need for open criticism of results [36].

In *The Advancement of Learning* (1605), and its much expanded Latin version nearly two decades later – the *De Dignitate et Augmentis Scientiarum* of 1623 – he defined what has come to be known as 'the scientific method' of observation, theory and experiment. He wanted Nature studied by experimentation to seek out 'crucial instances' that would distinguish the true from the false. With this publication he also ushered in the age of *reductionism* – the breaking down of complex systems into their simpler constituent parts so that these could be studied individually, with the tacit assumption that they would perform in exactly the same way when they were part of the system as a whole. *The Advancement of Learning* also set out a classification of knowledge that has had a great influence on the way libraries and encyclopaedias are arranged. Of anecdotal interest: Bacon's doctor was William Harvey (1578–1657), the physician who discovered the circulation of the blood.

In the early 20th Century there was a group of philosophers in Vienna called the 'logical positivists'. They were emphatically empiricist in their outlook believing, like Bacon, that only that which could be personally observed with the senses or established by deduction could be regarded as true. They therefore dismissed all the fundamental tenets of religion as superstition or, as philosopher of science, Karl Popper, puts it so graphically in his book *The Logic of Scientific Discovery*: 'metaphysics by its very nature is nothing but nonsensical twaddle' [379]. The views of the Vienna Circle were endorsed and popularised by the English philosopher Alfred .J. Ayer in his book *Language, Truth and Logic* [32]. In his criticism of religious belief in his opening chapter on 'The elimination of metaphysics', Ayer maintains that 'the assertion that fictitious objects have a special non-empirical mode of real being is devoid of all literal significance' [33]. However, all of this argument in favour of empiricism is based on the assumption that the five senses are all that humans possess and it ignores the very real sixth sense that has served humankind, as far as we are aware, since its very origins.

This criterion of *verification* was regarded as the essential demand for the establishment of the truth of statements about the world. The Vienna Circle were much influenced by the 1921 publication of *Tractatus Logico-Philosophicus* by Ludwig Wittgenstein (1889–1951), who likewise asserted that truth can only be established by empirical verification. Karl Popper, one of the Vienna Circle, fell out with the group over this insistence on verification since he believed that *falsification* – finding just one negative instance of an event – was of far more significance than innumerable instances of verification. However, he was not the first to assert this: Francis Bacon had done so previously in his *Novum Organum* (1620): 'in establishing any true axiom the negative instance is the more powerful' [37].

This last work also contained Bacon's 'doctrine of the idols' – an account of the various ways the human mind is led into error, which Bacon distinguished as the idols of the tribe (fallibility of humankind in general), idols of the cave (individual susceptibility to error), idols of the market (errors in use and interpretation of language), and idols of the theatre (mistakes induced by following established systems of thinking in philosophy or science). Several, and perhaps all, of these 'idols' are relevant to the presumed validity of scriptures, where recording by scribes will be coloured by their veneration for their spiritual leader, and cannot fail to be influenced by the prevailing cultural tenor of the society in which they work; and where successive translators must interpret every word in each context in producing their versions of text. Using Bacon's principles, it is logically untenable that such a huge body of men working over so very many generations will produce an accurate account of the words and actions of the founders of the various religions.

One of the first great British scientists to be inspired by Bacon's enthusiasm for the study of Nature was the English physical scientist and mathematician Isaac Newton (1642–1727), son of an illiterate pagan father and a Christian mother. He was born into turbulent times in England during the reign of Charles I, with hostilities between Puritans and Catholics, and between Royalists and Parliamentarians rampant. Newton's father died two months before he was born, on Christmas Day in 1642; his mother remarried shortly after and went to live with her new husband, so he was brought up by his grandmother. Though he was an indifferent scholar at first, in his teenage years he occupied his mind with mathematics while working on the family farm at Woolsthorpe near Grantham in Lincolnshire. He completed a B.A. degree at Cambridge University in 1665 and two years later was made a fellow of Trinity College, where his uncle was a tutor. Because he was not an orthodox Christian he had to have special dispensation in order to hold his posts at Cambridge – at a time when all university teachers were members of the clergy or at least practicing and avowed Christians. However, the spread of the Great Plague in 1665 forced closure of the college and Newton was sent home to Woolsthorpe.

In the 18 months between then and the spring of 1667, when the college reopened, the seeds were planted of most of the discoveries in mathematics, mechanics and optics for which Newton is now remembered, though many did not come to fruition for some time. In mathematics, he established the binomial theorem, which is used today constantly in statistics to work out the probabilities of one of two possible events occurring. He created a method, which was subsequently developed by Joseph Raphson (1648–1715), for finding approximate solutions to higher order algebraic equations. But the most significant of his discoveries in this field was the evolution of the method of the calculus to measure rates of change (differential calculus) and summation of areas and volumes (integral calculus). The calculus unites concepts of space and time, and was a momentous creation, but because Newton was secretive and introverted by nature, he kept his discoveries to himself. His work was not generally known until much later, after similar concepts using different notation had been elaborated, more or less simultaneously as it was subsequently revealed, by the German philosopher Leibniz. By the age of 27, Newton had become Lucasian Professor of Mathematics at Cambridge, and was the youngest ever to hold the post.

In mechanics, Newton formalised some of the discoveries of Galileo. He amplified the three laws of motion described by Galileo from his observation of falling objects. In his second law of motion, Newton was able to define and provide a mathematical formula for this new concept of *force* that produces acceleration in an object. A *force* represents an interaction between two or more objects, and the region in which this force acts is designated as a *field*, as defined by Michael Faraday (see below). Newton stated precisely the law of gravitation governing the motion of the planets around the sun: he showed that all objects attract each other with a force that is directly proportional to their *mass* (a concept that Newton also introduced and defined) and is inversely proportional to the square of their distance apart. This disposed of Descartes' theory of spinning vortices producing planetary motion. These definitions, calculations and explanations were finally published in the book called, briefly, *Principia*, published in three parts from 1687. Newton's friend and supporter, Edmund Halley (1656–1742), later astronomer royal, undertook publication of the first edition at his own expense at the recommendation of the Royal Society.

In the field of optics (*Opticks*, 1704), Newton explained how the spectrum of colours produced from white light by passing the light through a prism was due to different speeds of the constituent colours. This provided a precise explanation of the formation of the colours of a rainbow; Roger Bacon (see Chapter 3) had already suggested that the colours were due to sunlight passing through raindrops in the air, but had attributed the phenomenon to God. Newton proposed a theory that light was made up of particles (the *corpuscular theory*) to complement the *wave theory* introduced by Robert Hooke in 1665 and Christiaan Huyghens in 1678. Newton's corpuscular theory soon went out of fashion, but had to be revived in 1905 when Einstein published his Nobel Prize-winning work on the photoelectric effect; it was substantiated still further by ideas in quantum mechanics in the 1920s (see Chapter 8). Newton modified the design of a telescope to reduce the optical defect known as chromatic aberration – the fact that lenses bend the components of white light by different amounts and produce a fuzzy image: where Galileo's telescope had used refraction, Newton's had used reflection.

The time when Newton was confined to Woolsthorpe was almost certainly one of the most productive 18–month periods in the history of scientific discovery, though the seeds of these discoveries were not to germinate and flower for many years yet. Newton was reluctant to put his discoveries before the newly inaugurated Royal Society of London that had been founded in 1662 because he feared acrimonious criticism. Their Curator of Experiments, a physicist called Robert Hooke (1635–1703), discoverer of the law of elasticity that bears his name, was an enemy of Newton's because he had his own theory of colour, different from Newton's, and subsequently to be proved totally incorrect. The two men also disagreed on the nature of light – waves or particles? On Hooke's death in March 1703, Newton was elected President of the Royal Society and thereafter he became more socially adept and asserted his undoubted scientific authority. The departure of the Catholic King James and accession of the Protestant monarchs William and Mary in 1689 created a more relaxed environment in which to express views that might not accord with Catholic theology. Newton was so comfortable with his new-found social circle, which included philosopher John Locke and diarist Samuel Pepys as well as Edmund Halley, that he became a Member of Parliament. In 1696 he was made first Warden and then Master of the Royal Mint.

As well as his work in mathematics, mechanics, optics and astronomy, Newton had a lifelong interest in alchemy and, in the latter half of his life, made a serious study of theology. He believed that in establishing laws of planetary motion he had achieved proof of the existence of God. Newton, like other scientists of his day, explored the natural world to uncover God's grandeur. An understanding of Nature in scientific terms in no way lessens its intoxicating beauty or its capacity for providing spiritual uplift, just as the analysis of a poem or piece of music can deepen the appreciation of the reader or listener, for it engages the rational mind as well as the soul. As Paul Davies says: 'In Renaissance Europe, the justification for what we today call the scientific approach to enquiry was the belief in a rational God whose created order could be discerned from a careful study of nature.' [135]. This idea is echoed by Alister McGrath in commenting on 'the deeply religious worldview of the medieval and Renaissance periods; [this] ensured that even the most 'secular' of activities – whether economic, political or scientific – were saturated with the themes of Christian theology.' [339]. Newton however wanted to rid the worship of God of what he saw as distorting excrescences, like the Trinity and the deification of Jesus. Like Arius, Newton rejected the divinity of Jesus. The first authorised version of the Bible in English had appeared only in 1611 at the behest of Catholic King James, so the revelatory world-view of scripture was only just becoming widely available in England, at a time when both Protestantism and scientific discovery were just burgeoning. Newton's serious and extensive studies during the 1670s of early Christian literature led him to conclude that there were many additions and deletions made by the Church fathers – an idea for which there is an increasing amount of evidence today [see Chapter 1 and references therein]. Newton immersed himself in the controversies that had occupied the attentions of the medieval philosophers, trying to reconcile Greek philosophy (particularly that of Aristotle) with theological principles. Newton's theology was certainly not Christian – more that of an emphatic monotheist, or perhaps pantheist.

The German philosopher, mathematician and diplomat, Gottfried Wilhelm Leibniz (1646–1716), was born in Leipzig. He did not develop any one philosophical system and wrote no seminal treatise, like his fellow continental European rationalists, Descartes and Spinoza, but rather wrote a number of philosophical tracts on various subjects. However, it was in his mathematics that Leibniz made his most significant contributions to posterity. The system of the calculus that he invented, at much the same time as Newton but independently, is the one preferred today over Newton's Method of Fluxions. Leibniz discovered the basic principles of topology to complement, as he saw it, the analytical or algebraic geometry of Descartes. Though the discovery was ignored at the time, it has had a huge impact on the development of non-Euclidean geometries (geometries not confined to one plane) in the 20th Century and their applications. On a trip to London in January of 1673, Leibniz presented to the Royal Society (that had been formed only in 1660–62) the prototype of a calculating machine, which subsequently led to the more sophisticated calculators and computers we know today. His redevelopment of binary arithmetic (representing all numbers by combinations of the digits 1 and 0) provided the language used to program computers today. He did much to lobby for the setting up of scientific academies similar to the Royal Society in Germany at the turn of the century. Interestingly, in his science, Leibniz postulated that matter was no more than a concentration of energy or motion, an idea we shall meet again in Chapter 8, since once again it accords with 20th Century quantum physics.

In 1714 Leibniz published a tract called *Monadology*. His concept of a monad was of an entity that was simple, without parts and comprised 'the elements of things' [315]. These monads are eternal, for 'there is no way in which a simple substance could begin in the course of nature' [316]. We also have that 'every monad must be different from every other' and that 'the natural changes of monads come from an *internal principle*' [317]. Each of these monads exhibits perception (awareness of its surroundings) but not consciousness [319]. In effect, therefore, Leibniz' monads possess many of the properties now associated with atoms, and Leibniz identifies them as such: 'monads are the true atoms of nature' [314]. He even goes on to say that 'there must be differentiation within that which changes', and that '[this] differentiation must involve a plurality within the unity or the simple' [318]: again, a picture of subatomic particles within the atom. And all of this was a century before Dalton's Atomic Theory and two centuries before it was discovered that atoms were still not the most fundamental particles of matter. We are told [320] that 'each created monad represents the whole universe' – a precursor to David Bohm's implicate order concept of each component encapsulating the whole in coded form (see Chapter 8). Much of what Leibniz envisaged in his world of monads pre-empts the properties of atoms that have been elaborated in 20th Century physics, but with a spiritual dimension.

In the generation after Newton and Leibniz, Emanuel Swedenborg (1688–1772) was born in Stockholm. His father, Jesper Swedberg, was a Lutheran pastor, who became Professor of Theology at Uppsala University and, from 1702, Bishop of Skara, a sparsely populated region some 200 kilometres south-west of Stockholm. He is remembered today in Skara for his interest in, and influence on, education in the region. When his father was appointed to Skara, young Swedenborg stayed in Uppsala to complete his studies at the university until his graduation in 1709. He stayed with his sister and her husband, Eric Benzelius, the librarian at the university. Benzelius was a brilliant man with a keen interest in science who rose to become Bishop of Linköping. These two men, his father and Benzelius, were the formative influences on young Swedenborg and they contributed to the development of his rational approach to interpretation of the Bible, informed by his personal revelationary experiences: 'First the doctrinal things of the church must be learned, and then the words must be examined to see if these are true; because they are not true because the heads of the church have said so and their followers confirm it, because in this way the doctrinal things of all churches and religions would have to be called true' [466]. This was a highly perceptive comment to make in a world long before our current multi-culturalism and awareness of the great varieties of religious experience: 'The means of salvation have been provided for everyone, and heaven is such that all who live well, of whatever religion they may be, have a place there' [467].

Swedenborg was a polymath, a scholar of science, mathematics, cosmology, physiology, and engineering before he abandoned his science in the early 1740s to turn his attention to philosophy and theology after experiencing a series of visions. Despite the breadth of his knowledge, he preferred to base his conclusions on the evidence gathered by others who were experts in their respective fields: 'I therefore laid aside my instruments ... and determined rather to rely on the researches of others than to trust to my own' [468]. In physiology, he was the first to recognise the nature of the cerebrospinal fluid that bathes the central nervous system. In chemistry he created a picture of matter as consisting of atoms, entities that were themselves composed of subatomic particles that existed as spinning vortices: this was fifty years before Dalton's Atomic Theory and a century before Lord Kelvin proposed his spinning vortices theory of atoms (see Chapters 2 and 8). With his spiritual approach to the nature of matter, Swedenborg maintained that 'for anything to exist it must be continually created and sustained from within itself' [466] and also that 'every point must contain infinite energy within itself'. These are ideas that emerged again amongst 20th Century physicists with the quantum theory of matter, Einstein's Special Relativity Theory with its mass-energy relationship, and particularly with David Bohm's idea of implicate order (see Chapter 8). In harmony with the Eastern *Advaita* philosophy of Sankara (788–820), Swedenborg taught the underlying unity of all creation. He also maintained that 'there is no such thing as chance, and apparent accident or fortune is Providence in the ultimate of order' [466]. Swiss psychoanalyst Carl Jung was also to see 'chance' or 'coincidence' or 'serendipity' as manifestations of the universal spiritual energy (see Chapter 7).

The *Arcane Celestia*, though published anonymously at the time, was Swedenborg's first public declaration of his own spiritual revelations. He believed that the world was embarking on a new era of understanding of the divine, the age of the New Jerusalem. The central idea was an endorsement of thoroughgoing monotheism, and a revision of the role of Jesus. Swedenborg saw this as the Second Advent – a new image of God and Jesus: the enactment of the fundamental principle of living for the good of others, rather than a physical re-appearance of the Messiah on Earth. He is telling us that we should actually live the principles exemplified by the life of Jesus: 'No one can be said to repent unless he actually separates himself from those things of which he has repented' [466]; 'The loves of self and of the world constitute hell with man' [466]. Swedenborg's concepts of heaven and hell correspond to those presented in this book – they are states of bliss and torment in this life, and experienced in even more vivid fashion in the afterlife, produced respectively by living a life of selfish and materialist gratification or living a life dedicated to the wellbeing of others. 'The kingdom of heaven is within' and 'heaven is within the internal man' [466]: do we hear in these expressions the concept of the soul as 'God in Us', as presented by Anthony Freeman (see Chapter 7)? But we are told that 'heaven is not the same in one as in another' [469], thus preserving the uniqueness and individuality of the human soul – the *haecceitas* of Duns Scotus (Chapter 3). For

Swedenborg, the Trinity comprises God the Father as infinite and eternal creative energy; Jesus as the embodiment of divine qualities in human form; and the Holy Spirit as an all-pervading divine energy flowing from God the Creator – three aspects of the one God. There is also a divine Trinity in the love, wisdom and ongoing activity of God. This is rather different from the orthodox Christian view of the Trinity, either Protestant or Catholic.

The divine participates in the daily affairs of humankind because anything that Man does or creates is a reflection of his thoughts and feelings, and these in turn emanate from the mind of God: 'The things that are in the spiritual world can be seen as in a mirror from those that come into existence in the natural world' [469]. This Swedenborg calls his Law of Correspondences which 'applies universally to all created forms, linking them every instant to the corresponding form on the next higher level from which they receive their existence' [452]. This recalls the notions of Bishop George Berkeley earlier in the 18th Century, that we owe our sensory experiences to ideas in the mind of God, and that these perceptions define existence (see Chapter 7); the notion also recalls the writings of Plato about the immaterial world of the Ideas or Forms shaping our human concepts in the world of reason and experience (see Chapter 2). We hear echoes of Moses ben Maimon (Chapter 3) in Swedenborg's assertion: 'The Divine is infinite, and of the Infinite nothing can be said except that It Is' [466]; 'Nevertheless, the concept of the Infinite, as in mathematics, can and should have an important place in our intuitive perception' [466]. A Church of the New Jerusalem was founded around 1784 in America by his followers.

Swedenborg's clairvoyance (see Chapter 6) was only one aspect of his mysticism, though his expression of his experiences was that of a rational scientist rather than the somewhat dreamy and enigmatic expression of the true mystic. Nevertheless, he advocated the necessity of going beyond the material world of the senses if we were to ever experience a glimpse of ultimate reality: 'There are two things proper to Nature – space and time. It is from these that man in the natural world forms the ideas of his thought and thence of his understanding. If he remains in these ideas and does not raise his mind above them, he can never perceive anything divine [470].

Though some of Swedenborg's observations and conclusions in science are highly perceptive, obviously he did not have the benefit of the discoveries of science over the past two centuries, with the result that some of his conclusions in this arena we would now regard as erroneous. Nevertheless, his insight into theological matters, his view of the Bible as not representing historical fact but giving an allegorical account of the soul's journey to enlightenment (which, as we saw in Chapter 1, has been increasingly validated by archaeological and literary studies over the last century), and his perception of the more spiritual dimension associated with the material world were quite outstanding. The number of cross-references in this section to later work is an indication of how many of the concepts of others found echoes or, more often, pre-visions in the literary output of Emanuel Swedenborg, a testimony to the prescience of this remarkable man. He died in London in 1772 after suffering a stroke the previous year, but was subsequently interred in Uppsala Cathedral.

Even some of the English theologians of the time were writing works along the same lines, attempting, like Newton and Swedenborg, to get back to the basic principles of the Christian religion – the worship of one God and the living of a virtuous life. John Biddle (1615–1662), born in Wotton-under-Edge in Gloucestershire reflected the spirit of the times with his *Twelve Arguments Drawn out of Scripture, Wherein the Commonly Received Opinion Touching the Deity of the Holy Spirit Is Clearly and Fully Refuted* (1645). Biddle's name is associated with the founding of Socinianism or Unitarianism and the most distinctive features of their theology were the denial of the Trinity and of the divinity of Christ [283]. John Toland (1670–1722), born in Londonderry, Ulster, gave great offence with his *Christianity not Mysterious*, published anonymously in 1696 and in a new edition the same year bearing his name. He contended that the 'mystery' (that is, rational incomprehensibility) of Christian doctrine was redolent of 'tyranny and superstition'.

Toland was accused of having called into question the validity of the New Testament, which he referred to as 'the numerous suppositious pieces under the name of Christ and His apostles and other great persons'. The philosopher John Locke wrote a book that expressed similar opinions, despite its title – *Reasonableness of Christianity*. Matthew Tindal (died 1733) expressed yet another 'back to basics' view of the purpose of Christianity as the worship of God. Though Tindal was brought up as a Roman Catholic, like Toland, he became a Protestant zealot. His book *Christianity as Old as Creation: or the Gospel, a Republication of the Religion of Nature*, first published in 1730 but going through three subsequent editions in the next three years, became the standard deist text: 'There's a religion of nature and reason written in the hearts of every one of us from the first creation, by which all mankind must judge of the truth of any institutional religion whatever' [quoted in ref.19].

In Judaism, the German philosopher Moses Mendelssohn (1729–1786), a silk merchant by trade and grandfather of composers Fanny and Felix Mendelssohn, tried to apply the rationalist principles of the Enlightenment to the Jewish view of God, though he was a devout and orthodox practicing Jew himself. Mendelssohn argued that if we had to rely on personal divine revelation alone as a path to God, most of us would be excluded because we had no such experience, and this would be inconsistent with the concept of a loving God. So he used straightforward rational arguments to establish the existence and qualities of a God that all could experience by the use of the God-given faculty of reason. In *Jerusalem or On Religious Power and Judaism* (1783) he argued that no institution of church or state had the right to impose their religious views on any individual. He did not believe that there should be one universal religion and regarded the existence of many paths to the divine as a fundamental principle of human free-will. He also supported the notion of immortality of the soul. Mendelssohn was a close friend of the German dramatist Gotthold Ephraim Lessing (1729–1781) and it is generally believed that the eponymous hero of Lessing's *Nathan the Wise* (1779) is a portrait of Mendelssohn.

Almost inevitably, in accord with the principles of Hegel's dialectic theory of history (see Chapter 7), there was a backlash against what many saw as this dilution of Christianity and removal of the need for personal experience of the divine. The Wesley family, for example, inspired the establishment of a new Christian sect in England, the Methodists, who also rejected the notion of a divine Trinity but adhered to the word of the Bible, fired with new religious fervour. First there was Charles Wesley (1707–88), founder of the movement at Christ Church College, Oxford in 1729. He was the 18th of the 19 children of Samuel and Susanna Wesley. Samuel Wesley (1766–1837), son of Charles, and his son Samuel Sebastian Wesley (1810–76) were primarily composers and organists, the latter a regular conductor of the Three Choirs Festivals in the 1860s and 1870s when they were held in Gloucester Cathedral, of which he was organist. But Samuel and Susanna's 15th child, John Wesley (1703–91), at Oxford with Charles, was a Methodist firebrand and also a noted composer of hymn tunes and is often regarded as the formal founder of the movement. John and Charles Wesley spent three years (1735–38) as missionaries in the Colonies, in the southern region of America in the state of Georgia. Charles Wesley worked as secretary to the state's Governor, but had to return home early due to ill health. In the late 1730s, one of their disciples from their Oxford days, George Whitfield (1714–1770), whipped up a wave of Christian fanaticism in the New England states of America known as the Great Awakening. Evangelism has been a prominent Christian movement in America ever since and it undoubtedly contributed to the acceptance of new religious leaders with the power of oratory, like Joseph Smith, Brigham Young, William Miller and Mary Baker Eddy, described in Chapter 1.

Judaism too mounted a defence against any erosion of the role of God brought about by this increased faith in rationalism provoked by the success of science. Again in the 1730s, but this time in Europe, a particularly charismatic Polish peasant called Israel ben Eliezer (*ca.*1700–1760) inspired a pietist movement in Judaism comparable to those taking place in Protestantism. He was born in what is now south-west Ukraine. At first he was a teacher in a *heder* (a Jewish elementary school), and later an innkeeper, but from the mid-1730s Ben Eliezer became a spiritual healer, herbalist and exorcist. He was called *Baal Shem Tov*, Master of the Good Name, by his people and known simply as the Besht. In periods of mystical trance he had visions of events, both past and future. The movement of total devotion to God that the Besht founded became known as Hasidism, though *Hasidim* (the pious or devout ones) are mentioned in the Jewish scriptures, the *Mishnah* and the *Talmud*, where they refer to the ancestors of the Pharisees in the 2nd Century BCE. Karen Armstrong says of their philosophy: 'A devout Jew could experience God in the tiniest action of his daily life ... because the divine sparks were everywhere' and 'Every man is a redeemer of a world that is all his own' [20]. So, in pursuing our own health and spiritual fulfillment and in service to others, we are in communion with the divine and helping to fulfil the divine purpose. Every Jew, not just the academic elite, had a duty to practice *devekuth* or meditative contemplation in which they sit in solitude and 'imagine the light of the *Shekinah* above their heads, as though it were flowing all around them and they were sitting in the midst of light' [ref. 20, after Gershom Sholem]: the *Shekinah* is the Jewish Holy Spirit of God on Earth. Those who were able to reach the greatest heights of *devekuth* were known as the *zaddikim*. This kind of meditation is precisely what many present-day spiritual healers do in their contemplative devotions, imagining the light of the spiritual energy infusing into their bodies through the crown *chakra* (see Section 6.5.5). There is much in the practice of spiritual healing that derives from the *Kabbalah*, the Jewish mystical tradition.

So the battle-lines were drawn in 18th Century Europe between the theologians who thought that a more rational approach to some of the foundations of religion would make God more accessible to the common man, and those who were intent upon preserving the traditional beliefs. There was widespread concern that scientific discovery would drive people away from scripture and from God, so attempts to make science and religion more compatible were viewed with some urgency, just as theologians had been trying for centuries to make revealed scripture compatible with Greek rationalism.

Meanwhile in science, studies were being undertaken that would eventually help to forge links between some of the separate disciplines of the subject that were opening up. Robert Hooke (1635–1703) in England and Nicolaus Steno (1638–1686), a Danish scientist who spent most of his life in Italy, were the first to show that sea shells found in rocks, even those located many metres above present sea-level, were the remains of ancient marine creatures and their discoveries were instrumental in geology being designated as a separate discipline from about 1735; and the term 'zoology' for life sciences dates back to 1669. In using fossils to correlate strata, a link was forged between these two disciplines.

But it was in physics that some of these unifying principles were first discovered. In 1798, Benjamin Thompson, Count Rumford (1753–1814), boiled water with the heat generated by the boring of a cannon; and in 1799 Humphry Davy (1778–1829) melted ice by the heat of friction produced when two blocks were rubbed together. These experiments were important because they led to the abandonment of the old notion of heat as some type of fluid, called 'caloric', that acted to raise the temperature of objects. As the friction produced by doing mechanical work could generate heat, it was henceforth regarded as a form of energy. So two important and seemingly very different physical quantities, mechanical work and heat, had been shown to be interconvertible. This was a major step in the direction of *holism*, the bringing together of disparate parts of the whole subject of science that had been studied by reductionism.

These experiments led to the statement in 1847 of one of the most fundamental of the laws of physics, the Law of Conservation of Energy, with which science took another step towards holism. As mentioned in Chapter 2, it was the German philosopher-scientist, Hermann von Helmholtz (1821–1894) who suggested that energy can be changed from one form into another, but it can never be created or destroyed. This law had to be modified slightly into a Law of Conservation of Mass and Energy after the formulation of Einstein's Relativity Theory in which the interconversion and relationship between mass and energy, $E = mc^2$, was discovered. The conservation law subsequently became known as the First Law of Thermodynamics, when other seemingly inviolate properties of heat were discovered.

Other unifying scientific experiments were being conducted in the field of electromagnetism. Following on the studies of the English physician and physicist William Gilbert (1544–1603) on magnetism, Danish physical chemist Hans Christian Oersted (1777–1851) showed in 1820 that an electric current produced deflection of a compass needle, so he deduced that electric currents must generate a magnetic effect. Surrey born Michael Faraday (1791–1867) showed in 1831 that the reverse process was also possible: passing a magnet back and forth through a coil of wire could induce an electric current, the direction of which changed with direction of movement of the magnet. He also showed that a magnetic field was capable of moving a wire carrying electric current, thus establishing a relationship between electric, magnetic and mechanical energy. To this day we use mechanical energy from steam turning a turbine to produce electricity in the dynamos of power stations. The electric motor and the transformer are inventions directly derived from Faraday's work. Less well known are his Laws of Electrolysis (the splitting up of a chemical compound by passing an electric current through its solution in water or when it is molten – a process used commercially to prepare some metals from their salts); his discovery of the compound, benzene, the main component of the fuel we get from oil; and his introduction of the concept of the *electromagnetic field* – the region around a magnet or conducting wire where the magnetic or electrical effects are observed. This concept of a *field* – the region in which forces of attraction or repulsion operate – is one that we shall have much need of later. Newton's gravitational forces similarly act within a *gravitational field*.

It was Scots physicist James Clerk Maxwell (1831–79) who provided the theoretical basis of the unification of electricity and magnetism discovered experimentally by Oersted and Faraday. His mathematical formulation of the laws of electromagnetism appeared in scientific papers in 1864 and culminated in his *Treatise on Electricity and Magnetism* of 1873. So although scientists were still studying isolated systems, as recommended by Francis Bacon, the process of unification of concepts and laws in science had begun. Scientists today still search for a Unified Field Theory that will unite all of the four energy fields defined by science. The other two fields act within atoms and we shall meet those in Chapter 8.

The findings of Galileo and Newton had already produced some considerable disquiet in religious circles, but these were minimal compared to the religious shock waves produced by new discoveries and theories in biology and geology. The whole spiritual framework of belief in the Victorian era was profoundly shaken by the mid-century publications of the natural scientists. At the beginning of the 19th Century, people believed that the Earth had been in existence for only some 6000 years or, more precisely, since 4004 BCE. This date had been calculated by the Irish cleric, Archbishop James Ussher (1581–1656), from his chronological interpretation of stories of the Bible. His theory was published in the *Annales Veteris et Novi Testamenti* of 1650–54, and this date is still adhered to today by Jehovah's Witnesses and some other religious sects.

But Scots geologist, James Hutton (1726–97), had other ideas. Hutton trained as a doctor of medicine, became a gentleman farmer, and made so much money out of the new farm machinery and techniques of agriculture he devised that he was able to spend the remaining 30 years of his life as an amateur scientist. From his studies of land-shaping processes in action, Hutton was led to suggest that 'The present is the key to the past': the geological processes of weathering and deposition that we see today were essentially the same, he maintained, as those that had operated throughout geological history – only very, very, slowly. So slowly, in fact, that it would require far more than Ussher's 6000 years to build up the deposits we see today. Geologists now accept this concept, called Uniformitarianism, as a description of the changes that shape the surface features of Earth. It was originally proposed by Hutton in a paper entitled 'Theory of the Earth' that he presented to the

Royal Society of Edinburgh in 1785 and which appeared in their *Transactions*. A two-volume book with the same title was published in 1795. Publication of a third volume was prevented by his death in 1797, but the manuscript was later edited by another famous Scottish geologist, Archibald Geikie. Little notice was taken of Hutton's ideas at the time because they contradicted the established religious beliefs of the day: until, that is, they were revived by John Playfair's *Illustrations of the Huttonian Theory* of 1802.

The English surveyor, William Smith (1769–1839), added immensely to the information then available about rock strata and the fossils they contained. Smith spent his life in cuttings, quarries and mines, so he had a wonderful opportunity to study the rocks that lay beneath the weathered surface of the Earth. It was he who suggested that strata could be correlated by means of the fossils they contained. From this, and a mass of other discoveries that he made he became known as the Father of British Geology and, from 1838, palaeontology – the study of fossils – became established as a separate discipline within science.

An almost exact contemporary of Smith's, the French naturalist Baron Georges Cuvier (1769–1832), took the data that Smith and others were accumulating to suggest that a series of calamities had shaped the landforms and produced extinction of species of living animals and plants. His Catastrophe Theory of Earth's geological history appeared in the *Discours sur les révolutions de la surface du globe* of 1812. This was a much more acceptable idea to religious believers than Hutton's theories because it seemed to put biblical notions of Creation and the Flood on a scientific foundation.

However, when Scottish geologist Charles Lyell (1797–1875) published his *Principles of Geology* (in 3 volumes, 1830–33) and *Elements of Geology* (1838), these discredited once and for all, for rational minds, the biblical stories of the Creation, and of Noah and the Ark as being a historical account of the source of animal diversity, and of the Flood as producing the sediments now found as rock strata.

The biological pattern of evolution was accounted for by Charles

Darwin (1809–82) in his book *On the Origin of Species*, published in 1859, and this was further supported by Lyell in *The Antiquity of Man* (1863). There are still some puzzling aspects of both geological and biological succession but few scientists now doubt that the views of Lyell and Darwin on the formation of rock structures, flora and fauna are essentially correct. It is difficult today for us to imagine how profoundly disturbed devout but rational and intelligent people must have been by these scientific revelations, made in an era when scientific discoveries were becoming equated with truth.

Charles Darwin was born in Shrewsbury, Shropshire, the grandson of Erasmus Darwin (1731–1802), himself an eminent English poet, scientist and physician. Charles' mother, a daughter of pottery magnate Josiah Wedgewood, died when he was only eight years old. He attended Shrewsbury school, where one of his tutors was the English writer Samuel Butler (1835–1902). After publication of *Origin of Species*, Butler became one of Darwin's staunchest allies in the face of considerable hostile criticism from theologians and scientists alike. In his university education, Darwin first studied medicine at Edinburgh University and then theology at Cambridge, but left in 1831 without taking Honours. From 1831 to 1836 he travelled with *HMS Beagle* as a naturalist to study flora and fauna in the islands of the South Atlantic and it was these studies that gave him the material for his later seminal work. From 1838 to 1841, he was secretary of the Geological Society and became a close acquaintance of Sir Charles Lyell, an association that influenced him greatly.

Another formative influence on Darwin was his reading of the *Essay on the Principle of Population* by Thomas Robert Malthus (1766–1834), published in its first edition in 1798. The main thrust of Malthus' argument was that populations tend to increase by geometric or exponential progression while the means of subsistence for them increase only by arithmetic progression. Hence, he deduced, populations will always grow up to the limits of the materials necessary for their support. Populations are prevented from growing beyond this point by war, famine and disease. The publication roused a great deal of opposition because of the controversial conclusion that

Malthus drew from his observations, namely, that social provision for the poor tends only to aggravate this situation. Leaving aside here the social implications of this conclusion, the expression of the relation between populations and their means of subsistence was a key element in helping Darwin to formulate his idea of what has become known as 'the survival of the fittest' – those individuals of a population will survive who are best adapted to their surroundings. These survival characteristics were then somehow handed down to succeeding generations, though by what mechanism was not known at that time.

It is Darwin's scheme for evolution through adaptation to environment that is generally accepted in biology today. But in Darwin's day there was already a theory of evolution to which he himself subscribed and which he did not regard as incompatible with his own ideas. This was the theory of evolution proposed by the French naturalist Jean-Baptiste Lamarck (1744–1829). He had proposed the idea, with supporting argument, that characteristics acquired in the lifetime of an individual are passed on to descendants, and it is this theory for which Lamarck is best known today. It seemed such an obvious conclusion that it was widely accepted.

Yet Lamarck's greatest contribution to the subject of biology was his approach to the classification of flora and fauna, distinguishing invertebrates for the first time by the absence of the spinal column. He built on the systematic classification of living creatures that had been started by English naturalist John Ray (1627–1705) and developed by Swedish botanist Carl von Linne (usually known by the Latinised version of his name, Linnaeus: 1707–1778) and Baron Cuvier, whose name we encountered earlier. Such descriptive and evolutionary relationships unequivocally discredited for rational people any idea of the remotest vestige of literal truth in the Adam and Eve fable [Genesis, Chaps 2, 3].

However, the work of Lamarck's which has gained the greatest notoriety and which is still a subject of controversy is his idea of 'transformism' by the inheritance of acquired characteristics, a theory most completely worked out in *Zoological Philosophy* (1809).

This idea, which has become known as Lamarckism, has been part of popular belief for centuries, and still persists, even amongst some scientists. It seems to accord with common sense. To use Lamarck's own example: if generations of giraffes browse the leaves on tall trees they progressively stretch their legs and necks. Subsequent generations inherit and exaggerate these characteristics until we get to the giraffes we know today. How else do ostriches get callouses on the underside of their bellies or camels thickened pads on their knees, both characteristics visible in the new-born of their species, if these are not inherited from adults developing the pads to provide protection when sitting or squatting? These questions have still not been convincingly answered using Darwinian arguments alone.

The main objection to Lamarckism has been that no mechanism is known by which such acquired characteristics could be transmitted from one generation to the next; however, some 20th Century geneticists believe they might have found the key. Albert Szent-Györgyi, the Nobel Prize-winning biochemist who isolated vitamin C, suggested that the cell is subject to many kinds of chemical and physical influences in the body, including possible modification by energetic fields in the parent individuals. Thus the lifestyle of the parents could be transmitted in some way through cellular DNA to the offspring. That proteins and DNA are influenced by electromagnetic fields has now been established experimentally, and this might eventually provide some support for a contribution to evolution from Lamarckism. It will have great social and moral implications if it is established that the lifestyle of parents deeply affects the wellbeing of their offspring in ways far beyond the obvious living conditions that accompany the nurture of children.

The only cases where a kind of Lamarckism is generally accepted by contemporary biologists are (i) where an individual is subjected to some types of chemical pollution or radiation that damage the genes; this can then be transmitted to offspring with the tragic consequences of mutation or early death from cancer: we have had several tragic examples of this in the 20th Century from the cancer rates found in descendants of the Curies after their work on radioactivity, or still found in the children of Nagasaki and Hiroshima after the nuclear explosions in World War 2, or around Chernobyl after the power plant explosion; or (ii) the practices of young individuals within a society who reflect the behaviour that has been learned and practiced by their parents and other senior members of the society in which they grow up; in a sense, the young then inherit behaviour learned in the lifetime of their parents. But this is not genetic inheritance: it is transmission of cultural behaviour, which Richard Dawkins postulates as occurring through units he calls *memes* rather than genes [139]. We know all too well that children learn not only by instruction but also by example, which is why it is so important for parents to set examples for their children that are beneficial to them as individuals and to society as a whole. With these two exceptions, the idea of any form of adult experience that can be passed on to offspring is not generally accepted by the scientific community as a factor that contributes to the development of individual characteristics; these are acquired during the life of the individual through personal experience and are not inherited genetically at birth. Lamarck was one of the first naturalists to emphasise the interconnectedness of all facets of the natural world, including humankind. Although he was a believer in environmental holism, Lamarck saw Nature as quite distinct from God.

After the work, primarily, of Galileo and Newton, Lyell and Darwin, while the idea of God the Creator was still extant, the concept of God the Sustainer, immanent in the world had, for many, at least in academe, given way to the Laws of Nature ruling our everyday lives, laws that could be built on a secure and irrefutable mathematical foundation. It was French philosopher Blaise Pascal (1623–1662) who introduced the concept of '*déisme*' in the posthumously published collection of aphorisms, *Pensées*, to describe a role for God as Creator but not Sustainer. The English word 'deism' defining this principle of belief was first used in 1682, some two decades after the death of Pascal. In a time of upheaval in religious thought, it was necessary to emphasise the traditional religious view of God as responsible for all things and immanent in the world, interacting with humankind. Ralph Cudworth (1617–88), in his book *The True Intellectual System of the Universe* (1678), used the term 'theism' to describe belief in the Christian Church's image of God as Creator and Sustainer, immanent in the world. The role of God was now a fundamental topic of debate amongst academics in the Renaissance in the light of these scientific discoveries.

The Catholic theologian John Henry Newman (1801–1890) was quite comfortable with what science had to say about the creation of the material world of rocks, flora and fauna. He had no trouble accommodating the changes in thinking about the origins and functions of the natural world brought about by 19th Century scientific discovery. He did not see these as challenging his Christian beliefs: 'to live is to change, and to be perfect is to have changed often' [354]. He acknowledged that the whole process of living involves change and growth: 'growth is the only evidence of life' [355]. For most theologians of the time, however, scientific discoveries posed a substantial threat to established religious dogma since they seemed to eliminate the need for God as Sustainer and possibly even as Creator of the universe.

With rational, scientific explanations for many of the wonders of Nature, rather than their being attributed to God-given miracles, seeming contradictions between science and much that is written in scripture became evident in the post-Renaissance period. Whatever role for God may be prescribed by the various religions, and whatever scientists tell us about the workings of the natural world, our common human experience tells us that Man is undeniably a spiritual being. To be human is to possess some sense of moral right, whether based on humanistic or divine principles; to possess an awareness of the aesthetic and the numinous; to be able to create, often in the name of the divine, masterpieces that inspire awe or joy in others: in other words, to possess what many describe as 'soul'. In the next chapter we shall consider the concept of soul and its relationship with mind.

5 The nature of soul

5.1. A definition of soul

There have been many attempts over the past few decades to find a biological explanation for the activities of mind, and particularly for the nature of memory, the existence of our conscious awareness and the emotional aspects of our personality. These properties of mind are much more difficult to interpret than plain physiological functioning of the brain in responding to the input of the five senses, because they are non-material. It is one thing to explain vision as light entering the eye, falling on the retina, producing signals passing along the optic nerve to the brain and subsequently generating the firing of cerebral neurons. It is quite another to unravel the mystery of how those physical processes, and particularly the electrical activity of the brain, can produce the notion of the image that we see.

At the same time, some biologists have also been seeking some rational and scientifically acceptable basis for those phenomena that are usually designated as psychic events or psi, often referred to as 'supernatural' or 'paranormal', though they involve phenomena well-known to indigenous peoples, sages and prophets as entirely normal and natural and part of everyday life. Conventional biologists have either dismissed them completely as irrational nonsense, or they have been seeking and expecting to find evidence to deny their existence, to 'explain them away'. If there is unequivocal empirical evidence with theoretical underpinning for psi, this might then, by extension, provide a scientific interpretation of human consciousness and the everyday workings of mind on the one hand, and of the idea of soul on the other, since these all involve communion in some way with a spiritual realm. Why does this matter? Because conscious awareness and sophisticated language for communication are the distinguishing characteristics of human existence, and they are therefore fundamental topics for scientific study. Because scientists, theologians and laymen would all like to establish accord rather than discord between the world pictures of science and religion. And a belief in the reality of the human soul in its many manifestations, and the possibility of an afterlife and even reincarnation is at the heart of much religious belief, and this again is a uniquely human characteristic. These ideas of a Divine Being and soul form the foundation of many religious faiths, and that in turn determines the mind-set for how people live their lives. If religious faith can be shown to have a rational basis, this would silence or at least subdue the critics and cynics who maintain that a majority of people, who do have such beliefs, live their lives based on fallacy and fantasy. Furthermore, if a common thread can be established running through several major world religions, this provides a hope at least of lessening the violent discord evident throughout the world between different religious factions claiming their scripture as unequivocal and unilateral truth.

In pondering the question: What is soul? assuming essentially that one believes that such a thing exists at all, the first assertion must surely be that it is not a synonym for mind, though many of the Greek philosophers discussed in Chapter 2 used the terms interchangeably. Even in everyday speech, mind and soul have two distinguishable connotations. The term 'mind' refers to mental capability: when we say that someone has a good mind we mean that they possess the ability to problem solve in general, to find answers quickly to mathematical problems, to speak a number of languages or to display aptitude in a number of different fields. These are faculties that, to some extent at least, can be objectively and quantitatively measured through IQ tests. The word 'soul' on the other hand in

Western society relates to a person's moral intent, or to their being spiritually aware. A person we describe as being a 'good soul' shows a desire to do good for other people; has the ability to respond to aesthetic stimuli, such as from art, poetry, music, or natural beauty; or is able to make great leaps of creative imagination in the arts or sciences. They may also possess an ability to exclude external physical stimuli and reach a contemplative state that perceives a higher truth: it is a subjective quality that can be assessed only by its effects on the individual and others.

At the very least then, the term 'soul' is a useful linguistic convention to describe the spiritual nature of Man. But is it any more than this? We could also identify these characteristics with what American philosopher Danah Zohar and her English psychiatrist husband Ian Marshall describe as 'spiritual intelligence' in their recent book *SQ – Spiritual Intelligence* [532]: 'This is the intelligence with which we address and solve problems of meaning and value, the intelligence with which we place our actions and lives in a wider, richer, meaning-giving context, the intelligence with which we can assess that one course of action or one life-path is more meaningful than another.' Harvard psychologist Howard Gardner in his books *Frames of Mind* [205] and *Multiple Intelligences* [206] distinguished six kinds of intelligence – spiritual intelligence was not one of them, because Gardner's was a conventional materialist approach. But the ability of some individuals to access a reality beyond that accessible to the five senses is accepted by all whose world-view is not hidden behind a cloak of materialist reductionism or extreme scepticism.

Soul is quite simply the spiritual component of humanity, singly or collectively. It is that which gives us an awareness of the numinous in so many of our everyday activities: it does not have to involve blinding visions of a divine being. It gives us the sense of wonder at being alive in a world of Nature, and the feeling of rapture at the many beautiful creations wrought by our fellow humans, in art, architecture, poetry or music. It inspires the sense of mystery and awe as to the source and purpose of it all. Albert Einstein expressed it so aptly in one of his interviews: 'The most beautiful and deepest experience a man can have is the sense of the mysterious. It is the underlying principle of religion as well as of all serious endeavour in art and science' [92]. Soul is what many call our sixth sense. One day we will marvel that science has progressed so far in a few hundred years by focusing only on the sensory and rational while ignoring the sixth sense known to primitives, prophets, seers and shamans for many generations.

Soul and immortality

Soul is also a component of the human organism that many cultures, past and present, throughout the world believe survives death in some form: it is regarded as 'an ethereal surviving being' [488]. Anthropologists tell us that there are 'unmistakable indications of a conception of the continuance of life after death from early Man living in China half a million years ago' [271]. Paul Radin maintains that belief in some form of reincarnation (see Section 6.5.6) is 'universally present in all the simple food-gathering and hunting-fishing civilisations' [392 quoted in ref. 257]. We have seen already in Chapter 1 that Egyptian society saw death and the afterlife as part of the natural cycle of existence. So this characteristic of survival of death, with or without recycling into another earthly incarnation, is an essential defining quality of soul. Many pagans believe that a continuing spiritual force, of which the human soul is a part, is also present in the natural world: this idea, known as *animism*, has also pervaded human societies from their very earliest inception.

Soul and the Eastern religious philosophies

The spiritual dimension of the world is of greater importance in Eastern than in Western religious philosophies. Though there is belief in some form of reincarnation in the Eastern religions of Buddhism and Taoism, there is no concept of individual soul, or of a personal God, comparable to that in the West. Yet, the Buddhist Society's 'Twelve Principles of Buddhism' state: 'Buddhism does not deny the existence of God or soul, though it places its own meaning on those terms'. For God, Buddhism sees the Creator of the universe, the Unborn described in Buddhist scriptures; soul is that component of the individual that seeks the enlightenment of union with Ultimate Being [265]. In less mystical terms, it is self-reliance and tolerance in the individual and the one-ness and sanctity of the entire created world that form the basic tenets of Buddhism.

In Buddhism, the principal doctrine is that of a constant cycle of birth and death (*samsara*), a world of becoming rather than being, that one must undergo in the process of attaining *nirvana*, a state of realisation of emptiness, no-soul or non-self (*anatta*) where all is one. The no-soul doctrine is called *anatman*. It does not however mean 'extinction', as the Buddha specifically made clear: it is a form of consciousness or energy flux that is reborn until one can achieve *nirvana*. The *First Noble Truth* tells us that all things in the world are *anicca*, changing and impermanent, including worldly existence. This leads to a state of *dukkha*, which is suffering, unhappiness, incompleteness, or what later philosophers might call *alienation* from one's life or surroundings. The *Second Noble Truth* gives us a reason for this state of mind in longing – for permanence or security. The *Third Noble Truth* tells us that *nirvana* provides a means of escape from *dukkha* by focusing on the 'now', each moment following the next; and the *Fourth Noble Truth* provides an *Eightfold Way* of living so as to escape *samsara*. This cycle is driven by *karma*, the conduct of life in the preceding incarnation. But there is no soul to survive death and attain union with God, as there is also no God, either as Creator or Sustainer. These religions are emphatically *monist* in that all creation is one in Infinite Mind. There must however be a component of mind that survives to transmit the *karma* on to the next earthly incarnation. It is a flux of spiritual energy that moves from one life to the next, implementing the *karma* that it inherited from the previous incarnation.

In Hinduism, from which Buddhism was derived, there are concepts equivalent to the Western ideas of God and soul. The state of *nirvana* (enlightened consciousness) is attained by extinguishing worldly desires so as to achieve union of individual soul or self (*atman* or *jiva-atman*) with the Absolute or *Brahman*, as laid down in the Hindu scriptures. The earliest of these are believed to have been written down around 1000 BCE after centuries of oral tradition. These make up the *Shruti*, the four sets of *Vedas*: these are believed to have been transmitted to the Gurus or *Rishis*, the sages who served as channels of divine knowledge. The best known of these in the West is the *Rig Veda*, a collection of hymns praising the deities. Human existence is prone to error or evil through ignorance (*avidya*), so one must seek knowledge (*jnana*) in earthly existence, but also show devotion or faith (*bhakti*), and the practice of useful work and good deeds (*karma*), as described in the *Vedas* (Sanskrit: *veda* = knowledge). To follow *bhakti* without *jnana* leads to vacuous sentimentality; but *jnana* without *bhakti* is just specious dialectic. To study and adhere to dogmas, to recite creeds and practice rituals as prescribed by a religion is meaningless without the *karma* and *ahimsa* (non-violence, non-hatred). Each individual soul must undergo recycling into earthly incarnations until it achieves *moksha*, a release from worldliness attained by *dharma* (right action, or religious moral faith). In the *Vedas* we are told that we and the world comprise *purusha* (soul, spirit, self; Communal Soul) and *prakriti* (the potential(ity) of Nature, including all matter; the non-self) out of which the world evolves under the influence of *purusha*. *Prakriti* may be changed from one form to another, but never created or destroyed.

The *Upanishads* also form part of this literature and they are thought to have originated around 400 years BCE: these contain the elements of Hindu mystical philosophy. They were transmitted by the Gurus to their students much as the masters of Greek philosophy instructed their students. The *Brihadaranyaka Upanishad* defines *atman* as universal spirit or vital force and, as such, operates in every form of life, not just humankind, and *Atman* is therefore at times identified with *Brahman*.

God in Hinduism is *Brahman*, The Other or The One and is without attributes, unknown and unknowable. Hindus therefore have their *avatars*, *Rama* and *Krishna*, who are manifestations of their god on Earth. Their exploits are described, respectively, in the epic poems, the *Ramayana* and *Mahabharata*, which make up the *Smriti* of Hindu scripture. The longest poem of the *Mahabharata* is the *Bhagavad Gita*, 'The Song of the Adorable One', the best known of the epics from this literature.

The *Bhagavad Gita* says that life should be devoted to selfless work, carried out from a principle of duty and not undertaken for personal gain. The maxim is: 'plain living and high thinking', to be satisfied with what we have and not be continually questing after more of everything. Some branches of the Hindu religions place more emphasis than others on the devotional meditation (*bhakti*) aspect of the faith as a means of enlightenment, but Hindu philosophy is capable of many interpretations. One thing that is certain is that the principles it advocates are the antithesis of the materialism that pervades so much of Western society. There is much more emphasis in Eastern religion on the attainment of the wisdom of the sage, as so often caricatured in Western films and on T.V. The goal is to strive towards the wisdom of accumulated learning in old age, of making informed impartial judgements, of recognising and accepting the uncertainties and limitations of human existence.

Although this scripture is of Hindu origin, it belongs to and should be shared with all humankind. For it is a doctrine of supreme wisdom, found amongst primitive people in all the continents: it is the wisdom of the ancestors, preserved in myths and symbols, rites and rituals, songs and dances [216]. This surely is an eternal truth – to live a life devoted to selfless work for the spiritual enrichment of others as part of the fulfilment of the universal divine spirit.

Theosophy is a religious philosophy that owes much to Hindu scripture and to the writings too of Emanuel Swedenborg (see Chapter 4). It was established in 1875 in New York, primarily by a Russian emigré, Helena Blavatsky (1831–1891) or HPB as she preferred to be known. Its aims are to seek out the common ground between religion and science, and to use rational knowledge in an effort to understand scriptural truths. However, its terminology and methodology are very mystical. The Bible and the supposed divinity of Jesus are of little or no significance. Though theosophy is different from spiritualism, there is belief in the possibility of contact with souls in the afterlife. Its principles are based on revelations to HPB, primarily by her two spiritual Masters, Morya and Koot Hoomi, respectively Indian and Tibetan. Modern theosophists place great store by HPB's writings: *Isis Unveiled* (1877), *The Secret Doctrine* (1888), and *The Key to Theosophy* (1889). HPB died in London in 1891. The most important aspect of theosophy for this presentation is the belief in the spiritual component of humankind, and in a universal spiritual domain to which we can have access through meditation and through the gifts of seers and sages of indigenous peoples, particularly those of North American and Asian Indians, and from Tibet, whose lives have not become corrupted by Western materialism. After the death of Madame Blavatsky, the English social reformer Annie Besant (1847–1933) was active in promoting the work of the Theosophical Society.

Ensoulment

It is a common belief in many religious philosophies that all living creatures are sacred. If there is a universal spiritual field, this must pervade all plant and animal life, as well as the mineral domain, not just humans. What humans can do is to respond to this field through consciousness – at least to a greater extent than most animals. Many higher animals like apes display a high degree of protectiveness to their offspring. Parents feed their offspring, which may not always be in the best interests of their own survival if food is scarce. It is a matter of debate amongst biologists as to whether altruism exists in animals as a truly 'moral activity' or not: is it just that an individual recognises that their own survival is optimised by helping others in times of danger? Altruism is defined by the Chambers Dictionary as 'the principle of living or acting in the interest of others'. Is this enough to define altruistic behaviour? Unless some element of self-sacrifice is involved, the suspicion will always arise that the action also has potential for self-interest. Humans continually make sacrifices and take risks for the benefit of other people but, in most circumstances, an animal will put its own survival before that of any others and we see no sign of anything resembling activities of soul comparable to those in humans. But dogs, particularly, when they live close to humans, do sometimes risk their lives to save their masters, so we cannot say that some form of altruism is not present: this could hardly be a genetic trait. Dogs also have a 'sixth sense' about the impending presence of their masters, which is certainly an aspect of soul [430] Obviously, lacking the sophisticated language of human communication, animals do not have the possibilities for most of the activities of soul, so any spiritual faculty associated with the animal kingdom must be rudimentary. This is even more so in considering plants or minerals.

If, as is believed in Eastern religious philosophy and in theosophy, the divine spirit pervades everything within the universe, and if the human brain and mind have evolved and developed over the past few million years as the biologists tell us, then it is logical to speculate that *ensoulment* of the human organism has also progressed along with biological evolution, leading to a *hierarchy of soul*. We know that very early Man had visions of the divine and an aesthetic sense well enough developed to want to represent himself or his surroundings in artwork and to adorn the body with jewellery. But the breadth of spiritual and aesthetic vision is clearly more developed today.

We are all aware of 'good' people who have lived amongst us, quite apart from the Manifestations of God or the prophets. There are people like Mother Teresa and Albert Schweitzer and countless other humanitarians even in the past century who have given their lives to the service of others. It is not fanciful to suggest that they have a soul more finely tuned in to the spiritual field, or more highly developed, than most of us. The same is undoubtedly true of shamans, seers and psychics. At the other extreme, there are those who seem to spend their lives exploiting or speaking ill of others, making malicious mischief, or even committing heinous crimes, and such people surely can have only a poorly developed soul, or be scarcely tuned in to the spiritual field, or even attuned to the source of evil, if there is one. The argument of evolution of humans from lower animals and the observation of degrees of goodness or soul in humans both imply the existence of a hierarchy of soul. Theosophists too believe that there are infinitely varying degrees of spirituality. One highly developed soul adds to the stock of beneficence within World Soul, to counter the negative effects of those whose spiritual development is still at a rudimentary stage or who have been corrupted by the material world. In this picture of soul, the Christian concepts of Heaven and Hell correspond to the states of bliss or torment experienced by the soul in the afterlife upon assessing the quality of the life just lived. The Catholic state of Purgatory is just that condition of spiritual torment. A soul living a life of evil on Earth is unlikely to undergo immediate transformation to goodness on passing into the spiritual realm. Pagans, theosophists and spiritualists all believe in the existence of malign spirits.

The French mystical palaeontologist Teilhard de Chardin (1881–1955) contended that the world has passed through a series of evolutions: first there was geogenesis, the creation of the land and the sea; then came biogenesis, the creation of life; this was followed by psychogenesis, the development of thinking beings; now we are in the stage of noogenesis, the evolution of mind into what is identified elsewhere in this book as Cosmic Soul or Communal Soul [118]. These ideas all illustrate a hierarchy of soul that is evolving with humankind. Despite bitter conflict, often based on religious differences, in various parts of the world, there seems to be an encouraging groundswell of increasing spiritual awareness within humankind – a realisation amongst more and more people that we must not let ethnic or religious differences force us into conflict, and that as individuals we need to focus more on things spiritual and less on the material. This is in keeping with the ideas of theosophists and members of the Baha'i faith that the world is slowly evolving into a state of global harmony.

The idea of evolution of soul, if such exists, developing along with that of the human brain is not implausible; and, if soul if equated with the God in us, the evolution of soul implies evolution of God, as in Process Theology (see Chapter 1). However, if ensoulment of the species presents a philosophical and theological problem, then ensoulment of the individual is an even greater one. The belief among members of the Catholic Church, and many other Christians, is that soul enters the organism at conception. If ensoulment does occur at conception, then one individual is the bearer of two souls, those of the mother and of the child. If soul is a distinctive feature of self, of the individual, then the foetus is not an individual biologically until birth, so we have an inconsistency. Western religion does not accept the possibility of reincarnation, through which one soul is invested successively in different individuals. The argument against this is precisely that each soul is unique to an individual, so that one soul can never be incarnate in two different individuals, even consecutively and, conversely, one physical body should never, at any time, be associated with two souls. The ancient belief that the soul enters with the first breath of independent life is a more reasonable hypothesis on these grounds.

A further difficulty with ensoulment at conception arises in the case when, after conception, the fertilised cell develops abnormally, not into a human being but into a mass of potentially tumorous tissue called a hydatid mole or hydatiform cyst. This event, fortunately, is comparatively rare, but when it does occur, to associate a divine soul with such a degenerate cellular mass that never becomes anything resembling a human being is surely to undermine the sanctity of the human soul. With a similar argument, it is difficult to fathom any constructive purpose in assigning a soul to a foetus that is stillborn, an event that causes nothing but great stress and despair to the parents. If the soul's journey on Earth is to learn and bring joy and uplift to the lives of others, such an event must surely have exactly the opposite effect.

5.2.   The nature of mind and its relation to soul

We have seen that the Greek philosophers frequently used the terms 'mind' and 'soul' interchangeably. The reason for this may be that among the functions of 'mind', of primary importance is the idea of 'self-consciousness', an awareness of oneself as an individual, and this distinctive individuality, the *haecceitas* (see Chapter 3) within each of us, apart from our unique genetic makeup, is soul. The term 'soul' is used in the following discussion in the sense defined above, as aesthetic and numinous awareness, corresponding to the concept in Judeo-Christian belief systems.

The definition of 'mind' is itself a complex and highly controversial issue and there is no room here to do more than briefly review some of the principal ideas about how the non-material mind relates to the physical brain.

The mind and the brain

It was the view of the French philosopher René Descartes (1596–1650) that body and mind were two separate kinds of things – the body was a material entity (*res extensa*), while mind was a separate, non-material thinking substance (*res cogitans*) [142]. Mind and brain interacted, so Descartes wrote, by the grace of God, through the pineal gland, which was also therefore the seat of the soul. This point of view is called *dualism* (believing that the world is made up of two kinds of stuff or things, where the word 'things' does not necessarily mean 'material objects'). If the two, mind and brain, are held to run in parallel but independently, with no causal relation between them, this view of mind is called *epiphenomenalism*, and this was the view of the French philosopher Nicholas de Malebranche (1638–1715) [332]. In Malebranche's view it was God who saw to it that, say, the pain of touching a hot surface was reflected simultaneously in the mind. In recent times, this form of dualism in the mechanism of mental activity has also been the view of Karl Popper and John Eccles, whom we shall discuss shortly.

Like many of the Greek philosophers, Descartes regarded the terms 'mind' and 'soul' as synonymous. He built his system of philosophy on the belief that what he could formulate 'clearly and distinctly' in his mind must be correct, because 'God is no deceiver' – a phrase that recurs several times in his philosophy. He distinguished his thinking from dreaming in two ways [142]: by consciously provoked memories of real-life events when he was awake, and from the irrationality of dream events, which often involve bizarre situations. Apart from raising difficulties about how mind and body were to interrelate, this Cartesian dualism influenced scientific philosophy until the 20th Century in that material objects, living or inanimate, were considered to be the province of empirical investigation while scientific methods were not believed to be relevant for a study of moral or spiritual issues or even to the study of the workings of the mind.

In a seminal work on mind, the Oxford philosopher Gilbert Ryle (1900–1976) [406] described Descartes' view of mind as 'the ghost in the machine'. He maintained that 'body' and 'mind' were two different kinds of descriptive words or 'categories': there was only one object, the body, and that mind was simply the thinking, feeling aspect of the body, in other words, a description of the behaviour of the body. This was a theory of mind built on *logical behaviourism*: a mental event is defined as behaving, or having the tendency to behave, in a particular way. Ryle's behaviourist approach, highly regarded in its day, was subsequently criticised in some detail by John Eccles.

Neurologist Sir John Eccles (1903–1997) was born in Melbourne, Australia and after qualification worked not only in Australia but also at Oxford and in the United States. He went to work with Charles Sherrington (see below) at Oxford when the latter was already over sixty years old. He believed that there is a limit to what we can achieve in explaining spiritual matters by scientific investigation. In what is described as a dualist-interactionist theory he envisages two quite different but interacting domains: 'I maintain that the human mystery is incredibly demeaned by scientific reductionism, with its claim in promissory materialism to account eventually for all of the spiritual world in terms of patterns of neuronal activity. This belief must be classed as a superstition ... we have to recognise that we are spiritual beings with souls existing in a spiritual world as well as material beings with bodies and brains existing in the material world' [160]. This is not quite the same separated mind and body theory of Descartes, involving two different kinds of material: in Eccles' view the mind is a physical substance but inhabiting a different world [161]. Because mind and brain run independently, this constitutes epiphenomenalism [381]. Eccles shared the 1963 Nobel Prize in Medicine with Alan Lloyd Hodgkin and Andrew Huxley for his work on neuronal transmission. One of his nine children also worked in the field of neurology.

Wilder Penfield (1891–1976) was born in Spokane, Washington State in the USA. He had a youthful ambition to become a Rhodes Scholar and, in 1914, he achieved his ambition and began study as a graduate at Merton College, Oxford, where he was greatly influenced by Sir Charles Sherrington (see below). Another formative influence on Penfield was Canadian-born Professor of Medicine, Sir William Ostler. After two years at Oxford, Penfield entered the John Hopkins Medical School where he received his M.D. He joined the staff at McGill Medical School in 1928 and it is here that he made his reputation as a brilliant neurosurgeon. He operated on epileptics under local anaesthesia and found that certain areas of the brain elicited certain kinds of responses, especially particular memories. As a result, he suggested that there were specific areas of the brain responsible for certain human functions and he sought the units in the brain, which he called *engrams*, responsible for those memories. Today, in the new spirit of holism, the brain is regarded much more as functioning as a whole rather than as a collection of individually functioning units (see Chapter 8 for Pribram's holographic interpretation of brain function), but Penfield immeasurably advanced our knowledge of the functioning of the brain, as well as being a brilliant neurosurgeon. The search for an explanation of the mechanism of brain function and the nature of mind and consciousness continues.

Roger Wolcott Sperry (1913–1994) was another neurosurgeon who worked on brain function, with particular regard to epilepsy. While he was a Ph.D. student at the University of Chicago, Sperry had Paul Weiss as a mentor (see Chapter 8). The work for which Sperry received the Nobel Prize in physiology and medicine in 1981, jointly with David Hubel and Torsten Wiesel, was the discovery of the different functions of the left and right hemispheres of the brain (the so-called 'split-brain theory'), the left being involved in logical reasoning, as in mathematics, and language, while the right was the more creative hemisphere having to do with art, music and spirituality. These may be regarded as the embodiment of the *yang* and *yin*, male and female, principles of the universal energy as described in Chinese philosophy.

Oxford neurologist, Sir Charles Sherrington (1857–1952), won the 1932 Nobel Prize in medicine for his work on the function of neurons, and he was Waynefleet Professor of Physiology at Oxford from 1913 to 1935. Both Eccles and Penfield were enormously influenced by his teaching. In his Gifford Lectures Sherrington linked mind and brain with external spiritual energy: 'I have therefore to think of the brain as an organ of liaison between energy and mind, but not as a converter of energy into mind, or vice versa' [433]. Although these ideas are more than 60 years old now, they are particularly interesting, because there is a school of thought that the brain, through its functioning (as mind) does indeed link up with an external energy field so that mind can thereby serve as a medium for various events that we describe as psychic or mystical. The brain does not need to *convert* energy in order to produce the functions we describe as mind: mind just *is* the internal cerebral energy field that is produced in every instant by the activity within the brain. Individual soul is that distinctive mental activity that liaises between the field within the physical brain and the external energy field that is the universal spiritual field. External communication is achieved by tuning in the frequencies of the brainwaves to resonate with those of the external field, rather like tuning in a radio to the correct waveband. This idea will be described in more detail in Chapter 8. This is not to suggest that all mundane, everyday tasks require conscious or overt communion with the external energy field; the brain has a large enough store of energy within it to work automatically on such tasks that involve the neurons of the brain communicating directly and internally with neurons within the rest of the body. However, it is certainly possible that many human thoughts, feelings and actions do involve such interaction with an external spiritual field: if we believe that the divine is everywhere, then every event, human or otherwise, is in some sense an interaction with the divine.

The view that there is a one-to-one correspondence between each physical, neural (brain, CNS) event and a corresponding immaterial, mental (mind) event may be described as *determinism*; it is associated in recent philosophical thought with Ted Honderich [263]. It is a determinist theory because it proposes a direct cause-and-effect linkage: each brain event produces a mental (or mind) effect, and each mind event is caused by specific brain activity. In the *functionalism* theory of mind, a mental event is both a cause and an effect comprising the sensory or afferent input, the brain processing, and the motor or efferent output. Hilary Putnam is one of the principal names associated with this idea [389]. But still, each brain event is associated with a mind event, however defined.

Bertrand Russell (1872–1970), mathematician and philosopher, was moving towards the world-view of modern physics and Eastern metaphysics when he denied the existence of mind or matter because everything in the universe is just a series of events [404]. What we describe as mind or matter are simply two aspects of some under-lying fundamental reality. 'The fact that an event occupies a finite amount of space-time does not prove that it has parts' [404]. 'Popular metaphysics divides the known world into mind and matter, and a human being into soul and body. Some – the materialists – have said that matter alone is real and mind is an illusion. Many – the idealists ... – have taken the opposite view, that mind alone is real and matter is an illusion. The view which I have suggested is that both mind and matter are structures composed of a more primitive stuff which is neither material nor mental' [405]. While, in theory, it may be possible to envisage all material objects as a series of subatomic events (see Chapter 8), and part of the space-time continuum, it is not very helpful to describe all the objects of our everyday experience, including the brain, in this way, and it does nothing to explain how a material brain produces non-material ideas.

Rupert Sheldrake has an even more controversial idea of mind as being extended in space from the brain to that which is perceived.

Light enters the eye from the object, and mind places the object at some location distant from the observer; and that, says Sheldrake, is where mind is at that moment [429]. We shall say more about Sheldrake's ideas in Chapter 8.

In a recent book on the relation of science and mind, Brian Ridley, Professor of Physics at the University of Essex comes to the conclusion that 'Consciousness ... must, I think, be accepted as an irreducible element of the world' [401]. He likens the existence of mind or consciousness to the existence of the universal physical constants, like Planck's constant or the gravitational constant. That these exist and have the values they do is just a plain fact about the universe: it is not something to which an explanation can be given and therefore, perhaps, should not even be sought.

Without going into further details of the many variations on these basic ideas of the relationship between mind and brain, let us follow the most common biological and philosophical approach [60, 131, 141, 338, 424] and regard mind essentially as a set of conscious and unconscious states of the central nervous system (to include the reflex arc of the spinal cord as well as the brain) which, at the molecular level, are brought about by various chemical and electromagnetic processes occurring within the CNS. We must include unconscious brain states in mind because we have a vast store of memories that are not in consciousness at every instant but are often there for recall when required. Then there are unconscious dream states. We are also all familiar with doing things sub-consciously, like carrying on a conversation while driving, or knitting while watching television – and perhaps also carrying on a conversation. The more holistic female mind seems to be better at executing multiple foci of attention than that of the more reductionist male.

Each mind event (including those in dreaming, over which we have no conscious control) therefore corresponds to a brain 'event' or to a particular complex of processes within the brain – this notion is the so-called *identity theory* or *reductive materialism*. Mind is conscious and unconscious thought, the name we give to the working of the brain, just as 'digestion' is the name we give to the working of the gut, or 'breathing' is the working of the lungs and associated musculature. We should however exclude from this definition those unconscious brain events that actually control the autonomic nervous system, those that keep our hearts beating and control our breathing, or those that monitor our body temperature to produce shivering or sweating. Most definitions of mind would not include brain events such as these, though even these autonomic processes can be modified by conscious thought, as in meditation, or relaxation therapy, or biofeedback equipment and techniques. Pain on the other hand, and the awareness of the need for food or drink or sleep, would definitely rank as mind events, as would the *awareness* that we are too hot or too cold even if body temperature control is subliminal. With these restrictions on the mind-brain identity theory, it might be more accurate to say that every mind event is produced by a complex of corresponding brain activity but that not all brain activity results in what would generally be regarded as a mental process or mind event.

On the rationalist world view, these mind states are wholly brought about or 'caused' by environmental factors, in the broadest sense, to which the body is subjected: the effects of drugs, the food that we eat, and other life experiences of the individual that produce biochemical compounds that interact with the anatomical structure of the brain, a structure that has been established genetically through reproduction. There is ample evidence to indicate that the mind-body interaction occurs in both directions, since states of mind can also affect the health of the body, either positively or negatively. There seems to be an intimate connection between the nervous and immune systems. There is now a specialised branch of medicine called psychoneuroimmunology (PNI) that deals with this interaction. In states of mental or emotional stress, the immune system of the body is one of the first to be weakened such that the subject is more vulnerable to infection. Many alternative therapies probably owe at least part of their therapeutic effects to a relaxing rapport between patient and healer and the resulting psychosomatic effects on the body. At a deeper level, healers may be thought of as channelling a universal energy into their patients, or attuning or aligning the personal energy field of the patient with the cosmic energy, as discussed further in the Chapter 6. This represents a total body-mind-spiritual field interaction. The whole topic of beneficial effects for the body brought about by uplifting spiritual experiences, including spiritual healing, will be covered in some detail in the next chapter.

An ongoing problem in theories of mind is the question of *free will*. Some believers in the divine maintain that all our thoughts are known beforehand in the spiritual realm. It may seem then that there is little left for us to choose. But even if it is so, that our actions are in some sense pre-determined, this does not mean that the decision is made for us because, although our decision may be 'known' in the spiritual realm, we do not know what mind state we will select. It is like our closest friends or partners saying: "I know what he (or she) will do", because they know us so intimately, and they may well be correct in their forecast. But we have still to make our decision, and we can still surprise them occasionally. Let us leave aside for the moment the question of human choice if all is known to an omniscient God (discussed in the paragraph on Bradwardine in Chapter 3) in order to focus on the physiological train of events in decision making.

We certainly feel that we can determine a specific course of action for ourselves, so if all mind activity is to be ascribed to essentially random electric and electromagnetic interactions in the brain, how is a particular electronic mind state representing a free thought selected? The process of selection of some specific ordered brain state producing a mental event must itself involve a decision and the selection of a previous specific electronic state, and we are into a position of infinite regress – every 'decision' to select a mind state needs a previous decision or mind-state selection to activate it.

Our choice of a line of thought is almost certainly determined by many factors: partly by our genetic make-up, by factors such as upbringing and social conditioning, by neuronal pathways already established through past decision-making (what we might describe as our habits), and partly by our immediate environment and the actual provocative sensory input, together with the pre-existing state of mind at the time of decision-making. The 'decision' is then influenced by a combination of these factors and, if we believe in a divine influence over our lives, our decision may also reflect the extent to which we 'tune in' to the divine spiritual realm; this may thereby influence the electronic state chosen, if this is appropriate to the kind of decision made. The intensity of this tuning-in experience is determined by our degree of empathy or resonance with the spiritual energy, like the tuning in of a radio to a particular frequency, and is itself influenced also by the other factors. The selection we make (the brain state that occurs) is determined by all of these factors – genetic, environmental, habitual and degree of spiritual attunement.

Routine decisions that we make in our everyday lives, like what breakfast cereal to eat, or what stroke to play in order to hit the cricket ball coming towards us, is a matter of instantaneous programming of incoming sensory information and response along established neural pathways using the brain's store of energy. It is doubtful if any external energy input is involved. For such mundane actions, it is suggested that the factors described above are alone enough to establish a particular brain state that constitutes a thought – or a whole series of them if some affirmative action like hitting a cricket ball is required. If we have hit a cricket ball many times, there are probably sufficiently well established neuronal and glial connections to program our response. It is only in original and creative thinking, or in establishing various kinds of meditative state, that participation of the universal spiritual field is suggested. More will be said of this in Chapter 8. Thus, what mind, thought, consciousness *is*, is the particular electronic and electromagnetic configuration of the brain at that instant, and this, for everyday tasks we implement using pre-existing programming – the process we call learning. There has to be a storage and retrieval system within the brain in order that we can use knowledge and memories, possibly resembling that in a computer, though one has to be cautious about analogies between human brains and inanimate electronic equipment. The electromagnetic waves that wash over the brain continually, even when we are asleep, can be likened to the screen-saver on the computer's monitor.

We shall therefore regard 'mind' as the consciously (and to some extent the unconsciously) working brain; and 'soul' is the name we shall reserve linguistically for those specific kinds of activity of mind, and thus of the brain, concerned with moral behaviour or aesthetic sensibility, including an awareness of or communing with a higher spiritual power. In the individual therefore, soul provides a conduit of communication between the material world of the brain and the surrounding environment on the one hand, and an aesthetic response from mind in providing spiritual uplift on the other. The brain receives, let us say, the aural signal of notes from a piece of music. Mind interprets this signal as, say, a symphony by Mahler. The physical brain picks out specific instrumentation or melodies. While that ongoing mental interpretation of the music is progressing, this swirl of electromagnetic activity in the brain is also simultaneously resonating with that in the universal spiritual field or akashic field of World Soul from which the spiritual uplift is derived. This feeds back into the individual to produce the aesthetic pleasure that is derived from the experience of the music. A similar explanation would apply if one is walking through beautiful countryside, listening to birdsong, or sitting quietly by the fire of a winter's evening reading a poem. This, it is suggested, is the nature of the activity of soul in relation to the mind and brain. It is the provider of spiritual refreshment from such physical experiences, many of which are explored in the next chapter.

The material world as mind
Three great systems of thought – religious, philosophical and scientific – converge in portraying the physical world as simply our conscious sensory experience of it. In some Eastern religious belief, particularly Mahayana Buddhism, the world itself is only human consciousness or *maya*, often rather imprecisely translated as 'illusion': perhaps 'appearance' or 'impression' would be closer to the meaning. This does not mean that the objects of the material world do not exist, only that

what we can perceive of them is illusory: we can never know their true being. Our sensory impressions are only just that – mental impressions or images. The exact nature of what we sense we can never know. In Hindu belief, the universe is the manifestation of their God, *Brahman*, who alone is real. The world comprises a spiritual dimension (*perusha*) and a material component (*prakriti*) that are complementary.

There are obvious resonances here with the writings of some of the philosophers too: Plato, who maintained that our worldly concepts are only reflections of the Absolute Ideas or Forms (Chapter 2); and the ideas of Bishop Berkeley (Chapter 7) that our sensory perceptions arise only and directly from those in the mind of God; and those of Locke on real essences and Kant on the noumenal (also summarised in Chapter 7).

There are scientists too who have expressed similar notions about the expression of the material within the mental. The mathematical physicist James Jeans (1877–1946) wrote along similar lines: 'the universe can best be pictured ... as consisting of pure mind' [276]. One of Jeans' contemporaries, physicist and astronomer Arthur Eddington (1882–1944), saw human consciousness as the intermediate between the unknowable quantum world and the world of material objects, and regarded both as essentially the same: 'The stuff of the world is mind stuff' [163].

Mystical experience – the soul in action

If we are to consider mental events as being of two kinds – those that arise from the initiation of purely biochemical and biophysical pathways, and those that suggest some external spiritual input – we need to try to distinguish between the two. It is difficult to be precise as to where we would draw that diffuse dividing line between those experiences of mind that are purely physical or operational, and those that produce emotional pleasure or that involve communion with divinity, however defined. There are clearly human experiences that seem to involve purely physiological mental control, without any kind of emotional or extracorporeal input, like driving or eating, or physical activities like walking or cycling: these are the ordinary experiences of everyday life. Then there are emotional experiences that involve the faculties of the brain that we would distinguish as soul, like being in love or listening to music or empathy with people in distress. At the highest end of the scale there are clear transcendental experiences that we distinguish as psychic or mystical.

The standard contemporary biological view is to assign all such emotional and mystical experiences to activities of mind/brain, dismissing the whole concept of soul. It seems that the concept of mysticism did not emerge until the Middle Ages, though such experiences have been characteristic of human behaviour throughout our history. Accounts of mystical experiences are recorded even in the books of the Old Testament and the *Vedas* of Hindu scripture, reporting events some 4000 years old or more; all native tribes have shamans or elders or sages that possess powers that fall under the common description of 'supernatural'. But the concept of being 'mystical' was not defined until the late 15th Century, even though it had been practiced for many centuries, and the word 'mysticism' itself is even more modern: its origin is given in the Oxford English Dictionary as occurring around 1736.

If we are to envisage interaction with the universal spiritual field as occurring more broadly than the overt experience of religious visions then it would perhaps be appropriate to distinguish between two kinds of mystical experience. We might say that there is an *ultimate or religious mysticism*, in which the subject feels they have had direct experience of the divine, or of some transcendent state of being; and a more common *incipient mysticism*, where there is an emotion that far transcends ordinary pleasure, but one does not have any realisation of being in the presence of divinity or ultimate reality. Experiences of aesthetic pleasure that spiritually uplift the individual belong to the latter group. Many people experience events such as these that enhance or transform the way they live their lives and yet they do not involve a situation in which they feel that they have encountered their vision of the divine, or received insight into the essence of the material world. But if, as a result of such happenings, their lives become more spiritual, that is, less materially oriented, they achieve greater peace of mind and tranquillity, and adopt a state of mind that shows more concern for humankind and the environment in general, then these surely are worthy of regard as spiritual, mystical or religious experiences. In other words, through such experiences the individual develops or reinforces their *faith* – the mind-set of percepts that determines their behaviour, their code of ethics and how they live their lives. This, surely, is the all-important reason for exploring evidence for the existence of soul that may help to convince sceptics of the existence of a meaningful spiritual domain, help them to lead more fulfilled lives, and thereby enhance the quality of life for themselves and those with whom they come into contact.

As we saw in Chapter 1, the Cosmological Argument – the very existence of the universe, and the fact that there is something rather than nothing – has been used by theologians as evidence for the existence of God as Creator or First Cause. The cooperative workings of Nature provide reason to affirm the existence of a Grand Designer. We may not be able to deduce God's existence logically, as in a mathematical theorem, because we have no axioms or definitions or premises with which to start, and the divine is a unique entity, but reason combined with human experience gives us persuasive evidence. An examination of human history tells us that sages claiming insight into the ultimate nature of things seem to have been a part of every society since earliest times, and they are still with us today. So, the transcendental experiences of sages described in Holy Scripture must be regarded as another strand of the evidence for the existence of God, provided it does not conflict with reason. What criteria are necessary to regard the events they experience as mystical?

F.C. Happold [229] quotes Lasson's definition of mysticism: 'The essence of mysticism is the assertion of an intuition which transcends the temporal categories of the understanding' [p.37]. William James defined four criteria of mystical experiences: ineffability ('more like states of feeling than like states of intellect'); noetic quality ('insight into depths of truth'); transiency ('mystical states cannot be sustained for long'); and passivity ('the mystic feels as if his own will were in abeyance, and indeed sometimes as if he were grasped and held by a superior power'. . . 'They modify the inner life of the subject') [274]. Those who undergo a deep mystical or psychic experience always find that their lives are in some way transformed, and typically away from the material towards the spiritual. Belief in the sayings of spiritual leaders comes, not only from their message but also from the quality of the lives they lead. It is the detachment from the world of the five senses that Stace sees as paramount in what is described above as 'ultimate mysticism': 'The most important, the central characteristic in which all *fully developed* mystical experiences agree, and which in the last analysis is definitive of them and serves to mark them off from other kinds of experience, is that they involve the apprehension of *an ultimate nonsensuous unity in all things*, a oneness or a One to which neither the senses nor the reason can penetrate. In other words, it entirely transcends our sensory-intellectual consciousness' [449]

Participation in an incipient mystical experience is uplifting and spiritually refreshing, even if it is not life transforming. It gives us a sense of belonging to something greater than ourselves – it takes us out of our body into the numinous. It makes us feel we are not alone: 'No one on this earth is alone. We only become alone or lonely if we believe, at an unconscious level, that we are separated from the thought energy of the earth and the many people it connects us to' [227]. This is what mystical experiences – even incipient mystical experiences – allow us to feel. They lift our emotions at the time, but after, 'like wind or waves, or light in the morning or evening, [they] leave traces of energy behind them after they have gone' [228].

One of the most extensive collections of data in the U.K. involving religious, mystical or spiritual experiences is to be found in the library of the Alister Hardy Trust, originally at Oxford but now located at the University of Wales in Lampeter. Sir Alister Hardy FRS was born in Nottingham in 1896. He was educated at Oxford and became Professor of Zoology at the University of Hull, 1928–42. His primary interest was in marine biology and he sailed on the *Discovery* expeditions to the Antarctic in the 1930s to study marine mammals. He became Professor of Zoology at Oxford from 1945 to 1961. In 1969, Hardy set up the Religious Experience Research Unit at Manchester College, Oxford. His aim was to document religious experiences so that there would be a source of empirical data that future researchers into the nature of spiritual experience could draw on and from which they could reach conclusions, as in the manner of any scientific investigation. For too long, too many scientists have dismissed all spiritual and psychic experiences as of no relevance to the way the world works other than to the individual concerned: they are a social phenomenon contributing nothing to science or universal knowledge. Increasingly, this view has been shown to be misguided, and Hardy has contributed to this enlightenment with his archives. Sir Alister Hardy died in 1985 having left a unique legacy of religious experiences to which more incidents are continually being added.

Chapter 6 explores some aspects of mystical or psychic experience that could be regarded as manifestations of soul. Most of these would fall into the category of incipient mystical experiences, evidence for which abounds, and only spiritual enlightenment and some near-death experiences in these examples would be classed as religious mystical experiences. The classification used here is based on a few of the examples given in Alister Hardy's *The Spiritual Nature of Man* [232].

6 Manifestations of soul in the individual

There are a number of human activities that seem to go beyond plain physiological functioning of the brain, that is, routine activities of mind. These are activities that impact on an individual's spiritual world-view or faith, events that many would associate with soul, as defined in the previous chapter. In life, soul is that part of mind that communes with the divine, or with what believers call the akashic field or universal spiritual field. The activities described here are expressions of the human soul that can be regarded as communion with the divine spirit, activities other than the practice of the ritual of an organised religion. Although they are grouped differently here, such activities form part of the classification of kinds of religious experience given by Sir Alister Hardy in his book *The Spiritual Nature of Man* [232]. As these activities do not involve the communal worship that is the distinguishing characteristic of the term 'religion', it would perhaps be more appropriate to call them spiritual experiences, or even mystical experiences in the sense described in the previous chapter. Hardy was concerned to accumulate evidence of religious experience, albeit usually personal and anecdotal, to serve as a source of data for those who wanted to conduct a systematic investigation of the phenomena. It is no more or less reliable than any evidence gathered from human subjects, with all their individual traits.

Some of these activities are also included in Zohar and Marshall's very eloquently described examples of what they call 'spiritual intelligence' at work: '[the] place within the self, of light, a feeling of holiness in everyday objects and events, the sense of the sacred in the act of loving, the ecstasy in understanding something for the first time, the elation of bringing something new into the world, the satisfaction of seeing justice, the peace of serving God.' [532]. Spiritual intelligence (SQ), they say, is the next evolutionary step after rational intelligence (IQ) and emotional intelligence (EQ); it represents an awareness of the needs and feelings of others and of the environment and world at large.

Many great theologians, like Friedrich Schleiermacher (1768–1834) and, more recently, Karl Rahner (1904–1984) and Paul Tillich (1886–1965), have maintained that personal experience of the divine is the only valid route for affirmation of God, but also say that there are indications of the numinous in many of our everyday experiences. For most of us, these are our *only* route to the divine, so it is examples of some of these experiences that are discussed in this chapter. It is not the dogma and rituals of religion that should be paramount in our lives but the profound sense of the numinous in these common life experiences that involve soul. Many people find it easier to commune with the divine through Nature, music, poetry, art, architecture, love and meditation rather than through the prescribed ritual or dogmatic interpretation of scripture to be found in organised religion. Psychic events are also included by Hardy in his classification of religious experiences.

6.1.   Aesthetic sense

This section corresponds to some of the experiences grouped in Section 11 of Hardy's classification [232, p.28]. As St. Paul says in the letter to the Romans [1.20]: we know the hidden things of God by looking at the things that he has made' [10]. Aquinas was quick to point out however that this did not imply that God was *within* nature, as the pagans believed: 'God does not enter into the composition of other things: he is not the soul of the world' [13]. The human mind has two aspects: there is the sensory and rational aspect, and there is the emotional and introspective aspect. To be whole, we need to constantly exercise both of these faculties.

There are certain mind events that represent our ability to respond to works of art, music, poetry or scenes of natural beauty in such a way that we feel spiritually uplifted: this is soul in action in incipient mysticism. Such events may also produce physiologically measurable responses within the brain and the rest of the body. But what is it about, say, a specific piece of music that should provoke such a response? It is only sound, impinging on the ear, deciphered by the brain. The words of a poem are only so much ink on a sheet of paper – why should these create joy or spiritual uplift, or in some cases even make us feel uneasy? This is the faculty within mind that is capable of producing an emotional and spiritual as well as a physical or logical response to such things: the physical response would be to note that, say, a string orchestra was playing, or a poem was written in rhyming couplets; the aesthetic emotional response is what we would ascribe to soul. As stated at the end of the previous chapter, when we listen to music, even on our own, we are taken out of ourselves to a much more expansive realm: 'Who hears music, feels his solitude / Peopled at once' [98]. Part of this emotional response is due to the symmetry of form in a piece of music, or poem or the architectural structure of a great cathedral. The problem many people have with much modern art, poetry and music is its lack of obvious form or structure and, in the case of music, the discordance, atonality and disharmony that produces agitation and stress rather than relaxation or emotional uplift. As poet John Dryden said in his Dedication to Henry Purcell's *The Prophetess* (1690): 'As poetry is the harmony of words, so music is that of notes'. One must question whether seemingly random assortments of notes on a stave or of paint on a canvas, even if there is an underlying rational structure accessible to the cognoscente, really constitute art if the only response they provoke is revulsion or bewilderment. Music both popular and classical, from Bach to Berlin, from Purcell to Porter, that has been created over the course of the past four or five centuries is still alive and performed regularly today because it has beauty and harmony. One wonders how many of today's compositions in classical or popular music will still be heard even fifty years hence. According to physicist David Bohm (see Chapter 8): 'In listening to music, one is ... directly perceiving an implicate order' [77]. If that order is incomprehensible even at the sensory level, what are we to make of this assemblage of sounds claiming to be music?

Through music and poetry, the listener or reader should be able to commune with the spirit of the composer or poet, and with the world at large, as well as with the divine, and for some, this is their closest contact with the spiritual realm: 'A verbal art like poetry is reflective; it stops to think. Music is immediate; it goes on to become' [24]. And what it becomes is a contribution to a more enlightened soul. Some philosophers, like Pythagoras, Plato and Augustine, believed that there was a mathematical harmony underlying everything in the world, and that music was the audible expression of this harmony. The feelings it evoked defied expression: 'Man can say nothing of what he is incapable of feeling, but he can feel what he is incapable of putting into words' [31].

There are others who would say that their closest approach to a mystical experience was the emotions of the numinous that were aroused by being amid unspoilt countryside, the ability

> To see a World in a Grain of Sand
> And a Heaven in a Wild Flower,
> Hold Infinity in the palm of your hand
> And Eternity in an hour

William Blake, Auguries of Innocence

William Blake (1757–1827), living at a time when science was beginning to take over as the new religion, was a mystic as well as a poet, artist and engraver, an enemy of materialism and one who was frequently subject to visions. He was deeply religious, but rejected Christianity on the grounds that the Church's teachings had alienated humankind from their own humanity. Blake's religion was that of the pantheist.

The almost contemporary English Nature poets William Wordsworth (1770–1850) and Samuel Taylor Coleridge (1772–1834) saw the divine in all the natural world around them in the then-unspoilt English Lake District, before the invention of nuclear reprocessing plants. Their American friend, poet and philosopher Ralph Waldo Emerson (1803–1882), in his little book *Nature* [170] encouraged his readers to see 'God and nature face to face' – to see in Nature symbols for the spirit of God. This was the age of Romanticism that started in 19th Century Germany but carried on in much artistic creative expression in the twentieth. English poet Gerard Manley Hopkins saw the variety in Nature as expression of the divine: Glory be to God for dappled things (poem *Pied Beauty*). Many English composers of the 20th Century have found great creative inspiration for their music in the beauty of the English countryside. The post-Renaissance scientists regarded a study of Nature like another chapter of divine revelation.

The German philosopher Immanuel Kant (1724–1804) explored many different themes in his writings: one of his ideas relating to the spiritual domain is described in Chapter 7. His ideas were one of the main influences behind the Romantic movement that began with the appearance in 1774 of *A Theory of the Evolution of Humankind* (*Auch eine Philosophie der Geschichte zur Bildung der Menschheit*) by Johann Gottfried von Herder (1744–1803). As much as a whole social movement can be said to begin with one event, this is considered to be the most influential in initiating German Romanticism, though another key publication was the play *Sturm und Drang* (*Storm and Stress*; 1776) by Friedrich Maximilian von Klinger (1752–1831). As well as being a development of the ideas of Kant, Romanticism was also a rebellion against the formalism and cool detached elegance of the Classical period in art and music, and represented a yearning in the human soul for the spiritual dimension of existence in the midst of the mechanisation of the expanding Industrial Revolution. In his synthesis of Empiricism and Rationalism, Kant had seen all human experience as derived from sensory perception combined with a rational interpretation. Herder believed that human experience was shaped above all by feeling (*Gefuhl*) as the primary factor. It was the emotions, not reason or the senses, that primarily shaped human history. As David Hume says: 'Reason is, and ought only to be the slave of the passions, and can never pretend to any other office than to serve and obey them' [267]. It is our emotional feelings about the world that determine what events we take note of, and how we interpret them. There were no laws, like Kant's Categorical Imperative, that governed human behaviour: each society, each individual was different. The Spirit of the People (*Volkgeist*) was the determining factor in shaping the history of society and of the individual. The communication of knowledge within society is possible only through language, said Herder. Language expresses thought and thought expresses feelings; and when we talk of emotions and feelings, we are moving into that grey area between expressions of mind and manifestations of soul.

Immanuel Kant had many pupils and followers who were inspired by his philosophy. One of these was Friedrich Wilhelm Joseph von Schelling (1775–1854), a pupil of Johann Fichte (see Section 6.4). The Romantics turned first to Fichte as their leader but, when he rejected them, they adopted Schelling, who was happy to be counted amongst them: for Schelling's was, above all, a philosophy of Nature. In 1790 he entered the theological seminary at Tübingen from which he graduated in 1792. In 1798 he became Professor of Philosophy at Jena, which was the principal centre for the Romantic poets in Germany. Schelling subsequently held Chairs in Philosophy in Munich and Berlin. Schelling's *System of Transcendental Idealism* (Tübingen, 1800) expressed the same view essentially as that of Fichte – that the world as we experience it is the world of ideas created by the self. But, like Schiller, he also stressed the importance of the creative imagination expressed through poetry, art and music. The aesthetic was an indispensable part of the human consciousness with the natural world as the creative driving force. The Schlegel brothers, August (1767–1845) and Friedrich (1772–1829), both poets, were also prominent members of this circle of distinguished German Romantics.

An appreciation of Nature, Schelling maintained, was central to the creative process in art, music and literature, and this was an indispensable component of the human character. His predecessor in German Romanticism, Johann Christoph Friedrich von Schiller (1759–1805) formed a bridge between the cold rationalism of the Enlightenment and the unbridled passion of the Romantic period. A poet, dramatist and philosopher, and a close friend of Wolfgang Goethe (1749–1832), Schiller's view was that aesthetic expression, particularly in literature, was the highest aspect of the human soul. In his epoch-making book *The Aesthetic Education of Mankind*, he was keen to forge a link between aesthetic appreciation and morality, the latter a key concept in the philosophies of Immanuel Kant (Chapter 7) and Johann Fichte (Section 6.4). Schiller's *Ode to Joy*, set by Beethoven as the finale to his Ninth Symphony, encapsulates Schiller's philosophy of freedom of emotional expression as the highest pinnacle of human achievement.

Aesthetic appreciation of Nature is thus one of the paths to the divine. But there is a school of philosophical thought – *pantheism* – that actually identifies God with the natural world, totally immanent. This is generally interpreted as the view of the Dutch philosopher Benedict (or Baruch) Spinoza (1632–1677). Spinoza came from a Jewish family from Portugal. There they had been forced by the Inquisition to renounce their Judaism in favour of Catholicism, but always remained Jewish at heart. They fled Portugal and settled in Holland because of the somewhat greater religious tolerance in that country. Spinoza earned a living by teaching, but supplemented his meagre income by working as a lens-grinder. It was inhalation of the dust from this occupation that led to his premature death.

In a time when being a true Catholic meant having direct experience of God, Spinoza retained his fundamental Jewish belief that God was physically inaccessible to humankind. However, his greatest conflict with authority arose from his contention that the authors of the Pentateuch were not necessarily any better informed in matters of theology or the science of creation than he and his students. As a result, Spinoza was excommunicated from the Jewish community in 1656 for his religious views. He wrote a work on Cartesian philosophy, a subject that he also taught to his private students, and a *Theologico-Political Treatise*, published anonymously in 1670. This publication, once the identity of its author became known, drew down more scathing criticism on Spinoza for its advocacy of peace, tolerance and understanding in an era of violent religious persecution and intolerance of all non-Catholics. He also encouraged freedom of thought and speech on religious matters, particularly in biblical criticism, and many of his views have been endorsed by present-day studies.

Spinoza's most influential work, *Ethics*, written in Latin, was published posthumously just after his death. It is set out, like the philosophy of Descartes and the geometry of Euclid, as a series of propositions that are deduced from certain basic assumptions or axioms. As Spinoza said to Leibniz: 'Descartes starts from mind: I start from God.' This kind of radical foundationalism has been discredited on the grounds that the basic assumptions necessary can never be guaranteed to be infallible or indubitable. But if Descartes could not doubt his own existence as a thinking being, so Spinoza cannot doubt the existence of the creative essence of the world: 'God or a substance of infinite attributes, each of which expresses eternal and infinite essence, necessarily exists' [443]. His views on the relation between God and the natural world imply that Spinoza was a pantheist: 'Except God no substance can be granted or conceived.' [444]; 'Whatever is, is in God, and nothing can exist or be conceived without God.' [445]; 'God is the indwelling and not the transient cause of all things'[446]; 'God is not only the effecting cause of the existence of things, but also of their essence' [447]; 'In God there is granted not only the idea of his essence, but also the idea of all the things which follow necessarily from his essence' [448]. A variation in this view that we encountered in Chapter 1 in discussing paganism is that of *panentheism*. Here, Nature is still a part of God, but God is also transcendent: the divine is still immanent in the world but there is an aspect of God that is outside the world. With such seemingly instinctive and intimate association of Nature with God from the earliest times of civilisation, even associating aspects of Nature with anthropomorphic deities, it is not surprising that awe-inspiring views of natural beauty should generate a feeling of divine transcendence. Whether the natural world *is* God, or whether God is *in* the world of Nature, our efforts at conservation of the environment is a vital component of our acts of devotion to the divine.

The inference of the existence of God through the existence, beauty and coherence of the natural world is what is called natural theology. That there are human minds capable of appreciating this natural beauty is taken by some as further evidence of divine purpose. St Augustine, using the Genesis text as his authority, maintained that 'nothing (except the divine nature) can exist apart from the creation by God' [27]. The existence and order of the world formed part of Thomas Aquinas's Five Ways to infer the existence of God (see Chapter 1, Section 1.5.1). John Calvin believed that God had created the human mind with an innate sense of His being: 'There is within the human mind, and that by natural instinct, a sense of divinity.' [103]. It is a matter of philosophical debate whether we should regard our inference of God from the results of Creation as an instance of divine revelation, or as an axiom, a self-evident truth, or the result of applying our faculty of reason. Alister McGrath, as a Christian theologian, is concerned that it should be regarded as the first of these [341]. He rejects the approach of the 20th Century American philosopher William Alston in regarding natural theology as 'the enterprise of providing support for religious beliefs by starting from premises that neither are nor presuppose any religious beliefs' [3]. The premise that a cause-and-effect relationship exists between the existence of the universe and an incomprehensible agency that could be capable of producing such an effect is itself an innate human faculty. Whether or not one attributes this propensity to a divine origin is itself therefore a matter of faith.

The idea that the natural world in some way embodies the Universal Spirit is probably the greatest difference between Eastern and Western theology. In Western belief, whether Judaic, Christian or Islamic, God is utterly transcendent, separate from Nature,

while in Eastern thought, as in paganism, the Universal Spirit or
Universal Mind or Brahman is everywhere, 'unseen, inconceivable,
unimaginable, indescribable'. Western religion begins with a
transcendent God and develops images of the divine from the
prophets or the incarnation in Jesus, with the divine spirit invested
in us as soul. The focus is on the individual. Eastern religion starts
from a Divine Spirit or Brahman or Oneness in the natural world
and works towards the transcendence of humankind that is achieved
in *nirvana* through meditation and respect for the words of the
avatars, the messengers or manifestations of the divine. The focus
here is on the infinite expanse of the created universe and the divine
spirit.

As our lives become more pressured with concerns for material
growth and profit, more technologically sophisticated in sprawling
conurbations, each individual becomes more isolated spiritually and
emotionally, however active their social life may be, and time for
reflection and access to Nature become more difficult to secure – yet
also become increasingly necessary. The expansiveness and peace of
a natural environment is much more conducive to contemplative
meditation than the almost inescapable noise of urban life. Indeed it is
essential, for meditation can only be achieved in tranquil surroundings.
The popularity in recent years of classes, often held outdoors, in *yoga*
and *tai chi*, of stress management courses for executives in country
retreats, and a seemingly endless production of CDs of 'chillout'
music all testify to the realisation that such spiritual relaxation is an
increasingly essential component of our lives, whatever the demands
of business. The popularity of contemporary music that is infused
with a spiritual aura, such as many compositions by John Tavener
and Arvo Pärt, and of the philosophy described by M. Scott Peck
[363] and by James Redfield in his *Celestine* books [395] testify to our
need for release from the materialist treadmill. Tavener, who formerly
sought his inspiration in the Eastern Orthodox Church, has found
new inspiration in the natural world: 'I find walking in nature more
conducive to prayer than being in a church building. It's when I am
walking that musical ideas come.' [480].

It is through this enjoyment of the aesthetic experience of Nature, music and poetry that many find their God. As Cicero says: 'If any man cannot feel the power of God when he looks upon the stars, then I doubt whether he is capable of any feeling at all' [125]. Or as D.H. Lawrence expressed it poetically:

> The gods are nameless and imageless
> Yet looking in a great full lime-tree of summer
> I suddenly saw deep into the eyes of gods:
> it is enough.
>
> D.H. Lawrence: *The Body of God*

This appreciation of artistic creations and of Nature is a kind of mystical experience accessible to everyone, to a greater or lesser extent.

6.2. Inspired creativity [232, Section 9]

The term 'inspiration' is used in medicine to mean the taking in of air into the lungs; but it also represents the absorbing of spiritual energy that we can convert into creative output. Many people are aware of having had moments or even periods of inspiration that led to pinnacles of creativity, either in the arts or in science, or times when they were able to resolve some obstinate mental problems 'in a flash', often when the mind was not even focused on them; indeed, it is a common experience that focused concentration seems to *inhibit* this kind of enlightenment: 'Even in science, it is intuition...that gives new insights. These insights tend to come suddenly. . . but when relaxing' [106].

In the Introduction to this chapter we met the different kinds of 'intelligences' suggested by Zohar and Marshall – rational, emotional and spiritual. The Harvard psychologist Howard Gardner has presented some evidence for the existence of what he calls 'multiple intelligences' – specialised development of areas of the brain, as found in prodigies or savants, those who may even be mentally retarded overall but show an extraordinary ability in some specific field [205, 206]. There are six kinds of intelligence distinguished by Gardner: linguistic, mathematical or logical, spatial, musical, kinaesthetic (ability to exercise fine control over body movements), and personal (ability to know oneself and to understand the body language of others). However, spiritual intelligence – the ability to commune with the universal spiritual field to an extraordinarily high degree and thereby produce inspired creativity – is not one of them! The above-average physical development of areas of the brain does not preclude the possibility still of extra-corporeal input from the universal field. Indeed, it might be expected that such extra neuronal or glial development within regions of the brain would make it more sensitive to such spiritual input. Geniuses are almost always emotionally sensitive creatures.

The brain has within it great resources that can be called upon to provide energy for everyday logical functions, like routine decision-making and problem-solving; or making the instinctive decisions that are necessary in playing sports; or even focusing on several different tasks at the same time, as in carrying on a conversation while driving or knitting. But are the moments of supreme creativity or inspired insight in problem-solving any different qualitatively from the brain processes of everyday life, or are they merely quantitatively greater instances of thinking in gifted individuals? There are certainly areas of the brain that have now been identified as being associated with various sensory functions, and even the experience of pleasure or pain, but this is only a part of the picture: the role of emotion as a mind event is a subject of ongoing psychological and physiological controversy. Many creative people experience wild swings of mood that take them near the patient categories that psychologists call manic-depressive or obsessive-compulsive, and these states can be physiologically characterised: creativity is often in some way associated with highs and lows of emotion and characteristic patterns of behaviour which may result from psychic interaction with the spiritual realm. There are of course numerous instances of inspired creativity, and a few of the best-known examples, from the arts and science, of acknowledged divine inspiration derived from trance-like states are given below. Those who believe in the concept of soul and the universal spiritual field would say that all creative inspiration derives from this source; certainly, all artistic creativity is highly spiritual.

It was while French philosopher René Descartes (1596–1650) was resting up from a winter journey through Germany on 10 November 1619, seated in a small room that was heated only by a stove, that he had both daytime visions and night-time dreams that revealed to him a *scientia mirabilis*, as he called it. The exact nature of these visions is unknown because his record of the event in his notebooks is fragmentary, but it is believed to involve the unity of certain disparate subjects of study, like music, astronomy and arithmetic, and novel methods of study in science. His greatest contribution to science was his system for combining the disciplines of algebra and geometry into what is now known as co-ordinate or algebraic or Cartesian geometry, later to be extended by the German mathematician August Ferdinand Möbius (1790–1868). Descartes' method appeared in his book generally known by its abbreviated title of *Discourse on the Method of Sciences* (Leyden, 1637). His metaphysical work, *Meditations on First Philosophy*, appeared four years later (Amsterdam, 1641). It was in this work that the mind-body dualism idea was elaborated [142], as discussed in the previous chapter. *The World* (*Le Monde*), which he had withheld for fear of retribution by the Inquisition for its support of Copernicus, was finally published posthumously in Paris in 1664. How much of these works resulted directly from divine inspiration and the visions of 1619, and how much derives from the normal processes of reason we do not know.

The English historian Edward Gibbon (1737–1794) was born in Putney, Surrey. He was a sickly child, largely neglected by his mother and brought up by his aunt. His interest in the classics dated from his childhood. Enrolled in 1752 at Magdalen College, Oxford, before his 15th birthday, he read avidly and decided the following year to enter the Roman Catholic Church; he thereby disqualified himself from holding public office at this sensitive time in Protestant suspicions of anyone professing enthusiasm for Catholicism. Edward's father was therefore appalled at his son's decision and saw to it that he was instructed by a Calvinist minister in Lausanne, Switzerland, as a result of which Edward Gibbon reconverted back to Protestantism again the next year. Thereafter he abandoned his spiritual agonising and simply assented to the fundamental beliefs of the Christian faith. At Lausanne he met with the much travelled Voltaire; in Paris he was acquainted with the Encyclopédists Diderot and d'Alembert, and back in London he became part of Dr. Samuel Johnston's circle. Gibbon was held in high regard even by historian-philosopher David Hume when his history of Rome began to be published in 1776. At this time of his life, though Gibbon had written little of note, he was considered to be a man of letters and was of independent means. In his biography he related how he was walking through the ruins of the Capitol in Rome in October 1764 when he was struck by mystical inspiration that motivated him to write his monumental work *The History of the Decline and Fall of the Roman Empire* (1776–87), which describes its history from the 2nd Century CE up to the fall of Constantinople in 1453. This met with some public disfavour because it contained an account of the rise of Christianity, which was not in accord with the official Church view.

The German chemist, Friedrich August Kekulé was born in Darmstadt in 1829 and studied under another great chemist Justus von Liebig before taking professorial posts in Ghent and, later, Bonn. One of his best-known contributions to chemistry was his suggestion in 1865 of a formula for what are now known as aromatic compounds. The basic structure of such compounds has unique properties that could not be interpreted in terms of the chemistry known at that time. The structure that Kekulé proposed is called an aromatic ring and he maintained that it came to him in an inspired dream.

Austrian composer Gustav Mahler (1860–1911) certainly saw composition as part of this mystical interaction. Speaking of his

Second Symphony, popularly known as *The Resurrection*, he said: "Creative activity and the genesis of a work are mystical from start to finish, since one acts unconsciously, as if prompted from outside, and then one can hardly conceive how the result has come into being" [61] and "For me, the conception of the work never involved the laying down of a process, but at the most of a feeling ...The parallelism between life and music may be deeper and wider than we are yet in a position to understand" [62].

These few anecdotes give an impression of how some great creative minds have believed that divine inspiration played a significant part in their own creative processes.

6.3. Spiritual enlightenment [corresponding to ref. 232, Sections 1 and 12]

This term is used to describe what subjects believe is a direct vision of the divine, or some dimension of ultimate reality, as opposed to subconscious divine inspiration as source of the creative process, or spiritual uplift in our everyday lives from the arts or Nature. It also corresponds to what is described in the previous chapter (Section 4.2) as ultimate mysticism. The opening line of the *Tao Te Ching* says: 'The *Tao* that can be expressed is not the eternal *Tao*'. Or, as Fritjof Capra puts it: ' Absolute knowledge is ... an entirely non-intellectual experience of reality' [105]. Bishop Hugh Montefiore (1920–2005), a convert to Christianity from Judaism, regarded the miracles described in scripture, like Moses' encounter with the angel on Mount Sinai [Exodus 3, v. 2–3], or the shining light of the transfigured Jesus [Matthew 17, v.1–2] as examples of psychic experiences (see later) that also belong to the category of spiritual enlightenment. These events conform most strongly to the definition of mystical experience given in the 'Mysticism' part of Section 5.2. Because they are all highly individual, events such as these can be regarded as objective evidence of the spiritual realm only insofar as they have been repeated over and over through time in many lands and reported independently by people whose integrity is not suspect.

One of the ubiquitous practices of followers of Eastern religious philosophies is meditation. The aim is to dissociate oneself from one's material surroundings into a spiritual plane of tranquillity, as this sublime state is believed to produce spiritual refreshment and enlightenment through glimpses of the ineffable. Meditation is a core practice of devotees of *yoga* also in the West. *Yoga* has attracted enthusiasts in their attempts to create or retain lithe and supple bodies, and because it presents an opportunity to escape the stresses of modern life in the surrounding materialist culture by creating an oasis of calm. It enables practitioners to realign their sense of values of what is important in life by making time for a spiritual component. There are different types of *yoga* practice that focus on different aspects of the world-view. *Hatha yoga* focuses on the familiar *asanas* or postures and exercises to promote energy flow. *Karma yoga* concentrates on the doing of good works for the benefit of others – a life of selfless devotion to others. *Bhakti yoga* is for those who wish to live their lives as a devotion to the ever-present divine; and *inana yoga* concentrates on acquiring knowledge of ultimate spiritual truths. *Pūrna yoga* is a form of contemplation advocated particularly by Sri Aurobindo (see below) that seeks to maximise living practically but harmoniously in the real world, at one with one's environment. Ideally, one would wish to encompass all of these, but as each requires almost a lifetime of study and practice to perfect, realistically one must choose one's path to enlightenment.

Achievement of a contemplative or meditative state is assisted for some by tranquil music in the background, or by the chanting of a repetitive phrase, called a *mantra*, or by fixating on a symmetrical geometrical design, usually encompassed by a circle, occasionally a square, called a *yantra* or *mandala* (Sanskrit: magic circle) [182]. The designs symbolise mathematically the universal divine energy and help to focus the meditator's own mind and internal energy. Geometrical harmony is believed to be more conducive to calm meditative states than asymmetric designs: and the same could be said of aural or visual harmony in music or painting, as discussed above. The idea is to focus on the shape for as long as necessary to be able to hold the essential details in the mind with the eyes closed. The Swiss psychoanalyst Carl Jung believed that *mandalas* were of great significance in that they reflected some deep innate spiritual truth buried within the subconscious. Many of his patients reported visualising such designs in dreams or trance states, and Jung drew several such designs himself to help him when he was in states of stress.

Although they do not have the necessary experience of the world, children seem to be better attuned to the spiritual dimension than adults. There are many reports that children, whose brain activity is predominantly in the more relaxed alpha phase, seem to be more susceptible to 'spiritual visions', though these tend to be dismissed by sceptical adults as childish imaginings: the brains of adults seem to function mainly in the more critical and analytical beta mode. It has been shown by physiological measurements that deep relaxation and meditation does indeed produce a state of altered consciousness and increased alpha activity, which seems to come more naturally to children.

Sceptics would say that any observations made by those in such a mental state are relevant only to the participant and do not provide any evidence for the validity of the concepts of God and soul. Science has for many generations believed that experiment and observation with the five senses is the only path to truth. However, spiritual masters have been telling us for a very much longer time that there are other truths that are accessible only to the inner self or sixth sense. The eternity of mystical insight is as inscrutable as the infinity of the mathematician; but both have a part to play in our understanding of the world around us and our role in it.

Anthropologists have documented instances of instinctive knowing amongst indigenous tribal people in India and China, in Australia, New Zealand, and North and South America. The 'inner vision' or intuition of mystics through the ages has given rise to an extensive religious literature. The Western religions all have their mystical traditions, represented by the Jewish Kabbalah, the Sufi

Islamic tradition, and in some practices of the Gnostics. Moses is believed to have received the Ten Commandments by direct communication with God. Muhammad was given the *Qu'ran* by a vision of the Archangel Gabriel – who also visited Mary to tell her of the forthcoming birth of Jesus. All religions have a belief that certain gifted practitioners amongst them have the ability through meditation to access the divinity.

The medieval German Jesuit mystic Jakob Böhme (1575–1624) recalled the dualism of the Gnostics and Manichees in his theology of the ongoing conflict of the forces of good and evil, though the existence of evil he considered to be a necessary part of human spiritual evolution. The role of God in the world was to re-establish a state of grace in humankind, a state nearer to perfection even than the innocence before the Fall. The evolution of the created world to a state of greater peace and harmony was part of the evolution of God to a higher state. It was this suggestion, that God needed the created world in order to evolve to a higher state of perfection, that brought condemnation on Böhme, but it is reflected today in the ideas of Process Theology (see Chapter 1). The unchanging and unknowable God, Creator of all that is, the Godhead of Meister Eckhart (Chapter 4), was designated as the *Undgrund* or Abyss. The immanent God appears with Creation, which came about from the primordial oneness so that God would be evident to humankind. The world as becoming is the self-revelation of God in the material world of the senses.

Böhme had mystical experiences all through his life, but it was one such experience in 1600 that focused his mind on these ideas in theological philosophy while he worked in his mundane trade to raise a family; and it was another vision in 1610 that provoked his writing. Up to that time he had been a humble village shoemaker, as he had only a limited education. His first book, *Aurora*, published in 1612, met with such condemnation from the Church that he abandoned writing for the next decade and he was only persuaded to take up the pen again in 1619 by his friends. But his *Way To Christ* (1623) caused another scandal, so he retired, first to Dresden, and then to his home town of Görlitz. Nevertheless, he managed to produce in all more than two dozen books and tracts before his death in the following year. His complete works were not published until 1730. Böhme's experiences are described here rather than in the previous section only because they seem to have been more spiritually life-transforming than those of Descartes, Gibbon and the others whose spiritual experiences led to the creation of one specific work, not a whole new way of life. This surely is true mystical enlightenment.

Many subsequent philosophers and writers, like G.W.F. Hegel, William Blake, and Samuel Taylor Coleridge, were influenced by Böhme's ideas, and Carl Jung made many references to Böhme in his writings. Apart from its relationship with Process Theology, Böhme's ideology has something in it also of the Anthropic Principle (see Section 8.2) – that God has created the world with environmental parameters such that humankind can evolve, with the opportunity, through the existence of good and evil, to rise to a greater state of perfection and an awareness of His Creation.

A name that is often mentioned as having an influence on Böhme is that of Paracelsus, the epithet of Theophrastus Bombastus von Hohenheim (*ca.*1490–1541). He was a Swiss physician and alchemist, a man with minimal formal education, though he did study for a time at the University of Basel and even lectured there in later life. He was a contemporary of Martin Luther (Chapter 1) and Copernicus (Chapter 4), and his work was so popular, though controversial, that he provoked more academic discussion in his day than either of his now better-known contemporaries. His writings are generally held to be of little lasting value today except that, in his theology, he did lay great emphasis on the unity of the created world, humankind and the universe as a whole, with God, as did Böhme.

But it was as a physician that Paracelsus was best known, and he counted the Dutch humanist Erasmus and German printer Frobenius (Johann Froben) amongst his patients. He rejected the Hippocratic idea of imbalance of the four 'humours' as the source of illness. Instead, he believed that illness was caused by the *ens astrorum* (cosmic influences that varied with country and climate), *ens venemi* (toxic materials derived from food), *ens naturale et spirituale* (defects in the physical or mental consititution), or the *ens deale* (illnesses caused by Fate or spiritual imbalance). He stressed that the physician must be aware that illness is deeply affected by what he called the astral plane and by the state of the soul of the individual or, as we might say now, by the influence of state or attitude of mind and spirit on the health of the body as a whole. Paracelsus' most enduring contribution to medicine was probably the idea of using chemical compounds to treat disease instead of the plant extracts recommended by Galen. Many of these compounds, although potentially toxic, were used in extremely dilute preparations as the basis of homeopathic medicines in the 19th Century by Samuel Hahnemann (see Section 6.5), while Galen's use of diluted plant extracts was revived in the 20th Century by Edward Bach (1880–1936) in his 'flower remedies'. But Paracelsus' principle of using synthetic chemical compounds to treat ailments is regarded by some as the conceptual foundation of the 20th Century pharmaceutical industry. Unfortunately, Paracelsus' writings on chemistry and pharmacy were interspersed with ideas derived from his belief in spiritual beings like nymphs and sylphs and, as a result, any scientific merit in his innovations was obscured. But here was a man with virtually no formal education, like Böhme, largely self-taught, who had absorbed much of the writings on medicine and alchemy by the time he was sixteen, and who produced many valuable innovative ideas from the depths of his imagination.

6.4. The ability to love

The aspects of soul described in the earlier sections, and in Hardy's *Spiritual Nature of Man*, relate to individual experiences of inspiration – a drawing in of the universal spirit. The ability to love is an ongoing attitude of mind, enlightened by soul, that represents the pouring out of Soul from the individual into the world, so there is no specific 'experience' within the Hardy classification [232] that corresponds to human love. The phenomenon is like the effect of dropping a pebble into a pond creating ripples spreading outwards with ever-increasing radius. Our love similarly radiates out to our partners, to children, parents and siblings, to more distant relatives, to friends and the social community, and out into the world at large. Human loving is the most ubiquitous and all-embracing aspect of the human soul that envelopes our attitude to one another and, since it affects generations yet unborn, to our environment. The ideal is to encourage development of a world lived in accordance with the universal spiritual laws of empathy with one another and the environment [130].

The fact that humans can experience and reciprocate love may not be unique in the animal kingdom, but with our highly developed ability to communicate it is one of the most intensely satisfying of our emotional experiences. This surely is the highest expression of soul that we can experience. The concept of human loving embraces much more than the pairing of individuals in a life-long relationship. It also applies more generally in our ability to feel concern for the welfare of other people, creatures and places, and to display altruism. All animals as far as we know are genetically programmed to display affection and concern for their brood, but a sense of morality and wide-ranging empathy with other people is unique to humankind in the animal kingdom.

The joy and inspiration of personal love, one-to-one, person-to-person, is a spiritually uplifting experience. But throughout human history there have been those who selflessly care for others with whom they have no direct relationship out of humanitarian concern. In a settled society, each works in harmony with the other, partly out of self-concern, partly because it is the law, but also because it exemplifies the trait of morality that is part of the human soul. St. Augustine (354–430 CE) viewed the goodness of Man as a reflection of the goodness of God. The argument from morality – the so-called Axiological Argument (from the Greek: *axios* - worthy) – represents the fourth of Thomas Aquinas' Five Ways to proof of the existence of God [8]. Cardinal John Henry Newman (1801–1890), a convert to Catholicism from Anglicanism while he was at Oxford, saw this quality in humankind as one of the strongest arguments for the existence of God, as the representation of Supreme Good, from the lesser good found in the ethical behaviour of humankind. John Locke, while holding that the idea of God could not be innate, because the notion was so variable amongst different peoples of the world, and even absent in many, still saw human morality as a persuasive argument for God's existence [323]. David Selbourne says: 'Morality is the soul of society's existence' [427] and 'the self-realisation and well-being of each individual are dependent in great part on the existence of such moral relations' [426]

The existence of a code of morality, expressed through human free will, was central to the philosophy of the German philosopher Johann Gottlieb Fichte (1762–1814). He was one of the philosophical successors to Kant (see Chapter 7) and, in a sense, a protégé in that it was Kant who helped Fichte with the publication in 1792 of his first significant work, *Versuch einer Kritik aller Offenbarung* (*An Essay Towards a Critique of All Revelation*). Kant later dissociated himself from Fichte's ideas and also from the new philosophy that developed from his inspiration. Fichte studied at the Universities of Jena and Leipzig, and was briefly a professor at Jena but was dismissed on a charge of atheism, which Fichte denied. He was a champion of the forging of the independent German states into one nation, though the union was still some years distant; the cause was probably well suited to his rather abrasive personality.

In Fichte's view, it is the consciousness of the self and its accompanying conscience that define truth. In his *Wissenschaftslehre* (*Science of Knowledge*) Fichte regards morality as the restraint on the actions of the self; at the same time, conscience is the basis of my freedom, defining its bounds. All that is not self is classed as non-self, that is, the world of appearances from which the self is differentiated. With his pragmatic outlook, Fichte therefore had no time for the noumenal world of Kant. If this lay beyond the world of sensory experience, what was the point of speculating about it? Transcendental idealism was something for the individual self alone. Fichte was a great champion of freedom: he did not want humankind to be restricted by religious dogma. The only purpose in holding religious beliefs was the use to which they could be put – hence the charge of atheism that was leveled at him. Fichte was above all highly practical in his philosophy – almost a forerunner to the pragmatists Charles Peirce and William James whose ideas were outlined in Chapter 2. Freedom of the individual means freedom to act and freedom to think: the self is all important, but it is a self shaped by societal and individual morality. This was a forerunner to the view later elaborated by Karl Marx, that the self is shaped by society, rather than by our individual biology, as proposed by Sigmund Freud. He valued the concept of morality highly – it was the main purpose of the exercise of freedom to apply and develop moral integrity. It was only in his later years that Fichte came to realise that it was religious faith that determined one's morality.

Our love for humankind as a whole is expressed in doing things for others that will increase their happiness, wellbeing and fulfillment: this increases the positive, loving content of the universal energy. Conversely, each selfish or vindictive act, doing things that will hurt others, even spreading malicious gossip, detracts from the positive energy of the Universal Spirit. As we shall see later in this chapter (Section 6.5.5), when healing is carried out repeatedly in a particular environment it becomes more and more effective as the surroundings absorb the healing energies. The Hippocratic oath for physicians on the care of their patients also applies to each one of us in regard to others: If we can do no good, at least we should be sure to do no harm. The fundamental message of Isaiah, as expressed in the extended version found in 1947 amongst the Dead Sea Scrolls – the only book of the Bible to be discovered complete – is that we must *live* the life of goodness, charity and concern for others and our environment: it is not enough to simply follow the prescribed rituals and attend religious services. And we must do this with a positive frame of mind, really *believing* that what we do *and think* (especially in prayer and meditation) can really make a difference [89]. Spiritualists describe this as the power of intention [158]:

Great men are they who see that spiritual
is stronger than any material force, that thoughts
rule the world.

Ralph Waldo Emerson, *Progress of Culture*

How could a God of love, engendering love as a quality of soul in humankind, allow the existence of evil? Heraclitus maintained that the perfect harmony of existence demanded evil as a balance to good. In other words, it is a logical necessity as the opposite pole of goodness. Another point of view is that the existence of evil is not the work of God but is due to the imperfections of the material out of which the universe was created. St. Augustine (354–430 CE), following his earlier Manichean affiliation, regarded evil as the privation of good, just as darkness is the absence of light – an idea that itself derives from the even earlier NeoPlatonism of Plotinus (*ca.* 204–269 CE). Evil can have no place in the Supreme Being and exists only because light has been imprisoned by the forces of darkness. The existence of 'moral evil' – the voluntary doing of ill by humankind – Augustine, and many philosophers since, attribute to the existence of free will. Just as we can choose to do good, in varying degrees, so we must logically be able to do not-good or evil. Although it was not specifically considered by Augustine, his notion of evil includes the 'evil' of ill-fortune – the fact that many people live short or physically deprived lives of continual hardship, from circumstances of birth, or as a result of events in their lives, or from lack of will to do good. Later philosophers considered this as a problem of 'metaphysical evil'; and the evil of the trauma and hardship caused by natural disasters as 'physical evil'. Augustine's answer was that God has provided human life with as rich an existence as possible, with low points to accentuate the highs and opportunities to improve the lot of others so that they too may lead happier and more fulfilling lives. Augustine believed that God was all-good, and that in His eyes even these seemingly negative aspects of our lives were directed to our ultimate benefit. The Eastern philosophy is to regard all misfortune as a learning experience in order to move on to better things. If saints or angels or benevolent spirits have any input into our lives, then those who choose to do evil on Earth are unlikely to be instantly transformed on death, so their spirits also present a potential source of evil for those who wish to call upon them – the satanists.

Gottfried Wilhelm Leibniz argued that as God is good and 'absolutely perfect', it follows that He must have created the best of all possible worlds; any shortcomings are due to humankind: 'It follows also that created things owe their perfections to the influence of God, but that they owe their imperfections to their own nature, which is incapable of being without limits. For it is in this that they are distinguished from God' [313]. The 'best possible world' envisaged by Leibniz 'is that which permits a maximisation of being ... defined in terms not only of quantity but also of variety' [254].

Our biology is directed towards self-survival. While our care and concern for others who are directly involved in our lives may be expedient in enhancing the quality of our own lives, making personal sacrifices that may jeopardise our comfort or even survival would not be expected from organisms shaped from 'selfish genes' [137]. The Adam and Eve metaphor portrays a Fall in Man to render us intrinsically evil, from which religious belief is needed to save us, and this negative view of human nature was held by philosophers as diverse as Hobbes and Schopenhauer. But the idea that the neonate is evil from the moment of birth is absurd and obscene. Certainly, some degree of selfishness is essential for self-survival: this is programmed in by our genes. But, in fact, there are countless examples of people putting themselves through hardship or danger to help others. Indeed, there seems to be a growing belief that such concern for others is a necessity if we are to have social cohesion and international stability.

Although the dictionary definition of altruism states only that it is a 'concern for others, as a principle of action' [Oxford English Dictionary] or 'the principle of living and acting for the interest of others' [Chambers Dictionary], there must be some element of self-sacrifice involved if we are to be convinced that the actions of others are not motivated by their own self interest: a desire for reciprocity of concern, or some feeling of self-aggrandisement. This conforms with Dawkins' definition: 'An entity ... is said to be altruistic if it behaves in such a way as to increase another such entity's welfare at the expense of its own' [138]. The biological origins of altruism amongst any creatures other than humans are still controversial.

While racial and religious intolerance are still very evident, many believe that there is also a worldwide movement towards global harmony. In a more limited social context, there is increasing emphasis on duties and responsibilities towards others as well as expressing our rights as individuals. As President John F. Kennedy said: '. . . ask not what your country can do for you – ask what you can do for your country. My fellow citizens of the world: ask not what America will do for you, but what together we can do for the freedom of man' [292]. According to Aristotle's *Politics*, government is necessary to protect the weak from exploitation by the powerful, but all too often we have seen how political systems simply legitimise victimisation of the weak by the powerful. Every social system needs energetic individuals with vision and initiative if it is to prosper and develop, but their personal growth should not be at the expense of others and the society must always protect those that are willing but less able to be productive in their contribution. This concern for others is an integral part of social and international cohesion. As David Selbourne comments: 'while duties without rights make men slaves, rights without duties make men strangers' [428].

We have seen in earlier chapters something of the contribution of the early Greek and Roman thinkers to societal and scientific development since the Renaissance. John Stuart Mill (1806–73), in his work *On Liberty*, attributed our sense of societal duty to Greco-Roman origins: 'What little recognition the idea of obligation to the public obtains in modern morality is derived from Greek and Roman sources, not Christian.' [346]. Christian morality has tended to focus on salvation for the individual, and only more recently on societal obligations. For global harmony to be implemented, each individual has to believe in the one-world ethos and act accordingly.

As science writer Marilyn Ferguson said, interpreting the philosophy of psychologist Erich Fromm: 'The transformed self is the medium. The transformed life is the message.' [177]. It is not so much individual as global societal and environmental salvation that needs to be our focus now.

Concern for our natural environment has become not only an urgent practical issue since the damage done by resistance of pesticides to biodegradation was brought to our attention by Rachel Carson [113]. Many kinds of illness have been described in humans as a result of exposure to these toxic chemicals. It has also become a moral matter of safeguarding plant and animal life for future generations and of respecting the right to existence of other species and, as such, it is part of our love for other creatures. Again, in a purely selfish vein, we are becoming increasingly aware that flora and fauna from the natural environment can provide us with many remedies for our physical (and spiritual!) ills, remedies that often do not carry with them the range of undesirable side-effects produced by synthetic drugs. There is now a new philosophy that the Earth should be regarded as an organic interactive whole, of which humankind is but a part and, until now, the most destructive part [328, 329]. Our love for one another and desire for service to the divine can be implemented by acting as responsible custodians of the environment for future generations. Even if we adopt a more selfish attitude, with little concern for the aesthetic and moral issues of environmental desecration, our own survival within the lifetimes of our children is in jeopardy if we do not have regard for the damage we are doing to the balance of natural processes [146].

Ever since the 1960s, particularly, there has been an increasingly widespread expression of this need for empathy with a wider community than one's immediate family; concern for humankind generally and for our relationship with the global environment have been gaining ground steadily over the past few decades. Even in the 19th Century, the economic philosophy of German-born sociologist Karl Marx (1818–1883) may have been one of consumer materialism, but he too advocated a society in which every man helped every other: 'From each according to his ability; to each according to his needs' [335]. This universal interconnection of Man and Nature has been a cornerstone of Eastern philosophy for millennia.

In his second book on the theme of unity between East and West [110], American physicist Fritjof Capra looked beyond the physics to the social, ethical and environmental implications of his ideas on the relevance of Oriental philosophy to life in the West. His criticism of the obsessions with economic and material growth and with power in the Western world reinforces themes first brought to public attention in the 1960s by the American public welfare crusader and Harvard Law School graduate Ralph Nader. This was continued in the following decade by Erwin Schumacher in his book *Small Is Beautiful*. Quoting the Indian spiritual leader Mahatma Gandhi (1869–1948) Schumacher says 'Earth provides enough for every man's need, but not for every man's greed'. And again, encapsulating what he calls his 'economics of permanence' he says: 'Wisdom demands a new orientation of science and technology towards the organic, the gentle, the non-violent, the elegant and beautiful' [417]. Industrial organisations seem to have lost any regard they may once have had for employees or for service to the general public: there is really only one concern now and that is maximisation of profit for the benefit of directors and shareholders. Schumacher puts it more brutally: 'The ideal of industry is the elimination of living substances' [418], and he describes our present industrial organisation as one that 'consumes so much and accomplishes so little' [419]. In Ralph Nader style, American sociologist Lewis Mumford (1895–1990) criticised the inbuilt fragility and obsolescence of modern household equipment in Western society for its excessive and unnecessary consumption of natural resources and its pandering to society's materialist outlook [352]. We need to develop what the oriental sages describe as the *yin*, the intuitive, inquisitive and sensitive side of our personalities instead of giving way to the *yang*, the competitive, aggressive acquisitive part of our make-up.

This is a theme that continues to be emphasised by many writers concerned with the dangers – moral, social, economic and environmental – of our continuing along this path of materialist expansion and globalisation. One could cite, for example, the books of Swedish author Helena Norberg-Hodge: in *Bringing the Food Economy Home* [357] she emphasises the need to consume local produce, to use locally produced goods, rather than global merchandise with all that that implies in transport costs, squandering of resources and exploitation of local labour. Then there is her earlier *Ancient Futures* [358] in which she describes the devastating social effects on the Tibetan village community of Ladakh by the introduction of Western values – drug taking and crime have become a major issue, where previously they were unknown; the formerly closely knit families have been disrupted and the once-contented community has fragmented. Ervin Laszlo, Stanislav Grof and Peter Russell present their thesis in the format of a discussion [310]: Grof, for example, criticises 'The dominant scientific worldview [that] justifies and endorses a life strategy based on individualism and competition rather than synergy and cooperation', a strategy initiated and encouraged by Francis Bacon (see Chapter 4) [311]. Ervin Laszlo [303] emphasises the need to cultivate a global spiritual rather than materialist outlook: 'Our world is experiencing a fundamental crisis: A crisis in global economy, global ecology, and global politics'; 'Time and again we see leaders and members of religions incite aggression, fanaticism, hate and xenophobia. . . Religion often is misused for purely power-political goals' [304], and he encourages every individual to make their own personal contribution to this urgently needed philosophy of life. The book by the former Bishop of Durham, David Jenkins, *Market Whys and Human Wherefores* [277] comments on the unprecedented change in human living standards and philosophy of life brought about by the Industrial Revolution of the 18th century. This has allowed the philosophy of Francis Bacon, the dualism of Descartes, and the scientific discoveries of Newton to be implemented and exploited – without limit until resources are exhausted or human rationalism regains control over the quest after ever more material assets, of which Thomas Hobbes warned us, three centuries ago (see Chapter 2).

It is really a matter of cultivating a more constructive spiritual attitude of mind amongst those whose preoccupation is material growth. It is what the German-born psychologist Erich Fromm (1900–1980) described as a state of mind focussed on 'being' rather than 'having' [201]. Our material acquisitions should be those sufficient for our needs to allow us to live fulfilled lives (being) rather than satisfying our wants (having). In our pursuit of knowledge we need to focus more on creative ideas and understanding (being) rather than merely acquiring facts (having). Our spiritual faith should be more about the good works we do (being) rather than preoccupation with some religious creed or dogma (having). Our vision of the divine should focus internally on meditation, soul, self-realisation, the God in us (being) rather than on an external inaccessible deity demanding obedience and supplication (having). As Erich Fromm says, it is a problem for us that world leaders, to whom we have consigned the responsibility to guide us wisely, 'value personal success [having] more highly than social responsibility [being]'.

Father Bede Griffiths (1906–1993) in his book *The Marriage of East and West* [214] equally sees the need to attenuate the 'violent, aggressive, rational mind of the West' with the intrinsically gentle one-world philosophy of Eastern religion. As Father Bede says: 'there is something more in Indian culture than a search for harmony between man and nature, conscious and unconscious; there is a profound awareness of a power beyond both man and nature which penetrates everything and is the real source of beauty and vitality' [*ibid.*, p.6]. It was at Father Bede's ashram at Shantivanam in India that Cambridge biologist Rupert Sheldrake wrote his first book, which appeared in 1981 (see Chapter 7). It is a sad reflection of the attitude to spiritual matters shown by most scientists that the editor of the prestigious scientific journal *Nature* recommended this as a book for burning! In fact, we should regard Father Bede's radiant and global spiritual empathy and environmental concern as an inspirational model for us all, and we should be grateful to Sheldrake for putting these ideas once again at the forefront of human consciousness.

These books have been written by scholars from many different disciplines – economics, sociology, theology, science – but they embrace both spiritual and practical issues and present different aspects of just one over-riding theme: the importance of our global concern for humankind and our environment as part of our soul's propensity to love.

In either the Western or Oriental view of the meaning of life, our time on Earth is part of a learning process. Our lives are far from futile to ourselves or others if we see all events – even those that are seemingly trivial or unpleasant or distressing – as part of the cosmic interaction and if we thereby use those experiences to improve the physical or spiritual wellbeing of ourselves and of others at every opportunity. This concern for others also extends to the natural environment that we all share and which, as we are continually informed by the news media, is becoming contaminated and depleted at an alarming rate.

One of many environmental issues demanding our urgent attention is atmospheric pollution. In many large cities of the industrial world, the air is often no longer fit to breathe. It is well known that resources of coal and oil will be exhausted by the middle of this century. Our burning of fossil fuels and continuing reluctance to use maximum effort in finding and using renewable energy sources is probably the most significant factor in the current rise in levels of carbon dioxide in our atmosphere. There have been shifts in atmospheric CO_2 levels throughout recent geological history, so the current increase in level could be a natural phenomenon. The lowest CO_2 level in the past half-million years was 200 parts per million (ppm). After the Industrial Revolution of the 17th Century it was 280 ppm. It is now 360 ppm. While part of this change may be of natural origin, it is quite certain that we are contributing to this effect, partly or entirely. Carbon dioxide is one of the so-called 'greenhouse gases'; methane formed by decomposing rubbish tips is another. These form a layer within the atmosphere that traps the sun's energy radiated from the Earth's surface to raise atmospheric temperature, an effect described as 'global warming'. At the same time, the brightness of the sun is being reduced, in some places by more than 20% within the past 50 years, by particulate matter in the atmosphere produced by cars and aircraft. This effect is known as 'global dimming' and it is having a marked effect in reducing crop productivity and quality [451].

These effects are unquestionably the result of man-made pollution: only volcanic eruptions make a significant natural contribution to atmospheric particulate matter. While some areas of the globe may benefit from an overall rise in temperature, one disastrous consequence will be the melting of the polar ice-caps and a rise of several metres in the sea-level. Many coastal communities will be flooded, as will many low-lying tropical islands. Arctic fauna like polar bears will become extinct. Already, glaciers are receding world-wide from the effects of global warming, from the Alps to Alaska to Antarctica. The long-term effects of global dimming are as yet unknown but are hardly likely to be beneficial. Environmental conservation is a crucial issue for every person on the planet, and especially for those whose energy demands are excessive. The United States of America, with only some 6% of the world's population consumes over one-third of the world's resources. This material profligacy is not an attitude compatible with global concern and love of humankind, whatever pretensions there may be of establishing worldwide freedom and democracy.

The New Age philosophy regards humankind as guardians of the Earth as well as of one another: no one nation can abuse this trust without consequences to us all, and to future generations. This global environmental interdependence has been represented by the fanciful but powerful metaphor of a butterfly fluttering its wings in England producing a snowstorm in the Andes – the so-called 'butterfly effect' (see also Chapter 7). This is a very gentle, romantic image: the truth of the environmental situation is much less innocent and picturesque. The Saharan drought of the 1980s that killed over a million people almost certainly resulted from the atmospheric pollution caused by the industrial nations of Europe and America in the preceding decades. The Missouri River, the longest in America, is likely to become non-navigable within the next year after six years of drought over the catchment area. Acid rain in Scandinavia that kills fish in the lakes and rivers and leaches toxic levels of copper out of domestic water pipes has its source in Britain and Central Europe: environmental pollution is not a local affair. The incidents of extreme weather common all over the world in the 1990s and in the early 21st Century will become even more commonplace and more severe unless drastic remedial action is taken now. It is already too late to stop such calamities happening over the next few decades. It is not dramatic exaggeration to say that the planet is doomed if we cannot curb the greed for economic and material growth and quest for political power of the Western industrial nations. We all must urgently control this exploitation of Nature for our own material comfort and find new ways of sustainable existence. This is not an academic or intellectual debate – it has already become a matter of urgent concern to each one of us. This concern is part of the loving aspect of soul – to treasure Earth to pass on to our children and their children. Trying to eliminate poverty in Africa is laudable but, with corruption widespread in many of the countries in that continent, resources are not likely to be directed where they are needed. Perhaps our efforts should more urgently be directed at improving conditions in the countries of South America, where poverty is driving people to irreversibly destroy great tracts of the Amazon jungle to clear land for agriculture and, in other countries, where people are securing their livelihood by growing crops that produce cocaine and heroin, which destroy lives world-wide. At the present rate of exploitation and destabilisation, and deforestation in particular, Earth may not even survive our own lifetimes in a stable state. We need rich forest growth to absorb carbon dioxide and generate oxygen. It is a truism to say that we cannot continue with our present material growth in a world of limited physical resources, and those include the water we drink and the air we breathe.

It is estimated that humans are now exposed to some 50,000 to 70,000 different xenobiotic chemicals during our lifetimes, most of which are of unknown toxicity. Tests carried out on various animal species cannot reliably be extrapolated to humans, because their biochemistry is so different, so the 'safety' claimed for these materials is specious. Quite apart from the moral issues of causing stress to other creatures, we need greater reliability from testing that does not involve the use of laboratory animals [40, 86].

As we saw in Chapter 4, it was the English philosopher Francis Bacon (1561–1626) who laid down what became known as The Scientific Method in his 1605 publication, *The Advancement of Learning*. In this, he advocated exploitation of Nature for the benefit of Man, and recommended that systems should be broken down into simpler parts to facilitate their study. This principle of *reductionism* has produced remarkable advances in our understanding of the way the world works. But, fortunately, there are many enlightened individuals who believe that the only way forward now is through *holism*, to consider all things in their environment and with regard to their interaction with everything else, and especially our interaction with one another, and to have greater love and respect for the diversity of Nature and to secure its preservation. When Newton and Darwin studied the workings of Nature it was not so much for exploitation as for a greater understanding of the world that they believed God had created:

> Flower in the crannied wall,
> I pluck you out of the crannies,
> I hold you here, root and all, in my hand,
> Little flower – but *if* I could understand
> What you are, root and all, all in all,
> I should know what God and man is.
>
> Alfred Lord Tennyson, *Flower in the Crannied Wall*.

But, as Charles Taylor says of one of the recurring themes in Goethe and in Hegel: 'we only properly know nature when we try to commune with it, not when we try to dominate or dissect it in order to subject it to the categories of analytic understanding' [482]. We need to immerse ourselves in the spirit of Nature, as discussed in Section 6.1

above, to appreciate its beauty with soul as well as, or even instead of, with the rational mind. The attitude described by Tennyson is typical of Victorian England after publication of Darwin's *Origin of Species*, continuing the philosophy of Francis Bacon – to exploit Nature for our own ends: the 'having' described by Erich Fromm rather than the 'being' (see above). Better, to admire Nature mystically with the reflective philosophy described by Goethe in his poem *Found*:

> I walked in the woods
> All by myself,
> To seek nothing,
> That was on my mind.

Or, to put it in the (translated) words of French philosopher Blaise Pascal (1623–1662): 'All the misfortunes of men derive from one single thing, which is their inability to be at ease in an [empty] room' [361]. We have lost the ability to be at peace with ourselves. The reductionist materialist approach always demands some external object of interest rather than simple inward reflection.

The pollution and desecration of Nature are not our only challenges in the 21st Century. Any system, religious or political, that does not encourage restriction of population growth in a world of limited resources does a massive disservice to the whole of humankind, in perpetuity. World population at the time of the ancient Greek philosophers was only some 80 million. This had already doubled by the time Jesus was born. It took from then till the Renaissance to double again because of the deaths from plague, but it had reached 1600 million by 1900 because of the affluence brought about by the Industrial Revolution; with advances in nutrition, in medicine and in public hygiene, world population had soared to 2500 million by 1950. We have now passed 6000 million people on Earth. You do not have to be a statistician to foresee that the resources we have on the planet cannot possibly sustain this level of growth in population, or the growth in material affluence of nations already materially affluent when much of the world is impoverished and denied basic amenities of human existence. If we consider the effect of developing nations trying to attain the level of affluence of the industrialised West, it will be obvious that supplies of raw materials will run out long before the end of the century, with almost inevitable conflict over what remains, to say nothing of the ever-increasing level of pollution of our air, of our water, and of our soil. To live in a sustainable world environment and to stabilise if not reduce world population is a top priority as part of human service to the Oneness of the divine, of which we are all a part through Soul.

In a democracy, governments are appointed by the people to maintain social order for the wellbeing of all; religions purport to present and interpret the word of God for the spiritual uplift of sections of humankind. These political and religious institutions have been established to serve the good of the people, not the other way round. Global harmony will not be achieved unless adherents of the various religions accept that their path to God or Oneness is a regional and social construct, and is no more or less valid than any other belief system. As the Arabian mystic Muid ad-Din ibn al-Arabi (1165–1240) said: 'Do not attach yourself to any particular creed exclusively, so that you may disbelieve all the rest; otherwise you will lose much good, nay, you will fail to recognise the real truth of the matter. God, the omnipresent and omnipotent, is not limited by any one creed' [17]. Burgeoning of religious fundamentalism is not the way we should be going: fundamentalism soon breeds fanaticism, a belief that one's own viewpoint is the only one that is correct and true, and that all others must be extinguished. What the world urgently needs is to find a common core amongst the various religious philosophies to generate tolerance and harmony.

Over the past century we have repeatedly seen the terrible consequences of one group or nation trying to impose its political or religious will by force on others: it can never be successful without massive human tragedy, suffering and loss of life. As human ingenuity and technology become ever more sophisticated, the potential for widespread destruction, or even annihilation, increases. A universal spiritual theme *must* be found for humankind for our survival. As religious philosopher John Hick says: 'no longer must we place our own religion at the centre; instead, God must be there, with all religions equally distant from him.' [255]. The idea of a universal spiritual field is one that should not create disquiet in any religious system. Today, in the complex world in which we live, we tend to put our lives into compartments – time for work, for commuting, for relaxation, and so on, and religion is just one more compartment for Sundays, or even just for Easter and Christmas in Western Christianity. Spiritual faith needs to be lived as an integral part of everyday life if it is to be meaningful.

The points made in Chapter 1 concerning practices of the religious faiths of the West illustrate the fact that in orthodox Catholic doctrine, and in many other religious systems, one is dealing not with issues that have the best interests of humanity or of the environment in mind but many different human interpretations of the supposed word of God. Any religious or political system that lays down edicts that are clearly restrictive of human freedom and our ability to use, for the common good, the rational thought with which we have been blessed is not tenable in this highly interactive and environmentally threatened world. Furthermore, it denigrates our God-given power of reason. If we consider ourselves the most noble of God's creations, the one characteristic that distinguishes us from the flora and fauna of the field is our ability to think and communicate our thoughts. Insight and sophisticated language are uniquely human characteristics with unique potential for positive creativity that has universal human wellbeing as the goal. If we make ourselves slaves to man-made dogma and ritual, rather than actions that we believe will help us and, within our small circle of influence, the rest of humankind then we are denying the wisdom of God in giving us these faculties.

Whether or not one 'belongs to' one of the established religions, and even without a belief in the view of God prescribed by Western theology, it is entirely possible to live a good life devoted to the wellbeing of all humankind. All that is required – and for many people in a rationalist and materialist world, it seems that this is

a leap too far – is a belief in the oneness of creation, the existence
of an ever-present, overriding, interactive spiritual energy such
that our every act, provided it is well-intentioned, is of significance
as a step towards achieving the peace and spiritual harmony of
the world. There are many paths to this harmony and, as long as
they embrace tolerance of those who choose a different journey, it
matters not which way we take. As John Hick says, interpreting the
language-oriented philosophy of Ludwig Wittgenstein (1889–1951),
'what is important and to be respected here is not the conventional
religious organisations and their official formulations but the
religious way of experiencing and participating in human existence
and the forms of life in which this is expressed' [256]. With
increasing international travel and commercial integration, we have
all become aware of a multiplicity of cultures and belief systems.
Even the Church of Rome, formerly emphatic in its assertion that
'outside the Church there is no salvation', has modified its views
somewhat, largely due to the importance attached to the writings
of German Jesuit theologian Karl Rahner (1904–1984). As a pupil
of existentialist philosopher Martin Heidegger, and an opponent of
natural theology, Rahner asserts that it is individual transcendental
experience that is the key to the divine, not the prescriptions of
particular religious traditions.

This transcendental experience may be of the most intense kind,
as described in Section 6.3, but it can also be achieved through
inspired creativity by those infused with the divine spirit (Section
6.2), or by appreciation of the aesthetic beauty of the creations
of others, as described in the first section of this chapter. Most of
all, it is experienced in human loving (Section 6.4), however this is
expressed. Even Karl Barth, a noted theologian opposed to natural
theology, felt that believing in a transcendental level of being was the
only thing that made sense of human existence. Concern for others
of any religious system and for our natural environment is the true
expression of love and service to the divine.

We move on now to another of the types of religious experience as
defined in Alister Hardy's *The Spiritual Nature of Man*. This section

is rather different however from those discussed previously. The experiences described so far in this chapter are essentially subjective aspects of the human spiritual dimension – they involve individual experiences of creativity or joy. The subject of psychic experiences however lends itself to dispassionate scientific investigation using all the usual rigorous safeguards to obtain meaningful, objective data. Here, we can do repeatable experiments under prescribed conditions though, as we shall see, under such restrictions the results do not always follow the expected plan. What follows therefore are accounts of scientific experiments, though anecdotal accounts are included too. These phenomena are presented in greater detail than in the previous sections because they represent rational, objective, scientific evidence of a spiritual realm beyond the world of sensory experience and not explainable by the science that existed before the 20th Century and the creation of quantum physics. This Newtonian science is adequate still to explain most of the phenomena of the natural world.

6.5.   Psychic phenomena [232, Section 5]

Occurrences of telepathy, clairvoyance, premonition, psychokinesis, spiritual healing, near death experiences (NDEs), and claims to reincarnation may be described by the general term 'psychic events'. In the past, these events were generally regarded as beyond the realm of study or explanation from orthodox science; their very existence is still disputed by many scientists, despite the existence of overwhelming empirical, if frequently personal and anecdotal, evidence. Because of this, such occurrences are also described as 'paranormal' or 'supernatural' – above or beyond what is 'normal' or 'natural' – but, in fact, these events are entirely normal, and they occur frequently in the natural world. Aboriginal tribes use them in their everyday existence. The wise men, elders and sages of tribes have reported such happenings since the beginning of recorded human history. The events themselves, or the spiritual energy that is claimed to generate them, are also often known as *psi*. Though the situations involved in psi may be quite mundane, these events may also be regarded as examples of communication through some universal spiritual field representing World Soul or Communal Soul.

In our appreciation of the arts and Nature, in inspirational creativity, and in experience of the divine (Sections 6.1, 6.2, 6.3), we are drawing in the universal spirit into ourselves. In expressing ourselves through music and poetry (Section 6.2), and in loving (Section 6.4), we are radiating that spirit out to our fellow Man. Psychic events involve both of these processes – a two-way communion with the universal spiritual field.

In his first scientific paper, On the Limits of the Exact Sciences, presented after his graduation from Basel University, Carl Jung criticised scientists for their inflexible materialism and suggested that psychic events would be the phenomena of soul best suited to empirical study. Jung himself had many psychic visions and had a cousin, Hélène Preiswerk, who was a medium. It is these phenomena that have indeed been most rigorously studied using the standard testing techniques of science, so this is why psychic events are described most extensively in this chapter, though the anecdotes and publications cited are just a small representative sample of the huge number available. Extra-sensory perception or activity, *siddhis*, has always been an accepted human quality in Eastern thought, though given only to very few.

There are several books describing anecdotal psychic experiences by that persistent psi investigator, Lyall Watson [497, 498, 500, 501]. A review of one of his books in the newspaper *The Independent* in 1990 says: 'In recent times, belief in the supernatural has become a secular religion, with Lyall Watson as its high priest', which is a fair assessment of the significance of the man and the material he has gathered together in his publications. Dr. Watson was born in South Africa in 1939, and after completing degrees in botany and zoology, turned his attention to palaeontology, studying under Raymond Dart, who was the discoverer of the first African hominid, Australopithecus. Watson's Ph.D. in ethnology was completed under the supervision of Desmond Morris, another well-known writer and author of the popular book, *The Naked Ape* [351]. Watson's extensive study of psi effects are aimed at putting the data into an evolutionary and practical perspective. His evidence shows that ethnic tribes living much less sophisticated lives than most of us in Western society today rely heavily on psychic experiences for their very survival and are a part of their everyday lives. In *Supernature II* [Hodder and Stoughton, 1986] Watson says 'human society ... is a composition of ideas and beliefs – a new and essentially psychic phenomenon. A kind of supermind' [499]. This is an echo of Hegel's concept of societal *Geist*. Without this *Volkgeist* even our sophisticated Western societies would not cohere.

6.5.1. Telepathy [232, Section 5a]. The term 'telepathy' was coined in 1882 by Frederick Myers, one of the moving forces in the establishment of the Society for Psychical Research in London that same year, to describe mind-mind communication that does not involve the usual five senses.

One of the first 20th Century series of systematic investigations into psi were those of Joseph Banks Rhine into telepathy. He was a botanist who founded a (para)psychology unit at Duke University, North Carolina, during the 1930s. His results have been summarised in many publications [see, for example, refs. 399, 400]. His methodology has subsequently been criticised as lacking the rigour of present-day standards, but the results are nevertheless highly suggestive of the reality of telepathic communication. He used the selection of one out of five Zener cards (pictures of a star, cross, square, circle and wavy lines) or the throw of a die by one subject to be sensed by another individual. These tests were criticised because they may not have been truly random – for example, if the cards were not shuffled effectively, or if the weight distribution of the die was not uniform so that one or two faces would be more likely to be uppermost. Nevertheless, he was successful in showing that the ability of one set of subjects to guess the images viewed by other subjects was above what would be expected by chance. There have since been many similar scientific investigations into this aspect of Soul, with the benefit of studies that have shown how the possibility of positive responses can be improved. As we shall see in Chapter 8, there is also a new concept in the field of physics, the most basic of the sciences, that can be used to interpret the results.

The most comprehensive account of telepathy in recent years is to be found in Guy Lyon Playfair's *Twin Telepathy* [368]. As Playfair says, the best results in experiments on telepathy are obtained when there is a rapport between the subjects involved and the subjects feel comfortable and relaxed with the experimenter and conditions of the tests. Also, the subjects viewed need to be a little more interesting than the abstract images on the Zener cards used by Rhine. No two people are likely to be more in tune with one another's psychic aura than twins, especially identical twins. Even then, only about one-third of the people questioned or tested reported or showed psychic ability with one another. Also, it helps if the 'sender' of messages is extrovert and active in personality, and the 'receiver' more introverted and relaxed.

Playfair wryly comments about the reluctance of mainstream scientists to take telepathy, or any psychic phenomenon, seriously and subject it to rigorous scrutiny for fear of losing academic credibility: 'It's not a case of "I'll believe it when I see it" but of "I'll see it when I believe it"' [369]. One of the most extensive reports of twin telepathy cited by Playfair [370] is that of Mary Rosambeau who presented her results in her book *How Twins Grow Up* [403], with filled questionnaires from 600 twins or their parents. The characteristics of telepathic communication described by Rosambeau include anticipation of imminent contact (one twin sensing the other was about to phone), simultaneous identical thoughts (like buying similar clothes or presents at the same time, with no direct twin contact), and sympathetic pain or emotion (experienced by one twin when the other undergoes a traumatic experience). In recent years, Cambridge biologist Rupert Sheldrake has published two books [429, 430] giving details of experiments that his team has conducted on aspects of telepathy.

Another very convincing and unequivocal demonstration of telepathy that Playfair cites is the study by the Mexican psychologist Jacobo Grinberg-Zylberbaum who worked at the National Autonomous University in Mexico City [371]. He conducted experiments over a period of 18 years on pairs of subjects who were not necessarily related. The only condition to participation was that they should be emotionally close. In the first experiment, the subjects were asked to just sit and meditate together in an electromagnetically insulated room: the result was that their brain-wave patterns, as measured on an electroencephalogram (EEG) became harmonised. This simply would not happen with randomly chosen pairs of complete strangers. In a second experiment, the subject pairs were separated, again allowed to meditate while connected to the EEG, and then one of the pair was subjected to a short, sharp shock – either a loud noise, a bright flash of light, or a small electric shock. The subject thus treated always showed the result on the EEG with a spike in the trace, but in 25% of the subject pairs, the other, isolated subject showed a similar response simultaneously, though completely unaware by the usual five senses that anything was happening. Only some form of telepathy could have produced such results. No response whatever would be expected by chance, or only a very tiny positive value if subjects simply guessed that something might be happening in the next room, if subjects were not empathic. It was also found that the couples who could produce positive results, could do so on other occasions while those who could not respond empathically, were never able to do so [217, 218]. Grindberg-Zylberbaum attributed this psychic communication to the existence of what he called a *hyperfield*.

William G. Braud was a former Senior Research Associate at the Mind Science Foundation in San Antonio, Texas, an institute devoted to a scientific study of the human mind. He got together with an anthropologist, Marilyn Schlitz, to conduct a meta-analysis (an analysis of results from many other people's studies) of the effect of the human mind on other living things, not only humans – cats, dogs, even plants. The results showed a 37% success rate of influence compared to the 5% that would be expected by chance [409]. Braud, a member of the American Parapsychological Association, has published more than 60 papers on the subject since 1973. There is evidence that those who are tuned in to this kind of phenomenon – like the staff in Braud's own laboratory! – themselves become more susceptible to psychic effects [90]. It was mentioned previously that environments where healing takes place regularly become more conducive to successful healing on future occasions at that location. The same is true apparently for laboratory environments where the universal spiritual field is continually being accessed for telepathy experiments. This will be discussed further in Chapter 8 dealing with morphogenetic fields.

Experiments conducted by Charles Honorton (1946–1992) and his colleagues Stanley Krippner and Montague Ullman at the Maimonides Research Centre in Brooklyn, New York, on precognition of events in the dream state were amazingly successful, scoring accuracy rates of over 80% with the assistance of an English psychic, Malcolm Bessent [489].

Positive evidence of remote sensing by a psychic has also been rigorously investigated and results have been published by, for example, physicist Russell Targ and psychologist Jane Katra [478] and by Dean Radin, a Doctor of Psychology at Princeton University in New Jersey [393]. These results are published in peer-review books and journals, so while everyone may not be in agreement as to the interpretation of the results, this kind of work can no longer be dismissed as meaningless nonsense.

Jessica Utts, Professor of Statistics at the University of California at Davis, has long had an interest in using the statistical analysis of epidemiological data on psychic experiences to vindicate or discredit the claims of parapsychologists [491]. She collaborated with Professor Ray Hyman at the University of Oregon to review all psychic studies in the US for the government (to explore its military potential!) up to the mid-1990s and concluded that the results were far beyond what could have occurred by chance [490].

It has been suggested, even by eminent scientists like the American zoologist William Morton Wheeler (1865–1937), that some form of telepathy is at work in the social cooperation of animals or insects, as in the building of an anthill, or termitarium, or beehive, or in the simultaneous movement of flocks of birds or schools of fish. Wheeler was an expert in this particular field of social entomology [506, 507]. Lynne McTaggart gives other instances of telepathy in her book called *The Field* [344].

6.5.2. Clairvoyance [232, Section 5c]. In his work *City of God*, St. Augustine says 'The God we worship chose certain spirits and gave them the power of foresight, and through them He makes prophecies. To others He gave the gift of healing.' [25]. If Augustine accepts these as God-given gifts, it is regrettable that the Church today frowns on such practices, often regarding them as tantamount to witchcraft.

Clairvoyance is defined as the use of extrasensory perception (ESP) to glean information about current remote objects or events, usually without these objects or events being viewed at the time by anyone else. The term *telepathy* refers to person-to-person communication of remote objects or events. The term 'clairvoyance' is derived from the French, meaning 'seeing things clearly'. It is usually applied to knowledge of current remote events, future event perception being described as *precognition*. But the term clairvoyance is also used to refer to knowledge of events past. In the 1930s there was a gifted Russian-born Polish clairvoyant called Stefan Ossowiecki who worked with a Professor of Ethnology at the University of Warsaw, Stanislaw Poniatowski. Stefan's gift was to handle ancient artefacts and be able to describe where and when they were found, and the circumstances surrounding their use. During the sessions, Stefan was described as virtually 'dematerialising' becoming barely more than a shadow of his material body. He would then relate events as if he was there, living among the people he described [84, 377].

A similar use of archaeological clairvoyance was reported by J. Norman Emerson, Professor of Anthropology at the University of Toronto working with a psychic truck driver called George McMullen. Those with psychic ability are often from quite humble backgrounds and modest education. They are not sophisticated and highly educated people who would be in a more advantageous position to play tricks. McMullen would be taken to potential archaeological sites where he would pace back and forth for a while and then again describe the people and events that had once occupied that land. Although Emerson was highly sceptical at first, after having supervised successful digs at the sites described by McMullen he was forced to become a convert, convinced of the man's psychic powers [171]. This ability to see into the past is also described as *retrocognition*.

There is a famous and well-authenticated incidence on record of clairvoyance from the Swedish scientist, philosopher and theologian Emanuel Swedenborg (1688–1772). He related to dinner guests one night in Göteborg in 1759 that a huge fire was raging in Stockholm, some 300 miles away. Messages were eventually brought to the house that confirmed this event [94].

In one of her books, Lynne McTaggart describes other experiments on clairvoyance carried out on behalf of the American military by Hal Putoff and Russell Targ using the clairvoyant Ingo Swann [345]. In the experiments, Swann was later joined by another psychic, a building contractor from Lake Tahoe called Pat Price, another psychic of humble background who had been used successfully on several occasions by the Los Angeles police. The two psychics independently described a top-secret Pentagon establishment, the existence of which they could not possibly have known about through normal information channels because of its military significance.

Because psychics or mediums may be able to communicate possible future life paths to us because they are known to the spirit world does not mean that we do not have free will. God or our most intimate friends may know what we will do in any given situation, but we do not know until we have made that decision to act. Frequently we do not act as other people expect us to do. Nor are we being directed by the spirit world, though we may very well be guided if we have asked for help. The ultimate choice of action is always ours. How many of us have felt some 'inner voice' telling us that we should act in a certain way but, for some perverse reason, or perhaps out of compulsion or habit we decide to do something different. Foreknowledge does not necessarily imply determinism.

Other examples of clairvoyance may be found in Lawrence J. Bendit's book, *Paranormal Cognition* [51].

6.5.3. Premonition or precognition [232, Sections 5b, 5c]. *Precognition* is knowledge by ESP of a future event that is about to happen to oneself or others; *premonition* is a feeling of foreboding concerning misfortune associated with the event, and the term implies that the feeling is perhaps less intense than in precognition. It is more a feeling of unease than a picture of some specific disaster that would be classed as precognition.

As an example of precognition, Hans J. Eysenck and Carl Sargent in their book *Explaining the Unexplained* [176] tell of a woman in Cleethorpes, in Humberside in the UK, who had a vision around noon on 1st June 1974 of the huge explosion at the Nypro (UK) plant that occurred just before 5 p.m. that same evening; there were two witnesses to the incident. Eysenck and Sargent also report several instances of precognition in dreams concerning the terrible Aberfan disaster: on 21 October 1966, a coal tip in this small village in South Wales shifted after heavy rain and engulfed a school full of children. Sceptics may dismiss these latter reports as normal dream activity, for insecure coal tips have been a recurring nightmare of people in South Wales since they were first created after the development of the coal mining industry there. But the vividness and specificity of the reports does suggest something more significant.

The writer Dame Edith Lyttelton actually wrote down in February 1914 what seems to have been a premonition of the sinking of the liner *Lusitania*, sunk by a German torpedo in May 1915 [529].

A Mrs Jack Marshall witnessed the maiden voyage of the *Titanic* as it started out from Southampton on 10 April 1912. As it passed into the Solent, she had a vision of disaster, with 'hundreds of people struggling in the icy water'. Shortly before midnight on April 14th, the ship hit an iceberg and sank with the loss of more than 1500 lives [330, cited in ref. 528]. A man called J. Connon Middleton dreamed twice about an ocean liner sinking some ten days before the maiden voyage of the *Titanic*. As he was due to sail on the ship to attend a conference in America he was greatly concerned; but to his relief, the conference was cancelled. There are in fact 19 documented premonitions of disaster before the ship's maiden voyage: some of these people heeded their premonitions and did not sail with the ship; others did travel and were drowned.

In 1902, while encamped in the Orange Free State, J.W. Dunne, an aeronautical engineer who was to become an investigator into the paranormal reported having a dream about an imminent volcanic eruption on a French-occupied island: a few days later there was a catastrophic eruption of Mt. Pelée on Martinique, in the West Indies, with the loss of some 40,000 lives. Dunne had had a vision of 4000 people dying: had he 'seen' but 'misread' the forthcoming newspaper headlines? [530]. In his book *An Experiment with Time* (1927), Dunne describes many instances of dreams in which he envisioned an object or an event that was to feature in his life later, often on the following day. He did not consider that this was due to chance or coincidence, or to any form of paranormal precognition, but rather to some form of time-displacement that he thought would eventually be explicable through the laws of physics – quantum physics, perhaps?

A French actress by the name of Irene Muza once took part in a hypnosis experiment and was asked, while in trance, if she could see her future. She replied: 'My career will be short; I dare not say what my end will be – it will be terrible.' As the experimenters knew that this information would be extremely upsetting to the actress, they did not tell her anything of what she had said and she remembered nothing when she emerged from her trance state. A few weeks later, when she visited her hairdresser, there was an accident and one of the assistants spilled mineral oil onto a stove. It caught fire, the fire spread to Irene Muza setting her hair and clothes on fire, and she died in hospital a few hours later [360]. There is obviously no way that Muza would have provoked this terrible event even subconsciously – but she evidently knew of it subconsciously.

6.5.4. Psychokinesis (no equivalent classification in Hardy's *Spiritual Nature of Man*). This is defined as the ability to produce movement of some kind in objects remotely without any kind of physical contact between subject and object. It is perhaps one of the most difficult of paranormal events to comprehend, as it involves not solely mental events, or mind-to-mind or even mind-to-body events, but interaction between the human mind and inanimate objects.

Some individuals seem, unintentionally or intentionally, to be able to influence the normal working of electronic equipment in a laboratory [199, 394]. Incredible though it may seem, Radin has conducted experiments in which he and his colleagues have recorded statistically significant changes in the response of computers by human thought processes alone from remote subjects, that is, people not even in the same room as the computers [393].

Matthew Manning, now well known as a healer, participated in experiments with Dr. F.W. Lorenz at the University of California at Davis. He was being tested to see if he could induce a response in the nervous system of other subjects, to be detected by changes in conductivity of the skin produced by sweating. The subjects were supposed to have been selected randomly, but Manning's presence apparently affected the equipment there to carry out random number selection of subjects, so the experiment had to be abandoned.

Physicist Wolfgang Pauli is said to have had a detrimental effect on scientific equipment in laboratories where he was working; colleagues described him as a 'walking poltergeist'. His dramatic influence on equipment was attested to by fellow quantum physicists George Gamow and Werner Heisenberg – eminent and reputable men with scientific credibility at stake and hardly likely to be given to flights of fancy. Further details are described by Brian Inglis of the Koestler Foundation in his book *Coincidence* [268].

The Israeli psychic Uri Geller became a popular figure on television, and in personal appearances in the UK and USA, with his spoon-bending activities. It all started with a live demonstration on UK television in November 1973, supervised by Lyall Watson, the zoologist we described previously as committed to the study of the paranormal, and a sceptical John Taylor, Professor of Mathematics at King's College of the University of London. Not only did Geller bend the cutlery in the studio but, somewhat alarmingly, much cutlery all over the UK owned by viewers was also bent out of shape! But not the cutlery of *all* viewers. As with telepathy, all people cannot easily tune in to the spiritual field. The Apollo 14 astronaut Edgar Mitchell, who holds a Doctor of Science degree in aeronautics from the Massachusetts Institute of Technology, had previously tested Geller at the Stanford Research Institute in California, with similarly spectacular results. Mitchell is now at the Institute of Noetic Sciences in Sausalito, California. John Taylor published a technical article in *Nature* in 1978 in which he attributed Geller's ability to some kind of electromagnetic interaction. But these studies, and others with different subjects, have often been conducted in electromagnetically shielded rooms with subjects almost naked so that they could not hide 'equipment' about their person to work their 'magic'. Using the Principle of Parsimony that scientists generally call Ockham's Razor – that the simplest explanation is usually the correct one – the most obvious explanation for these and other psychic phenomena, when deceit and trickery have been excluded, is that they are due to a kind of force not yet defined in the realms of conventional science.

Helmut Schmidt, a former professor at the University of Cologne who moved to Seattle in Washington State to join Boeing, also reported psychokinetic effects on electronic laboratory equipment. He built a random number generator that switched on one out of four coloured lights – red, yellow, green or blue. Ordinarily, one would expect that a person guessing which light would come on would have a 1 in 4 or 25% chance of a correct answer. The first set of subjects Schmidt chose did in fact score close to this figure, but a second set of subjects who were all professional psychics scored rather better at 27% - a small but not insignificant deviation from a random result [94, 410, 411].

The American paranormal investigator J. Gaither Pratt was a research assistant with J.B. Rhine at Duke University in North Carolina. One Friday evening in October 1970, he and one of his assistants met with two Russian psychic investigators in Leningrad – Genady Sergeyev, a physiologist and mathematician at the A.A. Uktomskii Physiological Institute, and a mathematician and computer expert, Konstantin Ivanenko. There was another Russian also present – Nina (or Nelya) Kulagina (née Mikhailova), a psychic. This group witnessed and filmed Kulagina moving small objects across a table. Kulagina's psychokinetic powers had been investigated for nearly a decade within the Soviet Union, and films of these experiments were shown to an international parapsychology conference in Moscow in June 1968.

These experiments described above are just a few examples of very many studies carried out in Britain, the United States, Russia and continental Europe into psychokinesis.

The Indian mystic Sri Aurobindo maintained that all matter has some degree of consciousness; otherwise, it would not be possible for humankind to interact with matter in the way described above. Sri Aurobindo Ghose was born in Calcutta, India, in 1872. From the age of seven, he was educated in England at St. Paul's School in London and at King's College, Cambridge, returning to India in 1893. He was a child prodigy and by the time he graduated he was master of some six or seven languages. Once back in India he became an administrative official, which gave him time to participate in India's struggle for independence from British imperialist rule. In this, he was admired alongside his contemporary, Mahatma Mohandas Gandhi (1869–1948). In 1908 he was jailed for just over a year for supposedly plotting the assassination of an official. From 1910 onwards, Aurobindo withdrew from the active political struggle, content in his inner knowledge that India would eventually be free. He retreated to Pondicherry, a coastal town in South-east India, where he devoted himself to spiritual development. He began his spiritual quest to develop a new form of *yoga*, a quieting of the mind from worldly thoughts, such that one could use the discipline, not as an escape to higher worlds of consciousness but to sharpen the effectiveness of one's participation in everyday life. The yoga that Aurobindo developed is known as Integral Yoga or *pūrna yoga*. During this decade, from 1910 to 1920, he wrote prolifically. He was convinced that only a change in global consciousness could solve the world's political and environmental problems, a view expressed by many contemporary writers detailed in the previous section. Aurobindo departed earthly life in 1950.

From 1920 on, Aurobindo was joined in his spiritual quest by another whom we would describe as mystical, Mirra Alfassa, known by her spiritual name simply as the Mother. Mother Mirra was born in Paris in 1878 of an Egyptian mother, who was a disciple of Karl Marx, and a materialist Turkish father, a banker and brilliant mathematician – a somewhat incongruous pairing, one would have thought. Mother Mirra had psychic visions throughout her childhood and, in one of these, she had a vision of Aurobindo around the time he left jail to begin his spiritual journey. Ten years later, Mother went to Pondicherry to meet with Aurobindo and spent the next thirty years with him there teaching, and using yoga to interpret the world in which she lived. Mother Mirra was very down-to-earth. One of the Sri Aurobindo websites quotes of her: 'All the explanations I sought were always of a material nature; it seemed so obvious to me: no need for mysteries or anything of that sort – you must explain things in material terms. Therefore, I am sure there is no tendency for mystical dreaming in me!' [http://ourworld.compuserve.com/homepages/swar/Sae.htm]. This is the philosophy that has inspired the writing of this book – that mystical experiences should not at least conflict with rationality.

6.5.5. Spiritual healing (*Sections 3a and 6b in Hardy* [232]). The quote from St. Augustine given above in connection with clairvoyance is worth repeating here because its importance, coming from a noted Christian theological philosopher, cannot be exaggerated: 'The God we worship chose certain spirits and gave them the power of foresight, and through them He makes prophecies. To others He gave the gift of healing.' [25].

The development of the pharmaceutical industry in the 20th Century, from its beginnings with the discovery of aspirin by Hermann Dreser in 1893, has brought pain-relieving or even life-saving treatment to millions of people. With developments in anaesthetics, surgical techniques have become ever more sophisticated and surgeons are now able to correct problems with operations that could not have been attempted at the start of the 20th Century. But drug treatment and surgery carry significant risks. There is now a whole branch of medicine, iatrogenic medicine, devoted to the study of the illnesses caused by drugs and inappropriate or incompetent surgery. As a result, treatment of patients by non-invasive techniques is once again becoming more popular, and successful spiritual healers are in great demand. Until the 20th Century, such complementary or alternative medicine was almost the only kind available. Ether and chloroform were not available as anaesthetics to dull the pain of surgery until the middle of the 19th Century (see later), but the Chinese people have been using acupuncture for anaesthesia for at least a thousand years.

Although spiritual healing is often called faith healing, it does not matter whether or not the patient believes in God, or even in the ability of the healer: the remedial effects can still operate. It is well documented even in the orthodox medical field that if a person adopts a positive state of mind, even without any external agent, this can produce remarkable cures in the sick [248, 249, 334, 353, 434].

For those who lack the physical reserves or necessary power of will to heal themselves, the intervention of a spiritual healer can often restore or at least improve health. The effect seems to work even remotely, without patient and healer having to be in the same room – a phenomenon known as *distant healing*. If healing is carried out at the same location repeatedly, many healers report that the technique becomes more successful – as if the surroundings are in some way becoming tuned to the healing frequencies. The self-healing of Mary Baker Eddy described in Chapter 1 is an example of spiritual healing, though in her case it was the result of intense religious belief.

Many complementary healers work by retuning energy concentrations within the body [4, 5]. According to Eastern medicine, there are fourteen lines of energy called *meridians* that run vertically through the erect body. These meridians transmit the energy of the life force, *chi* (Chinese; the Japanese call it *ki*, the ancient Egyptians, *ka*). Chinese medicine interprets all illness as a disruption in the normal flow of energy through the meridians, and *acupuncture* – inserting needles into key points in the body along the meridians – is one way of retuning the energy field. But this is invasive.

Spiritual healers always retune the *chi* energy non-invasively by working on seven concentrations of the body's energy called *chakras*, located as spinning vortices of energy at seven points along the midline. The six petals of the lotus flower together with its centre are taken to represent these seven chakras in some Eastern philosophies. *Chakra* is a Sanskrit word that means vortex or spiral. Each chakra corresponds to one of the endocrine organs – pineal (the crown chakra), pituitary, thyroid, thymus, pancreas, adrenals, gonads, from the head downwards – and each has a distinctive colour associated with it. The healer focuses on the corresponding colour to retune the chakra [492]. The chakras are vortices with the apices inwards so that they can transmit energy from the universal energy field into or out of the body. The idea of spirals or spinning vortices is popular with some philosophers because it represents a metaphor of how several influences can be drawn together at one point, like the three-fold spirals of existence – past, present and future, or body, mind and spirit.

At the apex of each chakra vortex is a black hole that draws energy in, and a white hole for transmitting energy outwards to the energy field that surrounds the body, the *aura*. The aura gives an indication of our state of health and disposition in any life situation – whether we feel comfortable or uneasy, whether we are healthy or sick. As Johann Wolfgang Goethe (1749–1832) said: 'We all have certain electric and magnetic forces within us, and ourselves exercise an attractive and repelling force according as we come into touch with something like or unlike' [162]. Goethe's observations on the electromagnetic properties of the human body were made fully a century before they were recognised by physiologists. The aura however is not an electromagnetic field. Some of the best-known early examples of aura detection are those produced by Russian scientist, Semyon Kirlian, with the photographs of plants and human limbs that he took in the 1940s. Some spiritual healers can detect and retune the body's aura directly. Many complementary therapists, healers, theosophists, and others recognise layers of aura outside of the physical body that they distinguish as the etheric, emotional (or astral) and mental (conscious and subconscious) bodies, as well as the soul or spirit aura.

These ideas of spinning vortices bring to mind those of Lucretius and Kelvin (Chapter 2), and their view of a universe of spinning vortical atoms. As referred to previously, David Ash sees the whole universe as a conical vortex, with physical reality at its base, passing upwards through morphic, astral, psychic and spiritual levels that embrace the activities of the chakras [22].

Kinesiology. Another diagnostic technique sometimes used by healers is that of *kinesiology*, the study of human movement; this technique was discovered in 1964 by the American chiropractor Dr. George Goodheart. When subjects take hold of various foods or other substances to which they are allergic, a sensitive practitioner can pick up resistance to movement in the arm muscles. This is more a psychic than physiological phenomenon. Valerie Hunt, now Emeritus Professor in the Department of Physiological Sciences of UCLA in California, and a specialist in kinesiology, has spent the last 40 years studying the human aura associated with muscle activity. Electrical vibrations within the brain normally occur at a frequency of up to about 60 Hertz (number of waves or cycles per second). The electrical activity of muscle produces vibrations up to about 220 Hz or, for the heart, up to 250 Hz. With apparatus designed to measure electrical activity, Hunt picked up a fainter, smaller amplitude vibration that went up to 1600 Hz, or even higher. This field was strongest at the points where the chakras are located [347]. People whose outlook is mainly materially oriented show frequencies not much above those around 250 Hz recorded for normal muscle activity; psychics, sensitives and healers show much higher vibrational frequencies. Hunt was also able to distinguish, by readings on an oscilloscope, different auras as seen by sensitive psychics attuned to aura reading [477].

Crystal healing. Some healers make use of crystals in their treatment of patients' ailments [220]. Minerals are used rather than any randomly selected lump of rock because they are aesthetically appealing in their colours and regular crystal structures, and because their regular internal structure – the regular array of atoms and molecules known as the crystal lattice that produces the observed crystal shape – is more effective at producing coherence of spiritual energy for healing than a heterogeneous piece of rock. Most rocks are made up of several different minerals. As each mineral is associated with certain properties directed at specific ailments, the use of the mixture of minerals found in rocks would be a confusion. It is not suggested that therapies such as these can replace those of orthodox medicine. They are *complementary*; they can enhance the effects of conventional pharmaceutical drugs, or sometimes ameliorate their side effects. The crystals are an adjunct to the channelling achieved through the healers themselves. Crystals and healers both are concentrating the resources of the universal spiritual field into the patient. The healing does not come from the healer or from the crystal: it lies within the patient, and with the aid of the healing energy of the universal spiritual field (u.s.f.). As the healer connects with it and channels it, the body's electromagnetic and psychic fields become realigned. It is reputed to be the (possibly mythical!) Egyptian alchemist Hermes Trismegistus who coined the phrase often used by healers: 'as above, so below': restoring the order of the universal spiritual field within the human body [97]. Put in terms of David Bohm's concepts (see Chapter 8), what we experience here on Earth is the explicate version of the ultimate implicate reality of the u.s.f.

Some healers like to use their minerals in the form of a pendulum, often of the lilac coloured form of quartz known as amethyst or of amber. This is usually used for diagnosis rather than treatment. The pendulum responds to imbalances in the body's chakras or psychic energy and the technique is known as *radiesthesia*. The technique is a variation on that of *dowsing* or *divining*, often carried out by sensitives searching for water or minerals using V-shaped rods of wood (especially willow, hazel or alder) or metal (especially copper). Again, the visible response of pendulums or rods in the hands of the users is clear evidence of a form of reaction, channelled through the diviner or healer, that cannot be explained by pre-quantum science. The continual use of the technique of dowsing by cost-conscious industrial concerns and governmental organisations is testimony to its success.

Homeopathy. The founder of homeopathy was Christian Friedrich Samuel Hahnemann (1755–1843). He was born in Meissen, Germany, and studied medicine at Leipzig and Vienna before settling back in Leipzig. It was while he was preparing a German translation of William Cullen's *Materia Medica* that he was struck by the fact that quinine produced the same effects on the healthy body as the malaria it was being used to treat. From this observation Hahnemann proposed one of the two basic laws of homeopathy, the *Law of Similars* or 'like cures like'. This is sometimes mistakenly interpreted as meaning that botanical remedies should be derived from plants that resemble the shape of the organ they are being used to treat, an idea that owes more to Galen than Hahnemann; but homeopathy works on a whole-body philosophy, not the 'diseased-organ' philosophy of conventional medicine. As most diseases, and even the ingestion of many naturally occurring or non-biological compounds, produce fever, nausea, vomiting, and headache, it was not surprising that many of Hahnemann's preparations produced the same symptoms as the diseases. At that time, surgery was performed with nothing but alcohol as an anaesthetic – nitrous oxide was not used until 1844, ether in 1846 and chloroform not until 1847. Bloodletting with leeches was also fairly common, so even if homeopathy did not produce cures, at least it was non-invasive and not as unpleasant as the alternatives then in current use, and some of the time it unquestionably works, whatever the mechanism.

With most of the herbal treatments used at the time, the condition of patients often deteriorated before it improved. Hahnemann reasoned that if he used smaller quantities of his medicines, there would be less decline in health before recovery. He carried this idea to the extreme by diluting his medications to such an extent that there would be none of the active principle left in the preparation. This gave rise to the second law of homeopathy, the *Law of Infinitesimals* – that the potency of preparations increases with dilution. Now it is a recognised fact in orthodox medicine too that there are certain optimal doses of all pharmaceutical preparations – too small a dose will be ineffective, but too much, and you kill the patient, or at least produce intolerable side-effects. Even the vitamins and minerals that the body requires daily in small doses may produce unpleasant side effects in high doses. But orthodox science would say unequivocally that no effect could be produced if there were no medicinally effective compound present at all. A similar situation exists with a variety of homeopathic treatment called the Bach flower remedies, treatments by plant extracts instigated in the 1930s by a London medical practitioner called Edward Bach (1880–1936). If plants can respond to human intentions, this may provide some rationale for this treatment of ailments, where it is successful. But standard OTC homeopathic remedies, the so-called Schuessler salts, contain inorganic materials. They represent a variation in homeopathic treatment devised by Dr William H. Schuessler who also worked in Germany in the middle of last century.

It is this second law of homeopathy that has generated most of the controversy in the use of this technique of treatment. Most notoriously in recent years, an eminent French biochemist, Jacques Benveniste (born in Paris in 1935) and former Research Director at the French National Institute for Medical Research published work that suggested homeopathy was indeed effective. It was in 1984 that one of the laboratory technicians, Elizabeth Davenas, recorded positive results in allergy testing to solutions that contained no allergen. While research continued in France into the cause of these seemingly impossible results, scientists in other countries collaborated with Benveniste to see if they could independently produce the same results – and they did. So in 1988, a joint paper was published in the prestigious science journal *Nature* [134]. The editor of the journal, John Maddox, added what was effectively a disclaimer to the paper saying that there was 'no physical basis for such activity.' A highly prejudiced investigation initiated by Maddox subsequently could not verify these results. So Benveniste was forced to leave the Establishment and work independently on his findings in this new field he called 'digital biology'.

Other scientists, working under stringent conditions, have previously and subsequently produced similar results. For example, a study by J.C. Cazin *et al.* showed that homeopathic doses of arsenic eliminated doses of trapped arsenic that had been previously fed to rats [115]. The Scottish team of P.G. Gibson and his colleagues in Glasgow have produced a reduction in pain of rheumatoid arthritis sufferers with homeopathic treatment [210]. A recent book by Masaru Emoto [172] describes and illustrates with colour photographs the changes in molecular structures obtained from aqueous solutions under the influence of prayer and positive thoughts. And of course there are the scores of people who have been successfully treated by homeopathy who will also testify to its validity.

The situation now is that there have been many scientifically sound clinical trials that have demonstrated the effectiveness of homeopathy in many cases. It is not as reliable as treatment by pharmaceutical preparations, but neither does it produce the plethora of side effects associated with orthodox treatment. The problem is that the success rate for homeopathy is lower than for many other treatments, both orthodox and complementary. The question still remains as to how it works when it is successful. One would not expect any effects, positive or negative, at all. The placebo effect that is active in some 20–30% of cases even with pharmacological treatment cannot be ignored in homeopathic treatment (a patient 'willing' themselves better because they believe they have been given a curative preparation when in fact they have been given plain water, or some other inert equivalent). The spiritual power of the healer is quite likely to be another positive contributor to success. Electromagnetic fields have been considered as possibly involved in the mechanism of action of homeopathy, but the most likely explanation seems to be some kind of energy imprint of the active principle on the water or alcohol used as a carrier. It has been shown scientifically that spiritual healers can affect the molecular structure (specifically, the hydrogen bonding) of aqueous solutions, so it is possible that a similar effect occurs in homeopathic treatment. A problem arises with this hypothesis however if homeopathic remedies are given in solid form as lactose tablets. It's one thing to affect a solution in water or alcohol, but quite another to alter crystal structures! And, like any other treatment, homeopathy too has its share of failures.

The effectiveness of all kinds of spiritual healing depends upon the power of the healer to channel the universal energy (see Chapters 7 and 8); it also depends upon the patient and on the nature of their illness. What it does do is to help the patient muster their own resources, activate their own immune systems, and promote a state of mind that is receptive to healing from any source. This helps the patients to relax and reduce negative stress levels, which are harmful in all situations. (Positive stress levels, produced by joy or excitement or exercise can be beneficial, in moderation.) Often, seemingly physical illnesses may have an emotional cause. The aim of the healing is to encourage each patient towards what Carl Jung called *individuation* – becoming a fully integrated person, body, mind and spirit. Spiritual healers are often just that – healers of the spirit; they need to use counselling skills as much as they do chakra realignment.

Spiritual healing is a psychic phenomenon that, by its very nature, seems to involve communion with a spiritual field, and patients feel the beneficial effects whether or not they are religious, and independently of any belief in the divine or in the technique itself, and even if there is no contact between patient and healer. These positive effects can even be transmitted over long distances between individuals who do not see or even know each other, and distant healing is a regular practice in alternative or complementary medicine. But the effectiveness of the techniques does depend on the healer, the patient, the rapport between them, and the nature of the illness being treated. As with telepathy, there are certain preconditions for successful psychic communication in spiritual healing. A great deal can be achieved by the patients themselves with a positive attitude of mind. But positive energies channelled from healers and others does seem to have a beneficial effect on an individual's wellbeing.

In 1988, the physician Randolph Byrd published a randomised, double-blind study, carried out over the previous few years, on the effect of prayer on 400 patients in a coronary care unit. Those for whom prayers had been offered fared considerably better than those who had not been receiving spiritual help [102]. These data have been replicated by other studies [239].

Reports of the positive effect of prayer on both the individuals themselves (which is perhaps not too surprising, since it predisposes to a state of relaxation and calm, which is almost always beneficial to health, quite apart from any divine input) and on others in need of physical help has been documented and discussed in several books by Dr. Larry Dossey [148, 149].

Larry Dossey has pointed out the impracticability of trying to separate out body, mind and spirit in treating illness, so inter-related are these aspects of the human organism. He also notes that, in these examples of psychic communication, there is nothing physically measurable passing from person to person – rather, it is an interaction between the psychic fields of the individuals concerned, through the universal energy field that pervades both: 'Consciousness is everywhere; it's omnipresent. There's no necessity for anything to go anywhere, because consciousness is already everywhere.' [150].

Jeff Levin, a former medical school professor, has also been studying these phenomena for the past two decades and has published some of his results in a recent book [321]. The positive evidence continues to grow, as reported by other authors [295].

Elizabeth Targ, psychiatrist daughter of physicist Russell Targ, working in California together with psychologist Fred Sicher carried out a comparable study of spiritual healing effects on patients with AIDS. Again, distant healing was found to have a positive effect in ameliorating some of the symptoms of the disease and apparently assisting remission [435]. Elizabeth Targ's results were confirmed by further large-scale studies before her untimely death at age 40.

If prayer can exert such a positive effect on the wellbeing and healing of the sick, then all positive, loving thoughts add to the store of beneficence within the universal spiritual field. Conversely, thoughts of anger and hatred, as well as their detrimental effect on the physical health of the individual through raised stress levels, detract from the positive energy field and lead, locally, to the eruption of quarrels and disputes or, on a larger scale, to internecine struggle or war. Although, hopefully, the threat of nuclear annihilation of humankind has receded with the thawing of the cold war, international struggles for land, and resources, and power, or attempts to impose the religious beliefs or cultural lifestyle of one nation on another continue, and a global awareness of the need for positive, healing input to the spiritual field is urgently needed. And the choice is ours!

6.5.6. Near-death experiences, reincarnation and communion with spirits [232, Sections 1, 5d].

There are many books specifically on these subjects, documenting case histories of those who have had near-death experiences (NDEs) or who have detailed information of some past existence that it would be difficult, if not impossible, for them to come by other than by having lived the life themselves. Some physiologists who dismiss the whole afterlife concept attribute the phenomena of NDEs to normal near-death physiological processes, like the effects on the brain of oxygen deprivation. Recall of events from early life that were long forgotten, visions of some religious image such as Jesus or Mary, the vision of a bright light at the end of a dark tunnel, a sense of peace and calmness or euphoria, an out-of-body experience (OBE) of looking down on oneself (a frequent occurrence after cardiac arrest according to cardiologist Michael Sabom), and a heightened sense of spirituality and less attachment to material things after recovery – these are all commonly reported experiences of NDEs. There is also almost always a sense of disappointment when subjects find themselves back in the physical world again. Furthermore, negative NDEs are very much less common than positive experiences and occur comparatively rarely. It might be expected that people in such a stressed state as one would expect approaching death would be much more likely to have negative emotions rather than positive ones – but this does not seem to be the case. Carl Sagan suggested that the NDE may be a reliving of the birth experience, particularly the passage through a dark tunnel into the light. But this is the only part of the NDE that would correspond to the birth process. While some aspects of NDEs can be explained physiologically – the sense of peace or joy, the bright light or other visions, the tunnel experience – the subsequent detailed descriptions by patients of events occurring around them while they are in coma or deep anesthesia cannot.

Some of these NDE phenomena can indeed be induced by drugs such as anaesthetics or so-called 'recreational drugs' (a misnomer if ever there was one!) or are experienced by some people normally who are susceptible to epileptic seizures or migraine attacks, but not all of them. The OBE particularly is not uncommonly reported by people in deep anaesthesia undergoing serious and potentially life-threatening surgery. However, even when medical monitoring equipment registers that sensory input is suspended, patients are sometimes able to recall details of the operation procedure and even conversations between medical staff. There is no possibility that this could have occurred though the normal seeing or hearing physiological pathways.

While they are not usually near-death experiences, many emotionally intense creative people have severe illnesses involving a disturbed mental and emotional state during or just before an intensely creative period, sometimes taking them to the verge of what they think is madness or impending death: Sigmund Freud, Carl Jung, August Strindberg, Friedrich Nietzsche, Vincent van Gogh and theosophist Rudolf Steiner all underwent such experiences. Many spiritual healers undergo a less extreme version of such an illness before they acquire the ability and commitment to become healers.

Reincarnation. Reincarnation or *samsara* became a key tenet of the Eastern religions after it was clearly defined in the Hindu scriptures of the *Upanishads*, written some seven to five hundred years BCE. It was then taken up by those religions that were derived from Hinduism – Buddhism, Taoism and Jainism. At the time when the other principal Hindu scriptures, the *Vedas*, were written (13th-10th Century BCE), as there is no mention of reincarnation, the belief was presumably absorbed into Hindu belief from that of the ancient Egyptians and Babylonians that life would continue in some form in the next world – resurrection rather than reincarnation. Hence, in Egypt, bodies were embalmed and buried with food, utensils, jewellery, weapons and even small effigies or *shabtis* to function as servants in the afterlife. In Hinduism, deceased relatives were commemorated for the first year after departure from earthly life in the *shraddha* ritual [*Rig Veda* 10, 15, 1–11] because it was believed that the spirit of the deceased could exert either a positive or negative influence over the affairs of the living. The deceased were watched over by *Yama*, the god of the dead. The *Brihadaranyaka Upanishad* is the first to talk of the role of karma in recycling *atman*, an impersonal 'self' or mind, for earthly existence until the karmic debt to the Divine Spirit is repaid by good deeds and service in earthly life. In Taoism, the *Chuang Tzu* (written *ca.* 4th Century BCE) says: 'Birth is not a beginning; death is not an end. There is existence without limitation; there is continuity without a starting point', implying infinite existence in an infinite world.

What is it exactly that is reincarnated? Certainly not the same physical body, even if this is somehow reconstituted after death as some believe [see discussion in ref. 365]. Amongst those who believe in reincarnation, the generally held view is that of *metempsychosis*

– the passing of the soul after death into another physical body and, in some Eastern belief, not necessarily another human form. A physical metaphor for the process of recycling of souls can be drawn with the life processes of plants. In the spring and summer, buds develop into leaves and flowers that die off in the autumn and winter. The molecules that make up the leaves fall to earth and are recycled into other trees and shrubs that grow in that same spot in the following year. The molecules are the same but the form they assume is different What must transmigrate from earthly to 'heavenly' life are some sense of self and a body of memories. If we are to learn in each earthly incarnation, while we may not, under normal circumstances, remember anything of past lives in our day-to-day consciousness, still our soul must evolve, so some memory of earthly events previously experienced must remain. The element of mind that is directly and autonomously associated with brain function is gone, but the spiritual mind – the mind that engages in psychic events and NDEs, that communes with the universal spiritual field – lives on to assimilate and assess the experiences of the life just lived so that we do not repeat the ethical mistakes of our previous lives, to be re-embodied at some future time. The Purgatory of the Catholic Church is the state of torment of the soul in the afterlife at the realisation of the ethical mistakes it has made – the sins of omission and commission. Paradise is the state of satisfaction or joy at a life lived constructively for the benefit of humankind. Where we have failed in our duties but acted always with the best of intentions, a state of joy may still be produced by forgiveness for our transgressions by God or Communal Soul.

Recall of 'past lives' under hypnosis has been shown to be false on several occasions. Subjects simply recall stories they had heard or read in childhood that had long since become buried deep in the subconscious, though not all accounts have been discredited [525]. What is more impressive is recall of details of previous existence by children, and occasionally adults, in the normal waking state. Many of the most impressive cases originate in India, though reincarnation is part of the subconscious psyche in that part of the world, and therefore it may perhaps be expected that even children would be more likely to invent fanciful tales of this kind. On the other hand, it may be that Eastern religion is not so cluttered with the man-made tenets and rituals introduced into Western religions, so that their one-world viewpoint, characteristic of the pagans, brings them closer to the Universal Spirit. Among these more convincing cases of reincarnation reported by Indian children we might mention those of the little girls Swarnlata and Shanti Devi, aged three and four, respectively [359], and three-year old Jagdish Chandra [94]. At this age they would hardly be old enough to have worldly experiences to recollect.

Some of the best-known of the books dealing with NDE and reincarnation, most of which may well be available still, new or second-hand (many are long ago out of print) are by C.J. Ducasse [154] – an early appraisal of the phenomena; Ian Stevenson [457, 458, 459] – reports by a renowned researcher in the field of reincarnation claims in children; Raymond A. Moody [349] – the classic presentation of the subject; Michael Sabom [407] – case histories of NDEs from a heart surgeon; Colin Wilson [522] – a writer with a very accessible style who started as a sceptic but became a believer after researching the material for this book; Grant Solomon and Jane Solomon [439, 440] – a report of the five year experimental programme (1993–8) of the group based at Scole, near Diss in Norfolk, UK; Gary E. Schwartz with William L. Simon [422] – Schwartz is a professor in several departments of the University of Arizona, including psychology, psychiatry and neurology; Simon is a writer; Mark Fox [186] – a survey drawing on a wealth of material from the RERC at Lampeter; David Fontana [181] – a recent comprehensive overview. There are also further examples cited in Richard Broughton's *Parapsychology* [94] and in Hans J. Eysenck and Carl Sargent's *Explaining the Unexplained* [176].

The evidence presented in these books, with the related discussion and references therein, is too extensive to review here in any greater detail, but the number of examples, many anecdotal and uniquely individual, but many also from respected scientists working within the rigorous techniques accepted as standard in experimental practice is so overwhelming that one would have to be not just sceptical but to read with a closed mind to find it unconvincing. Even if we regarded some of these accounts as fanciful imaginings, even intentional deceit by some of the subjects, this much self-consistent data cannot be dismissed as fantasy. The evidence for some kind of spiritual domain associated with every human being, apart from our emotional selves, is highly persuasive to the open mind.

Spiritualism. One of the most convincing arguments for soul, an afterlife and even reincarnation surely is to be found in the work of spiritualists. Spiritualism is the name given to the formal religion of those who believe in the possibility of communication with the spirits of the dead, and that such contact can and does influence the lives of the living. Spiritualists believe that the spirits manifest themselves to many people from time to time, but especially to certain gifted individuals called *mediums* or *channelers*. Many responsible individuals have attested to the truth of the statements made by genuine mediums. Mediums are more frequently women than men, perhaps as a result of their greater propensity for intuitive *yin* activity associated with the right cerebral hemisphere. Men tend to have predominant logical left-brain or *yang* activity, though there have been some famous male psychics. In the USA, Andrew Jackson Davies (1822–1910) and Edgar Cayce (b. Kentucky 1877; d. 3 Jan 1945) used to go into self-induced trances to make predictions and diagnosis of illnesses. Again, the veracity of the diagnoses was testified to over and over. They were apparently receiving information from their spirit guides who are said to communicate with all mediums and spiritual healers. The medium Alice Bailey also focused her talents on healing. Born in England, she settled in California and became active in the theosophy movement there. She wrote many books claiming that the writing was not her own but that she was acting as amanuensis for a Tibetan Master, Dhwal Khul. There are certain similarities in her life with the work and writings of Helena Blavatsky, the founder of theosophy. Alice Bailey went on to establish an organisation now called The Lucis Trust.

Communion with the spirits of dead ancestors, like the mystical search for ultimate being, dates back to ancient times and is still widely practiced by peoples in less developed societies. The ancestors are believed to have knowledge that is not accessible to those on the earthly plane, both from wisdom gained during their earthly incarnation and experience, and from their access to the spiritual domain. The spirit guides are sages who have reached a higher plane of wisdom than others in the spiritual realm. All of the indigenous peoples of each continent have an ongoing tradition of communing with the spirits of the dead, a practice they would hardly have perpetuated, even out of ritualistic tradition, if it had not been found repeatedly to be of practical use. The Druids mentioned in Chapter 1 were sages with access to spiritual wisdom. The aborigines of Australia have a culture that is believed to go back as much as 50,000 years. Their sages access the Alcheringa or Dreamtime, the time of the ancestors, for spiritual guidance, especially in rituals dedicated to birth or death. For the aborigine, the Dreamtime was the time of Creation. Their distinctive musical instrument, the didgeridoo, is now used in healing practices around the world for its deep rich tone.

As a formal religion, Spiritualism began in 1848 after mysterious, rationally inexplicable events occurred in the Fox household in New England in the U.S.A. The Fox family comprised John Fox, a Methodist farmer, his wife Margaret, and their daughters Margaretta (aged 14 at the time), and Catherine (aged 12), and they lived in Hydesville, a small township near Rochester, New York State. They heard mysterious rappings at their home and it was alleged that they were being contacted by the spirit of one Charles B. Posna who was murdered in their house five years earlier during a robbery. The Foxes brought in more than a dozen neighbours to testify to the rappings. Again, as a devout religious family, they were not likely to perpetuate this kind of fraud, or to risk social exclusion as Satanists if these events were in some way fabricated. As a direct result of these events, the first Spiritualist meeting took place the following year, in November 1849.

The principles of the Spiritualist movement were laid down by Emma Hardinge Britten (born in Manchester in 1823) who maintained that they were given to her by her spirit guide. The principal beliefs are: (1) The unity and over-arching omnipotence of God; (2) Humankind is an inter-related family, irrespective of race or creed; (3) There is a communion of spirits with a ministry of angels; (4) There is continuous existence of every soul; (5) All individuals have personal responsibility for their fate; (6) There is joy or anguish after life on Earth for good or evil deeds performed in earthly existence; (7) Eternal progress is open to every soul.

To deter idle curiosity in supernatural phenomena or malicious persecution of those who claimed the gift of spiritual communication, the Spiritualists formed their movement for the serious investigation of life after death, of spiritual or psychic phenomena and to provide comfort for the bereaved and dying. Nurses who professionally attend to the dying have often reported seeing a diaphanous film of white matter, known as *ectoplasm*, leaving the corpse of the deceased immediately or up to some few hours after death. Although unscrupulous charlatans have exploited the bereaved, the desperate or the gullible with trickery, there is an increasing body of reliable evidence of the authenticity of many claimed communications with the dead.

Once spiritualism was recognised as a widely occurring phenomenon, many eminent and intelligent men, who would be unlikely to be easily duped with trickery, or risk damaged reputations, began to take it seriously: Sir William Crookes (1832–1919), an eminent physicist and chemist, discoverer of the element thallium and inventor of the radiometer; philosopher Sir Henry Sidgwick (1838–1900), who resigned from his post at Trinity College, Cambridge, because in his pursuit of spiritualism he felt that he could no longer subscribe to the 39 Articles of the Church of England; Sir Arthur Conan Doyle (1859–1930), doctor, historian and novelist, creator of Sherlock Holmes, and one who became a committed spiritualist and wrote a fascinating *History of Spiritualism* that was published in 1926; Charles Dodgson, alias Lewis Carroll (1832–1898), creator of *Alice in Wonderland*, who was convinced that all such phenomena simply could not be explained away as trickery. Conan Doyle was duped on one occasion apparently by a family claiming they had seen fairies at the bottom of their garden, but this was a case of quite ingenious trickery and would have made him all the more alert for fraud. The writers amongst these men clearly would have had a vivid imagination, but scientists and philosophers, with professional reputations at stake would not easily allow themselves to be duped. They all felt that there was a real phenomenon here that demanded investigation and explanation. Sidgwick married Eleanor Balfour, and her brother, Arthur Balfour, rose to become Prime Minister of Britain; he too followed developments in spiritualism with great interest.

*   *   *

Thus, there is a mass of empirical evidence to support the validity of a whole range of psychic phenomena that may be associated with the workings of an individual soul. Rather than dismiss all of these as fraud or naïve credulity, it is more rational to accept that these phenomena truly exist and try to find an explanation that is consistent with the rational world-view of science. The ideas are not incompatible also with the other more spiritual activities that may be ascribed to an individual human soul, as described in the early part of this chapter. Such a scientific interpretation is what is attempted in Chapter 8; but first, we should consider notions of philosophers, scientists and writers that represent, in very different contexts, one to another, the idea of a universal spiritual realm or Communal Soul.

7   Philosophy and the concept of a universal spirit

The idea of a spiritual energy encompassing the world and invested in each one of us individually, and forming a medium behind or interacting with material objects was a significant concept in early Eastern philosophical thought and for pagan peoples everywhere, as far as we know. It is to be found in the writings of philosophers and theologians since the time of the ancient Greeks, who in turn may well have adopted it from travellers from the Eastern civilisations, or more directly from the ancient Egyptians or Babylonians. These ideas recur in many very different contexts, but some of those most relevant to the present argument are described in this chapter.

First, it is worth pointing out that the idea of an all-pervading universal spirit could provide a unifying concept, both between different kinds of religious belief and, as we shall see in the next chapter, even between religion and science. It does not contradict the view of the divine held by many religions, but it is probably not compatible with fundamentalism in any belief system. In fact, it is the antithesis of fundamentalism. The teaching of Sri Ramakrishna (1836–1886), the mystical Indian philosopher, on the limitations of fundamentalism is most apposite: 'The fanatic sincerely believes that his path alone is true and the others are no paths at all. He feels it his duty to attack other religions. But this attitude is born of ignorance. The fanatic helps neither himself nor others. He deals out nothing but evil. Contrary to this, same-sightedness and acceptance of all religions are born of enlightenment' [465]. The 'same-sightedness' is the goal of the universal spiritual divine.

In the Hindu *Upanishads* (originating *ca.* 400 BCE), the divine breath is described as *Atman* or *Parama-ātman*, while *ātman* or *jiva-ātman* represents 'self' or the individual soul. *Atman* is also equivalent to the divine itself, *Brahman*, just as the Holy Spirit is the divine energy of God the Father in Christendom, distinct but not separate. Hinduism has its *Trinity* or *Trimurti* too in *Brahman* or *Brahma*, the creator, *Atman* the divine spirit, and *Vishnu*, *Rama* or *Siva* as manifestations or avatars. The creative essence of *Brahman* is *Brahma*, the equivalent of the Godhead of Western theology. Therefore, *Atman* may be regarded as a Hindu form of World Soul or Communal Soul. It may also be described as the all-pervading *akashic field* of Hindu philosophy and represents the energy of the astral plane as described by theosophists and spiritualists. The primaeval matter from which the universe was born was *akasha*, and the energy pervading it, through all time, was and is the akashic field. In the *Brihādaranyaka Upanishad*, *ātman* is described as a vital force that permeates all life forms. This idea lays the ground for the philosophy of vitalism, described later.

Hindu teaching of the *Samkara* and *Advaita* schools tells us that God alone is real and the universe is His incarnation; in essence however it is unknowable, for the world of the senses is *māyā* (illusion or idea). All that is, is really undifferentiated – subject and object, perceiver and perceived, observer and observed, which has resonances with some ideas in 20th Century quantum physics. In *Advaita*, our knowledge of the material world is made up of sense impressions only because of our inadequacy in perceiving ultimate truth, which is known only to *Brahman*. Samkara was a medieval Hindu philosopher and proponent of *advaita*.

In Judaism, the Divine Presence is represented by the *Shechinah*, The Indwelling One, immanent and omnipresent in both individuals and communities, as well as being concentrated in sacred places. In the mystical Jewish writings of the *Kabbalah*, the *Shechinah* is the tenth and final *Sefirah* (an emanation of God) and is sometimes taken to represent the feminine aspect of God. As psychologists tell us now that the feminine character is the more sensitive and spiritual, this seems an entirely appropriate concept – that the universal spirit, if it is associated with gender at all, should be feminine. The spirit of the divine is the light that illuminates the created world, that first outpouring from the undifferentiated matter of *En Sof,* a light that still shines throughout all creation. From earliest times, the divine has been associated with the sun and its emanating light and life-giving energy. As we saw in Chapter 1, the sun-god was the highest of the Egyptian deities. In the biblical account of the Creation, the first priority God was said to have attended to was creation of this spiritual and physical energy: 'Let there be light' [Genesis, Chapter 1, verse 3], or as the *Kabbalah* puts it:

> The universe was created out of nothingness from a single point of light. This nothingness is called the Endless World. The Endless World was filled with infinite Light. The Light was then contracted to a single point, creating primordial space. Beyond this point nothing is known. Therefore, the point is called the beginning. After the contraction, the Endless World issued forth a ray of Light. This ray of Light then expanded rapidly. All matter emanated from that point.
>
> From the sayings of the Jewish Kabbalist, Rabbi Isaac Luria, 1534–1572, as recorded by his disciple Hayim Vital in his treatise *The Tree of Life.* [quoted in ref. 52]

In Christianity, it is God the Holy Spirit that represents the World Soul, the spiritual aspect of the divinity. Any idea of a spirit equivalent in status to God would be unacceptable in Judaism or Islam with their emphatic monotheism, but the emanations of the *Sefiroth* provide a means for Jews to commune with the otherwise inaccessible God, as Jesus, Mary and the saints do in Christianity.

Many thinkers through the ages have had the inspiration of this unifying spiritual field in an essentially secular context. In historical (as opposed to pre-historical) times, one of the earliest visions of a spiritual realm lying beyond the material world of the senses was that of the Greek philosopher Plato (*ca.* 428–347 BCE) with his concept of the Ideas or Forms, the spiritual templates that form the source of our worldly ideas (see Chapter 2). Plato may well have been influenced by these Eastern philosophies described above.

The Greek theological philosopher Plotinus (*ca.* 205–270 CE), who was born in Egypt, developed some of the ideas of Plato and other earlier philosophers in his own philosophy. He revives the Stoic notion of an all-encompassing Universal or World Soul, also denoted as All-Soul. Plotinus' teachings were gathered together by his pupil, Porphyry, into six groups of nine books that thence became known as *The Enneads* from the Greek word *ennea* meaning 'nine' [373]. Thirty-six volumes of theological critique by Porphyry himself were burned on the orders of the early Church Fathers. To paraphrase the explanation given by Plotinus concerning the All-Soul: our individual soul is not a fragmentary part of All-Soul, like an arc is a part of the circumference of a circle but, in some sense, soul is a participant of All-Soul [paraphrase of ref. 202]. Individual souls are neither parts of nor yet separate from All-Soul because Soul is not a thing of quantity. Rather, Soul is the essence of God or The One, as whiteness is the essence of a portion of milk. Again using Plotinus' words: the whiteness of the portion is not a part or portion of the whiteness of milk in general. To use another of his analogies: soul is to All-Soul as are the theorems comprising the corpus of the subject of geometry. All-Soul is the composite of individual souls. Mind and Soul to Plotinus are lesser hypostases below The Good or The One, which is identified in places with God. The purpose of life to Plotinus is to free the individual soul from the material and sensual to achieve a unity through All-Soul with the higher Good.

Plotinus maintained that he had achieved union with The One four times in his life. It is at such times that it is said we glimpse not only the divine but derive insight into the nature of existence in some profound way. In our everyday existence, we cannot know the ultimate reality of matter: all observable properties are simply appearances (*maya*), because what fundamentally comprises matter is beyond the five senses.

As we saw in Chapter 3, the whole of the period that philosophers describe as 'medieval', from the time of Jesus to the Renaissance and Enlightenment, some 1500 years, was predominated by religious philosophy in the West – Jewish, Christian and Islamic. The synagogue, the monastery and the mosque were the centres of learning before the universities were established.

With the burgeoning of the Renaissance, philosophers directed their attention to secular issues as well as religious matters in their writing. It is with the first of the philosophers known as the British empiricists that we next meet a non-material component of the world, but now in a secular context. The 17th Century English empiricist philosopher, John Locke (1632–1704), was born in the Somerset village of Wrington. His father was an attorney by profession and a Puritan by religious belief, and he had a great influence on young Locke's childhood. In adulthood, Locke counted the scientists Robert Boyle and Isaac Newton among his friends; professionally, he was in the service of Lord Shaftsbury, sometime as a trade official. He was very active as a man of letters, writing mainly on political and religious issues.

In his book *An Essay Concerning Human Understanding*, published in 1689 [322], Locke gave an account of our use of words and ideas, and what constitutes knowledge and what represents opinion: 'Knowledge is the perception of the agreement or disagreement of two ideas' [324]; opinion is 'that which makes us presume things to be true before we know them to be so' [325]. This, in Locke's view, is what differentiates certainty from probability, faith or belief from knowledge. Locke believed that all of our knowledge is acquired by sense perception and that we start in this world with a *tabula rasa*, a blank white sheet on which the sensory experiences of the world are written [326]. In this, Locke differs somewhat from Plato, who felt that all knowledge was a relearning from past lives. However, this still implies that we start the relearning process from nothing in each lifetime.

In his discussion of degrees of knowledge, Locke maintained that every object possesses characteristics that give it its *nominal essence*, those properties that give rise to its name. The yellowness and heaviness of gold, or the whiteness of milk represent components of their nominal essence. Behind this nominal essence of every created object that gave it the properties by which it was defined there lay a spiritual *real essence* that generated those properties, the 'real constitution of substances, upon which depends this nominal essence, and all the properties of this sort'; 'the real essence is the constitution of the insensible parts of that body' [327]. A modern interpretation of this might be to say that 'real essence' refers to the ultimate atomic or subatomic structure of a substance but, as we shall see in the next chapter, there are grounds for considering this too to be part of the cosmic spirit.

As John Locke followed Francis Bacon in maintaining that the only knowledge that could be relied upon was that which we obtained with the senses, he is described as one of a number of philosophers known as the British empiricists, though this was not a 'school' of philosophical thought engendering mutual interaction. Locke's philosophy did however have a profound influence on the next member of the 'group'.

Bishop George Berkeley (1685–1753) was born in Kilkenny in southern Ireland. He was concerned that the world posited by English philosopher John Locke was too material, too experiential and allowed no room for God. If all our knowledge came from sensory experience, how were we to know God? This was the issue that concerned Berkeley. He therefore maintained that all our sensory inputs are experienced only by the grace of God: 'God *alone* [is] the immediate efficient cause of all things.' [58]; God is 'the Supreme Spirit which excites those ideas in our minds' [59]. Existence itself of any object depended upon our perception of it: *'esse ist percipi'* – to exist is to be perceived [57]. In Berkeley's view therefore, all of our rational and sensory perceptions are a reflection of the spiritual world held in the mind of God. Put another way, we seem to be accessing Plato's spiritual world of Ideas, which Augustine had already equated with 'thoughts in the mind of God' [28]. As we saw in Chapter 1, the notion that things in the world are a reflection of some underlying higher and greater reality is also one of the tenets of Whitehead's philosophy that has become known as Process Theology.

The German philosopher, Immanuel Kant (1724–1804) described Locke's nominal and real essences as the *phenomenal* and *noumenal* properties of a thing, respectively. The noumenal was also described as 'the thing-in-itself' (*das Ding an sich*), in other words, that which represents ultimate reality in relation to the object. He also realised that empirical observation alone could not provide knowledge without reason to provide an interpretation of sensory observation. Kant's ideas thus represented a fusion between the principles of the British empiricist philosophers, who believed all knowledge came from sensory experience, and the continental European rationalists like Descartes, Spinoza and Leibniz, and most of the Greek philosophers considered in Chapter 2, who suggested that we could understand the world only through reason because our senses could be deceived. Locke's real essence and Kant's noumenal qualities thus represent the concept of a universal spiritual dimension that lies behind the material world of experience. It was left to the Romantics to propose that even sensory input and rationalisation were not enough to make sense of the world but that it was the primacy of our emotions (*Gefuhl*) that determined how we interpreted our sensory perceptions, or even which sensory inputs we noted or perceived in the first place. Thus we have three sources of knowledge here: empiricism (the input of our five senses), rationalism (the thinking mind) and emotionalism (the bridge between the two) and, closely related to emotion but distinguishable from it, a fourth source of knowledge, revelation, intuition, or insight – what we call the sixth sense.

God as a universal spiritual force is also akin to the societal spirit that the German philosopher G.W.F. Hegel (1770–1831) described as *Geist*, in his reinterpretation of the ideas of Herder. *Geist* was a collective or universal mind, the spirit of an age that moves a society to behave in a particular way, just as individual soul is that which impels mind to a particular course of action in each one of us. Hegel's *Geist* exists only in human consciousness. Although in some

contexts Hegel uses this term in the sense of *Heilige Geist* (Holy
Spirit), this is not the God of Western theology, creator of all that is,
with an enduring and independent existence. Hegel is not a pantheist
– there is nothing divine about Nature in Hegel's philosophy. But
the created universe is mediate (*vermittelt*) – it is necessary as the
expression of God. In order to attain *Geist*'s (or God's) fulfillment,
humankind must evolve to a stage of realisation that they are part of
an expansive universe. The evolution of the universe, and particularly
of humankind, is part of the evolution of God or *Geist* [481]. Though
Hegel's work is not mentioned in this context, we are once again
back to the ideas of Process Theology.

   Hegel's first great work was the *Phenomenology of Mind* (or
Phenomenology of Spirit) (*Phänomenologie des Geistes*) of 1807,
completed on the eve of the Battle of Jena at which Napoleon defeated
the Prussians. Born and schooled in Stuttgart, Germany, Hegel had
completed his PhD at the seminary of Tubingen University by the
time he was 20. He held the prestigious Chair of Philosophy at the
University of Berlin from 1818 until his death from cholera in 1831.

   Though Hegel's *Geist* has religious connotations in some contexts
(the *Heilige Geist*), in others it is both a societal and an individual
driving force rather like Schopenhauer's *Wille* (see below), except
that Hegel's spirit is uplifting and creative where Schopenhauer's
is essentially pessimistic and destructive in its egoism. There is a
changeability (*Veränderlichkeit*) inherent in a society and in the world
in general. The world functions by this contradiction and conflict
between opposites, as suggested by Heraclitus. In Hegel's *Dialectic
Theory of History*, *Geist* continually evolves through such a process
of change involving a significantly large segment of society. The first
stage is that of *thesis*, where a society adopts a prevailing philosophy
of living. Then an element in the society rebels against the existing
order, the movement grows, and the all-pervading or most significant
ethos in terms of power becomes something that is opposed to the
established order: this is the stage of *antithesis*. Then society sees
shortcomings in this new philosophy too, recalls merit in some of
the practices of the former society and so adopts a way of life that

embraces elements from the two previous systems: this is the stage of *synthesis*. Then the process begins anew. There have been several illustrations of this theory in recent Western history; for example, the rise of Romanticism in the wake of the Industrial Revolution and of the increasing present-day focus on spirituality as a backlash against the excessive materialism of the 1980s in America and Britain. The socialist principles of Karl Marx inspired the communist revolution in Russia because of the extravagant excesses of the czarist regime. In some sense therefore, history can be viewed either as cyclical or oscillatory as it moves between opposing philosophical poles; or it can be considered vortical, if we believe that it is evolving slowly into an ideal state of greater harmony.

In his work *Philosophy of History* Hegel sums up his approach to human history with the opening sentence: 'the history of the world is nothing but the development of the idea of freedom' [436]. Societies produce these changes because they can; and the more they are repressed by dictatorial regimes, the more violent is their overthrow by an opposing system. This societal expression of mind and soul charts the course of human history. In a more limited context, Hegel's *Geist* is a successor to the *general will* idea proposed by Denis Diderot and Jean-Jacques Rousseau (1712–78) – it is both an individual and a communal motivating spirit. With his emphasis on the importance of individual and societal freedom of expression, Hegel was opposed to any religion that created dogmas that ran contrary to human nature.

Individuals not in harmony with the prevailing tenor of society, fighting against forces that are too powerful to be overcome, experience a feeling of *alienation*. This can be regarded as akin to the feeling of unease or disquiet described by Buddhists in the First Noble Truth as *dukkha*, which they see as an essential characteristic of human existence – a striving for self-expression. If we are forced into a way of life with which we are not comfortable, we try to make the best of it and convince ourselves, and the rest of the world, that we are contented. If we are not successful in taming the rebellion of our conscious selves and relegating our discontent to the subconscious, we will experience alienation from our surroundings. But we can tolerate a situation such as this only in the short term before psychological problems arise; which is why we need the Eightfold Way to peace and harmony described in the Fourth Noble Truth of Buddhist philosophy, or some equivalent set of moral values to guide us to a quiet soul.

In the wake of the changes in lifestyle brought about by the 17th and 18th Century Industrial Revolution, there was a widespread sense of alienation from the materialistic society in which people lived. Apart from massive pollution in industrial centres, the nature of daily work became repetitive and less satisfying. As Karl Marx was to say later, workers no longer used the fruits of their labours. They were now regimented to work a long day under poor conditions to increase the wealth of mill and mine owners who clearly lived more leisurely lives in prosperous surroundings. It was this sense of alienation, perhaps more than anything else, that gave rise to the emotional revolution we know as Romanticism in late 18th Century Germany. This feeling that the human spirit was not at one with such a material and regimented existence was not uncommon amongst philosophers of the 19th Century. One of these was Arthur Schopenhauer (1788–1860).

Schopenhauer was born in Gdansk, Poland, which was then called Danzig and a part of Prussia. He was independently wealthy from an inheritance that was left to him by his father, who died while Schopenhauer was sill in his teenage years. He was a committed atheist and pessimist; he saw in the 19th Century 'an age in which religion is almost entirely dead'.

His doctoral dissertation, published in 1813 and in an expanded version in 1847, was *On the Fourfold Root of the Principle of Sufficient Reason*. This defines the four reasons why events happen in the world as they do; as Schopenhauer put it: 'Nothing is without a ground or reason why it is'. According to Schopenhauer there are four types of reason: physical reasons (examples of the scientific principle of cause and effect – empiricism), logical reasons (our justifications for thinking or believing as we do, like our reasons for holding certain religious beliefs), mathematical reasons (like the properties of geometrical figures arrived at by Euclid in his *Elements* – these and logical reasons constitute rationalism), and moral reasons (we help others because we believe they would do the same for us – which involves emotionalism). These comprise the four ways we acquire knowledge of the world. There is no room in Schopenhauer's philosophy for any psychic intuition or knowledge through revelation, but he does acknowledge a kind of transcendental truth that includes intuitive axioms, like those of mathematics, or notions of space and time, or the existence of causality. Causality for Schopenhauer has to do with change (*cf.* Heraclitus) – the appearance and disappearance of states in time. So causality is a 'becoming' rather than 'being'.

His greatest work, *Die Welt als Wille und Vorstellung* (*The World as Will and Representation*), was published in 1818. '*Vorstellung*' can be translated as 'representation' or as 'idea'. Part I of the book, the world as idea, discusses the notion that all we really know of the world is from the ideas or representations formed in our minds from sensory experience, recalling the Hindu view of the world as *maya*. We divide the sensory world into discrete objects, but the world as will (Kant's 'noumenal') is a continuum that embraces all that is. As all is one in the world of the will, the spiritual world, in harming others we also harm ourselves. In Part II Schopenhauer discusses the idea that all of our actions are an expression of our will. Here it seems that by '*Wille*' Schopenhauer meant something akin to driving force or energy, which has more than a little in common with Bergson's *élan vital* and Freud's *libido* as life's driving force, though without the Freudian sexual associations. In the broader view it can perhaps be identified with Hegel's *Geist*, or with the ultimate reality or world of spirit behind the phenomenal world of appearance. D.W. Hamlyn defines it as 'a force which permeates nature and which thus governs all phenomena' [223]. Schopenhauer was heavily influenced by Kant, and identified Kant's *Ding-an-sich*, Kant's noumenal dimension of the world, with *Wille* [226].

While living in Frankfurt, Schopenhauer published there his work, *Uber den Willen in der Natur* (1836; English trans. 1889, *On the Will in Nature*). In this book he deduced philosophically that all matter must be transmutable into this energy of *Wille*, though it was the next century before Einstein showed mathematically that this was indeed a physical possibility. This interchange between matter and energy is at the heart of modern quantum mechanics (see Chapter 8).

Schopenhauer believed that our knowledge of the world is governed by our concepts of space and time. Various objects appear different to us because of their location in space and time, a view that was held by Thomas Aquinas but which differs from that of Duns Scotus with his notion of individuality within a thing, discussed in Chapter 3. If we could in some way put ourselves outside this space-time frame of reference, all reality would be one, said Schopenhauer. This notion is very similar to the eastern idea of *nirvana*, putting ourselves outside the world of physical experience. The only hope for humankind to escape *Wille* was to end attachment to material things. Schopenhauer was heavily influenced by oriental philosophy through his acquaintance with a specialist in Asian culture, Friedrich Mayer, whom he met, together with Goethe at the intellectual gatherings organised by his mother in Weimar. The Upanishads became a formative influence on Schopenhauer's work, together with the work of Plato and Kant. Schopenhauer's manuscripts reveal that he regarded Plato's Ideas and Kant's *Ding-an-sich* as one and the same [275]. Reality for Schopenhauer was impersonal, but intrinsically selfish and egoistic, a view he adopted from the degree of suffering and oppression he saw in the world. As he interpreted it, all life is suffering – a view again corresponding to the Buddhist *dukkha*. This he regarded to be incompatible with the existence of a loving God. Our everyday world of existence is essentially meaningless, it is illusion or *maya*, and it is only in times of transcendental meditation that we can be at peace and perhaps glimpse the ultimate nature of reality.

Schopenhauer believed that it was the function of art to give us an insight into the nature of ultimate reality. Through an appreciation of the aesthetic by an expression of *Wille*, we can put ourselves beyond the evil existing in space and time. The idea of an essential 'self' within the consciously thinking individual introduces the notion of the subconscious several decades before it appears in Freud. Through loving others we are able to define our own self in relation to others [225]. Schopenhauer's ideas exerted a great influence on many writers of the 20th century, such as Thomas Mann, Thomas Hardy and D.H. Lawrence.

This same spiritual driving-force concept was expressed in psychological terms for an individual by German philosopher Friedrich Nietzsche (1844–1900) and Austrian psychiatrist Alfred Adler (1870–1937) as a 'will-to-power' – our predominant motivating force. This cannot be achieved except through interaction with society. Society's and the individual's opinion of themselves and of the world at large influence all their psychological processes. Hegel and Kant similarly regarded society as the principal agent shaping our behaviour. Freud and Jung maintained that biology was the predominant factor determining behaviour.

The 'will-to-power' can also be viewed in a constructive sense as determination to succeed, to make things happen for the better of the world at large, or 'intention' as Wayne Dyer calls it [158]. This is the drive to work for human betterment that we achieve by tuning in to the universal spiritual field pervading society. But as Schopenhauer viewed the world as an evil place, *Wille* was more of an evil than a good driving force as he saw it. 'Evil' is perhaps too strong a word. The driving force of humankind he believed was personal gratification, usually at the expense of others; the ideal of moral behaviour – abstinence or altruism – was the antithesis of his philosophy [224].

The philosophy of Schopenhauer met with some approval by the psychoanalyst Carl Gustav Jung (1875–1961). Jung was born in the small village of Kesswil, on the shores of Lake Constance in Switzerland, but before Carl was four, the family moved to Basel where Jung's paternal grandfather, a respected physician, became Rector of the University. His father was a Protestant pastor. Jung's maternal grandfather was also a theologian but with a deep interest in the occult, while Jung's mother was somewhat emotionally unstable, so Jung's family life in an atmosphere that he described as 'unbreathable' was not a happy one. So, as he grew up, he became very self-absorbed and self-reliant. This introverted, introspective personality served him well in adulthood in understanding the minds of others as he had come to understand himself. He became subject to mental and emotional experiences that others might never even have brought into conscious awareness. He was much more at home in the world of dreams, day-dreams and visions than in the external world of real people. But his home background of spiritualism, theology and medicine influenced his adult career path.

Jung believed that humankind has a predisposition to act in certain ways under particular sets of circumstances based on intuitive images passed from one generation to another, and even from one culture to another. These patterns of action or primordial images that appeared in dreams or imaginings found practical expression with the recurrent themes found in myths and legends of many tribal groups. He called these *archetypes*: 'a priori, inborn forms of 'intuition' ... of perception and apprehension ... Just as his instincts compel man to a specifically human mode of existence, so the archetypes force his ways of perception and apprehension into specifically human patterns' [287]. Jung had many psychic experiences himself, so he was obviously a passionate believer in such phenomena, and also never doubted from an early age the existence of God. Jung had a firmer belief in the spiritual realm than his pastor father, apparently. Jung also considered that the human propensities for religion and myth were universal expressions of these archetypes. It was pointed out in Chapter 1 that very many of the stories to be found in the Old and New Testaments of the Bible are reworkings of myths that were current thousands of years earlier in Babylonian and Egyptian societies, and were even to be found in Hindu and Mayan cultures; these perpetuated myths are examples of such archetypes. Religion, which Jung regarded as an essential social structure, performed the function of allowing individuals to relate their inner feelings to the external world. Freud on the other hand was very dismissive of religion regarding it as a 'universal obsessional neurosis'

[198]. Freud, with his scientific training, was always looking for specific factual causes and origins of things and was therefore, in this sense, tending to look backwards in time. Jung, on the other hand, looked forwards in the sense that he was a dreamer who envisaged some ideal spiritual unifying theme amongst humankind as a whole and was more concerned with an individual's goals and objectives. Jung believed that as we grow older we grow towards a realisation of our full potential in the state Jung called *individuation*.

Conscious awareness is derived from our unconscious selves: it is the source of both creative and destructive impulses in humankind. As well as our personal unconscious, there is, Jung postulates, also an 'objective psyche' or *collective unconscious*, the contents of which 'do not belong to one individual alone but to a whole group of individuals, and generally to a whole nation, and even to the whole of mankind' [288]. It is through the collective unconscious that archetypes are perpetuated. This idea is closely allied to Hegel's *Geist* that provokes the dialectic evolution of a society; it is also the same concept as that proposed by Rupert Sheldrake as morphic fields of interaction of human minds (see below). In spiritual terms, the collective unconscious is the akashic field or universal spiritual field. The archetypes form part of, and are derived from, the collective unconscious. Psychiatrist Anthony Storr sees an analogy between archetypes and Kant's *Ding-an-sich* (which we have already identified with Schopenhauer's *Wille* and Locke's 'real essence') in that it is not so much an idea in itself but the predisposition to respond with a certain idea in a particular situation that constitutes the collective unconscious [462]. Storr also suggests that predispositions to experience archetypal images are not inherited but rather are derived from experiences in infancy [463], though this does not exclude the possibility that such ideas are accessed from the morphic field (see below). It has been noted (as reported in Section 6.5) that children seem much more able to experience psychic events than adults.

If the mask of personality we present to the word, which Jung called the *persona*, is too far removed from our inner selves and what we really want out of life, we feel *alienation* from our surroundings and psychological problems arise. As well as keeping our physical bodies healthy, we need peace of mind and spirit to function effectively. As Frieda Fordham says: our deepest human need is 'to relate the inner and outer man in equal degree' [184]. This is what Jung describes as achievement of *individuation*, the whole person. An essential part of this process is the realisation of the 'brotherhood with all living things, even with inorganic matter and the cosmos itself' [185]. Hegel called it *Selbstbewusstsein* – best translated as being self-assured, having self-awareness, or being comfortable with being the person that we are – which Hegel, like Adler, believed could only develop in a social context. Jung thought that the collective unconscious working through religion was one of the most important factors in helping us to secure this balanced state of selfhood, because it related us both to other people and to something beyond ourselves. While Jung believed that people were societally influenced through the collective unconscious, as expressed for example in religion, Freud believed that the unconscious mind was entirely personal and individual. Jung maintained that it was the internalisation of this universal spiritual field within society that motivated the individual; Freud however regarded all human motivations as essentially individual and innately biological, and those largely sexual in origin – the *libido*, as he called it.

When a group of people act independently in the same way at the same time, Jung called this phenomenon *synchronicity*, or meaningful coincidences [289]. Several examples are given below in the discussion of morphic fields. One of the first studies of synchronous events was that of Augustus de Morgan (1806–1871), who was born in Mandura, India while his father worked for the East India Company. He was the first Professor of Mathematics at London University, to which he was appointed in 1828 when he was only 22 years old. De Morgan also helped to found in 1831 the British Association for the Advancement of Science, and in 1845 it was he who introduced the solidus (/, as in ¾ for three-quarters) to simplify for printers the setting of fractions. De Morgan's *Essay on Probabilities* appeared in 1838; but his anecdotal accounts of coincidences appeared in the posthumous publication

Budget of Paradoxes, 1872 [269]. De Morgan's work was important in drawing attention to synchronicity as a phenomenon that merited investigation and explanation in statistical terms.

As for synchronicity being an acausal phenomenon: if minds are linked though the collective unconscious or akashic field, then once the germ of an idea exists in the psychic dimension after it has been formulated, its passage to other minds by a process similar to telepathy is not acausal. How many cases that we feel are examples of *déja-vu* in the waking state are really recollections of experiences that we have had previously in dreams, or visions experienced by others and transmitted through the collective unconscious? There is also a theory that attributes *déja-vu* phenomena to a vague recollection of a previous life experience. If this explanation holds, these are neither chance nor random events, nor are they acausal. The emphatic swings of the electorate at the general elections in the UK in 1979 and 1997, first to the political right and then to the left, and the intensity of the national expression of grief within the UK at the death of Princess Diana could well be cited as recent examples of societal communion through Hegel's *Geist* or Jung's collective unconscious.

James Redfield [395] attaches much importance to Jung's synchronicity, and by implication the collective unconscious or universal spiritual energy, in what he believes is the spiritual revolution that has been underway in the West for the past few decades, embracing many of the basic principles of Eastern philosophy and mystical tradition. He believes that this spiritual energy is also responsible for the fact that 'human civilisation has created ever more sophisticated examples of what we have always called genius. A greater percentage of the world's population now lives an inspired and energetic life. In the past, we have explained this progress in terms of secular materialism – that is, in terms of better food, better hygiene, and advances in medicine.' However, Redfield attributes this rather to the fact that, as result of synchronicity in spiritual energy levels between people living in mutual cooperation, 'we are able to live at ever higher states of energy.' [396]. This is the ultimate expression of our individuation, achieved with the help of resonating energies with those with whom we come into contact in our daily lives.

In his work *A System of Positive Polity*, published in 4 volumes from 1851 to 1854, the French philosopher, Auguste Comte (1798-1857), proposed an ideal positivist society with a religious, spiritual basis. The system was based on the worship of the Great Being, to replace the Catholic God. The Great Being was essentially humanity, past, present and future; and the most indelible and distinctive aspect of humanity is its spiritual component, Communal Soul. Comte believed that a study of social factors like economics and politics by scientific methods would lead to the formation of a just society. Comte was the founder of the movement of logical positivism – belief in only that which could be observed with the five senses – and he therefore had no time for psychology, because states of mind were unobservable and the resulting theories untestable. He also instituted the name 'sociology' for the social studies carried out by empirical scientific methods. Comte's Great Being concept may be regarded as another aspect of the universal spiritual field.

The English cleric, Anthony Freeman [191], saw human souls as a representation of God within each individual, motivating our actions – soul guides mind along the ethical path. To him, God is 'the sum of all my values and ideals in life' [194], in other words, God is a paragon of virtue to which the soul aspires in daily living. Such a God has 'no independent existence' [194]; 'God is now present in the hearts and lives of ordinary people' [195]. 'The God [portrayed in Genesis] is a human creation, however inspired' [193]. So the divine is within us and, through individual soul, we comprise part of the divine. This is an elaboration of the view of Emanuel Swedenborg (see Chapter 3) that 'heaven is in the internal man'. This is comparable to the *Seelenfünklein*, the spark of the soul within us, envisaged by the medieval German mystic Meister Eckhart achieving union with God, in his philosophy, through Jesus, the incarnate representation of Soul. Freeman continues: 'Holy baptism, confirmation [and] holy communion ... became the means whereby the Holy Spirit came into the lives of ordinary men and women' [196]. Freeman still maintains the necessity of the Christian rituals as a means of our becoming imbued with the Holy Spirit – unlike pagans who believe it is available to anyone wishing to participate in the divine essence through their faith. As we saw in Chapter 1, pagans believe we do not need the rituals and dogma of formal religion, just the practice of faith. Freeman, like Harpur [233], accepts that 'religion is a purely human creation' and 'the text of the Bible, the teachings of the Church, our forms of worship, etc. all have a human history' [192], an incontrovertible fact that fundamentalists choose to ignore. A similar notion to that of Freeman's is presented by Tom Harpur in his book *Finding the Still Point* [238] where he makes a strong case 'for the indwelling presence of the divine (Incarnation) in the life and soul of every human being.' Thus the individual human soul is the God-in-us, as envisaged by Anthony Freeman and Tom Harpur. By its ubiquity, it forms part of Communal Soul, the spiritual field formed by the souls of the living and the dead with whom many, from both orthodox and alternative religions, have long communed.

As we saw in Chapter 2, Aristotle saw science as the study of events or changes that occur in the objects of the natural world. He maintained that the subject under study possessed a constant potential, the true nature of which emerges as we observe a succession of its properties or actualities that are produced in the subject as a result of its purpose or intrinsic character or *entelechy* (Greek: *en* - in; *telos* - goal; *echein* - to have). The substance or matter of an object represent its potential(ity); its character, nature or form is its actuality, and it is entelechy that turns potentiality into actuality. Entelechy is a kind of spiritual and physical energy that brings forth the properties of objects from their being at a fundamental level. The entelechy of the human individual is our soul. With these ideas Aristotle introduced a concept that, in the 19th Century, gave rise to the principle discussed below of *vitalism* – the notion that the functions of living organisms could never be accounted for entirely by the laws of physics and chemistry, and that an extracorporeal force was needed to breathe life into living organisms. Vitalism is the philosophy that embraces the existence of what was described in the section on paganism as animism, hylozoism or panpsychism – some form of spiritual essence pervading not only humans but the whole of the created natural world. These three terms are used more or less synonymously, though strictly they mean something slightly different. 'Animism' means that there is at least some form of rudimentary soul in all things, animate and inanimate, or that all things are imbued with an extracorporeal spirit; 'hylozoism' [Greek: *hyle* – matter; *zoion* – animal] means that there is life in all things; 'panpsychism' means that all matter has some rudimentary sensory function.

This same universal spiritual field, many different aspects of which we have encountered in this chapter, is the medium through which telepathy, and other psychic phenomena are postulated to operate. As we saw in Chapter 6, in his study of human telepathy, Grindberg-Zylberbaum called this medium a hyperfield. It is also the spiritual realm that we enter with the rapture of our soul in the appreciation of aesthetic beauty in artistic creativity or within Nature. The extracorporeal field here is envisaged as the medium accessed by humans in their interaction with one another or with the material world, but it is continuous with the same field within us as soul.

While physicists search for a unified field theory that will tie together mathematically the forces of Nature, Ervin Laszlo believes that this same spiritual field *is* the fifth field of Nature that provides such a unification [305]. It is the medium through which the other fields interact – truly, a hyperfield. So here the unified field is a field of interaction of all matter. It is the akashic field: it is Communal Soul.

Vitalism is the idea that there is a vital, life-giving force in all animate matter, an energy inaccessible to study by conventional science. The idea already had a long history in medical practice before its resurgence in the 19th Century. We saw in Chapter 2 how Hippocrates believed that the state of health of an individual depended on the balance between the four humours. Traditional Chinese medicine has, since earliest times, treated illness as an imbalance of the body's spiritual energy or *chi,* to make it resonate with the universal *chi.* The use of meridians of energy and their concentrations in the foci known as chakras was described in Section 6.5.5. on spiritual healing. The success of acupuncture techniques based on these energy channels, as well as the effectiveness of spiritual healers, indicates that these long-established Eastern traditional ideas are not without some physical basis. Spiritual healers tune the body's energy fields by working with the chakras. Keeping these energy channels clear and supple is the Chinese way of maintaining the health of the life-force. For them, it is also a question of keeping a balance between the opposing poles by which *chi* is manifest in the individual: the *yin* and the *yang,* the soft, supple, intuitive, reflective, receptive female side of our character and the questing, decisive, rational, dominant, even aggressive male side, associated respectively with the right and left hemispheres of the brain by 20th Century physiologists.

The practice of meditation, acts of loving, being surrounded with natural beauty, and the enjoyment of gentle, structured, harmonious music, art or poetry optimise *chi*; aggression, conflict, anger, stress and discordant, structureless sound, even if it purports to be music, distort *chi.* The preoccupation of British television with domestic dramas that portray almost unceasing aggression, conflict and violence is a wholly negative phenomenon. It impresses this behaviour as normal on the subconscious of viewers, so we cannot be surprised if we see the same trend, and a lack of respect for those in authority, increasingly in society as a whole. The view of 'liberals' that television merely reflects society and does not influence it is utter nonsense. Why would advertisers waste millions of pounds creating advertisements for television if they had no effect?

The principle of *feng shui* (which means 'wind and water') is to envelop ourselves in harmonious surroundings with the same aim of optimising our individual *chi.* Although the principle of *feng shui* is to avoid unnecessary clutter in the home or office, plants, judiciously placed, are regarded as beneficial in the décor; for plants also enhance and respond to this universal spiritual energy, as well as generating life-giving oxygen. Some of the first formal experiments in the West on plant responses to beneficent or malign intentions were those of Cleve Backster [35] and the subject is discussed by Lyall Watson [498] and by Peter Tompkins and Christopher Bird [485]. This spiritual energy radiates from the living body of all plants and animal life as an aura (see Section 6.5.5.).

It was the results claimed by a number of experimenters in the 18th and 19th Centuries that led originally to the revival of the vitalism idea in the West. The Austrian mystic and physician Franz Anton Mesmer (1734–1815), impressed by the writings of Paracelsus on the effect of the stars and planets on human health, successfully carried out treatments of ailments by the laying on of hands. The cures, investigated and confirmed by no less a person than Benjamin Franklin, probably involved a combination of spiritual healing and hypnotism (mesmerism), but were thought to be calling on some extracorporeal energy. The importance of this work in the present context is that he believed that the universe was permeated by an invisible fluid that he channelled using 'animal magnetism' though his hands to produce healing. One of Sigmund Freud's pupils, Wilhelm Reich (1897–1957) channelled this same 'primordial energy' though a special box or cabinet, not equipped with any kind of electrical wiring or magnets, in his technique of treatment that he called orgone therapy. He maintained that he was harnessing the cosmic energetic field to boost that of an individual subject. It is entirely possible that these techniques, as well as the diagnosis of ailments or the location of water channels or mineral deposits by dowsing or radiesthesia, may involve the sensitivity of the diagnostician to the body's or Earth's electromagnetic field as much as their response to the object's aura or *chi* produced by the universal spiritual field.

It was in the 1890s that an eminent German biologist and philosopher, Hans Adolf Eduard Driesch (1867–1941) revived Aristotle's term and concept *entelechy* to explain how a complete and perfectly formed sea-urchin could be produced from a portion cut out of a blastula (early-stage embryo), a conversion as he saw it of potential turned into actuality. The cellular information for formation of the whole organism seemed to be encoded in each part of it [151]. Nowadays we would ascribe this to the function of DNA. Though Gregor Mendel had carried out his work on genes in a remote Austrian monastery at Brünn during the 1860s, the results of his experiments on hybridisation and the significance of what came to be called genes was not known to the world at large until 1900 (simultaneously by several researchers – see below), so Driesch would not have been aware of this. It was not until the latter part of his career, after he became a professor of philosophy at Heidelberg, then Cologne and finally Leipzig in the early 1920s, that Driesch worked out a more coherent theory of vitalism [152]. The idea of the whole encoded in each of its parts is an obvious physical metaphor for the implicate order theory of David Bohm (see next chapter).

The inheritance of behavioural characteristics that are acquired during the lifetime of an individual is known as Lamarckian inheritance, after the French naturalist Jean-Baptiste Lamarck, whose work was described in Chapter 3. This effect is thought by some biologists, like Rupert Sheldrake (see below), to be due to individuals of the same species 'tuning in' to this universal vital force. The effect is comparable to the tuning in of a radio station to the right signal to pick up a particular transmission. But first you need the set to be tuned to the correct waveband, AM or FM, long, short or medium wave, to pick up the signal of that wavelength or frequency you select with the tuning dial. The necessity of selecting the correct radio waveband is comparable in biology to being of the correct species to be able to tune in to your own species' wavelength. Whether or not you are able to receive the appropriate signal will depend on your genetic makeup. A relationship can also develop however between species, as in the case of domesticated cats and dogs and their owners, or between horses and veterinarians known as 'horse whisperers'. A possible mechanism for the interaction of the individual with the field at the molecular level will be given in the next chapter.

It was not only the biologists but also the philosophers who were interested in vitalism. It is the French philosopher Henri Bergson

(1859–1941) whose name is mainly associated with the revival of vitalism from a philosophical viewpoint. He was born in Paris of Irish-Jewish parents and was increasingly attracted to Roman Catholicism during his lifetime. It is somewhat ironic therefore that in 1914 the Holy Office placed his writings on the list of prohibited books because his theories appealed to modernists in the faith, and because his idea of a universal spiritual force was unacceptable to the Catholic concept of God (but what else is the Holy Spirit?). In 1913 he had been President of the British Society for Psychical Research. Before the First World War, Bergson's books made him one of the most widely read of all philosophers in his lifetime. It was the American philosopher William James, whom Bergson met in London, who was instrumental in bringing Bergson's work to the attention of the English-speaking world. Bergson won the Nobel Prize for literature in 1927 for the lucid exposition as well as for the intellectual significance of his work.

One focus of Bergson's philosophy was the concept of time. Bergson believed that while time is real in the sense that it is a creation of the human mind to serve as a frame of reference, time is in no way an intrinsic property of matter. He maintained that the future does not exist, in any sense: instead of every event occurring deterministically as a result of the conditions prevailing at any given time, and therefore in some way written into the present, Bergson felt that all that happens in the universe occurs as a continuously creative process. Not only we but also the whole universe has a kind of 'free will' to move in any direction. Time (*durée*) has existence only through memory. Instead of Descartes' *cogito ergo sum*, which may be rendered in French by '*je suis une chose qui pense*' ('I am a thing that thinks'), Bergson maintained that '*je suis une chose qui dure*' ('I am a thing that endures'). The sense of time that we experience in our everyday lives is a concept we create to make sense of our place in the world – it is not a physical reality like the dimensions of space [53, 54]. British astronomer Arthur Eddington (1882–1944) expressed a similar philosophy: 'In any attempt to bridge the domains of experience belonging to the spiritual and physical sides of our nature, time occupies the key position' [163]. Bergson described time as the life of consciousness [297]. Immanuel Kant thought that neither space nor time had any reality in the physical world: to him, they were both constructs of the human mind.

The other strand of Bergson's philosophy of relevance to this discussion is his belief that the existence of the universe only makes sense in the context of a creative divine spirit. This Universal Spirit or 'life-force' concept became popular amongst 19th Century scientists and philosophers. Bergson proposed his *élan vital* as an ineffable causative principle behind all objects, animate and inanimate, in the material world. In the use of intuition, humankind communicates with this spiritual energy and thence with God. God is not a person but the Creative Force itself, gathering together all the vital elements of the natural world and uniting the physical with the spiritual [55, 56]. This theory of *vitalism* that he championed had many followers in the Victorian era and is now enjoying a renaissance amongst (some) scientists as the existence of a universal spiritual force once again becomes a more prominently held hypothesis (see Chapter 8).

The American biologist Hans C. Spemann in 1921, Russian scientist Alexander Gurwitsch (in 1922) and German biologist Paul Weiss (in 1923) independently suggested that morphogenesis in living organisms is directed at the embryonic stage by an extracorporeal *morphogenetic field* rather than by specific molecules [441, 504]. Of these, Vienna-born Paul Alfred Weiss (1898–1989) is probably the best known as a result of his twenty-one years of teaching and research, first as lecturer and then professor of zoology at the University of Chicago (1933–1954). The British biologist Conrad H. Waddington (1905–75), Professor of Biology and Genetics at the University of Edinburgh, believed that the genetic pathways adopted by each species in the course of development were influenced by more than just the genetic code: he called these developmental pathways 'chreodes' [494]. These zoologists were all reviving the concept of vitalism that had been popular amongst 19th Century biologists like Driesch – the idea that the functions of living organisms could never be reduced to a series of physical and chemical processes: the whole was always greater than the sum of the parts. However much most scientists might use the reductionism principle to study the components of living systems, other eminent researchers believed that when the components were in place in the organism there were additional mechanisms operative that could not be studied in this way.

This idea of the morphogenetic field has been taken up and developed by the Cambridge biologist Rupert Sheldrake over the past twenty years. His books give full details of the history of these ideas and his interpretation of their relevance to us today [431, 432]. He believes that the morphogenetic field influences development and physical events in general by a process he calls *formative causation*. The comparable field acting on mental processes is called the *morphic field*, which corresponds to the universal spiritual field or akashic field. Sheldrake has published extensive experimental evidence detailing examples of the morphic field in action in his books *Dogs That Know When Their Owners Are Coming Home* [430] and *The Sense Of Being Stared At* [429]; the nature of the experiments he has conducted is evident from the book titles. That these are not electromagnetic fields that are operating in these phenomena has been established repeatedly by experiments in shielded environments; however, they may plausibly be identified with the universal spiritual field (u.s.f.) or the akashic field [307, 308].

Sheldrake believes that once an idea has been established in the morphic field, it is accessible to other minds under the right circumstances. The most obvious examples of the morphic field in action are those of the psychic phenomena elaborated in Chapter 6 and illustrated also by Sheldrake's books of experimental work. Earlier chapters have described how many of the ideas of post-Renaissance scientists and philosophers reflected earlier concepts created by the ancient Greeks. In some cases, the modern thinkers read accounts of the work of their Greek predecessors. In other instances, it is suggested, ideas may have been transmitted through the akashic or morphic field. This does not devalue the originality of the later work – it still had to be created anew by the later thinkers. On the contrary, it indicates a greater awareness of the spiritual dimension of existence, even subconsciously, and of how the world is in reality. As suggested in the previous chapter, all creative inspiration is believed to be derived by access to the universal spiritual field.

The origination of the concept of morphogenetic fields independently by Gurwitch, Spemann and Weiss in the early 1920s is itself an example of the phenomenon of such fields – morphic rather than morphogenetic. There have also been some monumental developments in mathematics and sciences that could be cited as instances of communication through the morphic field. For example, the simultaneous but independent creation of the calculus by Newton and Leibniz could be attributed to chance, both men developing existing mathematical theory because the state of the subject demanded it. But this was not the case. Both theories seemed to have come about by original creative thought from synchronous access to the morphic field as source of inspiration. Newton and Leibniz also simultaneously and independently derived series expansions for the trigonometric and exponential functions, of immense importance in the subsequent development of mathematics and science. Another example of monumental scientific advance that could be cited is that of the development of the theory of evolution simultaneously and again independently by Alfred Russell Wallace (1823–1913) and Charles Darwin (1809–1882): although the two were in contact with each other, they were working independently.

There is the simultaneous discovery in 1900 of the work of the Austrian monk, Gregor Mendel (1822–1884) on genes by Hugo de Vries in Leyden, Holland, Carl Correns in Berlin, Germany, and by Erich von Tschermak in Vienna, Austria – all geographically dispersed and working independently. The concept of the expansion of the universe after a primordial explosion was proposed by the Belgian cosmologist and priest, Georges Lemaître, in 1927, but it had already been suggested independently a few years earlier by Russian scientist Alexandr Friedmann – the notion that became known as the Big Bang. Russian science at the time was certainly not widely accessible to those outside the Soviet Union. The probability of these events occurring by 'chance', without some causative principle, is surely extremely small.

It is not known now precisely how much contact there was between chemists in different countries in the 19th Century, but the proposal of regularities occurring in properties of the elements was pointed out over a similar period of time by English chemist John Newlands (1838–99) in the *Chemical News* of 1863 and his book *Discovery of the Periodic Law* (1884), by the Russian chemist Dmitri Mendeleev (1834–1907) in 1871, and around the same time by German chemist Julius Lothar Meyer (1830–95). This is perhaps a less spectacular example of resonance in the morphic field because it could be argued here that the development of chemistry was such that certain similarities between properties of different elements were beginning to emerge, and could have been noted by any imaginative and observant chemistry researcher. But the previous examples are much more convincing. There are many other anecdotal examples given in Brian Inglis' book, *Coincidence: a matter of chance or synchronicity?* [269]. Telepathy, clairvoyance and other psychic events similarly would involve resonance between the individual and the morphic field.

One of the most spectacular spiritual demonstrations of morphic resonance may have been the turning of the people in the Middle and Far East to spiritual values presaged by the emergence in the middle of the first millennium BCE of many spiritual leaders. Amongst the Jewish peoples there were several prophets, most notably Ezekiel and Isaiah, and before them, Jeremiah and Elijah. In the Arabian culture, the cult of Zoroaster or Zarathustra flourished, though the prophet himself probably lived somewhat earlier. In the Far East, this was the time of Lao-tzu, the supposed founder of Taoism – certainly it was the time when the school flourished; of Siddhartha Gautama, the founder of Buddhism; and of Kung-fu tzu (Confucius) from whom the philosophy of Confucianism is derived. Perhaps there was a global awakening amongst civilised peoples of the need for spiritualism, triggered by continual local warfare. We have a similar situation today where even local wars pale into insignificance in terms of survival of human civilisation in the light of continual religious conflict and environmental desecration: there is obviously an urgent need for another holistic spiritual revival.

This morphic field as defined by Sheldrake is recognised by theosophists as the energy of the astral plane, also called by them the akashic field, on which the events of humankind have been written for all time, thereby providing the interconnectedness of human thought. Theosophy is a religious system that originated in New York City in 1875, with Helena Blavatsky as its prime mover. One of the objectives of the Theosophical Society is 'to encourage the study of comparative religion, philosophy and science'; another is 'to investigate unexplained laws of nature and the powers latent in man.' The investigations described in this book are all directed towards that goal. Though it originated out of spiritualist sessions, theosophy differs from spiritualism; theosophy is very much concerned with a rational approach to the mystical. HPB, as its founder preferred to be known, says of this psychic energy that all events are 'already traced in the Astral Light – not fatalistically, but only because the future, like the past, is ever alive in the present' [63]. This is a graphic description of the morphic field in action.

As discussed in Chapter 3, Duns Scotus maintained that even material objects had a certain individuality, their *haecceitas,* that lay beyond their location in space and time. This is comparable to Locke's real essence and Kant's noumenal properties, the thing-in-itself, as a transcendental dimension, outside of any space-time reference points and beyond sensory experience. Although Scotus's *haecceitas* is an individual quality, like Locke's real essence and Kant's noumenal qualities, by their very ubiquity they become representative of a universal spiritual quality, a cosmic spiritual field.

Gerard Manley Hopkins (1844–1889), was born in Stratford, Essex, the first in a family of eight children within a devout Anglican family. Like Scotus, he too studied at Oxford, from 1863–67. It was during this time that he wrote to Cardinal John Henry Newman, a famous convert to Catholicism, of his own desire to convert to the faith. Inspired by his reading of the *Spiritual Exercises* of St. Ignatius of Loyola, in 1868 Hopkins entered Manresa House in London as a Jesuit novitiate. From 1875 to 1877 he was a novitiate at St. Beuno's College, which overlooks the beautiful valley of the Elwy and Clwyd rivers in North Wales. Hopkins wrote spiritual impressionistic poetry in an innovative and highly graphic linguistic style. Some of the stylistic and metrical devices of multiple alliteration, rhyme and assonance within as well as between lines in his poetry are characteristic of those found in Welsh poetry known as *cynghanedd* (This technique is common in the work of Welsh poet Dylan Thomas too.) Hopkins did parish work in several English cities, and was appointed Professor of Classics at the University of Dublin in 1884. But Hopkins was a patriotic Englishman and probably found the anti-English atmosphere in Ireland at the time uncongenial. He died just five years later.

His first extant poem, *The Wreck of the Deutschland*, written at St. Beuno's, was inspired by the event that occurred in the Thames estuary on 7th December 1875. The ship's passenger list included five Franciscan nuns who had just been expelled from the newly created (1871) German Empire as that country tried to reduce the influence there of the Catholic Church with the Falck Laws (1872–5). Hopkins compares his safety at the seminary with the danger to which the nuns were exposed in the storm:

> Away in the loveable west,
> On a pastoral forehead of Wales,
> I was under a roof here, I was at rest,
> And they the prey of the gales

> [*Poems and Prose of Gerard Manley Hopkins*,
> edited by W.H. Gardner, Penguin, 1953]

During a short three-month spell ministering among the poor in Glasgow in the autumn of 1881, he found time to pay a brief visit to nearby Loch Lomond, which inspired him to write his poem *Inversnaid*. In its final stanza there is a plea to halt the desecration of Nature for industrial development – a view that resonates with our own current concerns regarding the damage to our global environment:

> What would the world be, once bereft
> Of wet and of wilderness? Let them be left,
> O let them be left, wilderness and wet;
> Long live the weeds and the wilderness yet.

Hopkins was a great admirer of Scotus' theological philosophy and particularly his concept of the distinctive inner quality of a thing, which Hopkins described as *inscape*: 'Nothing else in nature comes near this unspeakable stress of pitch, distinctiveness, and selving, this selfbeing of my own ...' [264]; 'There lives the dearest freshness deep down things' he says in the poem *God's Grandeur* – he senses that fresh vital spark in all the objects of Nature, the *Seelenfünklein*. The individuality of each thing shines forth from the inner depths of its own identity: as kingfishers catch fire, dragonflies draw flame. Hopkins also defined a spiritual energy, which he called *instress*, that produces and maintains this implicate quality. Hopkins saw Scotus as providing the theological ground for his own ideas of individuation; his admiration was expressed in his poem *Duns Scotus's Oxford*: 'these walls are what He haunted who of all men most sways my spirits to peace'. So in Scotus and Hopkins we have two more ideas of individual soul made universal by its ubiquity and maintained by interaction (Hopkins's 'instress') with the universal spiritual field.

In his book *The Religion of the Spirit* (1841), Jewish philosopher Solomon Formstecher (1808–1889), who died the same year as Hopkins, presents a view of God as World Soul, immanent in all things. The book presents an analysis of Judaism that suggests it should evolve into a universal religion for all humankind. There are obvious similarities between Formstecher's World Soul and the concept of Communal Soul developed in this presentation. Formstecher was a rabbi who was born and died in Offenbach, a town on the southern outskirts of Frankfurt-am-Main. After graduation from Giessen University he spent his whole life as a preacher in his home town. He also produced other books, such as *Twelve Preachers* (Würtzburg, 1833), and *Instruction in the Religion of Moses* (Giessen, 1860), and contributed articles to many periodicals. While Schelling described Universal Spirit and Nature as two complementary aspects of the deity, Formstecher saw Spirit, of which freedom of the human mind was part, as paramount, and quite separate from Nature. He wanted to distinguish between the unknowable essence of God, and God's handiwork in the world.

Another contemporary Jewish philosopher, Samuel Hirsch (1815–1889), was born in Thalfang in Prussia but emigrated to America in 1866 and died in Chicago, again in the same year as Formstecher and Hopkins. He studied at the Universities of Bonn, Berlin and Leipzig and in 1843 became Chief Rabbi to the Grand Duchy of Luxembourg, where he remained for the next twenty-three years. He spent another twenty-two years as rabbi in Philadelphia, and then moved to Chicago to join his son on retirement. His book *The Religious Philosophy of the Jews* (Leipzig, 1842) presents a rational approach to God, ignoring the Jewish mystical tradition. Humankind was independent and free to obey the words of Abraham and Moses: God is above and separate from Nature though immanent in it. Although he was influenced by Hegelianism, Hirsch rejected the notion of Hegel's societal *Geist* stressing instead our freedom as individuals to embrace God in everything we do. For Hirsch, God is within us (as for Anthony Freeman) rather than manifesting as a Communal Soul and it is this that leads us to moral action. Hegel maintained that Protestant Christianity was superior to Judaism because it represented active evolution of theological ideas. Hirsch on the other hand believed that the strength of Judaism lay precisely in this stability – that religious truth was eternal and could not evolve. Judaism was all about instructing Jews how to lead good and moral lives and Jesus was the Jewish exemplar. It was not Jesus but Paul's distorted views of Judaism that paved the way for the development of Christianity, according to Hirsch.

Thus, many great theologians, philosophers, poets and scientists through the ages have envisaged a ubiquitous spiritual realm, beyond the reach of the five senses, though the idea has arisen in many very different contexts. This spiritual realm may also be interpreted as a medium for the interaction between humankind and the divine as an all-pervading World Soul or Communal Soul. This energising force, variously interpreted as the entelechy postulated by Aristotle turning potentiality into actuality, and applied by Hans Driesch in the biosphere; the Ideas or Forms envisaged by Plato as source of our ideas, a notion recently rekindled by Roger Penrose; Berkeley's ideas in the mind of God that produce our sensory experiences; the World Soul of Plotinus and Solomon Formstecher; the morphogenetic field suggested by Paul Weiss, Hans Spemann and Alexander Gurwitch revived by Rupert Sheldrake, together with his morphic field that result in formative causation, the effects of which include the mechanism of Lamarckian inheritance; Jung's collective unconscious producing archetypes of behaviour and synchronicity of events; Hegel's *Geist* that produces concerted action from a society; Schopenhauer's *Wille*, constructively and optimistically interpreted as the spiritual drive of humankind, individually and societally; Henri Bergson's *élan vital* that energises the natural world; August Comte's Great Being, effectively all humanity, past, present and future, the most indelible and distinctive characteristic of which is the eternal Soul; the ubiquitous individual spiritual dimension of Locke's real essence, Kant's noumenal properties, Duns Scotus' *haecceitas*, and Hopkins' inscape; Grindberg-Zylberbaum's hyperfield and Laszlo's fifth field that embrace and coordinate the four fundamental fields of Nature in the current scientific paradigm; the *chi* of Chinese religious philosophies that pervades the universe and energises the body of the individual; the spiritual force that comes into play in telepathy, clairvoyance, premonition, spiritual healing and other psychic phenomena; that spiritual uplift we feel in appreciation of art, music, poetry, or the wonders of Nature, or of being in love; our empathy with humankind as a whole; the akashic field of theosophy and spiritualism that serves as source of inspiration to provoke the creative genius of scientist and artist alike; that ethereal, numinous field formed by the souls of the living and the dead with whom many commune, Eckhart's *Seelenfünklein*; *atman*, the breath of Brahman in Hindu theology; the Holy Spirit of Christian theology, the God-in-us of Anthony Freeman – this is what some today regard as a rationally plausible vision of the divine immanent in the world as Communal Soul. There is surely no more unifying and holistic concept to make us aware that our every action is of significance to all our fellow creatures, today and forever.

The fact that the concept of a universal spiritual realm has had so many protagonists does not of course make the idea true, but with such eminent thinkers from many disciplines as advocates it does at least provide us with a tenable hypothesis as an agent capable of producing mystical and psychic experience. For many it is more than just a speculative hypothesis – it is a living reality and the foundation of their faith. Furthermore, it is an idea that is becoming increasingly viable to rationalists in the light of some ideas of 20th Century scientists, as we shall see in the next chapter.

*   *   *

As the Welsh poet Dylan Thomas (1914–1953) implied so graphically, all of Nature is at one with this universal spiritual force:

> The force that through the green fuse drives the flower
> Drives my green age ...

> The force that drives the water through the rocks
> Drives my red blood ...

> And I am dumb to tell a weather's wind
> How time has ticked a heaven round the stars.

[from the *Collected Poems of Dylan Thomas, 1934–1952*, J.M. Dent, 1952]

8 The scientific exploration of mind and soul

In making sense of the world and living meaningful and fulfilled lives, we need to use the rational approach of philosophy, the sensory empiricism of science backed by the logic of mathematics, and we need the spiritual refreshment provided by our faith – these are the essential components of our existence in the world: 'Science investigates; religion interprets. Science gives man knowledge which is power; religion gives man wisdom which is control' [293]. We need control, at least over our own lives, and we need the power to be effective. To live in the world using only one aspect of our vast faculties without the illumination of the others is to live in the half-light with self-imposed tunnel vision. Scientists can no more ignore the empirical evidence of psychic phenomena and the other manifestations of soul than religions can adhere to fundamentalism and assert the literal, absolute and exclusive truth of all of the tenets on which their own particular world-views are based. It flies in the face of our God-given basic intelligence to deny that which is supported by undeniable logic and sensory observation. We were not invested with intelligence so that we could spend our lives in a fantasy world, afraid of truth. As American poet and philosopher Ralph Waldo Emerson (1803–1882) commented: 'The religion that is afraid of science dishonors God and commits suicide' [171]. Or, to quote Albert Einstein from one of his last publications: 'Science without religion is lame, religion without science is blind' [165]. We need rationality applied to religion if it is to be meaningful.

8.1.   The nature of scientific investigation

A majority of scientists would maintain that scientific investigation is *inductive*, moving from specific observed facts to a general conclusion, though American philosopher Charles Peirce described the process of extrapolating back from data to probable causative hypothesis as *abduction*. Karl Popper shared David Hume's scepticism over the cause-and-effect axiom at the root of scientific investigation and contended that 'a principle of induction is superfluous' [378] and 'there is no such thing as induction' [380]. He maintained that science began with a theory and then looked for consistent and coherent supporting evidence and in this respect was *deductive*. However, the way that science is actually carried out in practice is that we proceed from specific observed facts about the world to generate a hypothesis as to how these facts may be related to one another. We then conduct experiments or tests to see if we can verify or disprove our hypothesis and, as emphasised by Francis Bacon and Popper, we try to seek out experiments that will invalidate our hypothesis as the more significant tests of validity – falsification. If further observations confirm our hypothesis it becomes a theory and, with still further verification, our theory ultimately is designated as a natural law. The most important feature of scientific theories is that they should be able to predict new facts about the world that have not yet been observed. The only fundamental axiom that is assumed in scientific investigation is that there is such a thing as a cause-and-effect relationship in operation in the normally observed macro-world of the senses (we shall see later that this same principle does not apply to the micro-world of subatomic particles).

Induction implies that we move from many specific instances of sensory empirical observation to the generalisation of a probabilistic conclusion. Another way of putting this is to say that induction calls for a logical movement from the specific to the general. It should be noted however that the transition from experimental data to probable conclusion (which evolves from hypothesis to theory to law) frequently calls for a degree of speculative imagination, and even the original events observed by the senses are themselves subjective, at least in their interpretation.

Scientific theories are not derived directly and inescapably from observed facts: they are what logicians describe as *contingent* – the facts (and the subsequent theories) could be other than what they are. In this they differ from the conclusions of mathematics, which are *necessary*: assuming only the fundamental processes of logic in the human mind, the conclusions cannot be other than what they are. The relationships that we infer within the natural world are only those imposed by the human mind – they are not absolute. When new data emerge, we may well see those relationships differently. We have seen that some believe that even our concepts of space and time are human creations rather than intrinsic properties of the natural world.

Scientific theories are created in order to provide a most likely explanation of facts in a way that is consistent with existing ideas in science – what is called the current scientific *paradigm*. We do this to try to make sense of the world in which we live. Sometimes scientists feel that they can explain a body of facts convincingly only by going outside the current scientific thinking and creating a vision that is truly original. Such were the theories of Einstein and Schrödinger that we shall say more about in Section 8.3. The fact that existing scientific laws of nature are used to explain newly discovered observations does not make science deductive. The process of *deduction* involves working logically from universally assumed truths or axioms to certain conclusions. Even the process of deduction that we use in mathematics calls for the use of imagination, even though it leads to statements of certainty. The conclusions reached in mathematics often demand a certain amount of imaginative ingenuity – the exact path taken from premises to conclusion is not unambiguously and inescapably defined: only the ultimate conclusion is certain. Thus mathematics gives us certainty by the processes of rational logic while science can give us only probabilities of explanations by the use of reason from sensory observations. It is mathematics that provides an extra dimension of certainty to what would otherwise be speculative scientific hypothesis.

There are some who believe that the whole world of mathematics has already been created by God and is simply waiting to be discovered by humankind. This is the view presented by Oxford mathematician Roger Penrose in his book *Shadows of the Mind* (1995). Even Galileo, before the time when scientific theory was most often accompanied by mathematical interpretation, commented that the 'book of the universe [is] written in the language of mathematics' [342]. Penrose sees existence as comprising three worlds: the spiritual world, represented by Platonic Ideas, the material world around us, and the human mental world communing between the two, that is, mind coordinating soul and the senses. Causality and mathematics (or logic) provide the framework for human existence, supported by the inspiration of mystical experience.

Our attempts to understand the world at large is a part of our trying to understanding our place in it so that we can live meaningful lives. Science, basically, is no more than knowledge: the very word is derived from the Latin word *scire* meaning 'to know'. We have seen that we can acquire our knowledge in three ways – by observation with the five senses, by reason with the mind using axiomatic powers of logic, or by intuition or revelation perceived by what may be described as a sixth sense. All are equally individual at the moment of perception, but all can be replicated by other individuals to varying extents. Most sensory experience we can all perceive, unless we are physically handicapped; though as one who has never flown over the poles, for example, I must accept the word of intrepid explorers that there are in fact ice caps at the North and South Poles. The same is true of the majority of scientific discoveries, though even a research scientist will have first-hand knowledge of only a tiny part of the subject because of its breadth and complexity. A brilliant mathematician can prove Fermat's Theorem – but that proof is inaccessible to most of us: we simply have to take their word for it. In principle, however, all scientific observations and mathematical deductions are reproducible, though the path from observation of data to inductive conclusion is often hotly debated among scientists themselves – the conclusion is by no means unambiguously and inescapably defined, despite generally accepted scientific laws.

In a similar way we would argue that spiritual insight of great intensity (religious mysticism – Section 5.2) is available to only relatively few of us. The rest of us must accept the intuition of appropriately gifted seers and sages whose knowledge, wisdom and integrity we respect, as we do with science and mathematics, and use our own faculties to judge whether their words accord with our own world view. Spiritual experiences, especially those of great profundity, are not reproducible to order – but then, neither are most other acts of scientific or mathematical enlightenment. However, if we amass enough empirical data on psychic and mystical experiences, we find that there are many features in common, and we can proceed from these to a hypothesis that relates them to our present understanding of the way the world works, consistent with our other rational knowledge.

Such mystical insights provide the bases of the world's religions: but even religious beliefs should be essentially in harmony with existing science or knowledge if they are to form a framework for living. Their tenets may not be amenable to study by the methods of science, but they should not conflict with reason or sensory experience. Myths and parables have an important part to play in religion, for the moral message they convey, provided they are recognised for what they are. A religion that cloaks its dogma and basic tenets in a veil of incomprehension, claiming mystery or paradox or miracle, but at the same time demanding acceptance as literal truth, is not likely to be convincing to thinking individuals. If any religious system fears or rejects sensory or rational knowledge, because it conflicts with its dogma, then the tenets of that religion will be undermined for any intelligent, reasoning individual.

Instances of various forms of psychic communication have been recorded between people from all parts of the world, and through the ages, and are so numerous and well documented that no true scientist can ignore such a body of empirical evidence. Many peoples, from many lands, throughout recorded human history have described the same kinds of experiences. Intuition or instinct, beyond that which can be explained biologically through genetic programming, is at work in our everyday lives, and in those of domestic animals. Unsophisticated native tribes rely on such knowledge for their very survival. Science normally works with inanimate systems, so that exact reproducibility of results should be achievable at any time or place though, as any scientist knows, exact reproducibility is often surprisingly difficult to achieve. But data from living systems are much more variable, even from plants or animals or animal tissue; and if one is dealing with human individuals, with their complex of interactive daily life situations, to expect such exact reproducibility is unreasonable and, indeed, impossible. What can be said however is that there is an unmistakable pattern to these psychic events described by numerous witnesses who have shown themselves to be reliable and trustworthy individuals. It was to document such experiences that Sir Alister Hardy set up his Religious Experience Research Unit at Oxford in 1969, a unit that is now located in the University of Wales at Lampeter.

There is no reason to doubt the veracity of such people who report psychic events any less than the word of scientists describing experimental results that are inaccessible to most of us. For those who are still sceptical, or who will be convinced only by rational argument, there is an increasing body of evidence supporting psychic events that has been collected under rigorous scientific conditions and for which there is now some theoretical underpinning as is demanded of scientific data. One must at least believe that such phenomena exist in order to follow the argument as to their nature. As Isaiah is reputed to have said, in a different context: Unless you have faith, you will not understand. His words were echoed by St. Anselm of Canterbury (1033–1109): 'I do not seek to understand in order to have faith but I have faith in order to understand' [6]. This book is written for those who *do* seek to understand, in order to have faith.

It was Francis Bacon who first said that the contradictory experience was more valuable to scientific study than even repeated confirmation. To quote the classic philosophical example: the statement that 'all swans are white' may be verified by continual observation, but the first black swan discovered in Australia disproved the proposition. However, the statement 'all swans are white' is a *contingent* empirical property and it cannot be intentionally disproved: there is no experiment we could perform to test whether or not this is true, except to go on observing more and more swans. We must rely on a chance observation of a non-white swan *or* make being white part of the definition of 'swan', just as being yellow and heavy is part of the definition of the metal gold. Being yellow and heavy are *necessary* empirical properties of gold. If we have a lump of yellow rock that is not heavy, it may be sulphur, but it cannot be gold. To say that a piece of gold is heavy is therefore a tautology – a statement necessarily true by definition – though it still may convey information to someone who knows nothing of the properties of gold.

To say that God created the universe could also be regarded as a tautology, if 'God' is the name we give to the creative force that established the material world. This may not be the only property we associate with this divine creative energy, but it is the primary one, for without Creation there would be nothing to discuss and no-one to discuss it. So, like the heaviness of gold, this statement cannot be falsified because it is true by definition. Need there be a Creator at all? If there was no Creator, then either the laws of causality did not apply at the instant of creation (and as this was a unique event, when space and time would have been created, we cannot be sure) or the universe has existed for all eternity. However we view the origin of the universe, there is no statement that we can falsify. How about the statement that God, or some divine spiritual force, is active in our lives – can this statement be falsified? This is a working hypothesis that accounts for the phenomena presented in the previous chapter. Supporting evidence comprises the ever increasing examples of the kind discussed in the previous chapter. The problem of evil provides some contradictory evidence, of a kind, though not falsification, as we have seen.

Although most psychic or mystical experiences are characteristic

284 The Thoughtful Guide to God

of just one particular individual in a unique life situation, they are sometimes observable by others, and may be falsifiable, as shown by the experimental data given in Chapter 6. Other truly unique events, such as seeing a vision of the divine or a holy manifestation, are neither verifiable nor falsifiable in themselves. They can only be supported by behavioural evidence. However, if they are reported by many other people individually, at many different times and places, and a pattern is found to emerge of similarity between these kinds of experiences, as shown by the data accumulated by the Religious Experience Research Centre, this represents the kind of reproducibility found for human experiences in general.

In a similar way, we have no method of verifying or falsifying any statements of those who experience the emotions of pain, love, fear, anger, joy and so on, except by reference to comparable emotions that we as observers have experienced previously ourselves, and by judging the circumstances of the experience and behaviour of the holder of the emotion. We should qualify that statement by saying that, in some cases, there may be measurable physiological changes accompanying these emotions that can be used to provide supporting or conflicting evidence of that state of mind.

To attribute the positive emotions of loving (not just liking) and joy or ecstasy (not just pleasure) and other psychic events to the *same* divine energy as the God of Creation is problematical because the energy that produced Creation is of an entirely different order to that which might participate in our daily lives. This is why some believers envisage a Godhead that produced Creation as an entity about which nothing can be said, together with a God or divine energy as participant in the world. However we envisage it precisely, that there is some kind of universal spiritual energy field involved in such psychic and mystical human experiences must be regarded as a reasonable inductive hypothesis comparable to those generated by scientists in explaining experimental data.

To attribute the most ecstatic of human experiences in loving and aesthetic appreciation and artistic creativity to a divine spiritual energy field, albeit different perhaps from that which initiated

Creation, satisfies the human need to attribute causes to observed or experienced effects. It is how we make sense of the world around us. Scientists say that a 'gravitational field' makes the apple fall from the tree to the ground. They say that the poles of two magnets attract or repel each other because of the 'magnetic field'. These are theoretical notions proposed to explain observed effects, just as the divine spiritual energy is proposed to account for psychic and mystical experiences. No-one has 'seen' this divine energy any more than any scientist has ever 'seen' gravitational or magnetic fields – their existence is inferred from observed events. It is true that there is some mathematical underpinning of these scientific field concepts, but there is beginning to be mathematical theory and certainly much scientific experimental work also supporting a rational explanation for the divine energy field, as we shall see in Section 8.3.

All of the above argument presupposes that there is such thing as a 'cause-and-effect' or causality relationship, but Scottish philosopher David Hume (1711–1776) did not believe that any such relation between 'cause' and 'effect' existed other than that the two events happened to occur in 'constant conjunction'. However, that such a relationship exists is a fundamental axiom of science and of our everyday existence; it also lies at the heart of our belief in a divine force creating and planning the order of the universe. The British philosopher William Whewell (1794–1866) believed that the very existence of causality and our ability to gain knowledge by induction was itself evidence of the deity [508, 509]. Hume believed that the 'cause-and-effect' idea was simply a creation of the human mind and provided no evidence of a divine intelligence. But to quote John Polkinghorne: 'If the deep-seated congruence of the rationality present in our minds with the rationality present in the world is to find a true explanation it must surely lie in some more profound reason which is the ground of both.' [374]. For Polkinghorne 'Such a reason would be provided by the Rationality of the Creator' [374]. It would also be provided by the universal spiritual force envisaged as divine and interacting continuously with the whole of creation.

The evidence that, say, smoking causes many disabling medical conditions, like bronchitis, emphysema, cancer and arteriosclerosis, has been accepted for some time now for at least two fundamental scientific reasons: because of the number of positive associations between smoking and disease, and because the connection is consistent with basic chemical and biochemical principles – the existing scientific paradigm. Fortunately, all those who smoke do not necessarily fall prey to debilitating illness, and such illnesses can have other causes: nevertheless, *this does not disprove the proposition of a connection*. By a similar argument, if psychic events occur frequently under certain conditions, and the hypothesis is advanced that their occurrence may be related with some kind of spiritual dimension that is consistent with the precepts of religion, the fact that they cannot always be produced under prescribed conditions *does not disprove their existence, nor the existence of a divine spiritual field as source or causative influence.*

The idea of the spiritual field as causative influence cannot be tested in quite the same way as scientific data because God cannot be commanded to appear on demand as we can set the parameters of a scientific experiment. Also, scientific experiments on inorganic matter have a fairly reliable reproducibility; but when we deal with animals, or with living tissue, there is much more variability in the results. If we are trying to record responses from human subjects, with their plethora of life experiences, we cannot expect the same kind of reproducibility that we take for granted in dealing with inanimate matter. However, the results are consistent enough from a variety of psychic and spiritual experiences to satisfy the criterion of reproducibility for any socially based data.

A spiritual deity defined in this way is not the 'God-of-the-gaps' which unbelievers decry as having been invoked as explanation when science, argued in the traditional paradigm, has no explanation. The hypothesis may not yet have the mathematical underpinning characteristic of scientific theory, but it is just as valid a hypothesis to explain empirical observations of mystical and psychic events. It would be difficult if not impossible to generate an all-embracing mathematical theory as an interpretation of human behaviour as we are able to do for many of the properties of inanimate particles. The spiritual field hypothesis is just as valid as the physicists' ideas of quarks, strings and gravitons, which exist only in a world of esoteric mathematics. The incidence of mystical or psychic events in the lives of most of us is the empirical validation of this spiritual view of the divine.

A noted 20th Century theologian, Thomas Torrance from the University of Edinburgh, in one of his publications discussed the difference between the discoveries of science and the revelations of theology. He maintained that 'the difference between discovery and revelation [is] determined by the nature of the object with which each has to do' [486]. This is not strictly true, for each has to do with the natural world: science primarily explores the question 'how?' while religion gives us various interpretations as to the 'why?' of relationships, though confining itself almost entirely to human organisms. So it is not so much differences in the 'object with which each has to do' as the nature of the interrogation and the details of the approach – sensory observation or introspective conjecture (revelation plus rationalism). The methods of scientific investigation assume that empirical sensory observation is both necessary and sufficient to provide knowledge of the world, but for many millennia, shamans have known otherwise. As shown in Section 8.3 and in Chapters 6 and 7, empirical observation underpinned with theoretical reason is now also making its mark on notions of a universal spiritual field as interpretation of psychic and mystical phenomena and the nature of the divine.

But even this difference in approach and interpretation is not the only difference between science and religion. Scientists deal with issues that are limited in scope, by applying their philosophy of reductionism. Their results are objective in that, at least in principle, they are repeatable at any other time or place and (quantum mechanics excluded!) they are independent of the nature of the observer. They are also independent of social programming, though they usually have to comply with the existing body of knowledge in that field – the operational paradigm. As mentioned above, this last rule is occasionally broken, as was the case with the scientific revolutions brought about by Darwin's theory of evolution, Einstein's theory of relativity, or the postulates of quantum mechanics.

Religious, mystical and psychic experiences on the other hand are subjective, individual, one-time occurrences and it is only from the pattern within a whole range of experiences of people at different times and places that we can draw any conclusions. The individual events themselves are not repeatable and their interpretation *is* socially influenced. The details given in Chapter 1 of the historical development of Judaism, Christianity and Islam showed the extent to which these religions were socially programmed.

It is the very subjectivity and internalisation of mystical experience that gives us our personal faith, but my faith may be very different from that of the next man. As we have seen in Chapter 1, the views of the divine recounted by different prophets and their interpretation are themselves very different. But my belief in the principles of atomic theory as a scientist will essentially be in total accord with those of every other scientist. It is only at the forefront of knowledge that scientists usually disagree while there are very many fundamental differences in the interpretation of the Bible, the original source material for almost the whole of Western religion for two thousand years. Scientists may have quite passionate debates about their different points of view of a scientific theory but, happily, these differences never lead to the kind of carnage produced by disputes in religion. So variability of interpretation is a key difference between science and religion.

There is therefore a much greater difference between the nature of scientific and theological investigation than is indicated merely by differences in the object of investigation, like a geologist studying rocks and a biologist studying fruit-flies. What they have in common is that we have to accept the word of seers and mystics in religion as to their revelations just as we have to accept the word of scientists as to the results of their experiments or mathematicians about their calculations. The layman is in no position to directly verify any of these. To say that the layman *could*, with training, reproduce scientific results is no defence either, for many 'ordinary' people, with training in meditative techniques, have reached conclusions about the world similar to those of sages concerning the spiritual realm.

The greatest similarity between the methods of science and religion can be found in the approach of 'natural theology', where theologians infer the existence of God by reason or logic from the empirical evidence of creation and order in the world [see the books by Richard Swinburne, refs. 471, 472, 473]. Support for this point of view may also be drawn from the Bible: For the invisible things of him from the creation of the world are clearly seen, being understood from the things that are made, even his eternal power and Godhead [Romans, Chap. 1, v.20]. In the Middle Ages, many theologians from Judaism, Christianity and Islam were very concerned to try to present logical arguments for belief in God, to defend the faith against unbelievers and to try to interpret Greek rationalism and divine revelation in such a way as to make the two approaches compatible.

The Cosmological Argument (that the universe exists at all) and the Teleological Argument or Argument from Design (that the universe is too intricate to have developed by chance and that its components are coordinated to run essentially smoothly) as well as the Axiological Argument or Argument from Morality (that humankind exhibits altruism and has a sense of ethics), were mentioned in earlier chapters as logical reasons for believing in God. But some eminent modern theologians have also used rational arguments to present a more realistic image of God and of the purpose of religion, in particular, of Christianity [402]. The writer Gerald Priestland also argued for a more realistic and thereby meaningful image of God [385], and the Sea of Faith Movement that originated from Don Cupitt's television series of the same name is working to the same end. More recently, Anthony Freeman attempted a similar task [191], as we saw in the last chapter. However, rational arguments can also be advanced against the existence of God, as in the book by Antony Flew [180]. Other authors, like Gaskin [207], have presented extensive philosophical argument of both sides of the issue, as has

Mackie in his book, *The Miracle of Theism* [331], though with an ultimately atheistic conclusion.

These arguments for the existence of God are called 'natural theology' for at least two reasons. The procedure is 'natural' because the existence of the divine energy is inferred from the beauty and coherence of Nature. It is also 'natural' because the role of a deity is deduced by the use of humankind's axiomatic belief in the validity of the ubiquitous 'cause-and-effect' principle, and thence the deity as First Cause, and this is a faculty available to us all, irrespective of divine revelation. As William Whewell said: 'this Idea of Final Cause is not deduced from the phenomena by reasoning, but is assumed as the only condition under which we can reason on such subjects at all' [510]. American philosopher William Alston defines natural theology in this way: 'the enterprise of providing support for religious beliefs by starting from premises that neither are nor presuppose any religious beliefs' [3]. But human reason is not the only pathway to the divine and for some theologians, like Karl Barth, it is not even a valid one. They believe that direct mystical experience is the only path to affirmation of the divine, though they accept that the divine presence can be inferred from transcendental experiences in our everyday lives, such as those recounted in Chapter 6.

Thus, the evidence of the five senses coupled with reason – the tools of scientific investigation – provide us also with a route to the divine, but the most convincing evidence surely is from the experiences of the human soul, the sixth sense, that we all share to some degree, and from the rationally derived idea of Soul, the universal spiritual energy.

8.2.   Evolution in Nature by purpose or chance?

As there is a certain amount of controversy as to what the term 'Nature' means exactly [see, for example, ref. 340], perhaps we should first define precisely the sense which is meant here. It is used here in the sense given in the Chambers dictionary as 'the external world, in its virgin state' though often modified by Man. The concept includes all of the examples given by McGrath [339, p.38] – the destructive powers of wind and weather, and of earthquakes and volcanoes; the ultimate source of all our food and raw materials; and the environment that provides us with recreation and some of the most exhilarating and uplifting spiritual experiences of the soul. I differ from McGrath in that I would not regard these qualities as 'inconsistent with each other' in defining our concept of Nature.

The post-Renaissance scientific discoveries and theories of Isaac Newton (1642–1727) in physics and astronomy, of Charles Lyell (1797–1875) in geology and of Charles Darwin (1809–1882) in biology (see Chapter 4) seemed to explain rationally, often with mathematical support for the theories, the most significant aspects of creation of the solar system, of cataclysmic geological events like mountain building, and of the appearance of flora and fauna in the world. An explanation for the major aspects of Creation was at hand, though this did not eliminate God as source of Creation, or as Designer of the physical laws that were now emerging. What it did seem to remove was the necessary participation of the deity in the minutia of the day-to-day running of the universe: these it seemed were already programmed. The immanent and participatory God of theism gave way to the deist God as Creator and Designer of the world.

The creation and evolution of the universe is generally regarded by science as having been a matter of chance while theologians see it as exemplifying divine providence. The Belgian cosmologist and priest, Georges Lemaître (1894–1966), a monsignor in the Catholic Church, suggested in 1927 – the same year as he completed his PhD at the Massachusetts Institute of Technology – that the universe was expanding outwards as a result of a creative explosion from a mass of concentrated matter. This was later described as the Big Bang Theory and is generally credited to Lemaître, though modern scholarship has revealed that it had already been suggested independently a few years earlier by Russian scientist Alexander Friedmann. Friedmann made two predictions or assumptions about the universe – that it looks identical in all directions and that this would be true wherever we were in the universe – assumptions essentially borne out by subsequent investigations. These theories gained extra adherents from the discovery in 1929 by the American astronomer, Edwin Hubble (1889–1953), that the universe was expanding outwards. George Gamow, formerly a student of Friedmann's, suggested that the universe in its original state must have been extremely hot, and some trace of that heat in the universe of today would have been expected. When Arno Penzias and Robert Wilson discovered the background microwave radiation in space in 1965, the Big Bang Theory seemed to be vindicated.

Even the scientists in the Enlightenment believed that the creative event itself could still be interpreted as having been initiated by God. What happened afterwards to produce order out of the chaos and establish what we know as the laws and physical constants of Nature implies to believers the influence of some guiding hand or force – the role of God as Supreme Designer (the Teleological Argument). Theologians therefore, as one might expect, see the wonders of Nature as evidence of God's Creation and Design [471, 472, 473, 495]. The elegance of the design in both natural and social evolution is pointed up by Buchanan in his book *Ubiquity* [99]

Scientists, on the other hand, usually take the view that the universe, and in particular humankind, has evolved by chance [140, 348, 502]. Laboratory experiments have shown that if we mix together some simple gases, like carbon dioxide, methane and ammonia that were believed to be dominant in the early Earth atmosphere, and pass an arc discharge (the laboratory equivalent of lightning) through the mixture we can form amino acids, the building blocks of proteins. Proteins are known to have a propensity for self-organisation. Essential components of our cells called mitochondria that are responsible for the cell's use of oxygen were believed originally to be freely moving organelles that became assembled with other components like nucleic acids (the 'NA' part of DNA) into cellular complexes. Our cells, originally oxygen-hating (prokaryotes) when they were first formed, thus became oxygen-loving (eukaryotes).

And so, after enough attempts at getting the conditions just right, life was formed – or at least, that's in outline how the scientific story goes. In practice, there is a many billion-fold difference between the probability of forming a selection of amino acids in this way in the laboratory and the actual gathering together of all the right atoms into molecules of many amino acids and nitrogenous bases, and for these to then assemble into proteins and nucleic acids, then into cells, then into organisms, then down the evolutionary chain to humans. It would require a lot more than the fifteen billion years or so the Earth is thought to have been in existence. We must also bear in mind that it was many billion years after its creation before the Earth was cool enough for the life-forming processes to even begin. The most ancient rocks on Earth are only some 6 billion years old, which reduces the time available for life-forming experiments still further. By Ockham's Principle of Parsimony (that the simplest explanation is usually the correct one), a directing influence from the divine universal spiritual field is far more likely.

Although as individuals we may think that where and when we are born is indeed a matter of chance, some who believe in a universal spiritual causative force would argue that any birth is in some sense preselected in the spirit world. Hindus and some spiritualists and theosophers believe that we select, in broad outline, the kind of life we wish to live in our next incarnation. Others believe that the life we lead is actually determined for us by *karma*, as a learning experience in respect of our activities in previous recent incarnations – but not as punishment! The whole purpose of human life, if there is one, must surely be to learn to live in harmony with one another and thereby uplift the lives of others. It is our failure to do this as fully as we could that produces the torment of the afterlife and the need for reincarnation. This is our path of individual spiritual evolution.

Was the evolution of humankind part of the Grand Design from the outset? Quite contrary to the notion of a purposeless universe, created by chance, there is the opposing contention that the universe has evolved just so that humankind can exist. This idea is known as *The Anthropic Principle* and it was proposed originally by Brandon

Carter; it has since been developed into various forms, each of which demands necessary human participation to varying degrees [44, 114]. The evolution of Man is then part of the working out of God's plan for the universe, which makes our existence very far from meaningless or a matter of chance. This is close to the idea of Process Theology discussed in Chapter 1 – the evolution of the divine progressing along with that of humankind.

The physical constants of our natural environment are such that we have been physically able to evolve. If, say, gravity did not have the value it has, we would either float about in the air, like astronauts in a spaceship, or we would find moving around incredibly laborious, tiring and energy-consuming. With greater gravity we would need larger and heavier skeletons and greater supporting musculature. We would then need faster metabolism to process food to provide the energy required; and then we would be quite different beings. The oxygen level in the atmosphere at 21% is ideal to sustain human life as we know it. If it were lower, the cells that we have evolved with would not have survived. If it were higher, the earth would be beset continually with raging and uncontrollable fires caused by lightning strikes or volcanic eruptions. The greatest proportion of the atmosphere is made up of a relatively inert gas, nitrogen. But the element nitrogen is also an essential component of every living organism and we are fortunate that there are plants and microbes capable of turning this inert gas into a form that can be utilised by other plants and thence by us in building and maintaining our bodies. The universal solvent on Earth is water. Now most liquids are at their most dense at their freezing point; but water has its highest density at $4°C$, so that, as the temperature of water drops down to its freezing point, the surface freezes while the denser water at $4°$ sinks. This enables pond life and fish and mammals in lakes and seas to survive when the surface is frozen over. There is a pattern of relationships between the numbers known as the universal constants of Nature [461]. Paul Davies says that 'the fact that these relations are necessary for our existence is one of the most fascinating discoveries of modern science' [136]. The Scottish biologist D'Arcy Wentworth Thompson

(1860–1948) described many examples of mathematical relationships between the petals of flowers, the distribution of leaves on a stem or of the scales of conifer cones, and other features of plants, and within the arrangement of the hexagonal cells of a bee honeycomb, the spirals of conical sea shells, and other features of fauna [484]. They follow mathematically regular distribution patterns that can be represented by the terms of well-known mathematical series, often that of Italian mathematician Leonardo Fibonacci of Pisa (*ca.*1170–1230). It is little wonder that the overall smooth working of such a complicated and orderly scheme as evolution should be interpreted by believers as indicating the existence of a positively guiding Mind from the moment of Creation, despite the existence of natural disasters such as eruptions, earthquakes and floods, which periodically produce such devastating consequences in toll of human life.

We described the views on evolution of the French palaeontologist, Jesuit priest and mystic Pierre Teilhard de Chardin in Chapter 5. To recapitulate, de Chardin believed the world had passed through a successive series of stages of evolution involving geogenesis, biogenesis, psychogenesis and was now undergoing noogenesis, evolution of Soul, programmed by God [118]. De Chardin wrote his book a few decades before David Bohm published *Wholeness and the Implicate Order* (see next section). With the concept of holism dominating his thought, de Chardin writes of 'the irreversible coherence of all that exists.' [119]; and furthermore that 'Such coherence ... could not be the result of chance' [117]. Reason suggests that too many factors have cohered over the last 600 million years of Earth's existence during which life has appeared for the evolution of humankind to be the result of chance.

8.3.   Interpretation of soul from theoretical and experimental science

As the concepts and terminology of religion and ethics are quite different from those of science, it may be claimed that it is not even appropriate to try to find such a connection between these areas of human endeavour. It is certainly true that the jargon of one discipline is barely if at all relevant to another. It is as meaningless to talk about activation energy in religion as it is to expect transubstantiation to have any relevance to science. But science and religion are two aspects of the world in which we live so, where there is common ground between the two, there should be nothing inconsistent or incompatible between the concepts used in these two subjects. And the two should not be mutually exclusive. Thus, the calculations of Bishop James Ussher (1581–1656) of the age of the Earth as some 6000 years, based on his interpretation of information in the Bible, might have seemed reliable at the time, provided that the descriptions of biblical events were indeed historically authentic, but this calculation can no longer be considered accurate in the light of more recent geological information. We also know now, as did the early theologians living around the time of Jesus, that it was not intended that the biblical events themselves were to be taken as literal truth. Many of the stories described in the Bible are now considered as metaphorical or allegorical. So the rational scientific explanations we are seeking are not of scriptural events as such but of the basic religious and ethical concepts of the divine and of soul.

Instead of dismissing all reports of psychic and mystical phenomena as meaningless, it therefore behoves scientists to try to accommodate the mass of empirical evidence within their theoretical paradigms. At the same time, it might provide a rational basis for belief in a supreme deity and reinforce the faith of many, at a time when the impact of formal religion is diminishing in many countries in the West. So this concluding section attempts to provide an understanding of those natural phenomena that seem inexplicable by Newtonian science – those that some people class as paranormal or supernatural – at the same time providing a rational concept that may be interpreted as a spiritual divine.

Before we can proceed with the arguments, we need to review briefly some of the developments and, more especially, introduce the terminology of 19th and early 20th Century science to give us the language and conceptual framework we need to understand the theoretical basis of the universal spiritual force (u.s.f.). In this period, the theoretical mind-set or paradigm of scientists underwent a huge revolution. We have discussed the discoveries in biology and geology in Chapter 4. Here, we shall be concerned with the revolutions in physics and chemistry and their relevance to the life sciences.

First, the idea of indestructible atoms proposed by John Dalton in his Atomic Theory (1803) was shattered by the discovery of radioactivity by French scientists Henri Becquerel in 1895 and Marie Curie in 1897. Radioactivity is the spontaneous breaking off of pieces of atoms; but there are only two types of particles produced, called alpha and beta, and these are accompanied by bursts of energy called gamma rays. Then, other kinds of subatomic particles were discovered – electrons by J.J. Thompson, 1897, and positive nuclei within atoms by Ernest Rutherford, 1903. Some atoms, particularly of heavy elements, simply disintegrated of their own accord; other atoms could be made to generate streams of negative particles under the influence of a powerful electric field. The old idea of an indestructible 'plum pudding' atom of positive and negative charges spread randomly throughout the atom was no longer tenable. Rutherford's experiments showed that the positive particles were concentrated in the centre or nucleus of the atom while Thompson showed that it was possible to detach the negative electrons that circulated around this nucleus. A new picture of the atom had emerged. But, sensational though these discoveries were, an even greater paradigm shift came with the creation of quantum mechanics in the 1920s.

The properties of these newly discovered subatomic particles defied the laws of everyday experience, based on Newtonian mechanics. They possessed the properties of both waves and particles at the same time (Louis de Broglie's wave-particle duality, 1924). As both subatomic particles and light behaved in this way, a resolution had been found of the conflict between Newton's corpuscular theory and Huyghens' wave theory of the nature of light. These subatomic components could actually 'alternate' between being solid particles and packets of energy (as illustrated by Einstein's mass-energy relation, $E = mc^2$, from the Special Theory of Relativity 1905). It was impossible to exactly determine their speed and position, or their energy and lifetime of existence simultaneously (Werner Heisenberg's Uncertainty Principle, 1927). In the General Theory of Relativity (1916) Einstein showed that gravity could be represented as an effect equivalent to acceleration. The subatomic particles also possessed a multitude of possible properties, one of the options being selected by the observer in carrying out the experiment, that is, the experimenter determined the actual properties of the particle at that time (Niels Bohr and the Copenhagen Interpretation, 1913 on). As Heisenberg said: 'Natural science does not simply describe and explain nature; it is part of the interplay between nature and ourselves' [251].

Through these discoveries, physics took a giant step along the road to holism that had begun in the previous century with Faraday, Maxwell, Rumford and Davy (see Chapter 4). Now there was a gathering together of disparate properties of matter that had been studied through the process of reductionism: waves and particles, matter and energy, position in space and velocity, gravity and acceleration.

The properties of these subatomic particles, like the probability of finding them at a particular point in space, could be represented by a so-called 'wave function' and it was possible to construct a mathematical equation (Erwin Schrödinger's wave equation, 1926) to represent the possible options for their physical properties. Solving the equation corresponded to selecting one of the options for possible properties. There is a debate amongst scientists as to whether the solutions of the Schrödinger equation give the probable *properties* of the particle or the probable *existence* of the particle at a certain point, but this need not concern us here. The consequence of this in the present discussion is that, because particles have an infinite range of possible properties open to them, so does the world at large. Just as the experimenter determines the properties of the particle, we determine the properties of the world by the choices we make.

German scientist Max Planck (1858–1947) had already shown

that energy was transferred from one object to another in multiples of small packets of energy he called *quanta* (Planck's Quantum Theory, 1900). Bohr used this discovery to define certain prescribed orbits for electrons as they circulated around atoms: each orbit corresponds to one solution of Schrödinger's wave equation. As well as showing the unity of mass and energy in his Theory of Relativity (with the famous $E = mc^2$ relation), in 1905 Einstein also showed by his experiments on the photoelectric effect the equivalence of light as either particles or waves. It was for this, primarily, rather than for the relativity theory that he received the Nobel Prize in Physics in 1921. De Broglie subsequently integrated the particles of light called photons with the subatomic particles in his theory of wave-particle duality, mentioned above.

A system of subatomic particles, once established, behaves as an interacting whole, independent of time and space (space-time invariance): whatever happens to change the properties of one particle affects all the others. A 'thought experiment', that is, one that could be envisaged but not, it was believed, carried out in practice was suggested by Albert Einstein, Boris Podolsky and Nathan Rosen that would verify or disprove this idea of action-at-a-distance [167]. This will be discussed a little more fully shortly, because the principle affects the theory of brain function. Although the notion went against 'common sense', the idea was subsequently confirmed theoretically by John Bell at CERN in Switzerland nearly thirty years later [50], and experimentally by French scientist Alain Aspect and coworkers at the Institut d'Optique Theoretique et Appliquée, Paris, after another twenty years [23]).

Now, electrons that circulate around atoms like to go around in pairs, but spinning in opposite directions, like identical twins whirling around on an ice rink. In fact, no two electrons in the same system can have exactly the same parameters (the physical constants that describe their properties) according to Wolfgang Pauli's Exclusion Principle (most accessible description in English in ref. [362]). The EPR paradox speculated that if we could, in theory, trap a pair of these rotating electrons and keep one in, say, London and take the other to, say, New York, then change the spin of one of the electrons, its partner in the other location could not possibly know what had happened, so the two electrons could be forced into the same state, in contravention of the Pauli Principle. Contrary to common sense in the pre-quantum world, it was found that the pair of electrons did in fact behave as a unified system, so that whatever we did to one electron, the other would always respond and change its spin appropriately, irrespective of its location: this is space-time invariance in action. If brain function is to be described in terms of movements of electrons, then philosophically we can interpret this inter-connection of electrons as implying that we can influence the direction the world takes not only by our actions but also by our thoughts and intentions.

Although Bohr had envisaged electrons as rotating around nuclei in well-defined specific orbits, in fact it was found that these orbits become 'smeared' so that there is a region rather than a specific location where the electrons may be found. If we bombard a metal foil with a stream of electrons, we get a pattern of fuzzy concentric rings. What Alain Aspect did was to send the electrons through the foil one at a time instead of all bunched together. Incredible though it may seem, each electron appeared to sense where the others had landed so that Aspect ended up with an identical pattern of fuzzy concentric rings whether he used a stream of electrons or a succession of single particles.

Therefore, as with objects subjected to gravitational or magnetic forces, subatomic particles also exhibit 'action-at-a-distance', with each particle able to monitor what all the other particles in a system are doing. All of what we regard as solid matter is in fact made up ultimately of a seething collection of entities – particles, waves, energy fields – of indeterminate properties in a state of constant flux: the ultimate holism in a 'cloud of unknowing'. Just as the ancient Greek philosopher Heraclitus had said, echoing the tenets of Buddhism: 'all is change'.

This quantum picture of the atom, with a tiny dense positive nucleus surrounded by a more extended negative region of electrons,

implied that the atoms that make up solid objects were mostly space
– – but not 'empty' space. On the contrary, the space was filled with a
field of potential energy. The ancient Greek philosopher Aristotle did
not believe that such a thing as a vacuum existed: to him, space was
filled with the *entelechy* (which could be interpreted as some kind
of energy field in modern terminology) that turned *potentiality* into
actuality. As we saw in Chapter 4, it was Michael Faraday who first
invoked the concept of the *field* – as recently as the middle of the
19th Century: he believed that it was not the charge-bearing objects
themselves that were most important, but *the space around them
occupied by what he called a field*. This field is occupied by energy,
usually, potential energy. Energy is defined by scientists as 'capacity
to do work', so it means much the same as it does in our everyday
speech. The term 'work' has a specific meaning too as the ability of
a force to affect the speed or position of something. The concepts of
force, energy and field are fundamental to what follows.

Energy exists in just two basic forms in fundamental theory –
mechanical and electromagnetic (e.m.) energy – and both of these
can also be either dynamic or static in character, giving four types of
energy in all. All the kinds of energy we meet in our everyday lives are
just examples of these four kinds in particular situations. Dynamic
e.m. energy or radiation involves transfer of particles called *photons*.
They were given the name 'photon' by Gilbert Lewis in 1926, though
their existence had been suggested by Einstein's 1905 experiments on
the photoelectric effect – the generation of electricity from light. As
discussed above, such radiation can also be thought of as travelling
in waves. Static e.m. energy is the potential energy of interaction
between magnets or electrical charges – it is what makes two similar
or like charges (or magnetic poles) repel, and positives and negatives
attract each other. Mechanical energy also is of two types, dynamic
and static, interchangeable with each other: it may be kinetic (energy
of motion – dynamic) or potential (energy of position – static).
When one object interacts with another we say that there is a *force*
between them, using the concept defined by Newton (see Chapter
4), which creates a *field* of interaction. The four fundamental

forces of Nature – the strong and weak forces between subatomic particles, gravity and the Coulombic or e.m. force between electric charges or magnetic poles – all generate a field of potential energy, as do the forces of attraction between atoms and molecules (the static e.m. field) in chemical bonding. So a force is an entity that produces an interaction between two objects, generating a field or region of (potential) energy between them. The dynamic or kinetic e.m. energy transmitted by photons (light, and heat radiation) and mechanical kinetic energy (of moving objects) is convertible into potential energy. The other forms of heat energy transfer, conduction and convection, also involve kinetic energy, as does sound. Though it may seem rather remote, the fact that heat is only a form of kinetic energy is an absolutely fundamental concept in understanding the explanations of the workings of the mind and the possible nature of soul discussed below.

The most fundamental form of energy is therefore potential energy. There is a basic potential energy in all matter that cannot be destroyed called the *zero point energy*. As atoms are cooled, they lose all their kinetic energy of motion, which disappears completely at the lowest possible temperature, the zero point on the Kelvin scale of temperature, $-273°$ Celsius. (Lord Kelvin, William Thomson, 1824–1907, was the Belfast-born scientist who discovered the Second Law of Thermodynamics, and held the Chair of Natural Philosophy at Glasgow University for 53 years.) If such atoms at $-273°C$ were isolated particles, they would have no kinetic energy and we would know where they and their constituent subatomic particles were located; but we would also know that their energy was zero. This would be contrary to Heisenberg's Uncertainty Principle, which does not allow the position and velocity (or energy or momentum) of subatomic particles to be known simultaneously. So *all* particles must retain a tiny amount of energy (their zero point energy) for them to continue to exist. The *zero point field* (z.p.f.) of potential energy must always be associated with *all* objects in the world, both animate and inanimate, for matter to exist.

The heart or nucleus of every atom contains positive subatomic particles called *protons* and uncharged particles called *neutrons*. The neutrons can be thought of as a kind of insulation to keep the positively charged protons apart and stop them colliding and repelling each other. The protons and neutrons in the nucleus of every atom of matter, as well as continually exchanging particles called *mesons* between themselves are also continuously interacting with the z.p.f. for their very existence. The positive nucleus and the envelope of negative *electrons* distributed around it are continually interacting with the z.p.f. in order to maintain the forces of attraction that stabilise the system. The whole system of subatomic particles and waves is in a continual state of flux. Heisenberg's Uncertainty Principle and the wave-particle duality of Count Louis de Broglie arise because these subatomic particles are constantly metamorphosing between mass and energy, interchanging their masses with this background energy field. The protons and neutrons that make up the nuclei of atoms, where almost all of the mass is concentrated, are continually metamorphosing from one to another by the exchange of the *mesons* that comprise the strong nuclear force, and are also interacting with the z.p.f.

neutron $\leftrightarrow$ proton + meson + energy

matter (protons, neutrons, electrons) $\leftrightarrow$ energy (z.p.f.)

particles $\leftrightarrow$ waves

Hal Putoff, a laser physicist at Stanford Research Institute in California, suggested that the stable state of matter was maintained only by continual interchange of energy with the z.p.f. The motion of the subatomic particles creates the z.p.f., which then, in turn, stabilises the particles by the continual interaction between the two, particles and field [390]. Putoff had already perfected and patented a tuneable laser by the age of 35 – he was as much an inventor as physicist. He was a man who liked to try to apply physics to problems in real life. He saw the possibilities for an environmentally friendly renewable energy source in this z.p.f., if a way could be found to harness it. It was reading the papers of Timothy Boyer that first put him onto this idea of the role of the z.p.f. in quantum physics. Amongst the practical applications of Putoff's ideas is an explanation for the workings of mind [479].

In order to produce a symmetrical theoretical interpretation of energy fields, the interactions between objects are envisaged as the transmission of particles between them. The gravitational force between objects, the weakest of the four force fields but infinite in range, is said to involve the exchange of *virtual* (not experimentally detectable) particles called *gravitons* between the masses. Weak nuclear interactions, some 10^{25} times stronger than gravity, act over very short distances (about the size of an atomic nucleus) within atoms and involve exchange of *W particles*. The electromagnetic Coulombic force of attraction or repulsion between electric charges and magnetic poles is infinite in range and is about 10^{11} times stronger than the weak force; here, for consistency in the underlying theory, it is a virtual *photon* that is exchanged between poles or charges. As with the graviton, it is called a virtual photon because it is a conceptual, theoretical particle only: a screen placed between magnetic poles has no inhibiting effect. It is not possible to detect virtual photons experimentally, other than by the effects of repulsion or attraction between like or unlike electric charges or magnetic poles. The photons of e.m. radiative energy however are real: if a metallic sheet is placed between a light source and a screen, the light is blocked to form a shadow. As we have just seen, these Coulombic or electromagnetic forces hold the negative electrons in orbit around the positive nucleus of an atom, and they also bind atoms together to form molecules. Finally, the strong but short-range nuclear force binding an atomic nucleus together, about a hundred times stronger than the Coulombic force, is carried by particles called *mesons*. Like the weak force, it too has a range of the size of an atomic nucleus, which is why nuclei have the sizes they do – because they are held together by the strong and weak forces. All these four fundamental forces of Nature produce fields of potential energy.

When viewed from a more spiritual or everyday (as opposed to technical and scientific) aspect, the z.p.f. is sometimes designated the u.s.f. – the universal spiritual field or the universal energy field. It is also known as the akashic field – the spiritual field on which a record of the activities of the world is written. In Eastern religious philosophy, *akasha* is the primordial material from which *prana*, the totality of all forces and energies, formed the material universe. Physicists also describe this field as the quantum vacuum. It fills deep space and is the modern interpretation of what used to be called the aether. Its properties make it what scientists call a 'superfluid' – it offers no resistance to any object passing through it. Calling it the akashic field or u.s.f. is simply giving it a name – it does not explain what it is or how it arises. It's like saying an apple falls off a tree because of gravity – this is simply a name we give to a phenomenon. Although we may interpret the phenomenon in theoretical terms of graviton exchange, it still does not explain how the phenomenon of gravity arises. When we describe the akashic field as the z.p.f. or quantum vacuum we are simply describing it in terms of known phenomena of quantum physics.

There is a full discussion of the diverse role of the z.p.f. in science by Lynne McTaggart in her book, *The Field* [343]. Some of the experimental investigations described by her will be given below as illustrative examples of recent work in this area that supports the arguments given here.

Satyendra Nath Bose (1894–1974) was an Indian physicist, born in Calcutta. His greatest contribution to quantum mechanics was a statistical derivation of Planck's Quantum Theory [85]. He also derived statistical rules to describe the behaviour of large numbers of the subatomic particles called *bosons*, of which photons (light particles, exchanged in e.m. interactions) and mesons (strong force particles exchanged between protons and neutrons within the nucleus) and gravitons (exchanged in gravitational attraction) are prime examples. Bosons are particles of interactions. Bose's ideas were later expanded by Albert Einstein (1879–1955), so this mathematical technique in quantum physics is called Bose-Einstein statistics [166]. Bosons have a property of acting together as a unit, a phenomenon called Bose-Einstein condensation. We see this in lasers where the light particles act together to produce a strong and intense beam. The behaviour of these subatomic particles is different from that of whole atoms or molecules, which have a statistical scheme of their own to mathematically interpret experimental results: this scheme is called Maxwell-Boltzmann statistics [82, 337].

Technically, as well as mass and charge, subatomic particles have a property called *spin*, just like a cricket ball delivered from a bowler's hand. We met this property earlier in connection with the EPR experiment. Spin is designated mathematically as integral (a whole number, like 1, 2, and so on) or half-integral (±½). Bosons, such as photons and mesons, are all particles that have integral spin. Electrons, like the protons and neutrons inside the nucleus, belong to a group of particles called *fermions* (after the Italian physicist Enrico Fermi, 1901–1954) that have half-integral spin. The mathematical treatment of these particles to work out their probability distributions is carried out by yet another kind of statistics called Fermi-Dirac statistics, after Paul Dirac (1902–1984) who elaborated on Fermi's ideas. When fermions interact, they never coalesce; they produce interference patterns, as we shall see later when we look at how holograms are produced. These properties of fermions and bosons are important in explaining the mechanism of action of the mind.

As the central nervous system of brain and spinal cord functions by the constant activity of electronic impulses, the quantum properties of subatomic particles must be relevant for the activity of mind (and therefore also of soul). This electrical or electronic activity within the human body is how one part of the body communicates with another, how our biochemistry is controlled (at least, in part), and how we relate, physically and mentally, to the world around us. Ever since it was discovered that brain function at the molecular level involved electronic conduction, there has always been a metaphysical problem for philosophers of how the activity of 'inanimate' subatomic particles and chemical molecules and electromagnetic fields within the brain could generate the wealth of human mental experience and emotion within the physical brain. The quantum properties of subatomic particles described above have been used in two rather different ways to explain the functioning of the brain.

In one explanation, the mind-body or mind-brain duality has been postulated as a macro demonstration of the property of wave-particle duality of the electronic currents, and arising directly from it. American philosopher Danah Zohar, working with her psychiatrist husband Ian Marshall, envisages consciousness as a bridge between the physical world of reality (which includes the brain) and the ceaseless flux of the quantum world within what would now be described as the z.p.f. (which embraces mind/soul). This possible resolution of the mind-function problem provides a picture that parallels the function of soul given in Chapter 5 in non-quantum terminology as a bridge between brain function (mind) and the spiritual domain (z.p.f. or u.s.f.). Danah Zohar utilises the concept of the Bose-Einstein condensation elaborated above. As photons are produced by the interactions of electromagnetic brain waves, Zohar thought this phenomenon would be a good candidate to explain how these 'inanimate' subatomic particles in the brain could cohere to give rise to the activities of mind and consciousness, and thus create a sense of 'self' [531]. Sir John Eccles had a similar view of the mechanism of mind, but with mind existing outside of the body (and therefore equivalent to Soul or the akashic or universal spiritual field) and interacting with the human brain at the quantum level [161].

Within the human body, the neurons that make up the brain tissue, together with the glial cells that hold them together, function by the passage of streams of electrons that are interacting continuously with the z.p.f. within the brain. The quantum properties of photons and electrons mean that all energy states are possible, and human free will has been attributed by some physicists to the selection of one of these possible energy states. What determines that selection? The suggestion is that it may be interaction with the universal spiritual field. When electrons interact, as fermions, they produce interference patterns that are capable of storing massive amounts of information. This is brain function by mutual electron interaction such that it resonates with vibrations in the z.p.f., and it provides an alternative quantum mechanical picture of how inanimate electrons can produce the activities of mind. This explanation in terms of interference patterns between electrons will be discussed later in discussing the work of Karl Pribram.

Thus we have two suggestions as to how subatomic particles and waves in the brain might produce consciousness – Danah Zohar's idea of Bose-Einstein coherence of e.m. photons or by Fermi-Dirac interference between the electrons constantly coursing along the neurons and interaction of these electrons with the z.p.f. Scientific exploration of the role of the z.p.f. is important because the fields of communication in psi cannot be exclusively electromagnetic, if indeed e.m. fields are involved at all, because many experiments have been conducted in shielded environments. It is the working of the brain's e.m. fields that is picked up in EEG (electroencephalogram) recordings.

We saw in the previous chapter that the American entomologist William Morton Wheeler attributed the cooperative workings of colonies of insects, or the ability of flocks of birds or schools of fish to act in unison to telepathy, which is also thought now to be an example of communication through the z.p.f.. It is the same field as Grinberg-Zylberbaum designated as the hyperfield of telepathic communication and Ervin Laszlo refers to as the 'fifth field' (see Chapter 7). The suggestion that this field should be viewed as an extension of the four fields of Nature already known to science (each one associated with one of the four forces described above) leads Laszlo into formulating what he calls a unified interactive dynamics 'through which the facts investigated in physics, biology, and the sciences of mind and consciousness could be simply and coherently bound together' [306] These ideas are expanded on for their social implications in Laszlo's book published a few years later [309]. When physicists search for their Grand Unified Theory (GUT), this is only intended to unite all the laws of the 'inanimate' world of quantum particles: there is no room there to incorporate a theory of mind or consciousness let alone take account of spirit or soul. The z.p.f. theory does just that.

Quantum mechanics arose because the properties of subatomic particles did not seem to fit with classical Newtonian mechanics. But physicist Timothy Boyer of City University in New York has shown that classical physics does describe the subatomic world provided the z.p.f. is taken into account [88]. This is a huge step towards unification of scientific theory if the same laws can be shown to govern both the macro- and the micro-world. The theory becomes even more powerful if it can account for the workings of mind and human consciousness.

The attractive forces between molecules, known as van der Waals forces or dipole-dipole forces and hydrogen bonding, are thought to be further examples of z.p.f. activity. Most molecules are neutral or uncharged overall because all the positive protons and negative electrons in the constituent atoms cancel each other out in charge. But those charges are still there as discrete entities within the atoms. Under certain conditions, the centres of the charges can be made to shift with respect to one another so that a neutral molecule becomes *polar*, that is, it has a more positive part at one end and a more negative part at the other – it has become a *dipole*. With positive and negative regions now within the molecules, they attract one another by Coulombic forces. It is the initiation of this asymmetry of charge distribution that is thought to be due to the z.p.f.

Radioactive decay provides another example of the z.p.f. in action it is believed. Although scientists know that one-half of a given mass of a radioactive element will decay or disintegrate within a specified time (the *half-life* of the element), which may be only a few seconds or may be thousands of years, there is no way of knowing which of the atoms will be selected for decay. But the z.p.f. 'monitors' the mass so that, after an atom has decayed, the other atoms in some way are able to sense this and 'know' when it is time for another atom to decay. This is comparable, in terms of radionuclei, to the diffraction patterns obtained by Alain Aspect from his stream of electrons. In radioactive decay, the usual conservation laws of Nature apply – mass, momentum, charge and particle spin must all be conserved. But in some subatomic processes, 'handedness' or *parity* is not conserved.

Now we think of Nature as being inherently symmetrical. Many fundamental atomic particles were predicted or discovered through symmetry relationships with known particles – and it was not only subatomic particles that were discovered in this way. Russian chemist Dmitri Mendeleef (1834–1907) predicted the existence of certain elements from the symmetry of his arrangement of those known at the time into a Periodic Table of the elements, based on their properties. We have all admired the symmetry of a crystal, or starfish, or flower. But in terms of 'handedness', which chemists call *chirality*, Nature is not symmetrical. ('Parity' usually refers to pairs of separate particles; 'chirality' is more usually applied to molecules or crystals, but both terms mean 'paired symmetry'.)

All proteins in our bodies are made up of building blocks called amino acids. There are only some 20 of these commonly found in all the variety of proteins that make up our tissues – skin, hair, nails, liver, heart, and all the other organs. Because of the arrangement of atoms in each molecule of amino acids, all but one of them (the simplest, glycine) exist in two mirror image forms, related like one hand is to the other. These forms are called D- and L-forms after the Latin words for right and left. When crystals of these molecules are grown in the laboratory, a mixture of the two forms is produced. It was the French chemist Louis Pasteur (1822–1895) who first discovered the existence of the two forms of crystals of asymmetric molecules in 1848. They have the property of being able to rotate a plane of polarised light (light vibrating in one plane only) clockwise or anticlockwise, and the phenomenon is known as *optical activity*.

The amino acids in our proteins are all left-handed or of the L-form. Simple sugars like ribose and glucose, too, exist in D- and L-forms but, when they assemble to form natural carbohydrate polymers (like starch or cellulose) or are attached to bases in nucleic acids (DNA and RNA) in Nature, only the D-forms are used. Carbohydrates, proteins and nucleic acids are all polymers, made up of long chains of simple molecules, and Nature would not have been able to build such stable structures of large molecules if it had not had only one form of sugars and amino acids to work with. To create this degree of asymmetry in building the fundamental molecules of life, against the equal probability of both forms existing, is one of many strong Arguments from Design for the existence of a guiding force, which believers would call the divine or u.s.f. and which scientists might identify with the z.p.f.

The whole philosophy of atomic physics changed with the discoveries and theories of quantum mechanics in the early decades of the 20th Century. The old Newtonian certainty of either/or binary choices describable by binomial statistics was no longer applicable at the subatomic level. Newtonian mechanics is part of a world driven by the logical left hemisphere of the brain, the so-called *yang* or rational, masculine approach that has shaped Western scientific thought for centuries – the world of *reductionism* in which we could study the components of a complex system individually with the assumption that when we put them back together again they would work in the same way. We are now entering a world of *holism*, where it is recognised that the whole functions in a different way to the sum of its parts, and perhaps differently for different people at different times in different places. We are entering the world of what Lofti Zadeh called *fuzzy sets* [527; see also ref. 299], where the intuitive, feminine, *yin*, right cerebral hemisphere is predominant. This is the world of Eastern mysticism rather than Western logic and rationality. It is a world described by the normal or Gaussian statistical probability distribution, where the bell-shaped curve gives us not unequivocal results of 'yes' or 'no' (the binomial distribution) but only tells us that the greatest probabilities of a positive result occur at a certain point, but that positive outcomes may still occur with decreasing probabilities as we move to either side of this central point: the answer is always 'maybe'. The orbit of the electron around the nucleus is a perfect pictorial scientific example of such a fuzzy set – not a sharp black line representing a precise electronic orbit but a diffuse area of black merging into white through shades of grey on either side. There is a recognition by psychologists that each of us has within us both *yang* and *yin*, masculine and feminine characteristics, or *animus* and *anima* as Jung called them: the mind is *yang*, the soul is *yin*. The world it seems is more *yin* than *yang*!

The American physicist Fritjof Capra was struck by the resonances between the pictures of the atomic structure of matter that emerged from quantum mechanics and fundamental ideas in Eastern mysticism [104]. Capra completed his PhD at the University of Vienna in 1966. After postdoctoral study at the University of Paris (1966–68) he spent three years in California before joining the staff at Imperial College in the University of London (1971–74). Since then he has lived in California. He has written several books on the philosophical, spiritual and social implications of these discoveries in 20th Century atomic physics. He considered that the continual transmutation of particles and energy producing their fuzzy set of properties could be regarded as a metaphor for the impermanence of earthly life (*dukkha*) of the First Noble Truth in Buddhism and recycling of the soul in reincarnation. The inter-relation of all particles of all matter though all time reflected well the Eastern idea of the world as an interrelated unity: 'Quantum theory forces us to see the universe not as a collection of physical objects, but rather as a complicated web of relations between the various parts of a unified whole' [107]. 'In Eastern mysticism, this universal interwovenness always includes the human observer and his or her consciousness' [108]. This is similar to the situation when the observer determines the properties of a subatomic particle by the conditions chosen for the experiment: 'The crucial feature of atomic physics is that the human observer is not only necessary to observe the properties of an object, but is necessary even to define these properties' [108]. There is no Cartesian mind/body separation problem here. 'Mystical knowledge can never be obtained just by observation, but only by full participation with one's whole being' [109]. That physical unity of the created world perceived from the dawn of civilisation by Eastern mystics seems to be a reflection of the underlying subatomic unity achieved by particle resonances through the medium of the z.p.f. This constant flux between opposite poles of existence is also reminiscent of the views of Heraclitus. In recent years Capra has focused more on the social implications of his views in urging a more spiritual outlook for humankind [111, 112].

The American physicist, David Bohm, made his reputation from his work on plasmas at the Berkeley Radiation Laboratory in California. Plasmas are gases in which electrons have been knocked off atoms at high temperatures. Bohm was struck by the fact that the resulting electrons behaved, not as individual electrons any longer but as a coordinated cloud. After California, he became a professor at Princeton University in New Jersey in 1947 and in his time there wrote a seminal textbook on quantum physics [79]. But he was increasingly at odds with the prevailing interpretation of quantum mechanics. Already the following year he was publishing papers that suggested reinterpretation of the meaning of quantum mechanics [80]. He left America in the 1950s after the inquisition by Senator Joe McCarthy of suspected communist sympathisers and came to Britain: he worked first in Bristol, then in London.

Bohm had the opportunity to enlarge on his new ideas in his book *Causality and Chance in Modern Physics* [81]. He was expanding on ideas that were first put forward by Louis de Broglie [93] on modification of the emerging principles of quantum mechanics. But these ideas were before their time and met with much criticism from those who had already struggled with the accepted quantum interpretations. Bohm was formulating a picture of unity in all creation at both the microscopic and macroscopic level and, before Capra, drew attention to the parallels with Eastern religious philosophy.

In his book *Wholeness and the Implicate Order (WIO)* [68], Bohm presents a new view of the organisation of the universe: it is 'not to be understood solely in terms of a regular arrangement of objects (e.g. in rows) or as a regular arrangement of events (e.g. in a series). Rather, a total order is contained, in some implicit sense, in each region of space and time' [72]. The oneness of the created world, a fundamental part of eastern mysticism that became the battle cry of environmentalists from the 1960s onwards, was embraced here; the reductionism that has been so successful in science over the past four centuries was replaced by a new sense of holism at the subatomic level 'the classical idea of the separability of the world into distinct but interacting parts is no longer valid or relevant [71]. In 'the *implicate order*...everything is enfolded into everything' [75]. Einstein's Theory of Relativity connecting mass and energy, and the force of gravity with acceleration, hitherto quite separate physical parameters, also contributed to this new world picture: 'relativity and quantum theory...both imply the need to look on the world as an *undivided whole*'; 'there is a universal flux that cannot be defined explicitly but which can be known only implicitly' [69]; 'relativity theory requires continuity, strict causality (or determinism) and locality...quantum theory requires non-continuity, non-causality and non-locality ... what they have basically in common...is undivided wholeness' [74]. There were parallels drawn between the picture of natural order presented by the new quantum physics and that which had been envisioned by Eastern mystics for millennia: 'in the West, society has mainly emphasised the development of science and technology (dependent on measure) while in the East, the main emphasis has gone to religion and philosophy (which are directed ultimately toward the immeasurable) [70]'. Bohm coined a new word to describe the universe as he saw it: The *holomovement* is the unbroken and undivided totality of all there is – indefinable and immeasurable [73]. The laws of Nature (i.e. of the 'holomovement') express 'a force of necessity which binds together a certain set of the elements of the implicate order in such a way that they contribute to a common explicate end' [76]. Implicate order is the realm of Plato's Ideas, the templates from which our thoughts are constructed. Implicate order is Aristotle's 'potentiality', while reality is Aristotle's 'actuality' made explicate by entelechy, the universal spiritual field. In dealing with the significance of his ideas to theories of mind Bohm says: 'each moment of consciousness has a certain explicit content, which is a foreground, and an implicit content, which is a corresponding background' [78]. This implicate order in a thing can also be visualised as the object's z.p.f., interacting with the universal energy field.

Just as electrons can be thought of as either particles or waves, depending on the particular experiment in which they are being studied, so light can be considered to travel either as particles (photons) or as waves. It was explained above how photons could cohere by Bose-Einstein interaction. When light considered as waves travels along a pathway, the waves get in each other's way to produce *interference*. When they pass through or bounce off objects, under certain circumstances, they get bent by the subatomic particles in the object to produce *diffraction*, in the same way as water waves get bent around a groyne that projects out into the sea.

In 1947–48, a Hungarian-born physicist and engineer Dennis Gabor worked out the theory of how light waves subjected to interference and diffraction by an object could be reconstructed mathematically using so-called Fourier series to give an image of the object (a Fourier series is simply a mathematical equation in terms of sines and cosines that can be used to represent a waveform). The coded image of the object as an interference pattern is called a *hologram*. If this image is captured on a photosensitive plate or film then, when the image is suitably illuminated again by light, the object 'reappears'.

Karl Pribram was born in Vienna, the son of a famous biologist who had moved his family to America in 1927. After serving his academic apprenticeship with an eminent neurosurgeon, Karl Lashley, in Florida, he took up a research post at Yale University in 1948 at the age of 29, and a decade later moved to Stanford University in California. Two articles in *Scientific American* in 1964, one by Sir John Eccles about imagination arising from wave interference within the brain and the other dealing with Dennis Gabor's invention of holography, gave Pribram the idea that the brain might function entirely like a hologram by interference between quantum vibrations of the electrons that constitute conduction in nerves [382]. Such wave interference can store a huge amount of information, operating by the laws of quantum physics to sort and store information as virtual images. Although there are parts of the brain that are known to control specific functions, no specific location has so far been found for memory, and some functions can even be taken over by another part of the brain if the original operational region becomes damaged. It is as if each part of the brain, in some way, contains the information of the whole organ – a mechanism exactly like that of a hologram. Pribram and Gabor eventually met up to discuss this theory face-to-face [383]. The hologram image of the workings of the brain in memory accords nicely in the human organism with David Bohm's theory of implicate order in the world at large, each part containing an image of the whole, just as each cell in our bodies contains the DNA blueprint of the whole body. Pribram's hologram image of the working of the brain has now superseded the engram hypothesis of Wilder Penfield, discussed in Chapter 5.

Henry P. Stapp, at the Lawrence Laboratory of the University of California at Berkeley, presented an elegant mathematical description of how the approximation is arrived at in resolving one of the central problems in making measurements in the field of quantum mechanics: 'the observed system is required to be isolated in order to be defined, yet interacting in order to be observed' [453]. What the results show is the interconnectedness of the observer and the observed system, just as Niels Bohr suggested in his Copenhagen Interpretation. We keep going back to the holistic interrelated model of the world prevalent in the Eastern mystical tradition.

Stapp interpreted mind events as arising from the collapse of the wave functions represented by Schrödinger's equation, that is, the mental act was interpreted in quantum terms as the selection by the individual of a particular solution of the equation out of the many available. The physical universe is then viewed as a compendium of all these different wave functions that humankind selects by their sensory input [454]. In his book, Stapp draws parallels with William James' view of our lives as composed of mental processes that comprise 'experienced sense objects'. Reality is then a succession of collapses of wave functions. But the argument has been criticised as circular in that it is consciousness that causes the collapse of the wave function (selection of a particular solution) and that in turn creates the reality we experience with the senses; yet it is the collapsed wave function that produces the 'idea' that represents the mental event that comprises consciousness. Participation of the z.p.f. in these events would break the circularity.

In a paper published the following year [455] Stapp maintains that small modifications to standard quantum mechanics could accommodate a theory that would explain some of the unlikely psychic events, such as human will affecting electronic equipment. Papers giving the results of experiments that test these effects [e.g.refs. 156, 270] tend to be viewed with scepticism, not because of errors in procedure or protocols of experimentation but because the results do not seem to fit with established theory in physics. Stapp's paper presents a theoretical model, based on an extension of StephenWeinberg's nonlinear generalisation of quantum theory [503], that can embrace causal anomalies of the kind where the human mind seems to exert a degree of control over physical processes.

It is not implausible to suggest that the synchronicity, archetypes and collective unconscious postulated by Jung, and perhaps memory and psychic interaction of all kinds arise from some kind of quantum imprinting on the z.p.f., by a mechanism as suggested by Karl Pribram and others [312]. Jung, who had many psychic experiences himself and numbered quantum physicists Albert Einstein and Wolfgang Pauli amongst his friends, anticipated this quantum explanation of mind in a letter to parapsychology investigator J.B. Rhine in November 1945 [290]: 'I can explain extra-sensory perception only through the working hypothesis of the relativity of time and space... In the microphysical world the relativity of space and time is established fact. The psyche, inasmuch as it produces phenomena of a non-spatial or a non-temporal character, seems to belong to the microphysical world.'

The above discussion presents some quantum interpretations of mind, consciousness and, by extension, all those mental activities listed in Chapter 6 as functions of soul. This kind of interaction between molecules through interference patterns generated in the z.p.f. is not confined just to biological systems. Some form of 'action at a distance' even between inert chemical molecules has been suggested as the mechanism of the *Raleigh-Bénard instability*. Under certain conditions, a hexagonal honeycomb structure of convection currents can be set up in a heated liquid. The effect was discovered by French physicist Henri Bénard in 1900. It was investigated (and explained?) by Lord Rayleigh in 1916 and more recently by Gregoire Nicolis, a colleague of Ilya Prigogine in Belgium (see below) [356, 387].

A similar kind of interaction between inanimate molecules produces the *Belousov-Zhabotinsky reaction*. Discovered by Boris Belousov (in 1951) and investigated by Anatoly Zhabotinsky (in the early 1960s), a solution containing citric acid, potassium bromate, sulphuric acid and cerium ions as catalyst was found to produce a colourless-yellow oscillating chemical reaction. The solution changes quite suddenly back and forth between the pairs of colours of its own accord, indicating some kind of coordinated interaction between the molecules. Zhabotinsky later replaced cerium by iron to give a red-blue oscillating reaction and also used malonic acid instead of citric acid, so the mechanism is not even confined to a unique set of chemicals [see ref. 523]. Some form of interaction at a distance seems to be taking place between the molecules in these situations. Complex systems such as these can exhibit turbulence in rearrangement of the molecules so as to go on to produce a state of coherence. Such coherence is however unstable and therefore only temporary before the system rearranges itself into another temporarily stable state.

These are examples of what the Russian-born Belgian physical chemist, Ilya Prigogine, called *dissipative structures*: 'Dissipative structures actually correspond to a form of supramolecular organisation.' Seemingly unstable or chaotic systems can respond to even small perturbations by massive changes, even to the extent of producing temporary organised structures. Dissipative systems are examples of what was described in Section 6.4 as the 'butterfly effect', very eloquently explained by Ian Stewart again: 'The flapping of a single butterfly's wings today produces a tiny change in the state of the atmosphere. Over a period of time, what the atmosphere actually does diverges from what it would have done. So, in a month's time, a tornado that would have devastated the Indonesian coast doesn't happen. Or maybe one that wasn't going to happen, does' [460]. Dissipative structures appear to have the ability to organise themselves, without obvious energy input from outside the system, unless it is from the z.p.f.

The parameters that describe dissipative systems are macroscopic – crystal 'units' of centimetres with a stability of minutes or even hours: the distances between molecules in a crystal are microscopic – of the order of millionths of a centimetre, and the periods of vibration of the molecules in a normal crystal structure are of the order of 10^{-15} seconds. So there is some global influence contributing to the fluctuating stability of these supramolecular organised structures in addition to the usual interatomic forces between the participating molecules. The idea is that the system somehow shuffles energy around through the z.p.f. to move continually into and out of a state of equilibrium. Put another way, using the concepts suggested by David Bohm, there is some universal implicate aspect of reality that is made explicate in such dissipative systems [386, 387]. Prigogine was awarded the Nobel Prize in chemistry in 1977 for his work on the thermodynamic properties of such non-equilibrium systems comprising inorganic molecules.

Living systems take raw materials from their environment and assemble them into the polymer molecules that make up the essential structures of the organism – proteins for most land animals, carbohydrates for most plants. In so doing, they are creating organised structures that have lower *entropy* or less disorganisation than the raw materials they started with, and they require a source of energy to do this. This is a process that the Hungarian-born biochemist Albert Szent-Györgyi (1893–1986) called *syntropy* or negative entropy, for this process produces a state of greater organisation out of a more chaotic one. In illness, patients often reach a point of crisis in the progression of the disease. A small beneficial input into the patient's biochemistry at this point pushes them over into recovery and the systems reorganise themselves constructively; but an equally small negative input at the crisis point and the patient declines into death. This is another example of the dynamical instability of chaos, and we have seen in Chapter 6 how prayer or spiritual healing drawing on energy resources from the universal spiritual field at this critical point can make a difference.

Most inorganic systems on the other hand, left to their own processes, tend to states of greater disorganisation or larger entropy – like the rocks and minerals of the solid Earth surface with their mostly highly organised molecules being weathered by the forces of Nature to be dispersed across seas and plains into much tinier units of randomly distributed mineral grains. With higher entropy, these systems of dispersed particles have a lower energy.

In living systems, energy is produced by burning fats and sugars from our food; so the living human body too has a great store of potential energy, much of it stored as chemical energy in the carbohydrate polymer molecule, glycogen, mostly in the liver and muscle tissue. In addition, as well as the z.p.f. in every atom of every molecule in our bodies, there is a store of potential energy that could interact with the z.p.f. and which is carried around the organism as energy-rich chemical bonds in a compound called ATP (adenosine triphosphate – a molecule of the base-sugar complex adenosine with three phosphate groups). The bonds between phosphorus atoms and oxygen in phosphates, and between sulphur and oxygen atoms in sulphates, both of which are in plentiful supply in the body, possess a distinctive property of having very mobile electrons – pairs of electrons in the outer orbits that are not used in specific bonding to other atoms. Many molecules in the body contain ring structures of carbon, nitrogen or oxygen atoms, the distinctive property of which is again their mobile electrons. So, not only in the brain but throughout the body there is a store of these mobile electrons, with the possibility of contribution to or interaction with the z.p.f.

So it is not only in the brain that these e.m. and zero-point fields are operating. The molecules that comprise the essential fabric of the rest of our bodies – proteins and nucleic acids – as part of their mechanism of action also interact continuously with one another through the e.m. and zero-point fields. Proteins comprise the structure of most body tissues except bone, and there is some protein even there. Electrons once again move along the chains of the molecules by a mechanism described as electron channelling or tunnelling. This phenomenon was first postulated in inorganic systems in the late 1920s by George Gamow for electrons escaping from a nucleus, by applying the Heisenberg Uncertainty Principle. That it was also relevant for organic molecules was suggested by Szent-Györgyi in the early 1940s [475]. It is now a recognised biochemical mechanism involving the whole body [see, for example, ref. 187]. Proteins provide a network of superconducting molecules that exert a powerful influence over our health but which may also contribute to disease [see, for example, ref. 474]. It is not too great an act of speculative imagination to suggest that the positive effects of prayer and spiritual healing, and the negative effects of strong external e.m. fields such as those from overhead power lines or mobile phone masts, interact with the body's electronic circuitry as a whole, and with the circuits of the brain in particular. Albert Szent-Györgyi won the Nobel Prize in Medicine in 1937 for his discovery of the role of vitamin C in the body and because, as a single substance, this was the first vitamin to be chemically synthesised.

In the early part of the 20th Century, chemists generally believed that only so-called 'inorganic compounds' – those that contained no carbon and were not found to any great extent in living organisms – could conduct electricity, and then only if they were already partially broken up into ions by swapping electric charges (specifically, electrons) between atoms and were dissolved in water. It was quite a revolutionary idea that 'organic compounds' – those that do contain carbon and make up the tissues of living things – could also conduct electricity, especially since many of them did not readily dissolve in water.

Szent-Györgi's work suggested that electrons could flow in the body, not only within the central nervous system but also along the molecules of proteins and nucleic acids. Such an electron current, spread over a few adjacent atoms, is commonly found in organic molecules. Now it was being proposed as a mechanism operating over the whole body. All the so-called aromatic molecules possess such a 'mobile-electron' structure in the six-membered carbon ring, and the presence of N or P, O or S atoms in or adjacent to the ring supplies additional electrons from the so-called 'lone-pairs' in these atoms, electrons that interact with the ring current. The unsaturated and polyunsaturated lipids so important in our diet similarly contain regions of these 'delocalised' electrons, distributed over a number of adjacent carbon atoms. All carbohydrates, which provide energy for animal tissue and comprise the structures of plants, contain ring structures with many oxygen atoms. So, apart from the z.p.f. in all the molecules in the body, there is the possibility of the existence of all the quantum effects of electrons in most plant and animal tissue. The potential for quantum interaction with an external potential field is therefore great.

The phenomenon of electron channelling or tunnelling in proteins has been confirmed in recent years by the investigations of, amongst others, Harry Gray at the Beckman Institute of Caltech. Gray also suggested that the human organism might have an inbuilt mechanism towards organisation of materials – a process he, like Szent-Györgyi before him, called *syntropy*, as the opposite of *entropy*, a move towards greater disorder. If this is so, the DNA that forms the coding blueprint in our cells may be subject to change from subtler energetic influences than radiation or certain toxic chemicals, which are known to damage DNA structure and thereby produce cancer. If this is true, then it provides a plausible mechanism for Lamarckian inheritance of learned traits: the activities and life-style factors of parents are physically influential on these fundamental molecules of the body. If these same fundamental molecules, nucleic acids and proteins, interact with the z.p.f. through this electron mobility, there is an extracorporeal physical, and possibly also spiritual, input into inheritance.

Harold Saxton Burr, at Yale University in the 1940s, measured the electrical fields around many living things, both flora and fauna, and he found that these fields affected or were affected by the state of development and state of health of an organism, and that they influence cell development and genetic messaging from DNA [100,

101]. Burr was one of many eminent scientists in the 20th Century who supported the vitalism theory of the previous centuries: 'The Universe in which we find ourselves and from which we cannot be separated is a place of Law and Order. It is not an accident, nor chaos. It is organised and maintained by an Electro-dynamic field capable of determining the position and movement of all charged particles' [100]. Although Burr was concerned with using these fields to diagnose disease, there are also theoretical implications of the existence of such e.m. fields in the body. In work with L.J. Ravitz in the Department of Psychiatry at Yale, the measurement of these fields was used to explore the mental state of patients.

Fritz-Albert Popp has also been pursuing a study of the effects of biophotons, the constituent particles of e.m. radiation produced within the body. Popp worked first at University of Marburg and then with his team at the International Institute of Biophysics at Neuss, a small town across the river from Düsseldörf in Germany. Popp and his team are interested in bioluminescence – the fact that some biomolecules absorb energy at one wavelength and then radiate energy at a longer wavelength (lower energy). What does the body do with the 'missing' energy? It must supply extra energy for the potential energy store. Their study is primarily into the role of this effect in carcinogenesis and for environmental monitoring; but the photons emitted from the materials in their study showed a high degree of coherence – Bose-Einstein coherence – that enables molecules to communicate with one another.

This is the effect that Danah Zohar invoked to explain coordinated cellular communication in the brain. It is a phenomenon that is generally only studied at extreme conditions near absolute zero in the laboratory, but now it has been discovered as a process in biological systems. The biophotons emitted from healthy subjects produce an *aura*, which Popp has measured; we have seen earlier (see Section 6.5.5.) that some sensitives are able to detect this aura without scientific measuring instruments and thereby assess the character or state of health of the subject. The Russian engineer, Semyon Kirlian, was one of the first to photograph these fields surrounding leaves and human limbs in the early decades of the 20th Century. If soul is, at least in part, a property of mind, and if mind originates from activity of the brain, which is a mass of neurons conducting electric currents and bathed in a potential energy field, then we should not be surprised if the body radiates some form of e.m. field and that it should be susceptible to effects from external fields. The function of mind that interacts with the z.p.f. or u.s.f. is soul, but it seems increasingly likely that the body as a whole interacts physically with external e.m. and potential fields.

The fact that physical processes in the body can be influenced by external e.m. fields has been studied in several laboratories. For example, the orthopaedist, Robert Becker, showed that e.m. fields improved bone healing in humans and other animals, and simultaneously killed noxious bacteria that would have interfered with the healing process [47, 48, 49]. From 1958 to 1980, Becker was head of orthopaedic research at the Veterans Administration Hospital in Syracuse, New York. During this time he wrote over 100 research papers in medical journals and was twice nominated for the Nobel Prize in Medicine. Since the 1970s Becker has been warning of the potentially damaging effects on the body of external e.m. fields, such as those from overhead power lines but this is still not widely accepted by those in authority with commercial interests at stake.

Herbert Fröhlich at the University of Liverpool suggested that coordinated or synchronised vibrations of molecules and the radiation produced at certain critical frequencies (called Fröhlich frequencies) is used to achieve coherence and make the system take on quantum mechanical properties, like action-at-a-distance. This may be an extremely important property in understanding psychic phenomena, for in complex dynamic living systems, many kinds of coherence are possible [200]. Giuseppe Vitiello, in the Physics Department of the University of Salerno in Italy has followed a similar line of research: 'In the Quantum Field Theory approach to living matter one searches for basic dynamical laws which together with statistical mechanics originate ordering and functional efficiency' [493].

Stuart Hameroff, Professor of Anesthesiology and Psychology at the University of Arizona at Tucson has suggested that the neurons of the brain and elsewhere in the body are made up of hollow tubes called microtubules that comprise the structural fabric of the neuron. These function as waveguides to make disordered wave packets of electrons coherent and synchronous; in other words they act like optical fibres for photons and distribute information instantly throughout the body. Certainly, the speed of neural communication has cast doubt for many years on the idea that messages were transmitted by chemical molecules being released from the end of one nerve to travel to the next across the gaps or synapses in the neural chain. The speed of movement of molecules is just not sufficient to account for the speed of transmission of nerve impulses [221].

This theory of neural transmission was confirmed and further developed by Mari Jibu and Scott Hagan, from the Physics Department at McGill University in Montreal, Canada, working in collaboration with Stuart Hameroff [282].

Mari Jibu and Kunio Yasue, working in the Department of Anesthesiology at Okayama University in Japan, showed that neurons do indeed communicate using quantum processes by vibrational coherence in the z.p.f. [278, 279, 280, 281].

All of this is evidence to support the contention that the human body, and to a lesser extent that of plants and other animals, is a medium in which highly mobile electrons, with all their quantum properties, play a vital role in health and disease through both e.m. and potential energy fields. The evidence – both anecdotal and experimental, obtained under rigorously controlled conditions – for the existence of the psychic events and spiritual experiences discussed in Chapter 6 is unequivocal. As indicated above, the laboratory work on such processes has been backed up, as in any scientific investigation, by theoretical interpretations and explanations in terms of quantum mechanics.

With all brain events produced by electronic currents and electromagnetic fields, there is some kind of resonance between thought processes of different individuals and spiritual energy.

This can be represented either as quantum reaction between neural electrons and the universal zero point field, or as Fermi-Dirac interaction between electrons resulting in holographic interference between electronic wave patterns, or as Bose-Einstein interaction between the photons exchanged by interacting e.m. waves. Possibly, mathematical analysis may be able to distinguish between these detailed mechanisms but, when several equally probable interpretations are on offer, it often emerges that the result will be that the mechanism of mind, and thence of soul, involves all of these. Furthermore, they are only different shades of theoretical interpretation for what is essentially the same causal explanation.

We have seen in the opening chapter of this book that scripture and religion are essentially human constructs, however divinely inspired. Many people will find this a very disturbing conclusion if they have regarded their religion and the scripture on which it is based as in some sense representing a divine message, more or less directly transmitted to humankind. There are also very many different interpretations of this message as to how we should live our lives to achieve the greatest satisfaction for ourselves and others, and there is no logical reason for preferring one interpretation over another. This leaves us with the need to find some enduring universal concept derived rationally with minimal human interpretation and embellishment that is not incompatible with the major world religions or contemporary science and which enables us to express our sense of communion with the ineffable, for to be human is to possess an unquenchable spiritual component of our being. Perhaps Communal Soul, or Universal Mind, or the universal spiritual field or the zero point field represents such a concept.

Chapter 1 showed us that scripture and religion are human constructs, of immense moral value by their allegorical interpretation but that scriptures are neither historical documents nor presentations of unilateral truth as messages received directly from God. We have seen how the seeds of rational ideas sown by the Greek philosophers (Chapter 2) have been absorbed into theology (Chapter 3) and have evolved into empirical science over the past five hundred years since the Renaissance (Chapter 4). We have shown that soul can be regarded as the undisputed spiritual dimension of humankind and a function of mind, the working brain (Chapter 5). Many human experiences may be regarded as functions of the individual soul (Chapter 6). We have explored in Chapter 7 how the concepts of a spiritual dimension to the world have been envisaged by philosophers, theologians and poets, albeit often in completely different contexts, for more than two millennia. Our journey has culminated in 20th Century quantum physics which has been used to interpret spiritual, mystical and psychic phenomena in a way that is not inconsistent with rational thought. Such an interpretation also gives us the awareness that our every act, and even our every thought if focused, contributes, either positively or negatively, to the spiritual dimension of the world. It emphasises the need for positive thought and action. It also gives impetus to the urgent need for communion and collaboration between the peoples of the world, irrespective of differences in political or religious institutions, to find a solution for the preservation of Earth while we still have time – but not much time – as part of our expression of devotion to the divine spirit.

It is a small step for mind but a giant leap for humankind to associate the concept of the individual human soul that creates our faith, our moral blueprint for life, with a universal Communal Soul, a view of God as a universal divine energy, communing through this psychic energy field with which we all interact in every moment of our earthly existence – and beyond. From the above evidence and discussion it would not be irrational to conclude that there does exist a spiritual dimension, a cosmic energy, within the world. The physical manifestations of this spirit in psychic and mystical experiences are comparable to phenomena in the natural world that are interpreted in terms of scientific hypotheses; indeed, this universal spirit actually embraces the world of Nature. This spiritual dimension cannot be divorced from the physical. At every level, microscopic and macroscopic, organic and inorganic, the world comprises processes or interactions with this cosmic energy. What we do in our everyday lives, however seemingly trivial, affects everyone else: we all interact with one another and with this cosmic force in every moment of our existence. At every level of existence within our universe – subatomic particles, whole chemical atoms and molecules, flora and fauna in the environment, the agencies of geological weathering, global climate, human social contact – there is interaction and process, there is being and becoming.

As a result of the investigations described above, and many others, *it is now suggested that psi effects and, by extension, the other properties described above as representing soul, are produced by mind interacting with what is known spiritually as the universal spiritual field, the akashic field or the divine, or what is described scientifically as the zero point field.* The interaction occurs by processes that are recognised within the realm of quantum physics.

As the examples in the previous chapter show, the concept of an energising force that is beyond detection by the five senses has appeared in various and often quite different contexts of the works of scientists, philosophers and theologians over the last two thousand years or more. This does not, in itself, make it true, but as the product of so many great minds through the ages, it is certainly worth serious consideration as a working hypothesis. But this, it is suggested, is what many people today would regard as a rationally plausible view of God as Holy Spirit, or Brahman, or Communal Soul. To give this spiritual concept a rational interpretation does not demean the concept of the divine. On the contrary: this is a God based in rationality, God the Sustainer, a God who is evolving with our every action, to which we can all relate. This is God immanent in the world, interactive and personal. The ultimate Godhead, Creator and Designer of all that is, remains inaccessible and inexplicable.

9   Epilogue

A personal journey

My childhood was probably somewhat unusual. From the age of about seven I developed intractable asthma; I was even hospitalised in the local chest hospital for a few weeks in 1944 as a potentially terminal case. This was the hospital at Llandough for patients with tuberculosis (still quite prevalent in those days), and silicosis or pneumoconiosis contracted while working down the mines. As a result of my condition, I was not able to run around and play like other children. My recreations therefore were stamp collecting, reading and listening to music – all things that I could do by myself. In a Grammar School of over 400 boys, I was the only one with chronic asthma throughout my school career; today, you would be surprised to find any class that did not have at least one or two asthmatics even in primary school.

I was born and spent the first twenty-five years of my life in Cardiff. We were lucky to be living close to parkland, and this is where my love affair with Nature began. It was possible to walk the 3 or 4 miles from our house to Llandaff Cathedral beside the River Taff through woodland all the way, and this is a walk I did very often as a boy. It was my favourite haunt whenever I was studying for exams in school or college and wanted to think. It was quite safe then for small boys to walk about on their own in parkland in a major city. My mother was an accomplished amateur pianist and it was from her that I first derived my love and knowledge of music. My father was tone deaf and totally unmusical, but he was a published scholar of Welsh poetry, and it was probably from him that I derived my love of poetry and of languages in general.

I was brought up in a nonconformist Christian family, and attended Sunday-school and chapel like most other children of my age in South Wales, though I don't believe my parents attended church or chapel ever in my lifetime. I was confirmed into the Church of England in Wales in my early twenties, though this was a matter of expediency rather than conscience as my fiancée insisted on a church wedding. We had regular religious instruction in high school that was exclusively Christian, but religion was never discussed at home. But in my rebellious teenage years, in my heart I rejected the Christianity with which I had been indoctrinated and my objections were several-fold.

By now, I was beginning my training as a physical scientist, disciplined to accept only that which I could observe or deduce rationally. The whole God-concept was therefore suspect for me, as one who had never had anything resembling a personal mystical experience. By the 1950s, the idea of God as an old man with a beard in the heavens above had already been replaced in society by ... I wasn't sure what. I had no idea who or what this 'God' was that I was supposed to pray to. I have always had difficulty in attaching any meaning to the term 'God the Father'. There were also so many events in the Bible that seemed utterly illogical to me – seas parting, people being turned into pillars of salt, bushes springing into flame for no reason, multitudes of people being fed with just a few fish and loaves of bread, and many other events that just did not seem possible. We were told that miracles were not supposed to be rationally explainable – that's what made them miracles – but that all these events were nevertheless literally true. No-one at that stage thought to explain that these were only allegories or parables – that was not a commonly held attitude at that time. Devout Welsh chapel attendees have a long history of belief in literal Creationism and biblical truth.

We lived close to a gypsy encampment and, as my grandmother, a devout and regular chapelgoer, was convinced that gypsies had the power to inflict good or ill on a household, we were never short of pegs and 'lucky' heather! This belief in their magical powers I consigned to the 'superstitious nonsense' category with little hesitation, despite the fact that many of their predictions did in fact come true, which, as a good scientist, I had to acknowledge even in my extreme scepticism. Also, I did realise that they had no possible way of knowing anything of our family background, and the events that occurred did not seem like self-fulfilling prophecies: the unexpected death of my grandfather after a short illness; a trip to America where my mother and her parents had once lived for some ten years; and other more trivial events.

Then there was the mystery of the Trinity – God being in three different forms at the same time. I thought that this was completely illogical, and something I was never able to get to grips with in my mind. Being told again that incomprehensible mystery and paradox was part of the wonder of religion and all the more reason for believing was not at all helpful to me. To me, it was all the more reason for *not* believing. The concept of transubstantiation at the Eucharist always struck me as barbaric and cannibalistic, and I found the whole idea rather obscene.

But one of my biggest objections to Christianity was the contention, expressed repeatedly, that only 'good' people went to heaven, and 'good people' of course meant Christians. Sinners on the other hand were going to suffer hell-fire and damnation for all eternity – that seemed like a lot of punishment for what I thought were not very awful 'sins'. The most heinous of these sins was not believing in Jesus as the Son of God. We were taught that all those who did not believe in the divinity of Jesus and the Christian view of God were heathens and would be eternally damned, and that definition apparently included the passionately monotheistic Jews! Now, without doubt, some of my best friends at school were the Jewish boys, possibly because many of the other children didn't seem to want to associate with them. I was very aware that the Jews seemed to bring God into their lives, even as children, to a greater extent than I or, as far as I knew, any of my friends did. Family and fellowship seemed to rate highly with them. They attended synagogue regularly and willingly while I and my fellow Christian pupils had to be coerced and threatened to attend Sunday school, which we regarded as just a continuation of more lessons and a real drag! Religious instruction was, by general agreement, the most boring subject in the school curriculum. I don't know that I had any awareness at this time of Buddhism, Islam, or any other faiths. But the synagogue was only some 100 yards or so away from where I lived, so I couldn't fail to be aware of Judaism. It seemed monstrous to me that all these devout, God-fearing people that I admired were going to be punished forever once they died, and I found this totally unacceptable. And so, I ceased to be a Christian.

For the next decade, from my mid-teens to mid-twenties or thereabouts, at heart I effectively became an atheist as defined by Western religious belief, though still obliged to attend church services with my wife at the time. Just about everyone we knew was a professed Christian, as far as we were aware. I say 'professed Christian' because I was aware then that many of those who claimed to be Christians did not behave in a way that I would have expected from someone with a committed faith. Through all this angst though, as I wrestled with my thoughts and emotions concerning religion, I still had some sense of the ineffable. I still experienced periods of intense exhilaration, beyond the normal pleasures provided by ordinary entertainment, and it was music and Nature that produced this transcendental state for me.

It was through this mystical enchantment that I was first brought back to belief in a God, though one very different from that of my childhood instruction. My journey was supported increasingly by my rational scientific training, the essence of which I have tried to relate in this book – being confronted with numerous examples, even in my limited sphere of contacts, of events that as a scientist simply did not fit into the scheme of things that I had been taught, like the accuracy of the gypsy predictions, and success of complementary, or in my case alternative, therapies in treating my ever deteriorating health. Treatment by a naturopath in Australia marked the start of my recovery, and gradually I withdrew most of the cocktail of drugs I had been prescribed over the previous decade. It was the success of these seemingly 'unscientific' techniques in treating myself and others that convinced me that there was really something more to explore here than my science had taught me. It only served to confirm rationally what I had 'sensed' before.

So, as a graduate now, with degrees in physical sciences, and some training in medicine, I was forced to acknowledge the existence of events that were inexplicable under the existing scientific paradigm – psychic experiences – in my own life and, as I enquired not too deeply, into the lives of many others. As these psychic events piled up over the years, I soon began to search for an explanation that conformed to scientific rationalism. Clearly, it would be a denial of everything I had learned through my scientific education if I rejected all of these empirical observations as nonsense – imagination, wish-fulfillment, deception, and the like, the usual criticisms levelled by my colleagues – just because there was as yet no theoretical explanation acceptable to science.

I have now become totally convinced of a spiritual reality that is part of our everyday existence. This, for me, is God the Holy Spirit, the universal divine force, immanent in the world, personal in that it embraces the souls of the living and the dead. I feel reassured in my belief by the fact that there is now scientific theory that, again for me, underpins and rationalises that which would otherwise be a plausible but unsubstantiated theological hypothesis to account for those psychical and mystical events that are usually described as paranormal or supernatural. As I have never undergone anything I could unequivocally call a 'religious mystical experience', my closest approach to the spiritual realm is through the incipient mysticism I described earlier, with the uplift given to me by music and scenes of natural beauty, and the inspiration that has seemed to come to me in my writing. My path to God has been primarily through rationalisation. I have been treated by a local spiritual healer for several years now. After a personal near tragedy involving our only son, David, my second wife Jennifer has now become a healer too. She was at his bedside through those traumatic few days when we might have lost him but for the skill of the neurosurgeons at Frenchay Hospital in Bristol, and I'm sure his mother's presence aided his recovery. At almost the same age my mother had pneumonia and was nursed through it by her mother, and I had acute hepatitis and was nursed back to health by my family, so I have certainly known the warmth of human love.

On one occasion at least I think I have experienced what I certainly would call the most unequivocal incidence of divine inspiration. The topic I was set for my PhD in the 1960s was, at the outset, intimidating. It was suggested I should study the mechanism of a chemical reaction that had been investigated intermittently for the previous century by chemists far more eminent than I, without a plausible solution having been suggested. Though I found this prospect daunting, especially as a PhD study, I was reassured by my supervisor that I had the advantage of a century of scientific knowledge that my predecessors did not have, as well as an array of new and sophisticated analytical methods. The problem was indeed a knotty one, but after I had worked at it for some 18 months, a possible solution came to me while meditating to Anton Bruckner's massive Eighth Symphony. Bruckner was born in the little village of Ansfelden, near Linz in Austria in 1824, the son of the village schoolmaster. He was a choirboy and later a teacher and organist at St. Florian's monastery. He was a humble man, a devoted Catholic all of his life, and he dedicated his music to the service of God. With any sort of musical sensitivity it is difficult not to be inspired by any one of his ten symphonies or monumental choral works, particularly in the knowledge of the dedication that inspired their creation.

Whether mine will ultimately prove to be the correct explanation for the mechanism of the chemical reaction I studied only time and further research will tell, but the results were published in *Nature* and the *Journal of the Chemical Society* of Great Britain, and elsewhere in respected scientific journals, so at least the suggested solution must be reasonable.

Apart from the spiritual exhilaration I described earlier, I would regard the writing of this book as another mystical experience. I regard creative inspiration of all kinds as mystical in origin, but the comments of Gustav Mahler I recounted in Chapter 7 resonated particularly with me. There are many passages that I wrote here that, when I came back to them, I found I had no recollection of writing those words – just of having expressed a feeling or belief. The factual information of course is taken from other reliable sources, but the interpretations and impressionistic portions I could scarcely recall having written. This to me is spiritual enlightenment of soul by the divine spiritual energy.

In the 1980s, just two weeks after selling our house at a price one-third lower than the estate agents' valuation, I was suddenly made redundant from a publishing post in the Midlands. As I had a new wife and small baby son, and had just taken a huge financial loss to relocate, it was a devastating experience which, perhaps not surprisingly, aroused feelings of anger and apprehension. I had no income and no immediate job prospects. My colleagues suggested commuting into London each day from Milton Keynes, a return trip that would have taken some three hours out of each day in total door-to-door travel. I have always regarded commuting as an almost total waste of time, and energy, and resources, both mine and the environment's. So a change in career direction was indicated.

With the difficulties I experienced over the next couple of years trying to support a young family, doing a full-time teaching job and working evenings and weekends at freelance editing work, always to deadlines, it was again not surprising that the stress produced a heart attack. This time, I had to make a major life reassessment. Challenges like these force us to think about our values and priorities and to make and accept difficult decisions. From then on, my wife went out to work while I worked from home and looked after our son, and we have always shared the household duties and gardening. The time I spent at home recuperating gave me an opportunity I would not have had otherwise to write a couple of books on health and nutrition, elaborating principles I had always applied in my own life and which,

I am quite sure, have contributed to my continued active existence today. Apart from my hospitalisation as a child, when I was a teenager, our family doctor thought I would be lucky to reach 40, given a quiet lifestyle. I am now in my 60s having had a far from quiet life and, given the genetic predispositions I started with, and despite the ministrations of the National Health Service, I am still in reasonable health and active. So I must have been doing something right!

I am disappointed that my previous books [284, 285] do not seem to have changed significantly the eating habits and other behaviours of the nation, given the national prevalence of obesity and alcoholism; or to have produced, still, a ban on smoking in public places, though we are slowly moving that way. On the still more positive side, more people are becoming vegetarian and preferring grains, seeds and nuts to meat as a protein source, the cultivation of which is environmentally wasteful; recycling facilities are increasingly available, even in quite small communities; and renewable sources of energy are *slowly* being developed as alternatives to fossil fuels or atomic energy. At least I have touched the lives – positively, I hope – of the several thousand people who bought my books, or borrowed them from libraries, and the few hundred children to whom I have taught mathematics and sciences. I feel comforted and uplifted to be a part of the spiritual domain I have described in my previous books, more especially the second, and in this book, even if my contribution is only a relatively small one. My purpose in writing this account is to see if I can convince others of this rationale, to bring comfort or uplift to them in the process, and to do something tiny but positive for the global environment while we still have one, and people able to appreciate it. These things are all acts of love and worship of the divine spirit. I feel that my efforts to bring happiness and fufilment to others through my teaching, writing and publishing work, and to care for the environment as far as I can, really do make a positive contribution to the Universal Spirit, however relatively small the results of those efforts may be. My hope is that others will be similarly uplifted by this philosophy and will disseminate the message to still more people by their example.

References

Pages on which references are cited or serve as source material are given *in italics*. Scriptural references are included in the text.

1. Alexander, Samuel, *Space, Time and Deity*, Macmillan, London, 1920: *66*

2. Allen, D.J., *The Philosophy of Aristotle*, Oxford University Press, 2nd edn., p.47, 1970: *88*

3. Alston, William P., *Perceiving God: The epistemology of religious experience*, Cornell University Press, Ithaca, NY, 1991, p.289: *181, 290*

4. Angelo, Jack, *Your Healing Power*, Piatkus, London, 1994: *226*

5. Angelo, Jack and Jan Angelo, *Sacred Healing*, Piatkus, London, 2001: *226*

6. Anselm, *Monologion* I: *282*

7. Appelbaum, David, *The Vision of Kant*, Element Books, Rockport, Mass., USA, 1995: *249*

8. Aquinas, Thomas, *Summa Theologiae*, 1265–74, Timothy McDermott (ed.), Eyre and Spottiswoode-Methuen, London 1989; Methuen p.b.1991: *193*

9. *ibid.*, Chap.1, Section 2.1: *105*

10. *ibid.*, Chap.1, Section 2.2: *174*

11. *ibid.*, Chap.1, Section 3: *95, 103, 105*

12. *ibid.*, Chap.1, Section 3.6: *105*

13. *ibid.*, Chap.1, Section 3.8: *174*

14. Aristotle, *De Anima*, trans. Hugh Lawson-Tancred, Penguin, Harmondsworth, Middlesex, 1986

15. *ibid.*, Book II, Chap.1: *88*

16. Armstrong, Karen, *A History of God*, Heinemann, London, 1993

17. *ibid.*, p.275: *208*

18. *ibid.*, pp.290–291: *108*

19. *ibid.*, p.352: *134*

20. *ibid.*, pp.384–385: *136*

21. Ash, David, *The New Science of the Spirit,* The College of Psychic Studies, London, 1995, p.42

22. *ibid.*, p. 156: *227*

23. Aspect, A., J. Dalibard and G. Roger, *Phys. Rev. Lett.*, **49**, 1804, 1982: *299*

24. Auden, W.H., *The Dyer's Hand*, 1962: *176*

25. Augustine, *City of God*, Doubleday (Image Books), 1958, p.140: *217, 225*

26. *ibid.*, p.245: *101, 102*

27. *ibid.*, Chapter 23: *181*

28. Augustine, *On 83 Different Questions*, No.46: *248*

29. Augustine, *Retractiones*: *102*

30. Augustine, *Sermones* 12.4: *102*

31. Augustine, *Sermones* 117.7: *176*

32. Ayer, Alfred J., *Language, Truth and Logic*, Victor Gollancz, 1936; Pelican, 1971: *123*

33. *ibid.*, p.58: *123*

34. Ayer, Alfred J., *Hume*, Oxford University Press, Oxford, UK, 1980: *104*

35. Backster, Cleve, Evidence of a primary perception in plant life, *Intern. J. Parapsychology*, **10**, 4, 1968: *264*

36. Bacon, Francis, *New Atlantis*, written 1610 but published posthumously: *122*

37. Bacon, Francis, *Novum Organum*, 1620: *124*

38. Bacon, Francis, *De Dignitate et Augmentis Scientiarum*, 1623: *122*

39. Bacon, Francis, *The Advancement of Learning,* 1605: *122*

40. Bailey, Jarrod, Andrew Knight and Jonathan Balcombe, The future of teratology research is *in vitro*, *Biogenic Amines*, VSP (Brill), 2005: *206*

41. Barnes, Jonathan, *Aristotle*, Oxford University Press, 1982, p.66: *88*

42. *ibid.,* p. 67: *88*

43. *ibid.,* p. 68: *88*

44. Barrow, John D. and Frank J. Tipler, *The Anthropic Cosmological Principle*, Oxford University Press, Oxford, 1986: *294*

45. Barth, Karl, Systematische Theologie, 1960, p.38: *48*

46. Bates, Brian, *The Way of Wyrd*, Hay House, London, 2004: *16*

47. Becker, R.O., *Cross Currents: The perils of electropollution, the promise of electromedicine*, Jeremy Tarcher Publications, 1991: *324*

48. Becker, R.O., *The Body Electric*, William Morrow, 1998: *324*

49. Becker, R.O. and G. Selden, *The Body Electric: Electromagnetism and the foundation of life*, Quill, New York, 1985: *324*

50. Bell, John, *Physics*, 1, 195–200, 1964: *299*

51. Bendit, Lawrence J., *Paranormal Cognition,* Faber and Faber, 1945: *219*

52. Berg, Yehuda, *The Power of Kabbalah*, Hodder Mobius, 2004, p.60, quoting Rabbi Isaac Luria: *245*

53. Bergson, Henri, *Time and Free Will*, 1889, English trans. 1910: *266*

54. Bergson, Henri, *Matter and Memory*, 1896, English trans. 1911: *266*

55. Bergson, Henri, *l'Evolution creatrice,* 1907, English trans. *Creative Evolution*, 1911 by Dr Arthur Mitchell, assisted by William James until the latter's death in 1910: *267*

56. Bergson, Henri, *L'Energie spirituelle* (a collection of published articles), Eng. trans. by a devotee of Bergson's, Dr. Wildon Carr 1919: *267*

57. Berkeley, George, *The Principles of Human Knowledge*, 1710, section 3: *248*

58. *ibid.*, section 53: *248*

59. *ibid.*, section 57: *248*

60. Blakemore, Colin, *The Mind Machine*, BBC Books, London, 1988: *163*

61. Blaukopf, Kurt, *Mahler*, Thames and Hudson, 1976, p. 196: *187*

62. *ibid.*, p. 204: *187*

63. Blavatsky, Helena P., *The Secret Doctrine*, 1888, Vol.1, p.105: *154, 271*

64. Blavatsky, Helena P., *Isis Unveiled,* 1877: *154*

65. Blavatsky, Helena P., *The Voice of the Silence*, 1889: *154*

66. Blavatsky, Helena P., *The Key to Theosophy,* 1889: *154*

67. Boehner, Philotheus, *William of Ockham, Philosophical Writings: A selection*, Hackett, New York, 1964: *109*

68. Bohm, David, *Wholeness and the Implicate Order*, Routledge and Kegan Paul, London, 1980, Ark, 1983: *313*

69. *ibid.*, p.11: *314*

70. *ibid.*, p.23: *314*

71. *ibid.*, pp.124–5: *314*

72. *ibid.*, p.149: *313*

73. *ibid.*, p.151: *314*

74. *ibid.*, p.176: *314*

75. *ibid.*, p.177: *314*

76. *ibid.*, p.195: *314*

77. *ibid.*, p.200: *176*

78. *ibid.*, p.204: *314*

79. Bohm, David, *Quantum Theory*, Prentice-Hall, Englewood Cliffs, NJ, 1951: *313*

80. Bohm, David, *Physical Review*, **85**, 166, 180 (1952): *313*

81. Bohm, David, *Causality and Chance in Modern Physics* Routledge and Kegan Paul, London, 1957: *313*

82. Boltzmann, Ludwig, *Wiener Berichte*, **58**, 517–560, 1868: *306*

83. Bondi, Hermann, Thomas Gold and Fred Hoyle, *Monthly Notices of the Royal Astronomical Society*, **108**, 252, 1948: *80*

84. Borzmowski, Andrzey, Experiments with Ossowiecki, *Intern. J. Parapsychology*, 7(3), 259–284, 1965: *217*

85. Bose, S.N., *Zeitschrift für Physik*, **26**, 178–181, 1924: *305*

86. Bournais-Vardiabasis, N., An alternative *in vitro* method to detect teratogens utilising *Drosophila melanogaster* embryos, *Humane Innovations and Alternatives*, **8**, 630–634, 1994: *206*

87. Bowker, John (ed.), *Oxford Dictionary of World Religions*, Oxford University Press, 1997: *95*

88. Boyer, Timothy, *Physical Review* **182**, 1374–1383, 1969: *309*

89. Braden, Gregg, *The Isaiah Effect*, Hay House, Carlsbad, California, 2000: *30, 195*

90. Braud, William G., and M. Schlitz, A methodology for the objective study of transpersonal imagery, *J. Scientific Exploration*, **3**(1), 43–63, 1989: *216*

91. Braud, William G. and M. Schlitz, *J. Parapsychology* **47**, 95–119, 1983: *215*

92. Brian, Denis, *Einstein: A life*, Wiley, New York, 1996, p.234: *150*

93. Broglie, Count Louis de, *Compt. Rend.* **183**, 447 (1926); **185**, 380 (1927): *313*

94. Broughton, Richard, *Parapsychology*, Ballantine (USA), 1991; Rider (UK) 1992: *218, 222, 238*

95. *ibid.*, p.124: *222*

96. *ibid.*, p.262: *238*

97. Brown, Brian, *The Wisdom of the Egyptians*, Brentano, New York, 1923: *228*

98. Browning, Robert, *Balaustion's Adventure*, 1871: *175*

99. Buchanan, Mark, *Ubiquity: The science of history, or Why the world is simpler than we think*, Weidenfeld and Nicholson, London, 2000: *292*

100. Burr, H.S., *Blueprint for Immortality*, C.W. Daniel, 1972: *322, 323*

101. Burr, H.S., *The Fields of Life*, Ballantine, New York, 1972: *323*

102. Byrd, R.C., *Southern Medical Journal*, **81**(7), 826–829, 1988: *233*

103. Calvin, John, *Institutes*, I, iii, 1,2: *181*

104. Capra, Fritjof, *The Tao Of Physics*, Wildwood House, London, 1975: *81, 183, 187, 312*

105. *ibid.*, p.37: *187*

106. *ibid.*, p.39: *183*

107. *ibid.*, p.150: *312*

108. *ibid.*, p.152: *312*

109. *ibid.*, p.154: *312*

110. Capra, Fritjof. *The Turning Point*, Simon and Schuster (USA),

Wildwood House (UK), 1982: *200*

111. Capra, Fritjof., *The Web of Life*: *A new scientific understanding of living systems*, Anchor-Doubleday, New York, 1996: *313*

112. Capra, Fritjof., *The Hidden Connections*, Harper/Collins, London, 2002: *313*

113. Carson, Rachel, *Silent Spring*, Houghton-Mifflin, New York, 1962: *199*

114. Carter, Brandon, *Confrontation of Cosmological Theories with Observation*, ed. M.S. Longair, Reidel, Dordrecht, The Netherlands, 1974, p.291: *294*

115. Cazin, J.C. *et al. Human Toxicology*, July 1987: *231*

116. Chardin, Pierre Teilhard de, *Le Phenoméne Humaine*, 1955; English trans. *The Phenomenon of Man*, Collins, London, and Harper, New York, 1959

117. *ibid.*, p.161: *295*

118. *ibid.*, p.200: *156, 295*

119. *ibid.*, p.240: *295*

120. Cicero, *The Nature of the Gods,* translated by Horace C. P. McGregor, Penguin, Harmondsworth, 1972

121. *ibid.*, Book I, para.87: *13*

122. *ibid.*, Book I, para.89: *13*

123. *ibid.*, Book II, para. 87: *105*

124. *ibid.*, Book II, para.135: *13*

125. *ibid.*, Book II, para.145: *183*

126. *ibid.* Book II, para.154: *14*

127. *ibid.*, Book II, para.159: *14*

128. *ibid.*, Book II, para.163: *14*

129. Cohn-Sherbok, Dan, *Fifty Key Jewish Thinkers*, Routledge, London, pp.101–102, 1997: *97*

130. Cooper, Diane, *A Little Light on the Spiritual Laws*, Hodder and Stoughton, London, 2000: *193*

131. Crane, Tim, *The Mechanical Mind*, Penguin, London 1991: *163*

132. Cudworth, Ralph, *The True Intellectual System of the Universe,* 1678: *20*

133. Darwin, Charles, *Origin of Species,* 1859: *29, 141, 269*

134. Davenas, Elizabeth, *et al.*, *Nature*, **333**, 818, 1988: *231*

135. Davies, Paul, *The Mind of God*, Simon and Schuster, 1992; Penguin 2001 edition, p.71: *127*

136. Davies, Paul, *The Accidental Universe*, Cambridge University Press, 1982, p.130: *294*

137. Dawkins, Richard, *The Selfish Gene*, Oxford, 1976: *197*

138. *ibid.*, p.4: *198*

139. Dawkins, Richard, *The Selfish Gene*, Paladin (Granada) p.b., London, 1978, p.206: *144*

140. Dawkins, Richard, *The Blind Watchmaker*, Longman, 1986: *292*

141. Dennett, Daniel C., *Consciousness Explained*, Little, Brown and Co., Boston, MA, USA, 1991; Viking, London, 1992: *163*

142. Descartes, René, *Meditations on First Philosophy*, 1641, Meditation VI: *158, 185*

143. Descartes, René, *Discourse on the Method of Sciences*, 1637: *185*

144. Descartes, René, *The World (Le Monde)*, 1664: *185*

145. Diels, H. and W. Krantz, *Die Fragmente der Vorsokratiker*, Berlin, 10th edn 1952: Xenophanes, 11, 12, 14, 16: *74*

146. Dix, H.M. *Environmental Pollution*, John Wiley, Chichester, 1981: *199*

147. Dossey, Larry, *Healing Beyond the Body*, Shambala Publications, 2001: *233*

148. Dossey, Larry, *Healing Words: The power of prayer and the practice of medicine*, Harper-Collins, 1994: *233*

149. Dossey, Larry, *Reinventing Medicine*, Harper-Collins, 1999: *233*

150. Dossey, Larry, Interview with Dennis Hughes, Publisher of *The Holistic Health Magazine and Resource Review*, available on-line: *233*

151. Driesch, Hans, *Science and Philosophy of the Organism*, Black, London, 1908: *265*

152. Driesch, Hans, *The History and Theory of Vitalism*, Macmillan, London, 1914: *265*

153. Driesch, Hans, *Mind and Body*, Methuen, London, 1927: *265*

154. Ducasse, C.J., *The Belief in a Life after Death*, Charles C. Thomas, Springfield, Illinois, USA, 1961: *238*

155. Dunn, John, *Locke*, Oxford University Press, 1984: *247*

156. Dunne, B.J., *J. Scientific Exploration* **6**, 311, 1992: *317*

157. Dunne, J.W., *An Experiment with Time,* 1927: *220*

158. Dyer, Wayne, *The Power of Intention*, Hay House, Carlsbad, California, 2004: *195, 255*

159. Easterling, P.E. and J.V. Muir (eds), *Greek Religion and Society*, Cambridge University Press, 1985: *10*

160. Eccles, John, *Evolution of the Brain, Creation of the Self*, Routledge, London, 1989, p.241: *159*

161. Eccles, John, *How the Self Controls Its Brain*, Springer Verlag, Berlin, 1994, p.38: *160*

162. Eckermann, Johann Peter, *Conversations with Goethe*, trans. R.O. Moon, London, 1951: *227*

163. Eddington, Arthur, *The Nature of the Physical World*, Cambridge University Press, 1935: *168*

164. *ibid.*, p.91: *267*

165. Einstein, Albert, *Out of My Later Years*, 1950: *277*

166. Einstein, Albert, *Berliner Berichte*, Sept 1924, pp.261–267: *365*

167. Einstein, Albert, Boris Podolsky and Nathan Rosen, *Physical Review*, **47**, 777, 1935: *299*

168. Ellis, Peter Berresford, *A Brief History of the Druids*, Constable, London, 1994: *18*

169. Emerson, J.N., Intuitive archeology: A psychic approach, *New Horizon*, **1**(3), 14, 1974: *217*

170. Emerson, Ralph Waldo, *Nature,* James Munroe, Boston, 1836: *177*

171. Emerson, Ralph Waldo, *Journals*, 1831: *218, 277*

172. Emoto, Masaru, *The Hidden Messages in Water*, Beyond Words Publishing, Hillsboro, Oregon, 2004: *231*

173. Erler, Rolf Joachim and Reiner Marquard, *A Karl Barth Reader*, T. and T. Clark, Edinburgh, 1986: *48*

174. Epstein, Isidore, *Judaism*, Penguin, Harmondsworth, 1959: *33*

175. Evans, G.R., *Fifty Key Medieval Thinkers*, Routledge, London, 2002: *93*

176. Eysenck, Hans J., and Carl Sargent, *Explaining the Unexplained: Mysteries of the paranormal*, Multimedia Books, 1993: *219, 238*

177. Ferguson, Marilyn, *The Aquarian Conspiracy*, Routledge and Kegan Paul, London, 1981; Paladin edition, 1982, p.127: *199*

178. Fichte, Johann Gottlieb, *An Essay Towards a Critique of All Revelation*, 1792: *194*

179. Finley, M.I., *The Idea of a Theatre*, British Museum, London, 1980: *13*

180. Flew, Antony, *God and Philosophy*, Hutchinson, 1966: *289*

181. Fontana, David, *Is There An Afterlife? A comprehensive overview of the evidence*, O Books, Ropley, Hampshire, UK, 2005: *238*

182. Fontana, David, *Meditating with Mandalas*, Duncan Baird, London, 2005: *188*

183. Ford, Adam, *Universe: God, man and science*, Hodder and Stoughton, London, 1986: *1*

184. Fordham, Frieda, *An Introduction to Jung's Psychology*, Penguin, Harmondsworth, UK, 1953, p.71: *258*

185. *ibid.*, p.78: *258*

186. Fox, Mark, *Religion, Spirituality and the Near-Death Experience*, Routledge, London, 2003: *238*

187. Fragata, Mario, Structural pathways of electron transfer via tunnelling ..., in Proceedings of the 3rd Internet Conference on Photochemistry and Photobiology, 24th Nov – 24th Dec 2000, available at http://www.photobiology.com/photobiology 2000: 27: *321*

188. Frankfort, Henri, *Ancient Egyptian Religion*, Columbia University Press, 1948; Dover Publications, 2000: *7*

189. *ibid.*, p.67: *8*

190. *ibid.*, p.75: *8*

191. Freeman, Anthony, *God In Us*, SCM Press, 1993

192. *ibid.*, pp. 9, 10: *260*

193. *ibid.*, p.20: *260*

194. *ibid.*, p.25: *260*

195. *ibid.*, p.46: *260*

196. *ibid.*, p.47: *260*

197. Freke, Timothy and Peter Gandy, *The Jesus Mysteries*, Thorsons/Element, 1999: *22*

198. Freud, Sigmund, *The Future of an Illusion*, 1928: *257*

199. Frey, A.H., Field interactions with biological systems, *Federation of American Societies for Experimental Biology (FASEB) Journal*, 7, 272, 1993: *221*

200. Fröhlich, H., *Intern. J. Quantum Chem.* 2, 641–649, 1968; *Physics Letters* **51A**, 21, 1975: *324*

201. Fromm, Eric, *To Have or To Be*, Jonathan Cape, London, 1978: *202*

202. Frost, S.E., *Basic Teachings of the Great Philosophers*, Doubleday, 1942, p.134: *246*

203. Gardiner, Alan H. and K. Sethe, *Egyptian Letters to the Dead*, London, 1928: *8*

204. Gardiner, Patrick, *Schopenhauer*, Penguin, Harmondsworth, Middlesex, UK, 1963: *252*

205. Gardner, Howard, *Frames of Mind*, Basic Books, New York, 1983: *149, 184*

206. Gardner, Howard, *Multiple Intelligences* Basic Books, New York, 1993: *149, 184*

207. Gaskin, J.C.A., *The Quest for Eternity*, Penguin, Harmondsworth, Middlesex, UK, 1984: *289*

208. Gibb, H.A.R., *Islam*, Oxford University Press, Oxford, 1949, p.36: *52*

209. Gibbon, Edward, *The History of the Decline and Fall of the Roman Empire*, 1776–87: *113, 186*

210. Gibson, P.G. *et al. Brit. J. Clin. Pharmacol.*, **9**, 453–459, 1980: *231*

211. Gleick, James, *Chaos: Making a new science*, William Heinemann, London, 1988: *311*

212. Gleick, James, *Isaac Newton*, Harper Collins, London, 2004: *124*

213. Goldberg, David J. and John D. Rayner, *The Jewish People: Their history and their religion*, Viking, New York, 1987; Penguin, London, 1989: *33*

214. Griffiths, Father Bede, *The Marriage of East and West,* Templegate Publishers (US); Collins (UK) 1977

215. *ibid.*, p.6: *202*

216. *ibid.*, pp.84–5, paraphrased: *153*

217. Grinberg-Zylberbaum, Jacobo, M. Delaflor, L. Attie and A. Goswami, The E-P-R paradox in the brain – the transferred potential, *Physics Essays*, 7(4), 422–8, 1944: *215*

218. Grinberg-Zylberbaum, Jacobo, The syntergic theory, *Frontier Perspectives*, 4(1), 25–30, 1994

219. Guillaume, Alfred, *Islam*, Penguin, Harmondsworth, UK, p.139, 1954: *215*

220. Hall, Judy, *The Crystal Bible*, Godsfield Press, Alresford, Hampshire, UK, 2003: *228*

221. Hameroff, S., *Ultimate Computing: Biomolecular consciousness and nanotechnology*, North-Holland, Amsterdam, 1987: *325*

222. Hamlyn, D.W., *Schopenhauer*, Routledge and Kegan Paul, 1980

223. *ibid.*, p.95: *253*

224. *ibid.*, p.136: *255*

225. *ibid.*, p.146: *255*

226. *ibid.*, p.165: *253*

227. Hansard, Christopher, *The Tibetan Art of Positive Thinking*, Hodder and Stoughton, 2003, p.13: *171*

228. *ibid.*, p.14: *171*

229. Happold, F.C. *Mysticism*, Penguin, London, 1963, p.37: *170*

230. Hardy, Alister, *The Divine Flame*, Collins, London, 1966: *171*

231. Hardy, Alister, *The Biology of God*, Jonathan Cape, 1975.: *171*

232. Hardy, Alister, *The Spiritual Nature of Man: A study of contemporary religious experience,* Oxford University Press, Oxford UK, 1979, pp.25–30: *171-174, 183, 187, 213, 217, 219, 224, 234*

233. Harpur, Tom, *The Pagan Christ: Recovering the lost light*, Thomas Allen, Toronto, 2004

234. *ibid*, p.23: *16*

235. *ibid.*, p.61: *18*

236. *ibid.*, p.79: *18*

237. *ibid.*, p.80: *39*

238. Harpur, Tom, *Finding the Still Point,* Northstone Publishing, Kelona, BC, Canada, 2002: *16, 22, 261*

239. Harris, W.S., M. Gowda, J.W. Kolb, *et al., Archives of Internal Medicine,* **159**, 2273–2278, 1999: *233*

240. Hartshorne, Charles, *The Divine Relativity: A social conception of God,* Yale University Press, New Haven, Connecticut, 1948, p.28: *65*

241. *ibid.,* p.29: *65*
242. *ibid.,* p.46: *65*
243. *ibid.,* p.47: *65*
244. *ibid.,* p.55: *65*
245. *ibid.,* p.69: *65*
246. *ibid.,* p.79: *65*

247. Hawking, Stephen W., *A Brief History of Time,* Transworld Publishers (Bantam), London, 1988: *291*

248. Hay, Louise L., *The Power Is Within You,* Hay House, Carson CA, 1991: *225*

249. Hay, Louise L., *You Can Heal Your Life,* Hay House, Santa Monica CA, 1984: *225*

250. Hegel, G.W.F., *Phenomenology of Mind* (or *Phenomenology of Spirit*) (*Phänomenologie des Geistes*), 1807: *250*

251. Heisenberg, W., *Physics and Philosophy,* Allen and Unwin, London, 1963, p.75: *298*

252. Herder, Johann Gottfried von, *A Theory of the Evolution of Humankind* (*Auch eine Philosophie der Geschichte zur Bildung der Menschheit,* 1774: 3: *177*

253. Hesiod, *Works and Days,* pp.213–247: *74*

254. Hick, John, *Evil and the God of Love,* Macmillan, Basingstoke, UK, 1966, p.154: *197*

255. Hick, John, *God and the Universe of Faiths,* Macmillan, London; St. Martin's Press, New York, 1973: *209*

256. Hick, John, *Problems of Religious Pluralism,* Macmillan, 1985, p.18: *210*

257. Hick, John, *Death and Eternal Life,* Macmillan, 1985, pp.55, 56: *150*

258. Hobbes, Thomas *(trans.) Thucydides,* trans. R. Schlatter (Ed.),

New Brunswick, i, 22.4; iii, 82.2, 1975: *78*

259. Hobbes, Thomas, *Leviathan*, 1651; ed. John Plamenatz, Fontana (Collins) 1962, p.123: *79*

260. *ibid.*, Chap.13: *47*

261. *ibid.*, Chap. 27: *78*

262. Homer, *Iliad*, xvi, pp.385–392: 2: *74*

263. Honderich, Ted, *A Theory of Determinism*, Oxford University Press, 1988: *162*

264. Hopkins, Gerard Manley, Comments on the *Spiritual Exercises* of St. Ignatius of Loyola in *Gerard Manley Hopkins: Poems and Prose*, W.H. Gardner (ed.), Penguin, Harmondsworth, Middlesex, UK, 1953, p.146: *273*

265. Humphreys, Christmas, *The Buddhist Way of Life*, Unwin Hyman, London, 1969, paraphrased: *151*

266. Hume, David, *A Treatise of Human Nature*, 1739; Ernest Mossner (ed.), Penguin, Harmondsworth, UK, 1969, Book I, iii: *104*

267. *ibid.*, Book II, iii: *178*

268. Inglis, Brian, *Coincidence: A matter of chance or synchronicity?* Hutchinson, London, 1990

269. *ibid.*, p.33: *259, 270*

270. Jahn, R., Y. Dobyns and B. Dunne, *J. Scientific Exploration*, **5**, 205, 1991: *317*

271. James, E.O. in *Historia Religionum*, C.J. Bleeker and Geo Widengren (eds), E.J. Brill, Leiden, The Netherlands, 1969–71, vol.1, p.24: *150*

272. James, William, *Pragmatism*, 1907: *77*

273. James, William, *Principles of Psychology*, 1890: *77*

274. James, William, *The Varieties of Religious Experience*, Longmans 1902, Penguin 1982, Lectures XVI, XVII: *171*

275. Janaway, Christopher, *Schopenhauer*, Oxford University Press, 2002, p.17: *254*

276. Jeans, James, *The Mysterious Universe*, Cambridge University Press, 1930: *168*

277. Jenkins, David, *Market Whys and Human Wherefores*, Continuum, London, 2000: *201*

278. Jibu M., and K. Yasue, A physical picture of Umezawa's

quantum brain dynamics, in R. Trappl (ed.), *Cybernetics and Systems Research '92*, World Scientific, Singapore 1992: *325*

279. Jibu M., and K. Yasue, Intracellular signal transfer in Umezawa's quantum brain dynamics, *Cybernetics Systems International* 1(24), 1–7. 1993: *325*

280. Jibu M., and K. Yasue, Introduction to quantum brain dynamics, in E. Carvallo (ed.), *Nature, Cognition and System III*, Kluwer, London 1993: *325*

281. Jibu M., and K. Yasue, The basis of quantum brain dynamics, in K.H. Pribram (ed.), *Rethinking Neural Networks: Quantum fields and biological data*, Lawrence Erlbaum, Hillsdale NJ, 1993, pp.121–145: *325*

282. Jibu, M., S. Hagen, S. Hameroff, *et al.*, Quantum optical coherence in cytoskeletal microtubules: implications for brain function, *BioSystems*, **32**, 95–209, 1994: *325*

283. Jolley, Nicholas, *Leibniz and Locke*, Clarendon Press, Oxford, 1984, p.12: *128, 247*

284. Jones, H.A., *Prescriptions for Health*, Collins, London, 1986: *336*

285. Jones, H.A., *A Way of Health: Body, mind and spirit*, Tynron Press, Thornhill, Scotland, 1990: *336*

286. Jung, Carl Gustav, *Memories, Dreams, Reflections*, Routledge and Kegan Paul, London, 1963, 312: *65*

287. Jung, C.J., *Instinct and the Unconscious*, 1919, paragraph 270; in *The Collected Works of C.J. Jung (CW)*, Routledge and Kegan Paul, London, Vol. 8, 1960: *256*

288. Jung, C.W., *The Psychological Foundations of Belief in Spirits*, 1920, 1948, *CW* 8, 1960, para. 589: *257*

289. Jung, C.J., *Synchronicity: An Acausal Connecting Principle*, 1952; in *CW*, Vol. 8, 1960: *258*

290. Jung, C.J., *Letters*, ed. Gerhard Adler, Princeton University Press, Princeton NJ, 1953–75: *317*

291. Kant, Immanuel, *Critique of Pure Reason*, Königsberg, 1781: *177*

292. Kennedy, President John F., Inaugural Address, January 1961: *198*

293. King, Martin Luther, Jr., *Strength To Love*, Augsburg Fortress Publishers, 1963, 1.1: *277*

294. Klinger, Friedrich Maximilian von, *Sturm und Drang* (*Storm and Stress*) 1776: *177*

295. Koenig, Harold, Michael McCullough and David Larson, *Handbook of Religion and Health*, Oxford University Press, New York, 2001: *234*

296. Koestler, Arthur, *The Roots of Coincidence*, Hutchinson, London, 1972: *258*

297. Kolakowski, Leslek, *Bergson*, Oxford University Press, 1985: *267*

298. Körner, S., *Kant*, Penguin, Harmondsworth, Middlesex, UK, 1955: *249*

299. Kosko, Bart, *Fuzzy Thinking: The new science of fuzzy logic*, Hyperion (USA) 1993, Harper Collins (UK) 1994: *311*

300. Kuhn, Alvin Boyd, *The Lost Light*, Kessinger Publishing, Kila, MT, 1940 (Reprint): *18*

301. Lancaster, Brian L. *Mind, Brain and Human Potential*, Element Books, Shaftesbury, Dorset, UK, 1991: *157*

302. Lancaster, Brian L., *Approaches to Consciousness: The marriage of science and mysticism*, Palgrave Macmillan, Basingstoke, Hampshire, UK, 2004: *157*

303. Laszlo, Ervin, *You Can Change The World*, Positive News Publishing, Clun, Shropshire, UK, 2002: *201*

304. *ibid.*, p.89: *201*

305. Laszlo, Ervin, *The Creative Cosmos: A unified science of matter, life and mind*, Floris, Edinburgh, 1993, p.129: *262*

306. *ibid.*, p.134: *262*

307. Laszlo, Ervin, *The Inner Limits of Mankind: Heretical reflections on today's values, culture and politics*, Oneworld Publishers, London, 1989: *268*

308. Laszlo, Ervin, *The Interconnected Universe: Conceptual foundations of transdisciplinary unified theory*, World Scientific, Singapore, 1995: *268*

309. Laszlo, Ervin, *The Systems View of the World: A holistic vision for our time*, Hampton Press, 1996: *308*

310. Laszlo, Ervin, Stanislav Grof and Peter Russell, *The Consciousness Revolution*, Element Books, London 1999: *201*

311. *ibid.*, Elf Rock edn, Las Vegas, 2003, p.27: *201*

312. Laughlin, C.D., Archetypes, neurognosis and the quantum sea, *J. Scientific Exploration*, **10**, 375–400, 1996: *317*

313. Leibniz, Gottfried Wilhelm, Monadology, in G.H.R. Parkinson (ed.), *Leibniz' Philosophical Writings*, J.M. Dent, 1973 edn., Section 42: *197*

314. *ibid.*, 3: *129*

315. *ibid.*, 1–3: *129*

316. *ibid.*, 5: *129*

317. *ibid.*, 9–11: *129*

318. *ibid.*, 12, 13: *129*

319. *ibid.*, 14: *129*

320. *ibid.*, 69: *129*

321. Levin, Jeff, *God, Faith and Health: Exploring the spirituality–healing connection*, Wiley, New York, 2002: *233*

322. Locke, John, *An Essay Concerning Human Understanding*, 1690, Collins edn. 1964: *247*

323. *ibid.*, Book 1, Chapter IV, 8: *194*

324. *ibid.*, Book 4, 1.2: *247*

325. *ibid.*, Book 4, 15.3: *247*

326. *ibid.*, Chapter II: *247*

327. *ibid.*, Chapter VI: *248*

328. Lovelock, James, *Gaia: A new look at life on earth*, OUP, Oxford, 1979: *199*

329. Lovelock, James, *The Ages of Gaia*, OUP, Oxford, 1989: *199*

330. MacKenzie, Andrew, *Riddle of the Future*, Arthur Barker, London, 1974, p.47: *220*

331. Mackie, J.L., *The Miracle of Theism: Arguments for and against the Existence of God*, Clarendon Press, Oxford, 1982: *290*

332. Malebranche, Nicolas de, *Dialogues on Metaphysics and Religion*, 1688; English trans. M. Ginsberg, Allen and Unwin, London, 1923: *158*

333. Malthus, Thomas, *An Essay on the Principle of Population*, 1798: *70*

334. Manning, Matthew, *The Healing Journey*, Piatkus, 2001: *225*

335. Marx, Karl, *Critique of the Gotha Programme* 1875: *200*

336. Massey, Gerald, *The Historical Jesus and the Mythical Christ*, Kessinger Publications, Kila, MT, 2002: *39*

337. Maxwell, J.C. *Trans. Cambridge Phil. Soc.*, **12**, 547–570, 1878: *306*

338. McGinn, Colin, *The Character of Mind*, Oxford University Press, Oxford, UK, 1982: *163*

339. McGrath, Alister, *The Science of God*, T and T Clark (Continuum), London, 2004

340. *ibid.*, p.35: *290*

341. *ibid.*, p.74: *181*

342. *ibid.*, p.116: *280*

343. McTaggert, Lynne, *The Field*, Harper-Collins (Element), London, 2001: *305*

344. *ibid.*, p.163 on: *217*

345. *ibid.*, p.190 on: *218*

346. Mill, John Stuart, *On Liberty* 1859; H.B. Acton (ed.), Dent, London, 1972, p.118: *198*

347. Miller, Ronald S., Bridging the Gap: An interview with Valerie Hunt, published in *Science of Mind*, October 1983, p.12: *227*

348. Monod, Jacques, *Chance and Necessity*, Vantage Books, NY, 1971; Collins, London, 1972: *292*

349. Moody, Raymond A., *Life after Life*, Harper, San Francisco, 1975; Bantam, New York, 1976: *238*

350. Morgan, Augustus de, *Essay on Probabilities,* 1838: *258*

351. Morris, Desmond, *The Naked Ape,* Jonathan Cape, London, 1967: *213*

352. Mumford, Lewis, *Renewal of Life* series, 1934–1951: *200*

353. Murphy, Joseph, *The Power Of Your Subconscious Mind*, Bantam, New York, 1982: *225*

354. Newman, John Henry, *The Development of Christian Doctrine*, 1834: *145*

355. Newman, John Henry, *Apologia pro Vita Sua*, 1864: *145*

356. Nicolis, G. in *The New Physics*, ed. P.C.W. Davies, Cambridge University Press, 1989, p.319: *318*

357. Norberg-Hodge, Helena, *Bringing the Food Economy Home,* Zed Books, London, 2002: *201*

358. Norberg-Hodge, Helena, *Ancient Futures*, Century (Random House), London, 1991: *201*

359. *Omni Magazine*, **10**(4), 76, 1988: *238*

360. Osborn, Arthur, *The Future Is Now: The significance of precognition*, University Books, New York, 1961: *220*

361. Pascal, Blaise, *Pensées*, ii, 139: *207*

362. Pauli, Wolfgang, *Science*, **103**, 213–215, 1946: *299*

363. Peck, M. Scott, *The Road Less Travelled: A new psychology of love, traditional values and spiritual growth*, Simon and Schuster (USA) 1978, Hutchinson (UK) 1983: *182*

364. Peirce, Charles Sanders, *How To Make Our Ideas Clear*, 1878: *77*

365. Penelhum, Terence, *Survival and Disembodied Existence*, Routledge and Kegan Paul, London, 1970: *236*

366. Penrose, Roger, *Shadows of the Mind,* Oxford University Press, 1994: *275*

367. Plato, *Republic*, Book VII: *17*

368. Playfair, Guy Lyon, *Twin Telepathy* [Chrysalis Books (Vega), London, 2002

369. *ibid.*, p.44: *214*

370. *ibid.*, p.102: *214*

371. *ibid.,* p.144: *215*

372. Pliny the Elder, *Naturalis Historia*, XVI, 95: *18*

373. Plotinus, *The Enneads*, trans. Stephen Mackenna, Penguin, London, 1991: *246*

374. Polkinghorne, John, *Science and Creation: The search for understanding*, SPCK, London, 1988, p.22: *285*

375. Polkinghorne, John, *Science and Providence: God's interaction with the world*, SPCK, London, 1989: *285*

376. Polkinghorne, John, *Reason and Reality: The relationship between science and theology*, SPCK, London, 1991: *285*

377. Poniatowski, Stanislaw, Parapsychological probing of prehistoric cultures, in J. Goodman (ed.), *Psychic Archeology*, Putnam, New York, 1977: *217*

378. Popper, Karl, *The Logic of Scientific Discovery*, Hutchinson, London, 1959, p.29: *278*

379. *ibid.*, p.35: *123*

380. *ibid.*, p.40: *278*

381. Popper, Karl, and John Eccles, *The Self and Its Brain*, Springer, Berlin, 1977: *160*

382. Pribram, K.H., *Languages of the Brain: Experimental paradoxes and principles in neuropsychology*, Brandon House, New York, 1971: *315*

383. Pribram, K.H., *Brain and Perception: Holonomy and structure in figural processing*, Lawrence Erlbaum, Hillsdale NJ, 1991: *316*

384. Priest, Stephen, *Theories of the Mind*, Penguin, London, 1991: *163*

385. Priestland, Gerald, *The Case Against God*, Collins, 1984: *289*

386. Prigogine, Ilya, and Yves Elskens, Irreversibility, stochasticity and non-locality in classical dynamics, in *Quantum Implications*, Basil J. Hiley and F. David Peat (eds), Routledge and Kegan Paul, London, 1987: *319*

387. Prigogine, Ilya and Isabelle Stengers, *Order Out Of Chaos*, Bantam (USA), 1984; Heinemann (UK), 1984, p.142: *318*

388. *ibid.*, p.143: *319*

389. Putnam, Hilary (Ed.), *Mind, Language and Reality*, Cambridge University Press, 1980: *22, 162*

390. Putoff, H. *Physical Review D* **35**, 3266–3270, 1987: *303*

391. Quinton, Anthony, *Francis Bacon*, Oxford University Press, p.22, 1980: *122*

392. Radin, P.A. *Primitive Religion*, New York, 1937, p.270; quoted in John Hick, *Death and Eternal Life*, Macmillan, 1985, pp.55, 56: *150*

393. Radin, Dean, *The Conscious Universe: The scientific truth of paranormal phenomena*, Harper-Edge, New York 1997: *216, 221*

394. Radin, Dean, and R. Nelson, Evidence for consciousness-related anomalies in random physical systems, *Foundations of Physics*, **19**(12), 1499–1514, 1989: *221*

395. Redfield, James, *The Celestine Vision: Living the new spiritual awareness*, Warner Books, 1997: *182*

396. *ibid.*, pp. 181–2: *259*

397. Regardie, Israel, *The Tree of Life*, Samuel Weiser, 1972, pp.86–7: *3*

398. Reynolds, Alfred, *Jesus versus Christianity*, Cambridge International Publishers, London, 1988; 2nd edn. 1993: *22*

399. Rhine, Joseph Banks, *The Reach of the Mind*, Pelican, London, 1954: *213*

400. Rhine, Joseph Banks, *Extra-Sensory Perception*, Brandon, London, 1983: *213*

401. Ridley, B.K., *On Science*, Routledge, 2001, p.173: *163*

402. Robinson, John A.T., *Honest to God*, SCM Press, 1963: *289*

403. Rosambeau, Mary, *How Twins Grow Up*, Bodley Head, London, 1987: *214*

404. Russell, Bertrand, *Outline of Philosophy*, Allen and Unwin, London, 1927; 1979 pb. edn., p.222: *162*

405. *ibid.*, p.235: *162*

406. Ryle, Gilbert, *The Concept of Mind*, Oxford, 1949: *159*

407. Sabom, Michael, *Recollections of Death: A medical investigation*, Harper and Row, 1982: *238*

408. Schelling, Friedrich Wilhelm Joseph von, *System of Transcendental Idealism*, 1800: *178*

409. Schlitz, M., and W.G. Braud, Distant intentionality and healing: assessing the evidence, *Alternative Therapies*, 3(6), 62–73, 1997: *216*

410. Schmidt, Helmut, Mental influence in random events, *New Scientist*, 24 June 1971, pp.757–8: *222*

411. Schmidt, Helmut, Quantum processes predicted? *New Scientist*, 16 October 1969, pp.114–115: *222*

412. Schopenhauer, Arthur, *Die Welt als Wille und Vorstellung* (*The World as Will and Representation*), 1818: *253*

413. Schopenhauer, Arthur, *On the Fourfold Root of the Principle of Sufficient Reason*, 1813, 1847: *252*

414. Schopenhauer, Arthur, *Uber den Willen in der Natur* 1836; English trans. 1889, *On the Will in Nature*: *253*

415. Schrödinger, Erwin, *What is Life? The physical aspect of the living cell*, Cambridge University Press, 1944: *321*

416. Schrödinger, Erwin, *Mind and Matter*, Cambridge University Press, 1958: *167*

417. Schumacher, Erwin, *Small Is Beautiful*, Blond and Briggs, London, 1973, pp.26, 27: *200*

418. *ibid.*, p.91: *200*

419. *ibid.*, p.99: *200*

420. Schumacher, Erwin, *A Guide for the Perplexed*, Jonathan Cape, 1977: *85, 268al discovery that transforms science and medicine*, Hampton Roads, Charlottsville, Virginia, USA, 1999: *238*

422. Schwartz, Gary E., and William L. Simon, *The Afterlife Experiments*, Atria Books, New York, 2002: *238*

423. Scruton, Roger, *Kant*, Oxford University Press, 1985, p. 69: *78*

424. Searle, John R., *The Rediscovery of the Mind*, MIT Press, Boston, Mass., USA, 1994: *163*

425. Selbourne, David, *The Principle of Duty*, Sinclair-Stevenson, London, 1994

426. *ibid.*, p.16: *194*

427. *ibid.*, p.20: *194*

428. *ibid.*, p.33: *198*

429. Sheldrake, Rupert, *The Sense of Being Stared At, and other aspects of the extended mind*, Hutchinson, 2003: *163, 214, 268*

430. Sheldrake, Rupert, *Dogs That Know When Their Owners Are Coming Home*, Hutchinson, London, 1999, Arrow p.b. 2000: *155, 214, 268*

431. Sheldrake, R., *A New Science of Life*, Blond and Briggs, 1981: *268*

432. Sheldrake, Rupert, *The Presence of the Past*, Collins 1988: *268*

433. Sherrington, Charles, Gifford Lectures published as *Man on his Nature*, Cambridge University Press, 1940: *161*

434. Shine, Betty, *Mind Magic*, Bantam, 1991: *225*

435. Sicher, F., E. Targ, *et al.*, A randomised double-blind study of the effect of distant healing in a population with advanced AIDS: report of a small-scale study, *Western Journal of Medicine*, **168**(6), 356–363, 1998: *234*

436. Singer, Peter, *Hegel*, Oxford University Press, Oxford, 1983:

251

437. Smith, Peter, *The Baha'i Religion*, George Ronald, 1988: *58*

438. Snow, C.P., *The Two Cultures and the Scientific Revolution*, Cambridge University Press, 1959: 1

439. Solomon, Grant and Jane, http://www.netcomuk.co.uk/~gsolomon: *238*

440. Solomon, Grant, and Jane Solomon, *The Scole Experiment: Scientific evidence for life after death*, Piatkus Books, 1999: 40: *238*

441. Spemann, H.C., *Embryonic Development and Induction*, Yale University Press, 1938: *267*

442. Spencer, Herbert, *Principles of Biology*, part iii, chap. 12, 1865: *179*

443. Spinoza, Benedict (Baruch), *Ethics*, Part 1, Proposition XI: *180*

444. *ibid.*, Part I, Proposition XIV: *180*

445. *ibid.*, Part I, Proposition XV: *180*

446. *ibid.*, Part I, Proposition XVIII: *180*

447. *ibid.*, Part I, Proposition XXV:*180*

448. *ibid.*, Part II, Proposition III:*180*

449. Stace, W.T., *The Teachings of the Mystics*, Mentor Books, 1960, p.14: *171*

450. Stace, W.T., *Mysticism and Philosophy*, Macmillan, 1961: *171*

451. Stanhill, Gerry, and S. Cohen, Global dimming, *Agricultural and Forest Meteorology*, **107**, 255–278, 2001: *204*

452. Stanley, Michael, *Emanuel Swedenborg: Essential readings*, Thorsons (Crucible), London, 1988: *132*

453. Stapp, Henry P., S-Matrix interpretation of quantum theory, *Physical Review*, **D3**, 1303–20, 1971 March: *316*

454. Stapp, Henry P., *Mind, Matter and Quantum Mechanics*, Springer Verlag, 1993: *316*

455. Stapp, Henry P., Theoretical model of a purported empirical violation of the predictions of quantum theory, *Physical Review A*, **50**(1), July 1994: *317*

456. Stevens, Anthony, *Jung: A very short introduction*, Oxford University Press, Oxford, UK, 1994: *258*

457. Stevenson, Ian, *Twenty Cases Suggestive of Reincarnation*,

American Society for Psychical Research. New York, 1966: *238*

458. Stevenson, Ian, *Children Who Remember Past Lives*, University of Virginia Press, 1987: *238*

459. Stevenson, Ian, *When Reincarnation and Biology Intersect*, Praeger, 1997: *238*

460. Stewart, Ian, *Does God Play Dice? The Mathematics of Chaos*, Blackwell, Oxford, 1989, p.141: *319*

461. Stewart, Ian, *Nature's Numbers: Discovering order and pattern in the universe*, Weidenfeld and Nicholson, London, 1995: *319*

462. Storr, Anthony, *Jung*, Fontana, London, 1973, p.40: *257*

463. *ibid.*, p.48: *257*

464. Suzuki, D.T., *The Essence of Buddhism*, The Buddhist Society, London, 1947: *150*

465. Swami Chidbhavananda, *Ramakrishna Lives Vedanta*, Sri Ramakrishna Tapovana, India, 2nd edn. 1971, p.267: *243*

466. Swedenborg, *Arcane Celestia*, London, 8 vols, 1749–56: *130-132*

467. Swedenborg, *Divine Providence*, 1764: *130*

468. Swedenborg, *Oeconomia regni animalis*, in two parts, London and Amsterdam, 1740–41: *130*

469. Swedenborg, *Heaven and Hell*, London, 1758: *131, 132*

470. Swedenborg *Divine Love and Wisdom*, Amsterdam, 1763: *133*

471. Swinburne, Richard, *The Coherence of Theism*, Oxford University Press, 1977: *289, 292*

472. Swinburne, Richard, *The Existence of God*, Oxford University Press, 1979: *289, 292*

473. Swinburne, Richard, *Faith and Reason*, Oxford University Press, 1981: *289, 292*

474. Szent-Györgyi, Albert, *Electronic Biology and Cancer*, Dekker, New York, 1976: *321*

475. Szent-Györgyi, Albert, *The Living State*, Academic Press, New York, 1972: *321*

476. Talbot, Michael, *The Holographic Universe*, Harper-Collins (Grafton), London, 1991

477. *ibid.*, p.174 on: *228*

478. Targ, R., and J. Katra, *Miracles of Mind: Exploring nonlocal*

consciousness and spiritual healing, New World Library, Novato CA, 1999: *216*

479. Targ, R. and H. Putoff, *Mind Reach: Scientists look at psychic ability*, Delacorte Press, New York, 1977: *304*

480. Tavener, John, Interview with Richard Morrison, BBC Music Magazine, November 2004: *182*

481. Taylor, Charles, *Hegel and Modern Society*, Cambridge University Press, Cambridge UK, 1979: *250*

482. *ibid.*, p.10: *206*

483. Teichman, Jenny, *The Mind and the Soul*, Routledge Kegan Paul, London, 1974: *157*

484. Thompson, Darcy Wentworth, *On Growth and Form*, 1917: *295*

485. Tompkins, Peter, and Christopher Bird, *The Secret Life of Plants*, Penguin, London, 1973: *264*

486. Torrance, Thomas, *Theological Science*, Oxford University Press, 1969, p.130: *287*

487. Torrance, Thomas F., *Divine and Contingent Order*, Oxford University Press, 1981: *287*

488. Tylor, Edward Burnett, *Primitive Culture*, London, 1872, Vol. 2, p.24: *150*

489. Ullman, Montague, Stanley Krippner and Alan Vaughan, *Dream Telepathy: Experiments in nocturnal ESP*, 2nd edn., McFarland, Jefferson, North Carolina, 1989: *216*

490. Utts, J., An assessment of the evidence for psychic functioning, *J. Scientific Exploration*, **10**, 3–30, 1996: *216*

491. Utts, J., Psi, statistics and society, *Behavioral and Brain Sciences*, **10**, 615, 1987: *216*

492. Verner-Bonds, Lilian, *The Complete Book of Colour Healing*, Godsfield Press (David and Charles), London, 2000: *226*

493. Vitiello, Giuseppe, *Intern. J. Modern Physics*, **89**, 973, 1995: *324*

494. Waddington, Conrad H., *The Strategy of the Genes*, George Allen and Unwin, London, 1957: *267*

495. Ward, Keith, *God, Chance and Necessity*, Oneworld Publications, Oxford, 1996: *292*

496. Ward, Keith, *Images of Eternity*, Oneworld Publications, Oxford, 1993: *292*

497. Watson, Lyall, *Supernature*, Hodder and Stoughton, London, 1973: *212*

498. Watson, Lyall, *Supernature II*, Hodder and Stoughton, London, 1986, pp.61–68: *212, 264*

499. ibid., p.145: *213*

500. Watson, Lyall, *Lifetide*, Hodder and Stoughton, London, 1979: *212*

501. Watson, Lyall, *The Nature of Things*, Hodder and Stoughton, London, 1990: *212*

502. Weinberg, Steven, *The First Three Minutes*, Andre Deutsch, London, 1977: *292*

503. Weinberg, Steven, *Annals of Physics* (NY), **194**, 336, 1989: *317*

504. Weiss, Paul, *Principles of Development*, Holt, New York, 1939: *267*

505. Wells, G.A., *The Jesus Myth,* Open Court, 1999: *22*

506. Wheeler, William Morton, *Ants, Their Structure, Development and Behavior*, Columbia University Press, 1910: *217*

507. Wheeler, William Morton, The *Social Insects: Their origin and evolution*, Kegan Paul, London, 1928: *217*

508. Whewell, William, *History of the Inductive Sciences*, 3 vols, 1837: *285*

509. Whewell, William, *Philosophy of the Inductive Sciences*, 1840: *285*

510. Whewell, William, *Philosophy of the Inductive Sciences*, 2nd edn., 2 vols, London 1847; Cass, London, 1967, Vol.1, p.619: *290*

511. Whitehead, Alfred North, *Concept of Nature*, Cambridge University Press, 1920

512. *ibid.*, p.30–31: *64*

513. *ibid.*, p.168: *64*

514. Whitehead, Alfred North, *Process and Reality*, Macmillan, New York, 1929

515. *ibid.*, p.18: *64*

516. *ibid.*, p.28: *64*

517. *ibid.*, p.32: *64*

518. *ibid.*, p.40: *64*

519. *ibid.*, p.50: *64*

520. *ibid.*, p.67: *65*

521. White, Ruth, *Karma and Reincarnation*, Piatkus, London, 2000: *236*

522. Wilson, Colin, *Afterlife*, Grafton-Collins, 1987: *238*

523. Winfree, A., *J. Chem. Education,* **61**, 661, 1984: *318*

524. Wollheim, Richard, *Freud*, Fontana, London, 1973, p.220: *4*

525. Woolger, Roger, *Other Lives, Other Selves*, Wrekin Trust, 1990: *237*

526. Yolton, John W., *Locke: An introduction*, Basil Blackwell, 1985: *247*

527. Zadeh, Lofti A., Fuzzy sets, *Information and Control*, **8**, 338–353, 1965: *311*

528. Zohar, Danah, *Through the Time Barrier*, Heinemann 1982; Granada 1983, p.47: *220*

529. *ibid.,* p.53: *219*

530. *ibid.*, p.63: *220*

531. Zohar, Danah, *The Quantum Self*, William Morrow, 1990: *307*

532. Zohar, Danah, and Ian Marshall, *SQ – Spiritual Intelligence*, Bloomsbury, London, 2000: *149, 174*

533. Zukav, Gary, *The Dancing Wu Li Masters*, William Morrow (US), Rider Hutchinson (UK), 1979: *312*

534. Zukav, Gary, *The Seat of the Soul*, Rider (Random Century Group), London, 1990: *312*

Index

The Fall

The Evidence of a Golden Age, 6,000 Years of Insanity and the Dawning of a New Era

Steve Taylor

The Fall is a major work that overturns mainstream current thinking on the nature of civilization and human nature. It draws on the increasing evidence accumulated over recent decades that pre-literate humanity was relatively peaceful and egalitarian, rather than war-like and crude. It is not "natural" for human beings to kill each other, for men to oppress women, for individuals to accumulate massive wealth and power, or to abuse nature. The worldwide myths of a Golden Age or an original paradise have a factual, archaeological basis.

Taylor's ideas are provocative, and never fail to captivate the reader. It is my fervent wish that this important book will have a wide audience and reach the individuals and institutions that mould public opinion and behaviour. In a world where the very existence of humanity is threatened, Steve Taylor offers a visionary yet practical path out of the morass that distorts human nature. Dr Stanley Krippner, Professor of Psychology, Saybrooke Graduate School, California.

The Fall *is an astonishing work, full of amazing erudition, all brilliantly organised and argued. The argument that human beings have not always been – and do not have to be – such a psychological mess is presented with a beautiful inevitability and logic. The book is a remarkable feat.* Colin Wilson

The Fall *is a fascinating heretical work which demonstrates that the myth of the golden age reflects an archaic social reality. Read it and be cured.* Richard Rudgley, author of *Lost Civilizations of the Stone Age*

A fascinating, enlightening and inspiring investigation into the roots of human consciousness and a much needed proscription for a truly human future. Gary Lachmann, author of *A Secret History of Consciousness*

A thought-provoking diagnosis of the causes of warfare, patriarchy and materialism which holds potential for bringing humans more in harmony with each other, nature, and themselves. Tim Kasser, author of *The High Price of Materialism*

Well-argued, thoughtful, provocative and a pleasure to read. Christopher Ryan, Institute of Advanced Medicine and Advanced Behavioral Technology, Juarez, Mexico

Steve Taylor is a university and college lecturer in Manchester, England, and spent seven years researching and writing this book. He has written many articles and essays on psychology and spirituality for mainstream magazines and academic journals.

1 905047 20 7
£12.99 $24.95

The Censored Messiah
Peter Cresswell

Peter Cresswell has a revolutionary new theory about the life of Jesus and the origins of Christianity. It is a thrilling story, based on modern scholarship, of how a Jewish man tried to change the direction of the religious leadership of his people. It describes a breathtaking piece of brinkmanship carried out against the Roman occupiers of Israel, a journey into the mouth of death and beyond which appeared to succeed.

Peter Cresswell is a freelance writer with degrees from Cambridge and York Universities in Social Anthropology.

1 903816 67 X
£9.99 $14.95

Is There An Afterlife?
David Fontana

The question whether or not we survive physical death has occupied the minds of men and women since the dawn of recorded history. The spiritual traditions of both West and East have taught that death is not the end, but modern science generally dismisses such teachings.

The fruit of a lifetime's research and experience by a world expert in the field, *Is There An Afterlife?* presents the most complete survey to date of the evidence, both historical and contemporary, for survival of physical death. It looks at the question of what survives-personality, memory, emotions and body image-in particular exploring the question of consciousness as primary to and not dependent on matter in the light of recent brain research and quantum physics. It discusses the possible nature of the afterlife, the common threads in Western and Eastern traditions, the common features of "many levels," group souls and reincarnation.

As well a providing the broadest overview of the question, giving due weight to the claims both of science and religion, *Is There An Afterlife?* brings it into personal perspective. It asks how we should live in this life as if death is not the end, and suggests how we should change our behaviour accordingly.

David Fontana is a Fellow of the British Psychological Society (BPS), Founder Chair of the BPS Transpersonal Psychology Section, Past President and current Vice President of the Society for Psychical Research, and Chair of the SPR Survival Research Committee. He is Distinguished Visiting Fellow at Cardiff University, and Professor of Transpersonal Psychology at Liverpool John Moores University. His many books on spiritual themes have been translated into 25 languages.

1 903816 90 4
£11.99/$16.95

The Quest

Joycelin Dawes

What is your sense of soul? Although we may each understand the word differently, we treasure a sense of who we are, what it is to be alive and awareness of an inner experience and connection with "something more." In *The Quest* you explore this sense of soul through a regular practice based on skills of spiritual reflection and be reviewing the story of your life journey, your encounter with spiritual experience and your efforts to live in a sacred way.

Here you become the teller and explorer of your own story. You can find your own answers. You can deepen your spiritual life through the wisdom and insight of the world's religious traditions. You can revisit the building blocks of your beliefs and face the changes in your life. You can look more deeply at wholeness and connection and make your contribution to finding a new and better way.

So well written, constructed and presented, by a small independent group of individuals with many years experience in personal and spiritual growth, education and community, that it is a joy to work with. It is a life-long companion on the spiritual path and an outstanding achievement; it is a labour of love, created with love to bring more love into our world. Susanna Michaelis, *Caduceus*

1 903816 93 9
£9.99/$16.95

O

is a symbol of the world,
of oneness and unity. O Books
explores the many paths of wholeness and spiritual understanding which
different traditions have developed down
the ages. It aims to bring this knowledge in
accessible form, to a general readership, providing practical spirituality to today's seekers.

For the full list of over 200 titles covering:
ACADEMIC/THEOLOGY • ANGELS • ASTROLOGY/
NUMEROLOGY • BIOGRAPHY/AUTOBIOGRAPHY
• BUDDHISM/ENLIGHTENMENT • BUSINESS/LEADERSHIP/
WISDOM • CELTIC/DRUID/PAGAN • CHANNELLING
• CHRISTIANITY; EARLY • CHRISTIANITY; TRADITIONAL
• CHRISTIANITY; PROGRESSIVE • CHRISTIANITY;
DEVOTIONAL • CHILDREN'S SPIRITUALITY • CHILDREN'S
BIBLE STORIES • CHILDREN'S BOARD/NOVELTY • CREATIVE
SPIRITUALITY • CURRENT AFFAIRS/RELIGIOUS • ECONOMY/
POLITICS/SUSTAINABILITY • ENVIRONMENT/EARTH
• FICTION • GODDESS/FEMININE • HEALTH/FITNESS
• HEALING/REIKI • HINDUISM/ADVAITA/VEDANTA
• HISTORY/ARCHAEOLOGY • HOLISTIC SPIRITUALITY
• INTERFAITH/ECUMENICAL • ISLAM/SUFISM
• JUDAISM/CHRISTIANITY • MEDITATION/PRAYER
• MYSTERY/PARANORMAL • MYSTICISM • MYTHS
• POETRY • RELATIONSHIPS/LOVE • RELIGION/
PHILOSOPHY • SCHOOL TITLES • SCIENCE/
RELIGION • SELF-HELP/PSYCHOLOGY
• SPIRITUAL SEARCH • WORLD
RELIGIONS/SCRIPTURES • YOGA

**Please visit our website,
www.O-books.net**